Studies in the Legal History of the South

EDITED BY PAUL FINKELMAN, TIMOTHY S. HUEBNER, AND KERMIT L. HALL

This series explores the ways in which law has affected the development of the southern United States and in turn the ways the history of the South has affected the development of American law. Volumes in the series focus on a specific aspect of the law, such as slave law or civil rights legislation, or on a broader topic of historical significance to the development of the legal system in the region, such as issues of constitutional history and of law and society, comparative analyses with other legal systems, and biographical studies of influential southern jurists and lawyers.

Elbert Parr Tuttle

Oct 27, 2019

To David & Catherine

with every good

wish –

[signature]

Elbert Parr Tuttle

CHIEF JURIST OF THE CIVIL RIGHTS REVOLUTION

ANNE EMANUEL

The University of Georgia Press
Athens & London

© 2011 by the University of Georgia Press
Athens, Georgia 30602
www.ugapress.org
Designed by Walton Harris
Set in 10.5/14 Minion Pro
Printed and bound by Thomson-Shore

The paper in this book meets the guidelines for permanence
and durability of the Committee on Production Guidelines
for Book Longevity of the Council on Library Resources.

Printed in the United States of America

15   14   13   12   11   C   5   4   3   2   1

Library of Congress Cataloging-in-Publication Data

Emanuel, Anne (Anne S.), 1945–
Elbert Parr Tuttle : chief jurist of the Civil Rights
revolution / Anne Emanuel.
     p.   cm. — (Studies in the legal history
of the south)
Includes bibliographical references and index.
ISBN-13: 978-0-8203-3947-4 (hardcover : alk. paper)
ISBN-10: 0-8203-3947-4 (hardcover : alk. paper)
 1. Tuttle, Elbert P. (Elbert Parr), 1897–1996
 2. Judges—Georgia—Biography. I. Title.
KF373.T9E63 2011
347.73'14092—dc22 [B]   2011012911

British Library Cataloguing-in-Publication Data available

The publication of this book was made possible, in part, by a generous gift from Sutherland Asbill & Brennan LLP to honor the legacy of the firm founder Judge Elbert Parr Tuttle.

For those who turn to our courts
seeking justice and for those who
serve our courts with integrity

He brought honor to his calling,
and justice to millions of Americans.

CONTENTS

PREFACE

The hard truth of our cultural and constitutional history is that nowhere was it written that the civil rights revolution led by Martin Luther King Jr. would succeed. The movement cost its members more sacrifice and caused more terror than we care to remember. Dr. King's commitment to nonviolence held long enough and firmly enough to give the movement a moral imperative that resonated throughout the country, but its hold was not complete and was always fragile. Without the support of the federal courts of the Fifth Circuit, it is entirely possible that the promise of *Brown* would have gone unrealized, that the back of Jim Crow would remain unbroken. Without the leadership of Elbert Tuttle and the moral authority he commanded, the courts of the Fifth Circuit might not have met the challenge.

In December 1960, in a remarkable and fortuitous accident of history, Elbert Tuttle became the chief judge of the federal court with jurisdiction over most of the Deep South. The United States Court of Appeals for the Fifth Circuit covered six states—Alabama, Florida, Georgia, Louisiana, Mississippi, and Texas. Ordinarily, the men who sat on the Fifth Circuit were men of the region, steeped in its peculiar and pernicious history. Elbert Tuttle was not. With his wife and infant son, he had moved to Atlanta in 1923 at the age of twenty-five, a young lawyer who had fallen in love with a strong-willed Georgia girl and followed her home.

One lesson of Tuttle's life is that exposure to diversity matters. Born in California, he lived in Los Angeles, Washington, D.C., and Nogales, Arizona, on the border with Mexico before moving to Hawaii at the age of ten. In Hawaii the Tuttles lived on Oahu, where Elbert and his older brother, Malcolm, enrolled in the Punahou School. Unlike perhaps any other American school of that era, Punahou was racially and ethnically integrated; Tuttle studied and played alongside native Hawaiians as well as schoolmates of Chinese, Japanese, Philippine, and Portuguese ancestry.

From his earliest days in Georgia, Tuttle saw Jim Crow segregation as the unjust, oppressive apartheid it was. He had harbored political ambitions since his high school years, but in 1920s Georgia there was only one political party—the white Democratic Party, segregated by law as well as by custom. He would not join. Rather, he devoted considerable energy to building a viable Republican Party. Meanwhile, he and his brother-in-law Bill Sutherland, who had served as a law clerk to Justice Brandeis, built a highly regarded law firm. Though they specialized in corporate tax matters and were members of Atlanta's social elite, Sutherland and Tuttle did not hesitate to step forward when a nineteen-year-old black leftist, Angelo Herndon, was sentenced to twenty years on the chain gang for handing out leaflets calling for a demonstration to protest the loss of relief benefits. Their work on his behalf led to the landmark First Amendment opinion *Herndon v. Lowry*, decided by the United States Supreme Court in 1937.

Another lesson of Tuttle's life is that character matters. Elbert Tuttle never shirked responsibility, no matter the cost. After the Japanese attack on Pearl Harbor, he volunteered for overseas service at age forty-four. In 1944 and 1945 Elbert Tuttle commanded a field artillery battalion that participated in the Guam campaign and the battle for Leyte in the Philippines before joining the massive amphibious assault that began the battle for Okinawa. In mid-April 1945 his company braved gunfire from defending Japanese soldiers and landed on Ie Shima; on April 18 he was wounded in hand-to-hand combat with the Japanese. Two weeks later, Tuttle was joined in Hawaii by his son. A bomber pilot, Elbert Tuttle Jr. had finished his tour of duty on Iwo Jima in February 1945. Unwilling to go home while his father was fighting on nearby islands, he stayed on. When word came of his father's medical discharge, Buddy was promptly released. Father and son came back to Georgia together, arriving home on July 4, 1945.

Tuttle returned to Atlanta with a renewed commitment to civic affairs. His work with the Republican Party in Georgia kept him in contact with the state's leading black citizens, and his victory in a credentials committee battle proved instrumental to Eisenhower's ability to defeat Taft at the 1952 Republican Convention. After Eisenhower won the presidency, he selected Tuttle as general counsel to the treasury. Two years later, just after *Brown* was decided, Eisenhower nominated Tuttle for a seat on the Fifth Circuit. Tuttle joined the court in August 1954.

In 1960 Elbert Tuttle became the chief judge of the Fifth Circuit. The southern states remained locked in the rigid system of apartheid known as Jim Crow segregation. Six years had passed since *Brown I*, and nothing had happened. Throughout the South, from kindergarten through graduate and professional programs, only a handful of black students attended school with white students. Cabs, cafés, restaurants, hotels—all manner of public accommodations remained totally segregated. Early indications that moderates on race might offer progressive leadership had disappeared. Not only were southern statehouses held hostage to demagogues, southern senators and representatives in the United States Congress had decried *Brown* and defied the Supreme Court in their Southern Manifesto. The United States Supreme Court had decided *Brown*; it was up to the lower federal courts to implement it.

Judge Elbert Tuttle turned the tide of history just weeks after he became chief judge. Charlayne Hunter and Hamilton Holmes had waged a two-year struggle to be the first African American students admitted to the University of Georgia. They won when Federal District Court Judge Walter "Gus" Bootle ruled in their favor on Friday, January 6, 1961. Then, on Monday, January 9, the day that registration for the winter term ended, Judge Bootle entered a stay to allow the university to appeal. NAACP attorney Constance Baker Motley called Tuttle from the Macon Courthouse and asked how soon he could hear an appeal. As soon, he responded, as the attorneys on both sides could get to Atlanta. Later that afternoon, Tuttle vacated the stay, and Charlayne Hunter and Hamilton Holmes registered to attend the University of Georgia. Tuttle's swift, decisive intervention proved to be a harbinger of his stewardship.

As chief judge of the Fifth Circuit from 1960 to 1967, Tuttle led the way in disarming the southern states of the most effective weapon in their arsenal—delay. The circuit courts of appeals customarily sat in three-judge panels. Tuttle found in Rule 62 of the Federal Rules of Civil Procedure the power to do what was necessary when it was necessary, even if he had to do it sitting alone—as he did in the UGA case and as he did in May 1963 in the Birmingham Children's Crusade case, a ruling that arguably saved the movement. He gave vibrant life and meaning to the All Writs Act, which became in his hands the source of the Fifth Circuit's power to deal with obstructionist district court judges. Failure to rule, he held, was equivalent to denying relief, and an appeal could proceed. Realizing that those federal judges committed to segregation forever would delay inordinately in entering orders on remand, he proclaimed them issued by the Fifth Circuit itself with the simple phrase, "The mandate shall issue forthwith."

For his determination to recognize and protect the long-denied constitutional rights of black citizens of the South, Tuttle was reviled as an activist judge. When, decades later, he was honored for the work that had been anathema in its time, he accepted accolades with a modest yet incisive bemusement. "They were," he often said, "the easiest cases I ever decided. The constitutional rights were so compelling, and the wrongs were so enormous." Tuttle stepped down as chief judge in 1967, when he turned seventy, but he remained an active member of the court until the late 1980s. He continued to be productive; he continued to write lucid, influential opinions; he continued to develop what I call a jurisprudence of justice. But it was his work while he was chief judge, a period that coincided with the most critical years of the civil rights revolution, that thrust him onto history's stage.

While I devote a great deal of the book to the civil rights era, I trace Tuttle's family back ten generations to William and Elizabeth Tuttle, who arrived in Boston on the *Planter* in 1635 and established a home on land in New Haven, Connecticut, that became, after their deaths, the site of Yale College. The book also recounts his mother's family history and that of his wife, and it portrays the strength of Elbert's seventy-five-year marriage to Sara Sutherland Tuttle and their legendary devotion to each other. These are, I believe, emblematic American stories that enrich the reader's understanding of Tuttle's character—and it is his character that is the heart of the story.

AUTHOR'S NOTE

Race in America is central to this biography. Over the course of the twentieth century, the term used to describe individuals of African heritage changed (in civilized discourse) from "Negro" to "African American" to "black" and arguably then to "people of color." In writing this book, I have chosen to use "black" in most references. The exceptions occur, for the most part, when contemporaneous quotations that appear in the text use a different description.

ACKNOWLEDGMENTS

A work this long in the making accumulates more indebtedness than can be repaid, except, perhaps, in spirit. I owe large debts of gratitude for unstinting practical and moral support to my colleagues at Georgia State University College of Law and especially to Deans Marjorie Girth, Janice Griffith, and Steven Kaminshine; to my exceptional administrative assistant, Cindy Perry; to generations of able and enthusiastic law student research assistants, including, from Georgia State University College of Law, Roseanne Cross, Harold Franklin, Wendell Franklin, Forrest Graham, Russell Henry, Cheryl Barnes Legare, Delaycee Rowland, Heather Schafer, David Stevens, Nancee Tomlinson, Ben Windham, and Katie Wood; from the University of Texas School of Law, Katie Hutchinson; and from the University of Michigan Law School, Ben F. Johnson IV; and to Nancy Grayson and Jon Davies of the University of Georgia Press, who deftly and gracefully brought this project to fruition.

The burden of conducting innumerable interviews and voluminous research was lightened by the receptivity and generosity I encountered repeatedly from, among many others, men who served under Tuttle's command in World War II, his partners at Sutherland & Tuttle, his colleagues on the bench, attorneys who litigated before him, reporters who covered him, and other historians of the Fifth Circuit, especially Jack Bass, J. Robert Brown Jr., Joel Friedman, Lucy McGough, and Frank Read.

The cooperation and the patience of the Tuttle family have been profound. Dr. Elbert Tuttle Jr. and his wife, Ginny, and Jane "Nicky" Tuttle Harmon and her husband, John, shared their own recollections as well as their family records. The grandchildren (Guy, David, Beth, and Jane Tuttle; Betsy Harmon Kappel; and Cappy, Sara, and Peggy Harmon) have all been helpful, but special thanks must go to Beth and Jane, who collated and indexed much of the family memorabilia, and to Betsy's husband, Bruce Kappel, who edited and interwove Sara and Elbert's personal recollections and who provided many of the pictures included here.

The other Tuttle "family" cannot go unmentioned. Both Elbert Tuttle and his wife, Sara, held his law clerks dear, and the clerks reciprocated that deep affection. Many clerks shared recollections with me. Special thanks to Fred Aman, who provided copies of the substantial collection of letters from law clerks he collected in 1985 at the behest of the Eleventh Circuit Historical Society.

Finally, the unflagging support of my husband, Martin, and our sons, Brooks and Ben, is the foundation on which this work rests.

Portions of this work previously appeared, in different form, as "Lynching and the Law in Georgia circa 1931: A Chapter in the Legal Career of Judge Elbert Tuttle," *William & Mary Bill of Rights Journal* 5 (1996): 215–48; "Turning the Tide in the Civil Rights Revolution: Elbert Tuttle and the Desegregation of the University of Georgia," *Michigan Journal of Race and Law* (Fall 1999): 1–30; "The Tuttle Trilogy: Habeaus Corpus and Human Rights," *Journal of Southern Legal History* 5 (2002): 5–24; and "Forming the Historic Fifth Circuit: The Eisenhower Years," *Texas Forum on Civil Liberties and Civil Rights* 6 (2002): 233–59.

A NOTE ON SOURCES

I was fortunate to be able to conduct an extensive number of interviews, listed below, with Judge Tuttle and with members of his immediate family. Additionally, toward the ends of their lives, both Judge Tuttle and his wife, Sara, wrote personal recollections for their families. To avoid excessive use of endnotes, these materials are listed below. All quotations of family members and all family anecdotes that do not have individual endnotes are attributable to these materials, which are on file with the author.

Judge Elbert Tuttle at his chambers in Atlanta, Ga., March 19, 1993; May 5 and 18, 1993; July 8, 1993; August 9, 1993; April 20, 1994; and June 7 and 24, 1994

Judge Elbert Tuttle at his home in Atlanta, Ga., December 27, 1994

Sara Tuttle at her home in Atlanta, Ga., June 1, 1993

John and Jane "Nicky" Harmon at the home of Dr. and Mrs. Elbert Tuttle in Atlanta, Ga., July 27, 1995

John and Jane "Nicky" Harmon at Judge Tuttle's chambers in Atlanta, Ga., October 15, 1993

John Harmon by telephone, March 26, 2008

Dr. Elbert "Buddy" Tuttle and his wife, Ginny, at their home in Atlanta, Ga., passim

Jennie Sutherland Asbill at her home in Washington, D.C., November 1, 1993

Margaret Coleman at her home in Dallas, Tex., May 3, 1993

Additional interviews, which are cited in the notes when used, were conducted with Terrence B. "Terry" Adamson (telephone); Attorney General

Griffin Bell; Emmet Bondurant; Judge Walter "Gus" Bootle; Henry Bowden Sr.; Chief Justice Warren Burger; President James Earl "Jimmy" Carter (telephone); Bessie Mayfield Davis; John Doar (telephone); Edith Elsas; Herbert Elsas; Jack Frye (telephone); Judge John Godbold; Judge Irving Goldberg; Jack Greenburg (telephone); Lillian Gregory; John Griffin (telephone); Dean Erwin Griswold; Donald Hollowell; Hamilton Holmes (telephone); Forney Holt (telephone); Judge Frank Mays Hull; Dean Ben F. Johnson Jr.; Judge Nathaniel Jones (telephone); Worth Keeter (telephone); Charles Kidd; Anne Deas Koshewa (telephone); Judge Phyllis Kravitch; Edward "Larry" Laroussini (telephone); Laughlin McDonald (telephone); Donald F. Menagh (telephone); E. E. Moore; Judge Constance Baker Motley (telephone); Arnold Rose (telephone); Bill Shipp (telephone); Claude Sitton; Justice George T. Smith; Paul Szasz (telephone); Robert A. Thompson; Margaret Thrower; Randolph Thrower; Killian "Kil" Townsend; Henry T. Tuominen (telephone); Governor Ernest Vandiver (telephone); Edward Wadsworth; James "Jim" Wilson; and Judge John Minor Wisdom.

I benefited from conversations and correspondence with as well as research conducted by many of Judge Tuttle's law clerks, including Harold Adams, Dean Fred Aman, Senator Christopher S. Bond, Fred Codner, James C. Conner, Lawrence B. Custer, Stephen J. Ellmann, Charles M. Elson, Philip L. Evans, Judge Frank Mays Hull, Dennis Hutchinson, Hugh Kemp, Cameron "Cam" Kerry, Charles M. Kidd, Judith A. O'Brien, Dean Russell, C. V. Stelzemuller, and Paul Szasz.

Copies of the letters written by Elbert Tuttle to his wife, Sara, from the Pacific Theater during World War II, which are extensively quoted in chapter 7, are on file with the author.

The Tuttle Papers are held by the Emory University Manuscript, Archives, and Rare Book Library.

CHAPTER ONE

The Legal Lynching of John Downer

"Well, personally and frankly I think the boy with her screwed her."[1]

In 1932 this blunt assessment brought a Macon, Georgia, federal courtroom to a stunned silence. Marion Williamson, a captain in the Georgia National Guard and a Decatur attorney, sat in the witness chair. He had spoken the unspeakable truth, and he had spoken it under oath. It would, as it turned out, make no difference. A white woman had accused a black man of rape, and he would die for it. Nothing could save John Downer from the electric chair, not even the best efforts of Elbert Tuttle, a highly regarded Atlanta lawyer who took up Downer's cause.

Like Marion Williamson, Tuttle had become involved in the case a year earlier. On May 19, 1931, John Downer and an acquaintance had been arrested and taken to the Elberton jail, located on the second floor of the sheriff's home. News of the rape accusation circulated, and by 3:00 p.m. a mob several hundred strong had gathered. In Atlanta, Governor Lamartine Hardman issued a proclamation putting Elberton under martial law. Homer C. Parker, the adjutant general of the Georgia National Guard, ordered two Elberton units to duty and sent two Atlanta officers—Captain Williamson and the regimental commander, Col. Gerald P. O'Keefe—to assist. By the time they arrived, members of the mob were hammering away at the lock on Downer's cell. The soldiers managed to clear the jail, but they were not able to secure the sheriff's home downstairs, far less the grounds. General Parker dispatched Tuttle, a captain in the National Guard, to take tear gas grenades to the beleaguered troops.

Tuttle called his closest friend, Leckie Mattox, also a captain in the National Guard and his cousin by marriage. The two men decided that Mattox would wear civilian clothes so that he could blend into the mob.

They raced toward Elberton, arriving just after sundown and just in time to hear a burst of machine-gun fire from the jail. The mob had ignored the machine-gun positions set up to secure the second-floor jail and crowded into the yard and the sheriff's home. They had taken up two cries: "They won't shoot" and "They only have blanks." The last line of defense was a machine gun at the top of the stairs manned by Captain Williamson and Colonel O'Keefe. Just as Tuttle drove up, the mob began sallies up the stairs. O'Keefe fired several rounds of his pistol, calling out to the crowd, "These aren't blanks." When that had no effect, he ordered machine-gun fire; at least one man was struck.[2] Almost simultaneously, Tuttle and Mattox lobbed several canisters of tear gas. Suddenly attacked from two sides, the crowd was shaken. Tuttle made his way inside, where he and Maj. Andrew Drake, the local commander, managed to move the mob out of the sheriff's house.

Over the next hour the crowd continued to swell. Tuttle found the fire chief and had a hose brought to disperse the crowd, but the mob quickly gained control of it and directed it at the jail, breaking the windows and drenching the prisoners and their guards.[3] They didn't mind; the water quenched the tear gas that had drifted upstairs. The mob began to threaten to blow up the jail if the two suspects weren't turned over to them. Dynamite used in quarrying was readily available. Emissaries from the crowd warned Colonel O'Keefe of the plan, some saying the only thing preventing it was that soldiers from Elberton were inside the jail. Circulating in the crowd outside, Leckie Mattox was increasingly convinced the threat was real. As he later testified, he began "talking to groups of men . . . as if I were one of the Elbert County people; and the gist of my remarks was that we did not want to blow up a bunch of our Elbert County boys in there just to get a couple of negroes."[4]

The threats continued. Finally, a man O'Keefe believed to be the superintendent of a quarry told O'Keefe that the crowd had the dynamite and that they would detonate a warning blast that would give the soldiers five minutes to clear the jail. Two companies from Monroe, Georgia, arrived, assembled in formation, and marched to the jail, but the show of force had little effect; moments later a small explosion shook the jail.[5] Inside, Tuttle and the other officers devised a plan. Two guardsmen gave up their uniforms to the prisoners, who were then placed in the middle of the units of guardsmen. All of the lights not already broken were extinguished, and under cover of darkness the prisoners were taken out of the jail. Each prisoner was put on the floor of a car parked outside, both cars surrounded by groups of soldiers trying to look as if they were simply lounging. Near midnight more troops arrived, and the prisoners were moved from the cars to the troop buses. The National Guard units drove off, leaving behind a mob that had at its peak numbered 2,000, in a town of only 4,600.[6]

Elbert Tuttle left Elberton shaken by what he had seen. A man in whom a sense of fairness was bred in the bone, he was particularly appalled by the recognition that the mob would have murdered both men, despite the fact that, even taking the accusation at face value, only one could be guilty. He was glad to have played his part in preventing such a miscarriage of justice, glad to be able to deliver the accused from the destructive chaos of the mob to the orderly processes of the court. His sense of relief, like John Downer's deliverance, would prove to be short lived. The next morning, Tuesday, May 20, the local superior court judge convened a grand jury, which promptly indicted Downer for rape. Six days later, on Monday, May 26, trial commenced. The judge opened the proceedings that morning by appointing counsel to represent Downer. Because no local attorney wanted the job, the judge appointed three lawyers in an attempt to diffuse the stigma of representing Downer.

Tuttle, a seasoned litigator himself, was back in the courtroom commanding the national guardsmen assigned to keep order. As a technical matter, Downer's attorneys could have moved for a change of venue; they did not. Nor did they seek a continuance so that they could investigate and prepare their case; they asked only for time to interview their client and to subpoena his witnesses, who would testify that he had been home in bed at the time of the alleged attack. Between 10:30 and 11:00 a.m., without ever having left the courthouse, they announced they were ready. Tuttle watched with dismay, but he was not surprised; he understood all too well the pressures on Downer's counsel. "As was the case in most of those racially inflamed cases, the lawyer was almost forced to agree to an immediate trial, because every day the mob would be threatening to lynch the defendant. But of course it is true that he could have moved for a change of venue. . . . I don't want to pass judgment on the lawyer, but he would never have another client in that county if he moved for a change of venue and postponed the trial for another 3 or 4 months."[7]

The alleged victim took the stand and told her story. She had been parked in an isolated area with her boyfriend when a black man waving a pistol forced her out of the car and raped her. After reporting the rape, she had been taken home and sedated. That afternoon, when John Downer was brought to her window, she sat up in bed and identified the black man in the grip of two white sheriffs as her assailant. She was able to recognize him, she explained, by his size, color, and thick lips. Many of the guardsmen assigned to the trial suspected she had made up the story of a marauding black man because she was desperate to cover up the bleeding caused by intercourse with her boyfriend. It may have been simply coincidence that *Birth of a Nation*, D. W. Griffith's movie version of a book about the Klan in which "blacks were depicted as ignorant barbarians, lusting after fair young white maidens," had played in Elberton the Thursday before the alleged attack and had been trumpeted in the local newspaper with four-inch banner headlines.

By late afternoon, the trial was all but over. The attorneys made their closing arguments; the judge charged the jury. Now the matter was in the jury's hands—but not for long. In a scant six minutes, the twelve white men who had been sworn in as jurors that morning delivered their verdict: guilty, with no recommendation of mercy. Guilty, and sentenced to die. Elbert Tuttle was appalled—not surprised, but appalled. He was so appalled that he would take up Downer's cause and enlist other prominent Atlanta attorneys in it. At first he enjoyed a modicum of success. A federal court, agreeing with Tuttle that the trial had been a sham, ordered a new trial.[8] Former Georgia Superior Court judge Henry C. Hammond agreed to represent Downer at the new trial. A motion for change of venue was granted, but the trial was merely moved to adjacent Oglethorpe County. When the second trial began, twelve white men, selected from a panel of forty-eight white men, sat in the jury box. It was four years before the Supreme Court, deciding an appeal by Clarence Norris, one of the Scottsboro boys, would overturn his conviction, ruling that proof that Negroes had been continuously and totally excluded from juries created a prima facie case of unconstitutional discrimination that the state had failed to rebut.[9] It would be decades before the promise of the ruling in that case—*Norris v. Alabama*—would be realized.[10]

The state relied on two pieces of evidence: the alleged victim's identification of Downer and footprints that allegedly led from the scene to his home. Downer regularly walked past that point on his way home from work at a nearby farm. Assuming the tracks existed, they were not necessarily damning, but Downer had been terrified when confronted with this fact against him. According to Downer, when two sheriffs and two other white men had taken him "down the branch" to make him talk, he had claimed to have loaned the shoes to a friend. He reiterated that story in his unsworn statement at the first trial. At the second trial, he recanted:

> I didn't loan Isaac McCauley my shoes. I had them shoes on myself. And the reason I told the officers that, they was working on me so, and the crowd was around me, and I didn't have a chance to get to where none of my white people was. . . . I had never seen Isaac McCauley that night at all. I had never seen him but I told the officers that so the crowd wouldn't kill me. . . . So far as this crime, I don't know anything about it gentlemen, that is the truth. I always worked around white people; I had all the respect for them I could. I never had the first thing against me that I know of. . . . That is all I know about it, gentlemen. I am innocent of that crime.[11]

John Downer's second trial was more fair than his first. His attorney was not afraid to represent him, and there had been time for investigation, time to gather witnesses, time to allow some of the passion surrounding the first trial to subside. All of this was reflected in his attorney's small triumph; this jury stayed out longer than a mere six minutes, albeit less than an hour. The verdict and the sentence did not change. John Downer was again sentenced to die.

Downer's attorneys prepared to appeal. Henry Hammond was joined by Tuttle's brother-in-law and law partner, Bill Sutherland, and by the dean of Atlanta's black attorneys, A. T. Walden, on the brief. They argued that the court's charge to the jury had been unduly prejudicial. Not once but three times the court had pointed out that a recommendation of mercy would mean not only that Downer would not be executed but that he would not receive a life sentence either; the jury had only two choices, death or a sentence of one to twenty years. The statute carried forward a pre–Civil War scheme that embodied the twin evils of racism and sexism. Under two separate statutes, the penalty for rape of a white woman by a black man was death, and the penalty for the rape of a white woman by anyone other than a black man was two to twenty years.[12] By 1931, when Downer was first tried, a single statute provided that the penalty for rape was either one to twenty years or death. The assumption was that a black man who raped a white woman would always be sentenced to death, in part because the only alternative was a term of years after which he would be released. On the other hand, a white man who raped a white woman would be sentenced, in all but the most brutal cases, to only to a term of years. The statute reflected no concern about the rape of a black woman; no one expected that crime to be prosecuted. The trial judge had also instructed the jury extensively on the principle of consent, even though John Downer had not raised any issue of consent. By introducing the idea that this young white woman might have consented to intercourse with a black man, Downer's attorneys argued, the court's charge was both irrelevant and inflammatory.

John Downer's appeal was not without merit, but it would never be heard. The notice of appeal recited that the trial judge had denied the defendant's motion for a new trial, "and now within the time allowed by law, John Downer presents this his bill of exceptions." It omitted the phrase "to which judgment the plaintiff in error then and there excepted, now excepts and assigns thereon." Downer's attorney, the respected former judge Henry C. Hammond, filed an affidavit with the court explaining that this language had been part of the bill of exceptions prepared by the attorneys and that its omission was a clerical error. Unmoved, the Georgia Supreme Court dismissed the appeal.[13] Governor Eugene Talmadge was likewise unmoved by pleas for clemency, even those that pointed out that he had recently pardoned two young white men who were clearly guilty of rape.

On March 16, 1934, John Downer was executed. The long, futile struggle was over. Elbert Tuttle had been part of it from the very beginning to the bitter end. Experiencing the rage and racism of the mob in Elberton, he had thought there could be little worse. Later he would wonder what was worse—lynching by a lawless mob, or permitting "passion and violence . . . to operate through the machinery of the law."[14] What was more fearsome—the seething violence in the streets, or the willingness of a federal judge to attribute to "well-meaning people" the position that execution should proceed because the promise of the trial had prevented the lynching, and if the defendant were to be exonerated, a future mob would not be deterred, would take the law into its own hands? What was more horrific—the sheriff's terrifying extraction of a confession, or the Georgia Supreme Court's chilling dismissal of the appeal because a technical requirement that added nothing to the substance of the notice of appeal had been omitted by a typist?

More than a quarter of a century after John Downer's execution, Elbert Tuttle became the highest-ranking federal judge in the Deep South. On December 5, 1960, Tuttle was sworn in as chief judge of the United States Court of Appeals for the Fifth Circuit, the federal court with jurisdiction over Alabama, Georgia, Florida, Louisiana, Mississippi, and Texas. He had not forgotten John Downer.

CHAPTER TWO

The Great Migration

Elbert Parr Tuttle could trace his family line back ten generations, to April 1635, when the *Planter* left Gravesend, England, bound for Boston. On board were 117 passengers, including twenty-six-year-old William Tuttle, his twenty-three-year-old wife, Elizabeth, and their three small children: John, who was three and a half; Anne, who was two; and Thomas, who was only three months old. They arrived in Boston around the first of July. Two of William's older brothers were also on board with their families. John, thirty-nine, sailed with his wife and seven children; he did not stay in the New World but instead returned to Ireland, where he died at Carrickfergus on December 30, 1656. Richard, thirty-two, who, like William, was listed as a husbandman, sailed with his wife and three children. Isabel Tuttle, William, John, and Richard's mother, sailed with them; she was seventy.[1]

William and Elizabeth Tuttle were part of the Great Migration, when between 1630 and 1640 over thirteen thousand men, women, and children crossed from England to Massachusetts. For most, a search for religious freedom played a major role; the decade of the Great Migration coincided with the height of the Puritan crisis in England.[2] But a drive toward the promise of prosperity also played a role. The New World offered opportunities that were foreclosed to many in England. A detailed genealogy of the family of William Tuttle, published in 1883 by George Frederick Tuttle, notes that William Tuttle was described as a husbandman on the *Planter's* passenger list and concludes that he was a farmer who owned the land he tilled. Other historical sources maintain that the word "husbandman" described a tenant farmer.[3] That he was able to make the crossing, accompanied by his wife and three small children, indicates he may well have been a small landowner in England. A farmer who leased thirty acres in the first half of the seventeenth century might earn fourteen or fifteen pounds in profit a year, but subsistence would absorb eleven pounds, leaving only three or four pounds extra. The adult fare on the *Planter* was five pounds; it would take extraordinary circumstances for a tenant farmer to raise the funds for a family of four or five to make the crossing.[4]

An early entry on a registry in the secretary of state's office in Boston describes William Tuttle as a merchant; history does not record in what goods he traded. Whatever his occupation, he made a success of it. In 1641, only six years after they arrived in Massachusetts, William and Elizabeth moved to the new colony Quinnipiac (now Connecticut), where he bought the home and land of Edward Hopkins, who later became governor of the colony. Soon William expanded his holdings, buying ten nearby acres from Joshua Atwater. At her death in 1684, more than four decades later, Elizabeth still lived in the house Atwater had built early in the century. By 1717 the house had little value, and the property was sold to the trustees of a local collegiate school. They promptly demolished the Atwater-Tuttle homestead and erected a three-story building, which they named Yale College.[5]

William Tuttle's standing in the community was not merely a matter of material success. At various times a constable and a road commissioner, he was often called upon to sit as a juror or to arbitrate differences among the colonists. His standing was most evident in his seat at church. He worshiped at the New Haven meeting house, where a committee assigned seats under the rules of precedence. William Tuttle was assigned to the first cross seat, which "was near the pulpit and among the highest in dignity." For all of his success, he was matched by his wife. Elizabeth Tuttle bore eleven children and took into the Tuttle home the child of a deceased cousin, bringing the household to fourteen. All twelve of the children survived into maturity, a triumph over "privations, dangers, and trials, of which the mothers of the present day can hardly form a conception."[6] Elizabeth Tuttle died at age seventy-two on December 30, 1684. She survived her husband, who died suddenly in the early days of June 1673, by more than a decade.

For a generation or two, William Tuttle's many descendants stayed in New England. The most famous, his great grandson Jonathan Edwards, became one of the leading intellectual figures in colonial America.[7] William Tuttle's ninth child, Simon, settled nearby, prospered, and enjoyed the respect of the community. He also sired a large family. Most of his descendants stayed in New England for much of the next century; his son Timothy built the first or perhaps the second house in Cheshire, Connecticut, and his great-grandson Timothy became one of the original trustees of Clinton Academy, now Hamilton College.[8] Timothy's grandson Amos, born on February 13, 1806, moved to Michigan and married Abi Anne Cole in 1833. They set up house in Detroit, but in the spring of 1837, Amos decided to move. "Travelling facilities being poor, he walked [nearly four hundred miles] from Detroit, Mich., to Roscoe, Ill.," an area along the Rock River that was just beginning to be settled. Abi Anne followed a year later. Only seven or eight families lived in Roscoe, and Amos was able to buy a large tract of land on the east side of Main Street. A builder, he gave away lots to induce settlement. The descriptions of his character penned by the family genealogist and the officers of his church are eerily reminiscent of his great-grandson Elbert Tuttle. "He was honored and esteemed, faithful in all positions, honest in all business transactions." "Too much, say those who know him best, cannot be said of this noble, Christian man . . . undemonstrative but faithful and earnest, amiable in disposition and his life fragrant with the aroma of a noble Christian character."[9]

Amos and Abi Anne's son, Elbert Cole Tuttle, married Frederika B. Harley on January 1, 1871 and fathered three sons—Guy, Elbert, and Frank. Guy Harmon Tuttle, Judge Elbert Tuttle's father, was born on June 19, 1872, in Roscoe, Illinois, which lies some ninety-five miles northwest of Chicago.[10] As the nineteenth century neared its end, Guy Tuttle met and fell in love with Marguerite "Margie" Etta Parr. Two years older than Guy, Margie had been raised by her widowed mother. Margie's parents, Lucie Caroline McEldowney and Samuel Benton Parr, had married on July 12, 1865, and set up housekeeping in Corydon, Iowa, where Samuel's family had substantial roots; his father was among the earliest Disciples of Christ ministers in southern Iowa. Margie Parr, Elbert Tuttle's mother, took her faith very seriously; the Church of Christ had a profound influence on her life. The major reason for the founding of the Disciples of Christ, also known as the Christian Church, was the perception of its founders (most notably, Barton Stone of Kentucky and the father and son, Thomas and Alexander Campbell, of Pennsylvania) that the plethora of Christian denominations created unnecessary and inappropriate divisions.[11] Where others saw differences, they saw commonality; where others adopted rules that created divisions, they renounced creeds and relied solely on scripture. The new Christian Church enjoyed enormous popularity in the West, where the egalitarian tone it struck resonated among self-reliant pioneers.[12]

The influence on Margie Parr of her grandfather's religious calling was matched by the influence of the story of her father's brief life. Samuel Benton Parr enlisted at nineteen in the Iowa Militia, fighting with the Union army. His career on the battlefield soon ended with his capture, and he was imprisoned in the notorious Andersonville Prison, located in southern Georgia. Of the forty-five thousand Union prisoners of war held at Andersonville, nearly thirteen thousand died. Samuel Parr survived Andersonville, but by the time he was released at the war's end his health was broken. He returned home to Iowa, married, and fathered three daughters before he died at age thirty from the effects of disease, in all likelihood tuberculosis contracted at Andersonville.[13] Margie Parr Tuttle told her sons, Malcolm and Elbert, the story of her father's life and death often during their childhood. That he had died as a result of his fight against slavery caused her "to have a different attitude towards former slaves than most people of her generation." It also left her with an abiding antagonism toward the southern cause. When Elbert wrote to tell his parents he was marrying a "'rebel' from Georgia," his mother wrote back, "Don't ever mention to me marrying a 'rebel.'"[14]

Of the Parr daughters, Nellie Amanda was the first to marry and the first to leave Iowa. Her husband, Charles, contracted tuberculosis, and the only known treatment was to move to a warm, dry climate. Nellie and Charles moved to California and settled near Pasadena, where they raised chickens and grew apricots. Nellie's sister Margie and her widowed mother, Lucie, soon joined them, and Margie Parr was followed west by her suitor, Guy Tuttle. Margie and Guy married in Pasadena on April 2, 1895, and their two sons were born in short order, Malcolm on April 20, 1896, and Elbert on July 17, 1897. Elbert Parr Tuttle was born in a home owned by his parents at 306 Moline (now El Molino) Avenue in Pasadena.

In California, Guy Tuttle found work as a clerk for the Southern Pacific Railroad. At the same time, Earl Warren's father was a car repairman and inspector with the Southern Pacific in Los Angeles and Bakersfield.[15] Guy Tuttle's job qualified him for railroad passes. They allowed the young family to travel across the vast country, back to the East Coast as well as to Ames,

Iowa, where Guy's parents ran a boardinghouse. Although Guy Tuttle held a white-collar job with the railroad, he saw little opportunity for advancement. In 1900 he moved the family to Washington, D.C., where he worked in what was then known as the Department of War.

The Tuttle family stayed only a few years in Washington, just long enough for Malcolm and Elbert to start school there and for an event to occur that Elbert Tuttle would recall all of his life. Elbert spent many afternoons sitting on the front porch of their home at 1515 Corcoran Street with his mother. One day, as Margie Tuttle watched her son, she also watched a small drama unfold on the street. An older black woman waited at the corner streetcar stop, but she waited in vain. One streetcar, then another, passed her by without stopping. After the second went by, Margie Tuttle went into the house and came back out with her hat on and her pocket-book in hand; admonishing Elbert to stay put, she walked to the streetcar stop and stood there. The next streetcar stopped. Margie Tuttle stepped aside, watched the other woman board, and returned to her porch.[16]

In 1903 the Bureau of Immigration was transferred into the newly established Department of Commerce and Labor.[17] Guy Tuttle applied for a position and was hired and posted to Los Angeles. Then, in less than two years he was posted to Nogales, Arizona. The family spent only a year in Nogales, where, dismayed by the poor quality of the schools, Margie tutored the boys at home. At the end of the year, when Guy Tuttle was posted back to Los Angeles, the family returned to a home on Dewey Avenue near 10th Street in the northwestern part of the city. They were only about two miles from the area called Hollywood, then made up mostly of chicken farms. They lived close enough to the public swimming pools called Bimini Baths to walk there and close enough to Linda Vista, the small community just north of Pasadena where Margie Tuttle's sister Nellie lived with her husband, Charles, to visit often. Aunt Nellie and Uncle Charles had a son and a daughter who were close in age to the Tuttle boys, and the first cousins were fast friends.

As pleasant as life in Los Angeles was, Guy and Margie Tuttle did not linger there. Worried because Guy's job offered limited possibilities for advancement, Margie Tuttle shared her concerns with her friends, among them the Templeton sisters from Allerton, Iowa, who had moved to Hawaii as missionaries for the Church of Christ. Lena Templeton had married

W. A. Ramsay, who had enjoyed great success in the sugar industry.[18] In 1907 Lena Ramsay wrote her friend Margie Tuttle that the Hawaiian Sugar Planters' Association had an opening for a bookkeeper. Guy secured the position, and the Tuttles left for Hawaii. In San Francisco they boarded the steamship *Sierra* for a voyage across open ocean that took six days. They arrived on Oahu on September 23, 1907.[19] Islanders crowded the pier, draping arriving passengers with leis, and Hawaiian music filled the air. Steamer Day, even though it came once a week, was always an occasion.

CHAPTER THREE

Life Was a Breeze

The physical isolation of the Hawaiian Islands, the way their small surfaces sit surrounded by the vast ocean, made young Elbert Tuttle acutely aware of geography. Having the deposed queen of Hawaii, a woman of color, live around the corner made him acutely aware of politics.[1]

When the Tuttles arrived on Oahu, the public schools educated mostly Hawaiian children and the children of Asian laborers. For their sons, Guy and Margie chose the Punahou School, founded to educate the children of missionaries and already something of an elite academy. More than six decades later, Madelyn and Stanley Dunham would choose Punahou for their grandson, Barack Obama. By the time Malcolm and Elbert Tuttle enrolled, the school population included native Hawaiians and students of Philippine, Japanese, and Chinese ancestry. The admission of nonwhite students had not been accomplished without controversy, and students classified as "white" remained a substantial majority.[2] Still, Elbert Tuttle would grow up and be educated in the most racially integrated society in America.[3]

In both Nogales and Hawaii Tuttle's parents eschewed the public schools. The irony of the situation did not escape Tuttle. In 1974 he wrote his colleague on the bench, Judge Bryan Simpson, who had been vilified for his courage and integrity in overseeing the desegregation of public schools in Florida:

> You will be interested to know that when my brother and I arrived in Honolulu at the ages of 9 and 10 years our established friends in Honolulu convinced my mother that her boys should not go to the public schools of Honolulu because there were so many natives and Chinese and Japanese kids there. Fortunately, we did not miss any of the richness of school life by reason of this fact, because Punahou School from which I graduated in 1914

had a graduating class of which less than a third of us were Anglo-Saxon white. I guess we just mixed with the third generation orientals there instead of the second generation.[4]

Like many private schools on the mainland, Punahou Academy had been founded to provide a segregated haven for the Caucasian children of missionaries. The pioneer missionaries had recognized at once the need for schools for Hawaiian children, "particularly for the children of the chiefs . . . that are soon to sway the nation," and in 1839 a mission school called the Chiefs' Children's School opened.[5] It was strictly for Hawaiian children; "any notion of sending their [the missionaries'] children to school with Hawaiian students was out of the question."[6] For two decades, the missionaries persisted in sending their children back to the United States for schooling. The Congregationalists who first arrived had by and large been educated in the finest schools in New England, and they were committed to providing the same education to their children. When the children reached school age, either the entire family returned home or the children were sent back, across the Pacific Ocean and then across the continent, entrusted to family and friends half a world away. Communication between the islands and the continent was difficult at best; some children reportedly never saw their parents again.

The distress caused to both parents and children by this practice was severe. It was exceeded only by the contemplation of the alternative:

> Reports on the experience of the English missionaries in Tahiti reached Hawai'i as early as 1823, increasing already inflated fears of integrated schools. The reports included tales of unsupervised young girls "entertaining" native friends and using intoxicating beverages; two of the mission offspring were even said to be walking the streets of London. Clearly Tahitians and Hawaiians had a quite different approach to biological urges than properly educated and chaperoned New Englanders![7]

In 1840, as the ship carrying the missionaries' offspring pulled away from the dock, a distraught seven-year-old girl captured everyone's attention. Stretching her arms out over the rails, she shrieked in a piercing cry, "Oh father, dear father, do take me back." Caroline Armstrong's plea echoed in the hearts of the community, and that June the mission voted to establish a school at Punahou. The next spring, the Reverend

Daniel Dole and his wife arrived at the mission; he was designated the first principal. His wife worked by his side at the small school, and their son Sanford was born in their home on the campus. The school opened on July 11, 1842, with fifteen students; by the end of the year, the number had risen to thirty-four. All were children of missionaries; only children of missionaries were eligible for admission. Before the decade closed, the school had dropped its restriction, and Hawaiian students were admitted.

Among the first students was Samuel Chapman Armstrong. Armstrong's parents had been early missionaries, but in 1848 his father resigned his pastorate and became the minister of public instruction under Kamehameha III. Armstrong attended Punahou from 1844 to 1859 and graduated from Williams College in Williamston, Massachusetts, in 1861. Along with a number of classmates from Williams, he volunteered for the Union army. Having fought at Harpers Ferry and distinguished himself at Gettysburg, Armstrong applied for command of black troops. Late in 1863 he was appointed lieutenant colonel of the Ninth Regiment, U.S. Colored Troops. His success with his command won him a promotion to colonel and command of the Eighth Regiment, U.S. Colored Troops. After the end of the war, Armstrong retired from the army as a brevet brigadier general and continued to work with the men he had commanded through the Freedmen's Bureaus. He was appointed bureau superintendent in Hampton, Virginia, in 1866. In 1868 he founded Hampton Institute and served as its principal for twenty-five years. Booker T. Washington wrote of the rewards of his study there: "First was contact with a great man, General S. C. Armstrong, who, I repeat, was, in my opinion, the rarest, strongest, and most beautiful character that it has ever been my privilege to meet."[8] Although Armstrong never returned to Hawaii after graduating from Punahou in 1859, he attributed his commitment to racial equality to his upbringing by his missionary parents in the islands.[9] Just as he never forgot the influence of life in Hawaii, his school never forgot him. In 1993 the Punahou Alumni Association created the Samuel Chapman Armstrong Award to honor Punahou alumni who have made outstanding contributions to mankind. Elbert Tuttle was the first recipient.[10]

The Tuttle family flourished in Hawaii. The Hawaiian Sugar Planters' Association operated an experiment station through the work of a number of divisions, including a Division of Agriculture and Chemistry, a

Division of Entomology, and a Division of Pathology and Physiology. Guy Tuttle worked directly under the business director of the experiment station. The *Report of the Experiment Station Committee* for the year ending September 30, 1908, recorded his arrival: "Mr. G. H. Tuttle, who assumed his duties at the beginning of the fiscal year, has ably conducted the general business of the station; his quiet, business-like handling of affairs has contributed greatly to the smooth running of the station."[11] Regarding the Business Department, the 1909 report noted that "the affairs of this important department have been handled under the management of G. H. Tuttle in a most satisfactory and systematic manner."[12]

By 1910 Guy Tuttle had attained the title of cashier, assumed additional duties, and acquired an assistant. He gathered glowing accolades in the association's annual report: "[The Business] Department has been handled in the most efficient manner by the Cashier, Mr. G. H. Tuttle, and an unusually large amount of matters concerned with the dispatching of letters, reports, and publications; the filing of correspondence, records, and statistics; the keeping of Station accounts; and the general business affairs of the institution have been attended to."[13] In 1914 Guy Tuttle was transferred "from the Station to take charge of the central accounting office under the treasurer of the association."[14]

For Elbert and Malcolm Tuttle, life in Hawaii was a breeze. They settled into a house their parents rented on Keeaumoku Street, just three blocks from the Punahou School. In 1910 they moved around the corner when Guy and Margie bought a home at 1354 Wilder Street across from Guy's office at the Hawaiian Sugar Planters' Association. The deed, dated February 11, 1910, indicates a selling price of $4,500. Title was taken in Margie Tuttle's name.[15] Both homes were a scant few blocks from the home of one of the boys' schoolmates, Platt Cooke. Platt's grandparents had been among the first missionaries in Hawaii. His father was the president of sugar producer Alexander & Baldwin, Ltd.; in 1913 Cooke became the president of the Hawaiian Sugar Planters' Association. Their homestead included stables, and Platt Cooke generously shared his horses with his schoolmates. Malcolm and Elbert grew accustomed to riding out to Kapiolani Park and up Mount Tantalus. Unfortunately, Platt Cooke only studied at Punahou through the eighth grade; his family sent him to the Hotchkiss School in Connecticut for high school. When Platt Cooke's horses weren't available, Malcolm and Elbert hiked up Mount Tantalus. Coming down, they would make their way to Waikiki Beach, where they would join their friends to swim and surf at the Outrigger Club. Both boys were agile and quick learners, and in the summer of 1909 they participated in surfing competitions.

That fall, the brothers turned their attention from water currents to air currents. Punahou allowed students to choose an area to study; Malcolm and Elbert chose aviation. They studied aviation in the islands, from the legendary Maui, who was said to have flown over the islands in a giant kite, to a man who had floated over in a balloon at the turn of the century. Using silk, bamboo, wire, and an electric motor, the boys constructed a scale model of the Wright brothers' 1903 biplane. Though the motor proved too heavy and the model would not fly, it was an impressive effort; the Tuttle brothers were asked by Punahou to display and discuss it at commencement that June.

That summer the family moved. In May, Guy and Margie bought a lot in Kaimuki, a sparsely populated residential neighborhood up in the hills above Waikiki, about six miles from Punahou. For eight hundred dollars they acquired a lot that measured 100 × 166.8 feet at 1018 Sixth Avenue. Again they took title in Margie's name. Their new home went up quickly, and by the time the school year started they had moved into their new home. Meanwhile, the boys' new aviation project was well under way. Margie subscribed to the *Woman's Home Companion*, and the July 1910 issue carried an article by Harold Lynn titled "How to Build a Practical Glider." Malcolm and Elbert set to work, and by late October they had completed a glider. On Sunday, October 23, 1910, they took it out for a test flight. Fifteen feet long and eighteen feet wide, the glider weighed only forty pounds. Constructed of wood, cotton cloth, and piano wire, it was designed for calm days with winds below ten miles per hour. That Sunday the trade winds held steady at about ten miles per hour. Undaunted, the boys trudged with the glider seven blocks up to the Kaimuki Crater, where the hills sloped into the wind.

Malcolm went first; he lifted the wings over his head and ran downhill, with Elbert holding the tail up and running along behind him. They had taken only two or three steps when the glider jerked upward and lifted Malcolm off the ground, but only for a moment. On the second try, Malcolm glided a little farther, and then, on the third, he took off and flew at an altitude of ten feet for a distance of some forty feet. He was in the air long enough for Elbert to snap a dramatic picture before a gust of wind slapped the glider from the sky and knocked it askew. Malcolm was unhurt, but the glider was too damaged to fly. After Malcolm's crash, Malcolm and Elbert never took to the sky again, although the glider, patched up, did have one more outing. That Christmas, the Bible school party at Central Union Church included a special appearance. Dressed as Santa, Malcolm rode the glider down a cable from the Sunday school room balcony to a platform on the floor.[16] The stunt was a huge success and was followed by a New Year's Day story in the *Pacific Advertiser* describing Malcolm's flight in October, which, though brief, remains the first recorded flight in the Hawaiian Islands.

Although Malcolm and Elbert gave up flying, they continued to surf. Their headquarters was the Outrigger Club, which their father helped found. Guy Tuttle, busy with his duties at the Sugar Planters' Association and his young family, had found time to help Alexander Hume Ford organize the Outrigger Club. Not long after the club opened, the founders invited young Hawaiians from Waikiki Beach to join their swim team. Some did. World champion Duke Kahanamoku did not, although he would finally join in 1917 and remain a member the rest of his life.[17] In those early years, Duke swam and surfed with his Hawaiian friends. In 1911 William Rawlins, a haole attorney who often watched the boys swim, contrived to clock Duke. Rawlins marked out a one-hundred-yard course and encouraged Duke and two friends to swim it against each other. His stopwatch confirmed what he thought he had seen—Duke Kahanamoku was swimming at or barely under world record speed. Rawlins began coaching Duke and some of his friends. Meanwhile, the Outrigger Club flourished, despite the virtual disappearance of the founder and president, Alexander Ford. In late 1908 Ford simply boarded a liner bound for Vancouver, British Columbia, leaving no forwarding address or scheduled return date. The vacuum he left was filled by Guy Tuttle, who served as acting president in 1909–10. Early in 1910 the club elected Judge Sanford B. Dole, former president of the Hawaiian Republic and first governor of the territory of Hawaii, as its second president; Guy Tuttle was elected secretary.[18]

Guy Tuttle also worked with a group of sports enthusiasts pushing for Hawaiian membership in the United States Amateur Athletic Union. In 1911 a charter was granted to the Hawaiian Association of the AAU, and Guy Tuttle became the first president. On August 11, 1911, he served as clerk of the course for an American Amateur Swimming Meet at the Alakea slip on the Honolulu waterfront. Elbert Tuttle, now fourteen, was there; he had come to cheer on his friends from school, but instead he found himself applauding Duke Kahanamoku's breathtaking speed. Duke broke two American Amateur records that day. He broke the record for 50 yards by 1 3/5 seconds, swimming it in 24 1/5 seconds, and he broke the record for 100 yards by an astonishing 4 3/5 seconds, swimming it in 55 2/5 seconds.[19] Duke's friends and fans were jubilant, but their jubilance was short lived. The AAU rejected the times. Guy Tuttle had run the event with precision and accuracy, but the times were "simply so startling that the Mainland officials refused to go along with them."[20] The Hawaiian press thought it knew why:

> That Kahanamoku actually swam faster than is recorded of any man is beyond reasonable dispute. . . . There is bound to be a protest in . . . "The East" about his record. We are some sporting nation, but it must be admitted that that part of "we" which hangs around the corners of Tecumseh, Maine, and Forty-fifth Street, New York, are sometimes inclined to turn a collection of supercilious noses skywards over an American or world's amateur record of any sort actually being held by a "South Sea Islander" whom they might actually think at this moment is blowing the ashes under a pot destined for the parboiling of a missionary.[21]

Duke Kahanamoku was vindicated on a grand scale a year later at the Stockholm Olympic Games, when he smashed the world record in the one-hundred-meter freestyle.[22] Although the whole world did not notice, Guy Tuttle was vindicated as well.

The Tuttle family was well off thanks to Guy's industry and Margie's thrift. He had won a secure place at the Hawaiian Sugar Planters' Association; she managed the household so efficiently that it seemed she "saved a dollar from every dime he brought into the house," her son Elbert would remember laughingly. They were devoted to each other. She called him "dearest"; he called her "precious." If they were to use each other's given names, the boys would know something was amiss. Theirs was an exceedingly happy marriage, as happy, their son Elbert recalled decades later, as any he had ever known.

Margie and Guy Tuttle were both deeply religious. He was a Congregationalist, while she was a member of the Church of Christ. In Honolulu the Tuttle family joined the First Christian Church.[23] Margie insisted on regular church attendance; ordinarily, they went to services both Sunday morning and Sunday evening. Guy, an elder, sang in the choir. At that time, many church people thought it a sin to do anything on the Sabbath other than attend services and take meals at home with their family. Elbert and Malcolm often broke away to surf on Sunday afternoon; Elbert later surmised that no one "really thought that was a very sinful act."[24] Margie indulged her sons in their surfing on Sunday, but every night she made her boys take a pledge at their evening prayers that they would never use alcohol or tobacco. As a child, Elbert thought that if he did smoke a cigarette or take a drink, he would simply be struck dead. He outgrew that notion, but he never violated his pledge. Malcolm abided by his mother's rules with less rigor; when his mother chastised him as an adult, having caught him with a cigarette, he replied, "It's all right, mother; you've still got Elbert."

A gentle man, Guy Tuttle left all discipline of the children to his wife. Where he was easygoing, she was strict, and her standards were extremely high. She would punish the boys for uttering such mild expletives as "darn" and "gosh." Elbert "thought [he] would be struck dead if [he] ever said dammit."[25] Throughout his life, when confronted by conduct that might drive other men to profanity, he would utter "my word," his tone of voice expressing his surprise or outrage. Although Guy Tuttle, in contrast to most fathers of the time, never laid a hand on his sons, Margie was not averse to corporal punishment. In March 1901, when the family was packing for a move, Guy and Margie gave the boys fruit baskets for their toys. Elbert promptly presented his, neatly packed, with a little board about a foot long and two inches wide sitting on top. Malcolm protested—"Oh, Elbert, you don't want to take that old board." "Yes, I do want to take it," Elbert answered, "so in case I am naughty Precious can paddle me with it."[26]

For all her firmness, Margie Tuttle simply delighted in her boys, and they were extraordinarily close to each other and to their parents. "Every night," their mother wrote, "before going to bed they have a romp with their papa—Dearest they call him—and they never, never go to sleep without repeating over and over again—"Precious, I love you, you are sweet, good night. Dearest, I love you. You are sweet, good night." When six-year-old Elbert arrived home one afternoon to find new toy animals, he fairly burst with excitement and began claiming them: "I'm going to have the baby horsie; I'm going to have the bunny." Then he caught himself and announced, "I am not going to choose one until Malcolm gets here so he can have the first choice." Malcolm, at eight, saved soap wrappers for months, and when the time came to send them in and claim his prize, he put aside what he wanted and picked something out for Elbert instead.

The boys had started kindergarten together in 1901 in Los Angeles, and since they were dressed alike and were the same weight and almost the same size, many took them for twins. Their mother had but one worry; the next year, Malcolm would go on to first grade, leaving Elbert in kindergarten. "It breaks my heart to think of having them separated and I dread to think how they will stand the trial. O they are treasures."[27] The boys survived their separation in elementary school in Los Angeles. That would change in Hawaii. The family arrived in Honolulu in late September 1907, a week after school had begun for the year. Malcolm and Elbert enrolled in Punahou Academy, Malcolm in the sixth and Elbert in the fifth grade. Both brothers were excellent students. At the end of the year, a teacher took them aside to ask a rhetorical question: did the boys plan to go on to college? They did. The teacher pointed out that they would have to go to college on the mainland; in 1907 there was no college in the Hawaiian Islands. They might, he thought, wish to go together. They did. But if they were to start college together, Elbert would have to catch up. He was a very good student, good enough, the teacher suggested, to skip a year and join Malcolm in the seventh grade.

Elbert skipped sixth grade. He missed very little academically, although he maintained throughout his life that as a result of this promotion he never learned the kings and queens of England. He was a shy child, however, and vaulting forward a year did not serve him well socially. Throughout his high school years he never had a date, except a formal engagement for the final event—senior prom. Malcolm, on the other hand, enjoyed his share of dates, although he apparently was not always a successful swain. Once the school magazine contained a short poem, "Advice to M. Tuttle, Esq.":

> There are letters of accent,
> There are letters of tone,
> But the best of all letters,
> Is to let her alone.[28]

On another occasion, a column addressed the topic "What Makes Them Popular?" Of M.T. (Malcolm Tuttle) it advised, "Ask P.R." (a female friend's initials); of E.T. (Elbert Tuttle) it explained, "His sense."[29]

Even as an adolescent, Elbert Tuttle stood out for his intelligence and good sense. Although he was a year younger than his classmates, he excelled academically. In his junior year, the school magazine marveled, "15 and on the Honor Roll."[30] Senior year Elbert Tuttle was class president and managing editor of the *Oahuan*, the literary magazine that with its June issue also served as the yearbook. He was president of the Punahou Athletic Club as well, although by then his only sport was football, and he had only managed to move from third to second team. The truth was that he rarely took the field, which was a great relief to him, because one of the first times he played he was left reeling after a hard tackle by a two-hundred-pound halfback. Serving as the manager and treasurer of the Glee Club was a considerably safer harbor. One of his best friends was a boy his own age and therefore in the class behind him. Joseph Farrington and Elbert Tuttle shared a passion for journalism and for politics. Joe's father, Wallace Farrington, was the publisher of the *Honolulu Star Bulletin*. Elbert and Joe talked endlessly about Hawaii's relationship to the United States. At one point, they debated each other on the issue, taking opposite sides. In fact, both were committed to statehood for Hawaii, and each was determined to be the first congressman from Hawaii.[31]

At commencement, both Malcolm and Elbert were on the program. Malcolm was one of three students who had a "Commencement Part." His presentation was entitled "Vacuum Tubes (an Original Experiment)." Elbert, as class president, made the class gift. At the end of the program, just before the presentation of degrees, came the announcement of honors, including the highest honor awarded, the Trustees' Cup. It went to Elbert Tuttle. The next year it would go to his friend Joseph Farrington, who in 1942 became the first congressional delegate from the territory of Hawaii.

When Elbert Tuttle left Hawaii to attend college on the mainland, unlike Farrington, he left for good. He loved the islands, and he planned on returning, but it was not to be. One day during his senior year, Professor C. F. Schmutzler, who had joined the Punahou faculty in 1908 and who taught Elbert German, took him aside. Had Elbert given any thought to which college he might attend, Professor Schmutzler asked. Elbert replied that since they had been born in California, he and Malcolm would probably attend the University of California. But Schmutzler objected: "Isn't Malcolm planning to study engineering, and aren't you planning to study law?" Yes, Elbert replied, those were their plans. Well, Professor Schmutzler explained, the brothers couldn't go to Berkeley, because it didn't have a good engineering school. There were only two good engineering schools, in his opinion: Boston Tech (now MIT) and Cornell University in Ithaca, New York. But Boston Tech did not award a bachelor of arts degree, and Elbert would need a BA in order to go on to the Harvard Law School. So, Professor Schmutzler concluded, Malcolm and Elbert should go to Cornell. The decision was soon made, and in August 1914, accompanied by their mother and their motorcycle, the brothers left for Cornell.

The motorcycle was Elbert's second. Entrepreneurial from an early age, Elbert had arranged with the *Advertiser* to deliver the morning paper to Schofield Barracks, some twenty-five miles north of Honolulu, during the summer before his senior year. He bought a used Yale motorcycle and calculated that if he left by 6:00 a.m. he could arrive by 8:00 a.m.; the paper had been going by train, which didn't arrive until 1:00 p.m. It was a good plan, and it would have generated a healthy income for a high school student, but on his first day on the job, Elbert found himself ten miles away from Schofield by the side of the unpaved road with a motorcycle that had utterly broken down. He trudged along, pushing the bike, caught a few rides, and finally reached Schofield about noon. He could never recall what happened to the motorcycle or how he got back to Honolulu, but as soon as he got back he resigned. Later, in the spring of 1914, Malcolm and Elbert decided to buy a second motorcycle. They ordered a brand-new bike from the Excelsior Motorcycle Company, on the mainland. The model they bought was one of the first to have a clutch; no longer did the rider have to turn on the gas, run alongside the motorcycle as the engine caught, and then jump on board while it was running.

When Margie, Malcolm, and Elbert disembarked in San Francisco, they parted ways. The boys planned to motorcycle to Los Angeles and meet their mother at Aunt Nellie's home. Leaving San Francisco, they traveled on good roads for thirty or forty miles before paving gave way to sandy, bumpy stretches. The terrain was treacherous on a motorcycle, and the brothers proceeded with caution. In the end, the trip took them three full days, and they arrived in Los Angeles, fast running out of both money and gasoline, to find that the family had gone on to Long Beach. Bedraggled and exhausted, their spirits were restored by the warm welcome they received when they finally arrived in Long Beach. The next week, Margie and her sons took the train east; the motorcycle, crated, went with them. They arrived as the school year started and took rooms in a house a block and a half from campus, at 306 College Avenue. There were no dormitories at Cornell in 1914, and Margie decided to stay in Ithaca with her sons for their first year.

A seventeen-year-old college freshman, Elbert Tuttle had lived on the East Coast, on the West Coast, in Arizona on the border with Mexico, and in Hawaii; he had toured the White House, sunned himself at the Bimini Baths, summered in rural Iowa, surfed Waikiki, and criss-crossed the country by train more than a few times—all of this by 1914, long before interstate highways and air travel would make long-distance traveling common. Now the East Coast would claim him.

CHAPTER FOUR

College Years

The first year at Cornell—and for that matter every year at Cornell—was a busy one for Elbert. When he graduated four years later, his list of activities would take more than seven lines of fine type in a class where most lists ran two or three lines and only a couple required six. One classmate, Bill Ellis, vividly remembered seeing Elbert for the first time. Early in their freshmen year, they both attended a large student meeting. Ellis did not recall the issue at hand, only that it got out of control and produced a hot argument. "The snarl got worse and worse until a slender, modest but poised and plain-spoken young man rose to his feet. He proposed a solution to the difficulty, whatever it was, and when he finished speaking, the argument was settled. That was Elbert Tuttle. It was the first time I ever saw him. . . . And from that time to this, I have known that Elbert is a leader among men."[1]

Elbert arrived at Cornell with an interest in journalism. As a senior at Punahou, he had written an occasional school story for the *Advertiser*. That experience, combined with an incident that occurred soon after he arrived at Cornell, propelled him to try out for the *Cornell Daily Sun*. One day on campus he noticed a student conversing casually with an esteemed member of the faculty. Impressed and intrigued, he asked who the student was. He was, someone explained, the editor in chief of the *Cornell Daily Sun*. Elbert Tuttle set his sights on that post; he wanted to occupy the position of respect on campus so clearly occupied by the present editor. Simply getting on the *Sun* staff, let alone attaining the editorship, was no easy task. The paper ran a competition for freshman, or, to be more accurate, for the one spot open to a freshman. In the spring of 1915, fifty-eight hopeful freshmen went all out in the competition. Elbert Tuttle won.

During their freshman year, Malcolm and Elbert pledged a fraternity, Alpha Theta. One benefit of membership was the opportunity to live in the fraternity house beginning with their sophomore year. Their lodging was now secure, so at the end of their freshman year they said good-bye to their mother when Margie departed for Hawaii to rejoin her husband. Two years later, Alpha Theta merged with Pi Kappa Alpha. Ironically, Elbert Tuttle had joined the fraternity that throughout the twentieth century would be most associated with the old South. Pi Kappa Alpha had been founded by six friends, three of whom had fought for the Confederacy in the Civil War, at the University of Virginia in the spring of 1868. When the PIKA charter was granted to the Cornell chapter on March 26, 1917, Elbert Tuttle, attending the national convention, received it.

It cost far too much for Malcolm and Elbert to travel to Hawaii and back, so they spent the summer of 1915 with their father's brother Elbert and his wife, Alice, in Philadelphia. Uncle Bert, an engineer, worked for Bell Telephone Company of Pennsylvania. An engineering major, Malcolm managed to get a summer job with an iron works in Camden, New Jersey. Once again, Elbert tried the entrepreneurial route. Just as he arrived in Philadelphia, the streetcar employees went on strike. Private citizens had started carrying passengers for five cents a ride. Elbert put twenty dollars down on a car at a dealership; before he paid the balance he discovered that the city council levied a large license fee on "jitney" buses. When he went back to the dealer to try to recover his down payment, the dealer laughed at the thought. Elbert never got the twenty dollars or the car. Uncle Bert came to the rescue with a job at the phone company, and Elbert spent the summer writing rate schedules.

Malcolm and Elbert returned to Cornell in the fall and moved into the three-story, Tudor-style Alpha Theta fraternity house, which sat just one block west of the campus. Malcolm continued his studies in mechanical engineering, while Elbert took courses in American history, psychology, political science, and French. The teacher Elbert recalled with the greatest admiration from his first year was Professor Martin Sampson, who taught freshman English. Sophomore year, particular honors in his estimation went to Professor J. F. Mason, the French teacher. But most of Elbert's energy did not go into his classroom work; when the time came to select a science, he registered for geology because it was rumored to be the easiest. Most of his effort went into his work on the campus newspaper, the *Sun*. Published daily, it demanded prodigious effort from the student staff.

That summer, Malcolm and Elbert returned to Hawaii. The steamships that plied the waters from San Francisco to Honolulu sailed from

San Francisco every ten days. By the time the boys' cross-country train and steamship fares arrived, sent by their parents from Hawaii, they did not have time to arrange for reservations. They decided to try to make the first sailing they could. Their train had a daytime layover in Denver, where they had an invitation to lunch. A young woman at the Alpha Theta commencement party, hearing about their travel plans, had invited them to her cousin's Denver home. Malcolm and Elbert arrived in Denver at about 10:00 a.m. The timing was perfect; the only impediment to the plan was their luggage. They finally decided to stack it carefully in the middle of the terminal floor and simply leave it there; they reasoned that it would be safe because anyone who saw it there would assume the owner had a watchful eye on it. Having enjoyed a luncheon at Helen Spratt's home that proved to be the beginning of a friendship that would endure sixty years, they returned to the station to find the stack of luggage intact. Malcolm's ukulele and Elbert's mandolin rested on top, untouched.

They reached San Francisco the day before the *Lurline* sailed, but the only tickets left were in steerage. Steerage passengers slept below decks in bunks stacked three deep and dined on the fare prepared for the crew. It was not an attractive prospect, but the alternative was a ten-day wait for the next steamship. After their first night in steerage, Elbert organized a small string band. Malcolm played ukulele, Elbert played mandolin, a classmate from Punahou who was traveling first class chimed in on violin, and a part-Hawaiian student also returning from college and booked in steerage played the steel guitar. Steerage passengers were confined to the main deck, but Elbert thought that if they played Hawaiian music, they might be invited to the passenger decks. He was right. They passed the rest of the voyage dining on buffet meals set out for first-class passengers and sleeping on deck—except for Elbert. He bunked with a Punahou classmate who had an empty cot in his cabin.

Elbert went directly to the *Advertiser* offices to apply for a summer job. He hoped his high school contributions to the paper, combined with his experience on the *Cornell Daily Sun*, would help him secure a position. His qualifications proved less critical than his timing. The day before, the sports editor had sailed east, apparently one step ahead of the sheriff. The editor asked Elbert if he could handle the sports page; full of confidence, Elbert said it would be easy for him. It turned out that it was. Even though he was responsible for the copy for one entire page, he usually finished up in the early afternoon and spent the late afternoon surfing at Waikiki Beach, and he earned a respectable twenty-five dollars a week. That summer marked the beginning of a lifelong love affair with baseball. Although he had never been to a Major League game, he wrote copy on up to ten National and American League games a day. The box scores arrived by Morse code by about ten in the morning; armed with those and the names of the pitchers, Elbert would reconstruct the games. He also wrote stories describing local games he actually saw. Among the teams he recalled covering were a Japanese team for Keiou University and a team representing a black infantry regiment stationed at Schofield Barracks. Malcolm found work as well. He was taken on by the engineering firm starting the construction of a major naval base at the great natural basin known as Pearl Harbor.

Fall found the boys back in Ithaca, back at the fraternity house, back in classes, and Elbert back at the *Daily Sun*, where he scored a great coup. Elbert was night editor at the *Daily Sun* on November 7, 1916, the day of the presidential election. Former Supreme Court justice Charles Evans Hughes, the Republican candidate, had run a strong campaign against the incumbent, President Woodrow Wilson. As the returns came in, Hughes appeared to have won, and Wilson went to bed thinking he had been defeated. Only a junior in college, Elbert had followed the campaign and focused on what many seasoned reporters overlooked. The Republican governor of California, Hiram Johnson, had offered Hughes only lukewarm support. Because he thought Hughes might not carry his home state, Elbert ran a banner headline saying only what he knew to be true as they went to press: "Early Returns Show Hughes Slight Favorite." Many East Coast newspapers reported a victory for Hughes, but Elbert proved prescient. Woodrow Wilson carried California by 3,400 votes and was reelected.

In the spring, junior board members of the *Sun* wrote editorials in a competition to be named editor in chief. Elbert wrote several editorials favoring the creation of a student council. Those editorials, in combination with his overall record, earned him the office. He was selected days after a German submarine sank the *Lusitania*, a British ship with many Americans on board, and the United States declared war on Germany. Taking office immediately, Elbert published his first editorial as editor in chief on April 12, 1917. It was not about the student council. "In view of the presence of the Nation in the list of belligerent countries," he wrote, "affairs of national import far outweigh, in the minds of Cornell students and Faculty alike, matters of local and University interest."[2] A number of students left the university and enlisted in the war effort. Among them was C. M. Micou, whom Tuttle had considered his principal competitor for the editorship. Micou enlisted in the United States Marine Corps. Too soon, word came back that he had been killed in combat in Europe.

Elbert Tuttle had decided to enlist in the United States Air Force. He wasn't eligible until he turned twenty-one, however, and that would be the July following his graduation, so he stayed on at school, where he had been elected president of the student council, and he remained active in his fraternity. That fall, in recognition of the seriousness of the ongoing conflict, the Cornell fraternities canceled Junior Week. William A. Hammond, the secretary of the faculty, wrote a letter of thanks to Tuttle on November 12, 1917:

> My dear Mr. Tuttle:
>
> Permit me to say that I am proud of the action taken by you Cornell Fraternity Boys (you deserve the capitals) in canceling the traditional pleasures of Junior Week for the current year, and trebly proud that the action was a free and deliberate expression of your own feelings and ideals. The formulation of these feelings and ideals were, I believe, in large measure due to you personally, and I wish to congratulate you. After the hardships of the terrible struggle are over, you will look back upon this act with gladness.
>
> Very sincerely yours,
> Wm. A. Hammond[3]

During Tuttle's senior year, while he served as editor in chief of the *Cornell Daily Sun*, E. B. White won the freshman competition and joined the board. Like every other Cornell undergraduate named White, E. B. was called Andy in honor of the first president of Cornell, Andrew White. Later he became known to the world as the author of *Charlotte's Web* and the coauthor of Strunk and White's *Elements of Style*. Recalling that he had been "Andy" White's first editor, in future decades Elbert Tuttle enjoyed occasionally, with tongue in cheek, taking credit for teaching E. B. White all he knew about writing.

CHAPTER FIVE

Sara Sutherland

The summer of 1917, following their junior year, Malcolm and Elbert couldn't afford the cost of returning to Hawaii. When Elbert's fraternity brother Strawn Perry invited him to spend the summer with Strawn's family in Jacksonville, Florida, Elbert accepted gratefully. Strawn's father, the president of the Florida National Bank, arranged summer jobs for both boys at the bank. As soon as school let out, Elbert and Strawn traveled by boat from New York to Charleston, South Carolina, a two-day journey. They were met there by Strawn's friend Charlie Murchison. Murchison later married Helen Spratt, who had hosted the Tuttle boys in Denver the previous summer.

Charlie, Strawn, and Elbert arrived in Jacksonville the next morning about 10:00 a.m., and Strawn promptly put together a swimming party for noon. He arranged a date for Elbert and took as his own date his neighbor, eighteen-year-old Sara Sutherland. Fortunately, Strawn and Sara did not have a serious relationship, because Elbert Tuttle fell in love with Sara Sutherland at first sight. He was devastated when, after a week, Sara seemed to disappear. She had blithely taken off for a house party in Atlanta. He never forgot how desolate he was until she reappeared some ten days later.

Only nineteen years old when the summer began, Elbert Tuttle was president of his fraternity, president of the student council, and editor in chief of the *Cornell Daily Sun*, but when it came to girls he was shy and inexperienced. He courted Sara formally. Every evening, just after supper, he appeared at her home. For most of the summer he called her "Miss Sutherland"; he was waiting for her to give him permission to use her first name, while she was wondering how long this could last. "No one," she would laugh some sixty years later, "had ever called me Miss Sutherland before." Often the two young people would sit in her parlor and converse while listening to classical music. Elbert was enthralled; he simply knew the moment he laid eyes on Sara that he wanted her to be his wife. As lively as she was pretty, Sara enjoyed their evenings, but that didn't stop her from slipping out with friends after he had gone home. Elbert's strict code of conduct led him to leave around 10:30; Sara, on the other hand, maintained that on blazing hot summer days in Jacksonville, the day didn't really start until late afternoon, and it didn't end until 1:00 or 2:00 in the morning. For Sara, falling in love was a gradual process, but she was increasingly charmed by her serious suitor.

Elbert returned to Cornell for his senior year having just turned twenty. That fall, tragedy struck the Sutherland family when Sara's father suddenly fell ill and died. Born in 1868 in Louisville, Georgia, deep in the impoverished South, Sara's father had been named Phocion Leonidas Sutherland, for Phocion, an Athenian general and statesman, and Leonidas, the king of Sparta. It was an extraordinary name, especially for a man who had almost no formal education. Phocion Leonidas Sutherland was known simply as P.L. He had made his way in the world bit by bit, starting at age thirteen or fourteen selling candy, cigarettes, drinks, and gum on trains and moving on to work as a tobacco salesman. By 1895, when a friend named Norman Miller introduced him to Jennie Mattox, he had already made a success of himself. P. L. Sutherland and Jennie Mattox were married on December 5, 1895, in her hometown, Newnan, Georgia.

Jennie's mother, widowed three years earlier, had taken over their Coweta family farm. Momma Betty was a woman of strong character and strong will. "There was practically nothing she couldn't do," her granddaughter Sara recalled, and to top it off "she was a marvelous cook." But she was also a woman alone in rural Georgia. P.L. insisted that Momma Betty come live with them in College Park, just outside Atlanta. Sara's older brother, Bill, was born on October 4, 1896. Sara and her twin sister, Caroline, were born on July 24, 1898; Caroline died on July 14, 1899, when the twins were just short of one year old. After her death, the family moved to Florida, where P.L. had turpentine and lumber interests. Another daughter, Jennie, was born on August 30, 1900. The family sometimes lived in the turpentine camps, sometimes in cities; Sara recalled homes in both Saint Augustine and Jacksonville from those early years. Life in the camps was like life on a plantation. The Sutherland family lived in a comfortable home, while the laborers lived in dilapidated dwellings. Sara remembered that her mother was kept busy trying to provide for the health needs of the workers and their families to the limited extent that she could.

By 1906 P.L. was able to buy the colonial home in Newnan where his wife had been born. Built in 1826, the house had twelve-foot ceilings, a fireplace in every room, and, after P.L. renovated it, indoor plumbing and electricity. He and Jennie went to New York to buy furniture and returned with a baby grand piano, mahogany furniture for most of the house, and gold Louis Seize pieces for the music room. Sara was still using much of that furniture in her Atlanta home when she died near the end of the twentieth century. All the care that had gone into the Newnan home notwithstanding, the family lived there less than a year. In 1907 they moved to western Florida, near Quincy, where P.L. had tobacco plantations. Sara thought they moved because the bottom fell out of the timber market. At any rate, her father lost a good deal of money. Still, Quincy was home to one of Sara's fondest childhood memories. A friend of her parents, Col. Walter Corbett, gave her "a marvelous little fast moving horse."

P.L. began to worry about his children's education. Except for a short stint at Georgia Military Academy in College Park, Bill had been educated entirely by tutors. Often Bill's tutor lived with the family, particularly in the turpentine camps. The girls relied on their governesses. In 1909 P.L. moved the family to Jacksonville so the children could attend schools that would prepare them for college. It was soon apparent that intellectually Bill was a prodigy. At age fourteen he applied to the University of Virginia; when he was turned down, he went to the University of Florida for one year and then on to the University of Virginia, from which he graduated at seventeen. He went from Charlottesville to Cambridge, Massachusetts, where he studied law at Harvard. Despite his youth, Bill did very well at Harvard Law; upon his graduation United States Supreme Court Justice Louis Brandeis hired him as his law clerk.

Brought up in Georgia and Florida, Sara was steeped in the traditions and lore of the Confederacy. Her family was intensely loyal to the old South. Confederate veterans held annual reunions in Jacksonville; in 1914, when Sara was sixteen, her mother decided to host one for their family. Some forty relatives from Georgia, Virginia, and North Carolina came. Everyone stayed at the Sutherlands' six-bedroom house, which Sara's mother, Jennie, set up dormitory style, with the men on one side and the women on the other. Many of the elderly men who came bore scars from the Civil War.

Sara chauffeured the older folks during the day and, after they retired, partied with their sons and daughters. "We got to bed about two or three a.m. and were waked by the first rebel yell at five a.m.," she often recalled. "It was a huge success."

Sara graduated from Duval High School in 1915 and entered Wellesley College, just outside Boston, that fall. She traveled north by train with Bill, who was going back to Harvard for his second year of law school. Sara was not prepared for the cold and the snow or, highly intelligent as she was, for college algebra and trigonometry. She struggled through the year, and the D she managed to earn in math, she often said, looked better to her than any A ever did. Money was somewhat scarce in the Sutherland household, and Sara decided to transfer to the Florida State College for Women in Tallahassee (now Florida State University). At the end of that year, Jennie graduated from high school, and she and Sara decided to go to college together. They settled on Goucher, a well-regarded college for women in Baltimore.

Jennie and P.L. visited the girls that fall; then Jennie stayed with Bill, who was living in Washington, D.C., and clerking for Justice Brandeis, while P.L. boarded the train for a business trip to Dallas. When a bad cold turned into pneumonia, P.L. disembarked and turned around. Jennie and Bill met the train in Baltimore with an ambulance that took P.L. directly to Saint Agnes Hospital. For a few days he lingered near death with an extremely high fever. When the fever broke, he was able to sit up and converse; he seemed to have recovered. Then the fever recurred. P.L. slipped into a coma and died three days later, on November 1, 1917. He was forty-nine years old. His widow, Jennie, was forty-one. Sara found a way to get word to Elbert, in Ithaca. He came to Baltimore immediately, arriving in time to accompany the family as far as Washington with P.L.'s body before he returned to Cornell. After P.L.'s funeral, in Jacksonville, Jennie and Momma Betty moved to D.C., where Bill's Washington apartment became the Sutherland family home.

In May, Elbert graduated from Cornell. Shortly before graduating, he enlisted as a flying cadet in the air force, then a part of the United States Army Signal Corps. Waiting to be called for active duty, he managed to get a position with the War Planning Board that allowed him to be in D.C. with Sara. On July 17, 1918, his twenty-first birthday, Elbert was called to active duty. The call took him back to Ithaca, to the Cornell campus. To qualify as a flying cadet, Elbert had to attend ground school at the Military School of Aeronautics. His program was conducted at Cornell, and one class, a course on gasoline engines, was taught by his brother, Malcolm. At the end of the term, Malcolm wryly told Elbert that he wouldn't make much of an engineer.

Elbert had no interest in becoming an engineer, but he did want to get in the air. In 1918 there were far more prospective pilots than there were aircraft to fly. Elbert's class was sent to Air Observers School at Post Field, Oklahoma, adjacent to the artillery school at Fort Sill. That fall the great flu epidemic of 1918 held the country in its grip. More than 675,000 Americans and more than 20 million people worldwide succumbed to it. As the troop train crossed the country, it passed through station after station where coffins bearing the bodies of soldiers stood stacked by the dozens. In Dallas, twenty-one-year-old Elbert Tuttle escorted the sergeant in command of his squadron to the hospital and took over command.

Because flying cadets would direct artillery fire from the air, they had to pass the field artillery program for commissioned officers before they could take flying training. Shortly after the squadron completed field artillery training, the Armistice was signed, on November 11, 1918. The war was over. On December 20 Elbert, now a second lieutenant in the air force, his lack of flight training notwithstanding, boarded the train to leave Fort Sill. "Thank heavens," he said to a friend, "I'll never see this place again." He was wrong; more than two decades later he would return to Fort Sill to begin his active duty in World War II.

Elbert spent Christmas of 1918 in Ithaca with his mother and Malcolm. Guy Tuttle had joined the YMCA, which provided the services to soldiers that the USO would provide in later wars; he shipped out from New York shortly before the Armistice was signed and did not return until April. In January Elbert moved to New York City. With a friend from Cornell, Stan Shaw, he took a room in a brownstone on 43rd Street and landed a position as a copy editor with the *New York Evening Sun* at twenty-five dollars a month. He worked from 6:00 a.m. until early afternoon. Reporters on the beat called their stories in, and Elbert typed them. On his second day, a reporter called in a "Jack the Ripper" murder story. Elbert got the details and started typing; as he typed a sentence, a copy boy would rip the sheet out of his typewriter and run it to the city editor. Within thirty or forty minutes, his story was on page 1 of a paper on the streets of New York. Elbert was barely two weeks into his job at the *Sun* when he got an offer to join the staff of the *Army and Navy Journal* at thirty-five dollars a month. The salary increase was an inducement, but it was nothing compared to the fact that the *Journal* was in Washington, D.C. So was Sara. Elbert Tuttle moved to Washington.

The *Army and Navy Journal* was a civilian publication devoted entirely to stories of interest to the military. In 1918 soldiers who had been drafted into World War I were coming home with complaints about the military justice system, and Congress was considering revamping it. Elbert was particularly interested because he had already decided to pursue a career in law. He attended numerous hearings of the Military Affairs Committees in the House and Senate. On one occasion he arranged an interview with the secretary of the navy; the secretary turned out to be unavailable, so the assistant secretary, Franklin D. Roosevelt, sat in for him. Roosevelt, who had not yet suffered his bout with polio, impressed the young journalist with his modest and retiring demeanor.

The occasion that made the most lasting impression on the young reporter arose from a press conference. Elbert was present when President Wilson announced his intention to present the Treaty of Versailles, which would have created the League of Nations, to the Senate for ratification. When asked by a reporter, "Mr. President, what if the Senate refuses to ratify it?" Wilson had answered emphatically, "The Senate will ratify it." But the opponents of the treaty, led by Senator Henry Cabot Lodge, won the day. Lacking the support of the United States, the League of Nations failed. Elbert was dismayed. Throughout his life, he believed that had Wilson succeeded, World War II might have been avoided. After the war, he would commit himself to the Eisenhower candidacy with redoubled energy in part because he so feared Ike's opponent, Robert Taft, who campaigned on an isolationist platform.

Elbert's work kept him busy; he and one other staff member made up the entire Washington office of the *Journal*. But he found time for Sara, and shortly after his return they became engaged. Sara was finishing her studies at Goucher and would earn her bachelor's degree that spring, so they planned an October wedding. Sara had contracted the flu late in 1918, but she recovered fairly quickly from the acute phase and managed to take her exams to finish the first semester. Then she suffered a relapse that forced her to drop out of school. For six weeks she spent most of each day in bed. Even though she had not graduated, Sara and Elbert went ahead with the wedding. At 5:00 p.m. on October 22, 1919, a bright, sunny day, they were married at the Episcopal Church of the Epiphany on G Street. Sara's sister, Jennie, was her maid of honor; Malcolm was Elbert's best man. Bill gave his sister away, and Jennie and Momma Betty prepared a small reception at the Sutherland apartment.

Elbert and Sara spent their wedding night at the Lafayette Hotel, across the street from the White House. The next day they traveled by train to Jacksonville, where Sara's Uncle Julian, P.L.'s youngest brother, loaned them his car. They enjoyed a two-week-long wedding trip in Florida, visiting friends and family and staying at Uncle Julian's country home in San Mateo.

Back in Washington, the newlyweds' first home was an efficiency apartment on L Street near 14th, only two blocks from Elbert's office. They had a living room, bedroom, and bath. There was no kitchen, but they had an electric hot plate on which they could cook. Bill's apartment on Irving Street, where he lived with his mother and grandmother, was only a few blocks away; on many evenings, the young couple would join the Sutherlands for dinner. Jennie was still studying at Goucher in nearby Baltimore, and Sara enrolled for the spring term, hoping to finish the sixteen hours she needed to graduate. In December Elbert took a new job. The American Legion, a veterans' organization, was growing rapidly. Organizers decided to start a magazine, the *American Legion Weekly*. Elbert was offered a job as copy editor at fifty dollars a month. He would be working with a number of nationally known writers who had signed on with the magazine. Despite its promise, the magazine failed financially almost at once. By February he was out of a job, and he had a wife to support.

It was just over a year since Elbert had left New York and his friend Stan Shaw. He recalled that Stan had told him that he had received several offers before he took his first job, so Elbert called Stan for advice. Stan told Elbert that Cornell was looking for a publicity director for its ten-million-dollar endowment campaign. Elbert called Cornell and landed the job; he left for Ithaca almost immediately, and Sara followed a few days later, although leaving Washington meant dropping out of Goucher again. This time, a very determined Sara petitioned the trustees to allow her to take her last sixteen hours at Cornell and then be awarded a degree by Goucher. Sara managed to have her petition signed by each professor she had studied under at Goucher before she delivered it to the president of the college. When she arrived in Ithaca, about two weeks into the term, she enrolled and started classes. Soon word arrived that the Goucher board of trustees had granted her petition.

In Ithaca, Elbert and Sara rented a house on Waite Street, just a block and a half from the College of Arts and Sciences, where Sara would take most of her courses. Three coeds also had rooms in the house. Sara described them as "a Norwegian girl, . . . a cute little Chinese girl, . . . and a wild flapper from Chicago." On one occasion, a coed counselor from Cornell called Sara to ask her to see that the flapper stopped violating the women's curfew. Sara declined. She was, as she told the caller, the same age as her housemate, and she was not a chaperone. By the spring of 1920, Sara had finished enough hours at Cornell to be awarded her degree from Goucher. Because Goucher's graduation had already occurred before the Cornell term ended, she was awarded the degree in 1921. Her sister, Jennie, graduated in 1921 as well and on her graduation day married Mac Asbill, who had been Bill Sutherland's roommate at Harvard Law School.

That first summer in Ithaca, Elbert and Sara moved from the house they shared with the three coeds to an apartment owned by a professor who was away for the summer. At summer's end they moved again. Elbert, who had learned thriftiness at his mother's knee, had managed to accumulate five hundred dollars, which they used for a down payment on a three-thousand-dollar house on State Street. Built on a hill that sloped down toward the rear of the lot, the house was shaped like an old-fashioned piano box. In the fall of 1920, Elbert and Sara moved into the State Street house, and Elbert, having negotiated for time off from his job with the endowment campaign to attend class, started law school. Despite Elbert's heavy schedule, on Sara's initiative they went to almost every party, every concert, every play. Although she loved to be on the go, Sara began to worry about the effect of their social schedule on Elbert. There was family pride to uphold; her brother and brother-in-law had both done well at Harvard. Not one to mince words, she chided him, "Don't you bust out now or you'll embarrass me." She didn't want to stay home, however, and the end of the first term found them at a concert in Bailey Hall. The secretary of the law school was there too; he took the opportunity to congratulate Elbert on his grades—all As. At the end of the year, he won the Boardman Scholarship for standing first in the class.

On September 1, 1921, Elbert Jr. was born in the Ithaca hospital. Soon after his birth, the young family received an offer too good to refuse. Professor Orth, whose home was on the Cornell campus, was taking a sabbatical. He had rented two rooms upstairs to a Cornell graduate student, and he offered the Tuttles the rest of the house. They quickly moved from their "piano box" to a home with a baby grand piano in the parlor. Sara Tuttle expected to live well, and she did. Between Elbert's salary and the rent from their home on State Street, Sara was able to hire a coed to help with the baby and an older lady to cook and clean. That Christmas, Sara's family gathered in Atlanta. Bill and Elbert had already decided to start a law firm together; looking for an up-and-coming city, they had focused on Dallas and Atlanta because both cities were home to a fair number of major corporate offices, and neither city had many attorneys. They chose Atlanta largely because, in an era when air conditioning had not yet been invented, Dallas was simply too hot. At the family Christmas, Elbert had his first look at the city that would be his home for some seven decades.

Back in Ithaca, Elbert wrapped up the endowment campaign and became the managing editor of the *Cornell Alumni News*. He supplemented his income by writing articles for newspapers in Baltimore, Washington, Boston, Philadelphia, and New York; each paper paid twenty cents an inch. The sale of the State Street house brought the return of his five-hundred-dollar down payment and another five hundred dollars in profit, and he earned an additional thousand dollars by raising funds for the Cornell University Christian Association. That enabled him to put a down payment on a lot on Cayuga Heights Road about a half mile from campus. Housing was still in short supply in Ithaca, and Elbert had decided to build a seven-unit apartment house, hoping he and Sara could live there for his last year in law school. They didn't get in until the second term and by then had scarce funds left for furniture, but they loved their two-story apartment and the Norman French–style building. Still a law student, Elbert became landlord to the dean of the law school. That had its liabilities. On one occasion, the dean interrupted Elbert in the middle of an exam to say, "Mrs. Burdick just called and said her sink was stopped up. Will it be alright if she calls a plumber?" "Yes, Dean," Elbert replied, "it will be all right." Elbert wasn't the only one with a plumber story. Cornell's acting president, Peter

Smith, lived next door to the Orths. One day when Sara was out playing bridge, her student helper, Mildred, called to say that the boiler was leaking. Sara told her to go next door and get the handyman, named Smith, who took care of the president's house. Mildred fetched "Mr. Smith," and Sara came home to find the president on his hands and knees in her basement. He brushed her apologies off: "Well, after all, I was dean of engineering and if anybody could fix a furnace I ought to be able to."

At the end of the year, Elbert Tuttle stood in an enviable position. First in his class and editor of the law review, he was offered a position at $150 a month by Sullivan & Cromwell, one of New York's most prestigious firms. He turned it down. If Elbert Tuttle were to practice law, it would be in Atlanta. The job at Sullivan & Cromwell went to the student who was second in the class, Arthur H. Dean; in 1949 Dean succeeded John Foster Dulles as chairman of the firm. Elbert would have liked to go back to Hawaii, but Sara demurred. "It's too far," she said. "Too far from where?" Elbert asked pointedly. Her response, "Too far from here," was firm. They would not be moving to Hawaii. Meanwhile, Cornell offered Elbert the position of assistant comptroller. The salary was double what he could hope to make starting out as an attorney, and it was a very secure position. They both loved Ithaca, and they now owned the apartment building they had built. They hesitated, they talked, and finally Sara decided the matter. "I know you will never be satisfied until you try practicing law," she told Elbert. "If I'm going to starve, I'd rather starve when I'm young."

Elbert Tuttle (front row, right) with Malcolm (front row, left), his parents (second row, left), and paternal grandparents (second row, right). Courtesy of the Tuttle and Harmon families.

Malcolm and Elbert Tuttle with a scale model of the Wright brothers biplane, June 1910. Courtesy of the Punahou School Archives.

Elbert and Malcolm Tuttle with
surfboards, Oahu, 1913–14. Courtesy of
the Punahou School Archives.

Left: Elbert Tuttle and his mother, Margie ("Precious") Tuttle, 1914. Courtesy of the
Tuttle and Harmon families. *Right*: Guy Harmon Tuttle, Elbert Tuttle's father, circa
1910. Courtesy of the Tuttle and Harmon families.

Phocion Leonidas (P.L.) and Jennie Sutherland with their children, Sara, Bill, and Jennie, 1918. Courtesy of the Tuttle and Harmon families.

Sara holding Buddy; her mother, Jennie Sutherland; and her grandmother Betty Mattox, Ithaca, New York, 1921. Courtesy of the Tuttle and Harmon families.

Elbert Tuttle in his World War I uniform, 1918. Courtesy of the Tuttle and Harmon families.

 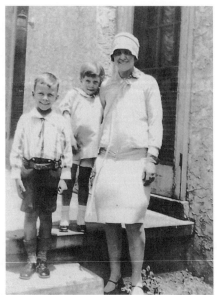

Left: Elbert Tuttle holding Elbert Jr. (Buddy), February 1922. Courtesy of the Tuttle and Harmon families. *Right:* Sara Tuttle with her children Jane (Nicky) and Elbert (Buddy), circa 1926. Courtesy of the Tuttle and Harmon families.

Sara Tuttle in Atlanta, 1930s. Courtesy of the Tuttle and Harmon families.

Elbert Tuttle, Mac Asbill Jr., and Elbert Tuttle Jr. From *The Ties that Bind* by Joe Renouard; courtesy of Sutherland, Asbill & Brennan LLP.

Elbert Tuttle with range finder, Tybee Island, Georgia, circa 1941. Courtesy of the Tuttle and Harmon families.

Left: Lt. Col. Elbert P. Tuttle, 179th Field Artillery, at Camp Blanding, Florida, July 1941. Photograph by Sydney L. Greenberg; copyright Atlanta Journal-Constitution; courtesy of Georgia State University. *Right:* Elbert and Sara Tuttle, at his brother Malcolm's home in New Rochelle, New York, 1943. Courtesy of the Tuttle and Harmon families.

Elbert Tuttle and Elbert Tuttle Jr. (Buddy), 1943. Courtesy of the Tuttle and Harmon families.

Elbert Tuttle Jr. (Buddy) and fellow pilot Mark Guffey with torpedo bomber, Tinian, 1944. Courtesy of the Tuttle and Harmon families.

John Harmon in his American Field Service uniform, July 1945. Courtesy of the Tuttle and Harmon families.

Elbert Tuttle, Okinawa, April 28, 1945. Courtesy of the Tuttle and Harmon families.

Brig. Gen. Isaac Spalding, Maj. Gen. A. D. Bruce, and Col. Elbert Tuttle, Fort MacPherson, Georgia, December 1945. Courtesy of the Tuttle and Harmon families.

These medals recognized Tuttle's service as a field artillery battalion commander during the Guam Campaign, the Leyte Operation, and the assaults against the Ryukus, including the amphibious landing on enemy-held territory in the Ryukus Islands. Top center: The Legion of Merit, awarded September 5, 1945; bottom left: The Bronze Star, awarded October 14, 1944; bottom right: The Purple Heart with Oak Leaf Cluster, awarded May 20, 1945. Tuttle was also awarded a Bronze Service Arrowhead on December 8, 1945. The complete text of the citations that accompanied the medals appears in appendix 2.

CHAPTER SIX

Founding a Law Firm
and Raising a Family

Sara and the baby left for Atlanta on May 20, 1923. "We didn't have two nickels to rub together," Sara remembered, "but we had youth and confidence and love and Elbert had lots of ability, so we knew life would be good to us." They left snow on the ground in Ithaca and arrived at a city in bloom. Elbert followed in early June, arriving just in time to take the Georgia bar exam. Before he left Ithaca, a package arrived; E. Smythe Gambrell, an Atlanta attorney for whom the Emory Law School would later be named, had sent Elbert a copy of *Park's Annotated Code of Georgia*. Smythe Gambrell had run into Bill Sutherland on the street in Atlanta; when Sutherland told him Elbert was coming, Gambrell marked his *Code* to indicate what he thought Elbert should study and shipped it off. Elbert read it on the long train trip down, sat for the bar, and passed.

Sara's entire family was already in Atlanta. Her brother, Bill, and her brother-in-law, Mac Asbill, were practicing law, but not with the same firm. Bill had married Sarah Hall, the daughter of a former attorney general of Georgia, in June. Mac and Jennie, Sara's sister, had a son, Mac Jr., who was the same age as Elbert Jr., and Sara's mother, Jennie, and grandmother Momma Betty were living with the Asbills. Elbert, Sara, and Buddy moved in too for the summer. In September, when they moved to a duplex on Moreland Avenue and North, Jennie and Momma Betty moved with them. Their five-person household grew to six on November 26 when Jane Sutherland Tuttle was born. The two Tuttle children, Elbert Jr. and Jane, were known only by their nicknames. Everyone called Elbert Jr. Buddy, and everyone called Jane Nicky, from Schnicklefritz, a lighthearted, affectionate name her father began using when she was a toddler.

By 1923 Mac Asbill had become a partner in the firm of Watkins, Russell & Asbill. Bill Sutherland had formed a "loose association" with Jones, Evins & Moore; the Jones in the firm name was Robert P. Jones, father of the golf champion Robert Tyre "Bobby" Jones. The firm gave Sutherland office space and funneled work to him. Sutherland also maintained a professional relationship with Miller & Chevalier, a national tax firm based in Washington. He was doing well, but not well enough to be able to start his own firm. Sutherland and Tuttle would have to bide their time. In the summer of 1923, Elbert Tuttle had a wife and a child and another child on the way; he needed a regular income, and he needed a substantial income. When he interviewed for a position as an associate with Anderson, Rountree & Crenshaw, he asked for $175 a month, $25 more than the going rate in a silk stocking New York firm. Daniel W. Rountree, the partner for whom he would work, agreed, and Tuttle became the first salaried associate at an Atlanta law firm.[1]

A bachelor, Rountree was a wealthy man, in part as a result of an early investment in Coca-Cola. By 1923 he no longer tried cases. He was, however, handling one or two complex matters involving the financing of buildings on which bonds were being issued. "I think," Tuttle recollected, "he needed someone to help him and when I told him how much I needed to live on why he just agreed to it because the dollars and cents didn't really make that much difference to him." A named partner in one of the city's largest and most successful firms, Rountree was particularly well known in the Atlanta bar. He had always attracted attention by his manner of dress— he was something of a dandy who in his youth dressed in colorful outfits and as an older attorney wore suits and shoes crafted in London. Rountree took such pride in the unusually stylish collars and cuffs of his shirts that he had his valet mail them weekly to New York for laundering. Shortly after he had moved to Atlanta in 1890 after more than a decade of successful practice in Quitman, Georgia, he had purchased all available back issues of the *Georgia Supreme Court Reports*. Anyone starting a library had to come to him. It was a good investment, not the least because of the attention it brought him.[2]

Although Rountree had hired him and Anderson still practiced actively, Tuttle had little contact with either of them. They were senior lawyers, gray eminences. "In those days, the leaders of the bar did not fraternize very much with brand new members." Both men were somewhat intimidating.

Known as General Anderson because he had attained the rank of brigadier general in the Georgia National Guard, Anderson was remote and reserved. Gracious and generous, Rountree was also a perfectionist with a temper. On one of his many trips to Europe, when told he would have to pay an export tax that approximated the cost of the Mercedes he had planned to ship home, he simply drove it off the pier. When Tuttle needed advice, he went to Robert Crenshaw, the youngest partner, "a very friendly, outgoing person, quite different from General Anderson."[3] The firm numbered the Trust Company of Georgia among its clients, and Tuttle worked mainly on matters sent over by the trust department. In later years he was bemused to recall that he regularly wrote wills for clients whom he never met. The trust officer would tell Tuttle what the client wanted, Tuttle would draft a will, and the trust officer would take the document to the client.

In the fall of 1923, soon after he had arrived in Atlanta, Tuttle tried his first case. The owner of a newsstand across the street from the Fulton County Courthouse sought Tuttle's help when the owner was sued by a printer who had delivered lottery tickets to him. Tuttle won the case by arguing that his client could not be sued on a contract to print lottery tickets because it was part of a plan to facilitate gambling, and gambling was illegal. The case meant a lot to Tuttle, not because it was his first trial, and not because he won. It was being selected by his client, a man who knew every lawyer in Fulton County, that meant the most to him. That case notwithstanding, Tuttle spent most of his time with corporate clients. Rountree represented the G. L. Miller Company, which built downtown office buildings by issuing bonds to finance the construction. The company prospered, and downtown flourished until 1929; as the Great Depression wore on, many of the bond issues went into default. By then, Tuttle was long out of that business. He and Bill Sutherland had dreamed of opening their own law firm, and they moved quickly once an opportunity was at hand.

In 1923 Bill Sutherland obtained a referral through his father-in-law, the former attorney general of Georgia. Sutherland filed a mandamus seeking the payment of interest allegedly due on county warrants that had been issued in payment for goods and services. The matter was highly contested, and two justices of the Georgia Supreme Court dissented, but Chief Justice Russell, father of Senator Richard Russell for whom the Senate Office Building is named, wrote for the majority and found the claim valid.[4] Bill Sutherland collected a fee of $2,500. He calculated that this sum would cover $100 per month rent for a year for an office next to his for Elbert and $100 per month for a year for a secretary; the $100 left would cover most of the cost of telephone service. On the strength of this nest egg, Elbert resigned his position with Anderson, Rountree & Crenshaw, and the partnership of Sutherland & Tuttle was established. Although both Bill Sutherland and Elbert Tuttle traced the partnership back to 1924, the firm is not listed in *Martindale's American Law Directory* until 1927. Until 1928, the firm listing for Jones, Evins & Moore continued to show Bill Sutherland as an associate.

In 1925 and 1926, *Martindale's* also listed Bill Sutherland as a "resident partner" of Miller & Chevalier. Robert N. Miller had been solicitor of the Bureau of Internal Revenue, a job now described as general counsel to the Internal Revenue Service. His law firm, with offices in Washington and Louisville, was among the nation's leading tax firms. Miller offered Bill Sutherland a position in the Washington office, but Sutherland was committed to building his own firm. At Sutherland & Tuttle, from the beginning Bill Sutherland was the tax specialist and Elbert Tuttle the general practitioner. Most of the firm's most substantial work was tax work. In 1927, in a case involving complex valuation issues, Sutherland won a judgment of $275,000 for the Atlantic Steel Company. At that time it was the largest judgment that had been won in a tax refund suit in Georgia. The underlying transaction, the acquisition by Atlantic Steel of a smaller steel company, had been the handiwork of Robert Woodruff, who in 1920 had engineered the purchase of Coca-Cola and taken it public. The connections the firm made in handling the Atlantic Steel case promised to be even more lucrative than the fee received. Sutherland & Tuttle had established itself. Both Bill Sutherland and Elbert Tuttle had social standing as well as professional standing. Atlanta's most exclusive club, the Piedmont Driving Club, had been organized in 1887 and chartered in 1895. Being a member of the Piedmont Driving Club both recognized and conferred high social status. Bill Sutherland and Elbert Tuttle were both members, Sutherland elected in 1922, Tuttle in 1925. Like most private clubs of the era, the Piedmont Driving Club admitted only white Christian males to membership.

Bill Sutherland supplemented his income by teaching a course at Emory Law School. He offered a bright young student, Tom Windham, office space with the firm. When Windham decided the practice of law was not for him because his true interest lay in construction, Elbert and Sara commissioned him to build a home. They were still living in rented quarters, although in the summer of 1924 they had moved from Moreland Avenue to a home at Penn Street and Sixth Avenue. Sara's mother and grandmother were both living with them. That August Momma Betty died peacefully from a heart attack that struck as she sat on the front porch. Mac and Jennie Asbill had built a home in a new subdivision just off Atlanta's famous Peachtree Street known as Brookwood Hills. Now very much an in-town neighborhood, in the 1920s Brookwood Hills lay at the city limits of Atlanta. Elbert Tuttle commissioned Tom Windham to build a home for his family on a lot located on Palisades Road, half a block outside the city limits. The family moved to their new home in September 1925. Bill Sutherland followed suit; as soon as the Tuttle home was complete, Tom Windham began construction on a home for the Sutherlands on Brighton Road, two blocks farther out.

The early years went so well for the young partnership that by 1928 Bill Sutherland and Elbert Tuttle felt secure enough to hire an associate. Joseph B. Brennan, who had just graduated from Harvard Law School, was the first of a series of outstanding young attorneys Bill Sutherland recruited to develop his tax practice. Brennan, a quiet, scholarly man who became a named partner in 1932, and Sutherland, a go-getter and business developer, were well matched. The firm prospered. Over and over they were able to obtain large judgments for corporate clients in cases involving technical tax questions. The firm also earned a reputation for expertise on federal constitutional issues. As early as 1929, Sutherland & Tuttle filed a brief in the United States Supreme Court. *Old Colony Trust Co. v. Commissioner* addressed whether an appeal from the tax court to the circuit court of appeals was a case or a controversy within the meaning of the Constitution.[5] In the course of working on *Old Colony*, Bill Sutherland met Arthur Ballentine, one of the nation's leading tax attorneys, and began a lifelong friendship. In 1931 Bill Sutherland argued his first case in the United States Supreme Court. His client was the Second National Bank of Saginaw; its appeal, on the issue of the constitutionality of section 611 of the Revenue Act of 1928, which barred certain taxpayer suits for refund, was one of a group of nine appeals heard by the court over three days. After hearing Sutherland's argument for Saginaw, counsel for another taxpayer asked him to argue its case as well. He was effective enough that the opinion of the court directed itself almost entirely to the argument he had made for his clients, but he did not prevail.[6]

Even though the country was in the throes of the Great Depression, the firm prospered. Everyone felt the Great Depression, but some felt it more than others. Buddy knew that times were hard, but in 1933 he was twelve years old, and he desperately wanted a shortwave radio. To his surprise, he got one for Christmas. His parents had tightened their belts, but they were able to maintain their home, their car, their housekeeper, even their club membership. They were also able to think of helping others. The Tuttle home was near the train track that served Atlanta. So many hungry men appeared asking for handouts that Sara Tuttle, joined by her sister, Jennie, made it a practice to prepare simple sandwiches to hand out at the back door. When the president suddenly announced a bank holiday, virtually every citizen, even the well off, felt fear. On March 6, 1933, all the banks closed. No one had access to his or her funds. Mac Asbill had several hundred dollars cash in hand for a business trip to New York. He canceled his trip, sought out his brothers-in-law, and divided his money among the three of them. It seemed a godsend. Elbert Tuttle took his share home and gave it to Sara for household expenses. By the next day, a chunk was gone; irrepressible Sara had rushed out and gotten a permanent. Who knew, she pointed out, when she would be able to get another?

As the 1930s wore on, the firm continued to grow in prominence. Bill Sutherland and Joe Brennan were back in the Supreme Court in 1932, in *Fox Film Corporation v. Doyal.*[7] Although they argued unsuccessfully that their clients' copyrights did not produce taxable income because they were instrumentalities of the United States, Sutherland and Brennan's position and briefing forced the Supreme Court to overrule its own recent opinion in *Long v. Rockwood.*[8] In 1932 they argued and lost *Woolford Realty Co. v. Rose,* and they filed an amicus brief in support of an unsuccessful petition for certiorari in *Ralston Purina v. United States.*[9] The next year they unsuccessfully sought the grant of a writ of certiorari in *Fulton Bag & Cotton Mills v. United States.*[10] In 1934 they argued and won, albeit temporarily, in *Clifton Mfg. Co. v. United States*; on remand the Fourth Circuit ruled against them.[11] In 1937 Sutherland and Brennan were back in the Supreme Court in two cases. In *Anniston Mfg. Co. v. Davis* they challenged the constitutionality of the restrictions on the refund of processing taxes unconstitutionally collected; the court upheld the statute but construed it in a manner that allowed taxpayers to secure large refunds, a substantial victory for the firm.[12] Mr. Justice Reed, who was the solicitor general when *Anniston* was argued in the Supreme Court, told Bill Sutherland that this case involved the largest claim against the government of any case that came up during his tenure. They also briefed, argued, and won in *McEachern v. Rose*.[13]

As Sutherland & Tuttle achieved national prominence in the tax field, Elbert Tuttle continued to anchor the general practice arm of the firm. Bill Sutherland maintained a high profile in the American Bar Association; Elbert Tuttle was far better known in Atlanta, where he focused his practice and found time for his family, for civic life, even for polo. When he arrived in Georgia, he pondered how to make himself part of his adopted state, and he decided to join the Georgia National Guard. Tuttle held a second lieutenant's commission in the United States Army, which he thought would translate into a commission in the National Guard. He shared these thoughts with Bill Sutherland, and Sutherland put him in touch with Charlie Cox, a major in command of a National Guard infantry battalion in the 122nd Infantry Regiment. Cox assured Tuttle that if he enlisted, he would be commissioned quickly, as he was. Membership in the Georgia National Guard carried an unusual benefit; the officers fielded a polo team, which competed with a cavalry unit stationed at Fort MacPherson. Many a weekend afternoon found the young attorney on horseback, mallet in hand, on a field laid out in Atlanta's Piedmont Park.

During their college years, Malcolm and Elbert's Cornell fraternity had merged with a national fraternity, Pi Kappa Alpha, which at that time housed its national office in Atlanta. In 1926 Tuttle was elected national counsel (then called grand chancellor). In 1930 he was elected national president, a post he held until 1938. Attending the national conventions gave him an opportunity for cross-country trips. Travel meant a great deal to Tuttle. He had grown up taking frequent train trips across the width of the country, travels that had culminated in the family's move to Hawaii, but for the decade following his junior year at Cornell he had been confined to the East Coast and the Southeast.

In 1926 or 1927 Jones, Evins & Moore turned to Sutherland & Tuttle for help with a federal tax claim against a patent medicine company that was their client. Tuttle took the matter on happily; it required him to travel to Los Angeles and San Francisco, Seattle, and Edmonton, Alberta, Canada, to take depositions. Sara stayed at home with the children. She had never traveled west of the Mississippi, and she had no burning desire to, but after his return Elbert convinced her they should attend the Chicago Century of Progress Exposition, which opened in 1933. Then he convinced her they should route the trip through New Orleans and Los Angeles, where they could visit his father and mother, who were living there then. Leaving Los Angeles, bound for Chicago, they stopped in San Francisco. Of all the cities they visited, San Francisco was Sara's favorite. On the way back east to Chicago, they stopped in Colorado to visit cousins of Sara's, transplants from Georgia. Finally, they arrived at their primary destination, Chicago, where the exposition had proven so popular that they had to settle for an out-of-the-way hotel. The trip was a great success in the most important way—now Sara, like her husband, had been bitten by the travel bug.

When the Tuttle family moved to Palisades Road, they joined the Peachtree Christian Church. It was the church of Elbert's childhood, the church his maternal great-grandfather had brought to southern Iowa. It was also nearby. Elbert became an elder, and Nicky and Buddy were both baptized there. Elbert and the children attended services every Sunday morning; Sara often stayed at home, enjoying a few rare hours of solitude. At a church picnic, Elbert met another church member named Otis M. "Jack" Simms. Jack Simms worked for a small company that made refrigerators, the Warren Company. The Warren Company bought the coils for the refrigerators from Larkin Coils, Inc. When Larkin Coils went into bankruptcy, Simms retained Tuttle to attend the sale of the company by the bankruptcy referee and buy the company. Tuttle recalled getting it for Simms for thirty thousand dollars. Under Jack Simms's leadership, Larkin Coils prospered. Tuttle served on the board of directors, and Sutherland & Tuttle represented the company.

Tuttle brought at least one other significant client to the firm in the early years. In perhaps 1928 Hewlett Hall asked Tuttle to try a matter for one of his clients who had sued the directors of a bank in West Point, Georgia. The trial judge referred the matter to a special master, an Atlanta lawyer named Cam Dorsey, brother of Hugh Dorsey, who had been Georgia's governor from 1917 to 1921. Cam Dorsey counted among his friends Franklin Delano Roosevelt, a Columbia Law School classmate. In later years, when Roosevelt visited Warm Springs, he would often work in a visit with his old friend.[14] Cam Dorsey ruled in favor of Tuttle's client. After that litigation had been concluded, he got in touch with Tuttle and explained that he was chairman of the Fulton County Board of Education and that he had also been representing the board. Now he thought the board should have independent counsel. Dorsey had been impressed with Tuttle and offered him the work. Tuttle accepted, and Sutherland & Tuttle had its first retainer— twenty-five dollars a month.

In 1932 Sara's mother, Jennie Sutherland, who had been widowed since 1917, remarried. Her new husband was an old friend, Colonel Corbett, who had long ago given Sara her beloved horse, Captain Corbett. Elbert and Sara Tuttle found themselves living without extended family for the first time since they had moved to Atlanta in 1923. Even so, the house was rarely empty. Ginny and Mac Asbill lived nearby and visited often; the families dined together almost every weekend. Buddy and Nicky were in and out, and all their friends were welcome. Sara loved having her home be a center of activity, not least because it allowed her to keep a close eye on her children. Through their teenage years, she waited up whenever they were out. That often led to late-night conversations that helped her keep up with what was going on with them and their friends.

Buddy's best friend was his first cousin, Mac Asbill Jr., known as Mackie as a child. Mac and Buddy were independent and as different as night and day, but they were also inseparable. Sara Tuttle liked to say that she and her sister, Jenny, each felt they had three children. Nicky had a circle of friends and was particularly close to Betty Haverty, for whom the Tuttle household was a second home. Despite being two years apart, as children Buddy and Jane played with each other as well. Once Buddy and Mackie came stomping in the house; they were mad at Nicky, they told her mother. Why, she inquired. "Because she won't play center on our football team." And who, Sara asked, was the center for the other team? "Billy Lowndes." Sara shook her head and informed the boys that little Nicky had more sense than they did; Billy Lowndes must weigh 140 pounds, she pointed out, about a hundred more than Nicky.

Buddy, whose birthday was September 1, started first grade in public school when he was barely five; he was one of the youngest students in his class. Still, year after year his elementary school teachers wanted to promote him a grade ahead. The teacher would call, Sara Tuttle would don her hat and her gloves and go out to the school for a conference, and then she would say no. Sara's opinion was set in concrete: she firmly believed that social growth was as important as intellectual growth. She also believed, as did many of his friends and associates, that her brother, Bill, brilliant as he undoubtedly was, had missed out on too many valuable playground lessons. If she also thought that her husband's social reserve was partly a product of his having skipped a grade, she never said so. But one thing was clear—as long as his mother had any say in the matter, Buddy would stay with his grade.

Elbert had loved riding horseback ever since his teenage years in Hawaii, when he and Malcolm had the use of Platt Cooke's horses. In Atlanta he owned his own horse—a quarter horse named Pet. He rode Pet for pleasure, he rode him when he played polo with the National Guard team at Piedmont Park, and for several years he rode Pet when he and two other officers on horseback led the Memorial Day Parade down Peachtree Street. When Buddy was ten or eleven, in 1931 or 1932, his father bought a Chincoteague pony and housed the pony, Doc, with Pet at the stables in Piedmont Park used by the National Guard. Many a weekday morning Elbert would awaken Buddy at 6:00 a.m. Father and son would drive about two miles to the stables, saddle up, and ride north through the Piedmont Park woods to an area called Morningside. They rode on Saturday afternoons, too; often they were joined by Leckie Mattox, Elbert's best friend, who also kept his horse at the Piedmont Park stables.

At the office, while Bill Sutherland built a prosperous, highly regarded national tax practice, Elbert Tuttle continued to practice general commercial law and to serve as the firm litigator. He lost very few, if any, cases, partly because of his skill and partly because he often found himself representing taxpayers against the Internal Revenue Service. The federal income tax was relatively new (the Sixteenth Amendment, which authorizes it, was ratified on February 3, 1913) and controversial.[15] In post-Depression 1932 the highest tax rate moved from 25 percent to 63 percent; in 1936 it went up to 79 percent and then to 81 percent in 1940. At the time, if the taxpayer challenged the tax and refused to pay it, the matter would go to the tax court. On the other hand, if the taxpayer paid the assessment and then challenged it by filing a complaint in federal district court, the matter would proceed to trial by jury. Elbert Tuttle always advised his clients to pay the tax so that he could litigate their claim before a jury. Then it was John Q. Citizen against the Internal Revenue Service, and John Q. Citizen almost always prevailed. In the tax cases, Tuttle knew he could rely on a bias of the region. "There was still some feeling in the southern states," he recalled, "that a Georgia resident ought not to be mulcted of his money by the federal government."[16] More pernicious biases affected litigation as well. In a 1982 address accepting the Brotherhood Award from the Georgia Region of the National Conference of Christians and Jews, Tuttle recalled that when he began to practice law in Atlanta, "it was commonly said among lawyers that in order to successfully try a case before a jury in Fulton County, it was necessary to associate a lawyer who had some close connection with, if not a member of, the Ku Klux Klan."[17] Frustrations with Jim Crow segregation aside, Tuttle loved practicing law. He was having such a good time that he recalled telling Sara one day in a burst of enthusiasm, "I feel sorry for anyone not practicing law." There was "always something new," and there were no time cards. That, he realized, was one of the real pleasures of his work: he would do the best job he could and then bill a fair price that the client could pay.[18]

Meanwhile, the Tuttle children were growing up. For his sixteenth birthday, September 1, 1937, Elbert and Sara gave Buddy, who was beginning his senior year in high school, a car—a brand-new 1937 blue Plymouth sedan. The car was a surprise. For a sixteen-year-old boy in 1937, having his own car was simply wonderful. Sara, always most concerned with how everyone got along with each other, treasured how generously he shared it with his cousin Mackie. By then, Mac Asbill Jr. was living with the Tuttle family. When his parents moved to Washington, D.C., he stayed with the Tuttles to finish out the school year. Then he moved to join his parents and spent his junior year at St. Albans School. He would have stayed there to graduate, but when his father's brother fell gravely ill, his mother went to Knoxville to help, and Mac came back to Atlanta. That June, Buddy and Mac graduated from North Fulton High School, Buddy as valedictorian and Mac as salutatorian. In the fall they started Princeton together. Nicky, who had two more years in high school, inherited the Plymouth. In June 1940 she graduated as salutatorian of her class. She entered Wellesley in the fall, her studies partly supported by a merit scholarship.

CHAPTER SEVEN

Gearing Up for War

By the summer of 1941, Elbert and his best friend, Sara's cousin Leckie Mattox, were already on active duty. Their Georgia National Guard infantry regiment was called up in September 1940. Shortly thereafter it was converted to a field artillery regiment and on February 28, 1941, posted to Fort Blanding, just south of Jacksonville, Florida. Before joining his regiment at Fort Blanding, Elbert reported for an advanced artillery course for field officers at Fort Sill, Oklahoma. When he had been discharged from active duty in 1918, he had been sure he would never see Fort Sill again. Sara arrived that spring, driven out by Buddy over his spring break. She managed to find a room over a Walgreen's, where the lunch-counter menu included "macaroni sandwiches." Sara was used to the red clay of Georgia, but she never became accustomed to the red dust that seemed to always fill the air in Oklahoma, even, she maintained, when it rained. That aside, she enjoyed riding horseback across the plains, returning in time for dinner with Elbert at the officers' club on the base. Elbert finished first in the advanced artillery class and was posted back to Fort Blanding, where he took command of his Field Artillery Battalion. With Elbert and Leckie both at Fort Blanding, Sara Tuttle and Gabrielle Mattox each rented a house at Ponte Vedra, about sixty miles from the base, for the summer of 1941. Elbert and Leckie drove to the beach houses every weekend and every Wednesday evening, rising early enough to be back at the base by 5:00 a.m. the next morning. It was a tiring commute, but well worth it. Not everyone would survive the war, and difficult years would pass before those who did would be together again.

The Tuttles shared their summer house first with their friends Helen and Wiley Ballard and then with the Asbills. Mac and Buddy invited John Harmon, a classmate at Princeton. John came, but not to see Buddy and

Mac or to vacation at the beach. He came because he had gone Elbert Tuttle one better. Elbert had fallen in love with Sara at first sight. John had fallen in love with Nicky's picture, prominently displayed on Buddy's dresser. He hitchhiked to Ponte Vedra to meet the girl in the picture and arrived with an issue of George Seldes's leftist magazine *In Fact* tucked securely under his arm. Despite the fact that he had hitchhiked his way there, and despite his flaunting of what was practically Communist Party literature, he recalled being welcomed with kindness, particularly by Nicky, who quickly became as enchanted with him as he had been with her picture. Besides, Buddy drew attention away from him by dyeing his hair; according to Sara, it came out pink, leaving her speechless for the only time in her life. Everyone else was amused, but she shuddered as she saw him off for his senior year at Princeton, with his bronzed skin setting off his pink hair.

It was an idyllic time, and it was well that it was. Europe was at war, and the entry of the United States was not far off. Elbert's active duty orders were only for one year, but Elbert and Sara both thought a world war was coming, and they both realized that the United States would have to enter the conflict. Elbert made it clear that when that happened, he wanted to volunteer for overseas duty. Sara did not want him to go; she did not want to risk losing her beloved husband. But he had made up his mind, and she would not stand in his way.

Nor would she lose him a moment sooner than she had to. Until Elbert went overseas, Sara decided, she would travel from base to base with him. They were well off, and the firm committed to paying him the difference between his draw and his officer's salary as long as he was on active duty. Still, they could not keep their Atlanta house and make their home around the country as well. In October 1940 they sold their home, put their furniture in storage, and moved into the Colonial Terrace apartments on Peachtree Road. As they locked the warehouse door on their furniture, Elbert turned to Sara. "Honey," he said, "they say this is for one year and I hope it will be for one year, but if we get back in five years we will do well." It would be eight long years before they recovered their furniture.

At summer's end, Buddy and Mac went back to Princeton and Nicky to Wellesley. To be close to Fort Blanding, Sara took an apartment in South Jacksonville. In November 1941, when Elbert was sent to North Carolina for a month on maneuvers, Sara visited him there and then drove north. She planned to spend the month visiting family, starting with her son, Buddy, her nephew, Mac, and Nicky's young man, John Harmon, at Princeton. In early December, Sara, Buddy, and Johnny were touring the countryside around Princeton when the program on the car radio was interrupted with news of the attack on Pearl Harbor. By the time night fell, pandemonium reigned; all over Princeton, young men built huge bonfires and threw in everything in sight. Bravado notwithstanding, everyone feared invasion. Sara continued her trip east; her next stop was New Rochelle, where Elbert's brother, Malcolm, and his wife, Aurilla, lived. The next day, as Sara approached the Holland Tunnel, radio broadcasters announced that unidentified planes were flying over the city, and all police and fire personnel were ordered to their stations. Sara had to muster all her courage to drive down into the tunnel, fighting her fear that it might collapse around her. For the rest of their lives, Elbert insisted she had been safer underground than she was on Riverside Drive. Sara held her ground; even if he was right, she preferred the open air.

When she rejoined Elbert at Fort Blanding, everything had changed. America had entered the war; it was only a matter of time before he would be shipped overseas. Any time they could spend together was doubly precious. They would waste none of it. Quarters for married couples were scant on bases, usually confined to homes for a few officers. When they arrived in a new town, Sara would rent an apartment, if possible, or rooms in a house. She was nothing if not efficient; by the second afternoon she would have located a place to live, a bank, and a doctor. Then she would buy a ham, make homemade mayonnaise, put out a green plant, and feel at home. Baked ham with homemade mayonnaise showed off one of her few culinary skills. For practically her entire life, Sara Tuttle had someone in the kitchen. Only during the early years at Cornell, the very first years of their marriage, had Sara actually cooked and kept house. When they moved to Atlanta, Momma Betty moved in with them and took over the kitchen, assisted by a young woman named Katy Brown who also looked after Buddy (young and high spirited, whenever a fire engine came by she would drop everything, grab the baby, and rush out to see if they could see the fire). When they moved to Palisades Road, Maude Rooks came to work for Sara. She stayed with the Tuttles until they sold their home after Elbert enlisted for active duty. As Sara and Elbert traveled the country during the war years, Sara was on her own, but since they always took dinner at the officers' club, being able to bake a ham sufficed.

In the distance she managed to keep from housework and cooking, Sara may have shared an affinity with her mother-in-law. Precious was given to writing light poems, usually about her husband or her sons, sometimes with a religious theme. One that survived, titled "To My Husband," read:

> I'd climb the highest mountain, dear,
> I'd cross the desert wide,
> I'd sail the raging ocean, too:
> An elephant I'd ride.
> And in jungle I would tweak
> A spotted leopard's nose,
> If only you will never ask
> Me, dear, to mend your hose.
> I'd do just anything you ask,
> To prove I love you, dear.
> I'd cross the plains by caravan:
> I'd pinch a tiger's ear,
> Or even ride an aeroplane,
> Or fondle slimy seals,
> If only you will never ask
> Me, dear, to cook your meals.

In March 1942 Elbert was ordered to Camp Shelby at Hattiesburg, Mississippi. There Sara found a "funny" little apartment for which they were very grateful: it let them be together. On weekends they could drive down to the Gulf Coast to swim and sun, and they found new friends. "It wasn't bad," Sara would remember. It was better than the next stop. From Hattiesburg, Elbert's orders took them to Fort Sam Polk, near Alexandria, Louisiana. "It was hotter than Hades," Sara recalled. "It was a town of 25,000 people . . . [with] 125,000 troops within a radius of 25 miles . . . and very few living and recreational facilities." Elbert wouldn't go out on weekends because the streets were packed shoulder to shoulder. They took most of their dinners at the one air-conditioned place in town, the Bentley Hotel. Always determined to make the most of any situation she found herself in, Sara enjoyed watching the "boy meet girl" machinations that went on at the hotel. Still, she welcomed Elbert's next orders, which took him to the Command and General Staff School at Fort Leavenworth, Kansas.

There was no room on the base at Leavenworth, so Sara found a room and bath with an older couple. Mr. and Mrs. Kane were as nice as they could be, Sara remembered, and very midwestern, by which she meant that they didn't wear fancy clothes. Mrs. Kane had a Sunday hat and an everyday hat, a Sunday pocketbook and an everyday pocketbook. That was not all she could afford; it was all she needed. Sara, on the other hand, "just loved hats. I wore these little flower hats everywhere I went," she recalled. Most of her "little flower hats" were handmade by Archie Eason, a well-known haute couture hat maker in Jacksonville, Florida. Sara's collection of flowered hats astonished the Kanes; every evening they would peek out to see what she was wearing as she left to join Elbert for dinner at the officers' club. On a trip to New York, Sara bought a new hat and had her old hat sent to her at the Kanes' home. Over the years, Sara enlivened many a gathering with her tale of what happened when the hatbox arrived in the mail. Mr. Kane, she recalled, was all but overcome; "My God, Mary," he exclaimed, "she's bought another hat."

From Leavenworth, Elbert and Sara went to Fort Sam Houston in San Antonio, Texas, "a lovely and delightful" assignment. They found a "charming little house," and they frequented the officers' club. Nicky spent Christmas break with them. Buddy couldn't join them; he was in flight training in Corpus Christi.

In late spring, Elbert was ordered back to Columbia, South Carolina. A few months later, Buddy was sent to El Centro, California, for final flight training. Sara realized that her son would be sent overseas very soon. She was determined to see him before he left, so off she went, traveling by train. It was not an easy trip. "To travel at that time one needed plenty of time, some extra money, and a sense of humor," she often recalled. As she made her way home, Elbert managed to wire her that he had gotten her a berth on a train leaving Chicago. She tried to claim it, but just as she did, a young man arrived and said it was his, and then another man claimed it was his. Sara responded tartly. "Well," she said, "we are going to be cozy, aren't we?" The conductor saved the day. "If you'll sit up till midnight," he told Sara, "I'll put you in another car which will take you all the way to Columbia and you won't have to get up at five in the morning in Asheville." Sara accepted; as she put it, "I never minded staying up until midnight."

Sara's stay at El Centro was bittersweet. "All of those cute boys came into the Barbara Worth Hotel at night and talked and talked. . . . They were doing what they felt was their duty, but they didn't want to kill, and they knew that was what they were training for." Most nights she went with the young pilots across the border, where "we ate in these horrible places and they thought it was wonderful." At that time, she would do anything to be with Buddy; years later, she winced at the memory. "I wouldn't eat in one of those places now for a million dollars."

She had not been back with Elbert long when he received new orders. On December 5, 1943, Elbert reported for duty at Camp Pickett, Virginia. When he left Camp Pickett, he would be headed for his childhood home, Hawaii. But Hawaii was only a way station on his journey; his final destination was the Pacific theater. His son was already there; in January, Buddy had shipped out to the Pacific.

When his National Guard unit was called up in 1940, Tuttle was the first to leave the firm. After Pearl Harbor, there would be an exodus. In 1942 there were five partners (the three named partners plus Herbert Elsas and Ed Kane) and three associates (Randolph Thrower, Norman Stallings, and Ben Johnson) at Sutherland, Tuttle & Brennan. By 1943 Bill Sutherland and Joe Brennan were holding down the fort almost alone; all three of their partners were on active duty. Two of the associates, Thrower and Stallings, had already joined the war effort, and Ben Johnson was soon to leave. It was all Sutherland and Brennan could do to keep their heads above water. Then Joe Brennan decided he, too, wanted to serve. Bill knew he couldn't keep the firm going without Joe, particularly since Joe handled most of the lucrative tax-processing cases. But he couldn't talk Joe into staying, either.[1] He tried to reach Elbert, but Elbert was on the road. Bill knew that Elbert carried only one gasoline company credit card, so he had his secretary call each of the stations on Elbert's route. When Elbert stopped for gas in Fort Smith, Arkansas, the station attendant said, "Oh, you're Mr. Tuttle. I have a message for you."[2]

Tuttle left Sara in Fort Smith and flew back to Atlanta to talk to Joe. Elbert was not closer to Joe Brennan than Bill Sutherland was, but he was persuasive where Bill was bombastic. Someone, Tuttle pointed out, had to stay; someone had to make it possible for the others to go. He himself had no choice; he had been called up because he was an officer in the Georgia National Guard. He didn't have to volunteer for overseas duty, as he had, but he was certain to be working with the military and not with the firm. Joe had a choice and a calling. By staying, he helped Bill keep the firm afloat and supported, in a literal sense, the men who signed up. Throughout the war years, the firm paid its members the difference between their salary and their military pay. It wasn't easy. Had Elbert Tuttle not been able to convince Joe Brennan to stay at his desk, it would not have been possible.

Having Joe Brennan on board was critical, but the firm was still badly understaffed. No one was more aware of the problems than Lillian Ledbetter, who kept the books and knew how thin the firm's resources were stretched. One day she had a novel idea. Herbert Elsas's wife, Edith, was a graduate of Wellesley and a member of Phi Beta Kappa; she was also a young woman from a wealthy family who had married into a wealthy family. The firm needed help monitoring trust investments. Lillian suggested that they ask Edith. Bill Sutherland resisted. "She's the smartest person I know," he allowed, "but she doesn't know anything about paperwork." "But Mr. Sutherland," said Lillian, "she actually owns stocks. None of the rest of us do." Lillian's insight proved valuable; Edith understood the world of investments. She did come on board, and by the time the war ended, she had so impressed the brokers with whom she had worked that a major firm made her an offer.[3] Edith Elsas would have been a pioneer as a woman in investment banking in the South in 1945, but she turned the offer down. She had two small children, a house to run, and a husband home from the war.

Lillian Ledbetter and Edith Elsas became great friends. When Lillian married, Edith came to the wedding with Bill Sutherland and Bill's youngest daughter. Bill was notorious for running late. In the 1930s and 1940s he often took the train north from Atlanta's Brookwood station. It was not uncommon for him to call ahead and tell the conductor to hold the train. Another firm legend had Mr. Sutherland arriving late to catch a plane; he could see the plane, still on the runway, and insisted it be brought back to pick him up. The ticket agent was not as malleable as the conductor. Bill Sutherland threw a fit, but he missed the plane. He missed Lillian's wedding too. The Sutherland party arrived as the newlyweds left the church.

Despite Bill Sutherland's autocratic ways, he was a generous and kind man who took a real interest in others. When Lillian interviewed at the firm, he realized that she would know Jim Wilson, because both of their fathers were Methodist ministers, so he took the opportunity to brag about

Wilson's record at Harvard, "the best grades since Brandeis," he liked to say. "He was as nice as he could be," Lillian recalled, but "he didn't mind yelling a bit." Tuttle never raised his voice, let alone yelled at anyone. "He was very much a gentleman." Joe Brennan was "always very soft-spoken," and while he was very friendly, he was neither as formal as Tuttle nor as friendly as Sutherland. From the attorneys' point of view, Sutherland was the driving force behind the success of the firm, Tuttle the firm's conscience, and Joe Brennan the lawyer's lawyer, a scholarly balance wheel. Everyone, with the notable exception of Elbert Tuttle, worked long hours; late nights and Saturdays and Sundays were the rule. He had his own, primarily local, practice and was uninvolved in the complex tax and commercial litigation that consumed most of the other attorneys in the firm. He arrived early, sometimes after a horseback ride at daybreak with his son, and whenever possible he left in time to be home for dinner with his family. Nothing, he made clear, came before his family.

His sister-in-law, Sarah Sutherland, had heard him say that, and it rankled. Her husband threw himself completely into the firm and, she felt, was primarily responsible for its success. Tuttle, however, always seemed to garner an equal share of the rewards, whether professional or economic. The two families, the Sutherlands and the Tuttles, saw each other surprisingly little, even when Bill and Sarah still lived in Atlanta. At the firm, no ruptures were apparent. Elbert and Bill always got along with each other, Herbert Elsas would recall some four decades later. "I don't know how they did, but they did."[4] Postwar, they got along from a distance. Bill decided the firm needed to staff the Washington office full-time and moved there himself.

CHAPTER EIGHT

The War Years

In late 1941 army surveyors scouting for locations for a post large enough to train multiple infantry divisions checked out a Civilian Conservation Corps camp near Blackstone, a small town in south-central Virginia. It did not take them long to realize they had found a site—Camp Pickett was all but perfect. It had enough land and enough water, and it connected by rail to mountain and coastal training sites. By December the army had cleared nearly forty-six thousand acres. On December 7, when Japanese forces attacked Pearl Harbor, Fort Pickett became a national priority. Construction sped up, and within a year more than fourteen hundred buildings and a four-runway airfield had been completed. On December 5, 1943, Lt. Col. Elbert Tuttle reported to Fort Pickett, where he took command of the 304th Field Artillery Battalion of the Seventy-Seventh, or Statue of Liberty, Division—named for the patch emblazoned with the Statue of Liberty that the soldiers wore. Tuttle mentally gave his new unit high marks: they were well trained and capable. The men, for their part, welcomed the new commander. At forty-six, trim and fit, he stood five feet ten and weighed 145 pounds. He carried himself with dignity and treated his men with respect. Something about Elbert Tuttle inspired confidence, and the men of the 304th were happy to have a commanding officer in whom they could repose confidence. They were awaiting orders to ship out to the Pacific theater, and they would not wait long.

In January, Buddy went to the Pacific, and Sara joined Elbert at Fort Pickett. "Of course, I was a wreck," Sara remembered, "but I had to carry on." She found a garage apartment at the home of a young couple, the Matthewses, who had just adopted a baby girl. Sara was charmed by the child; she was a happy diversion. In March the orders for the 304th arrived, sending them to the Pacific theater. Sara managed to throw a party for the division before they left. Elbert got a last-minute chance to call Sara, just before the troop train pulled out. "Good-bye, honey," she said, "Have an interesting time." In later years, Elbert would often tell that story—that the last thing that his wife said to him as he shipped off for World War II was "have an interesting time." It always got a laugh from everyone, including Sara. Once in a while she would slip in a quiet but pointed reminder that "we had already had our good-byes."

The Statue of Liberty Division, along with the rest of the 304th Field Artillery Battalion, shipped out from Fort Pickett in March. Elbert and Sara had agreed that while they were apart, they would write every other day. Elbert broke that rule, as he explained to her in a letter written later that month from a ship crossing the Pacific. "I have not written earlier at sea, Sweet, because there was so little I could tell you. And, as you know, our mail travels with us until we arrive at our destination." Besides, he explained, "I really have felt as though I were living in a hiatus, if such a thing is possible. I really have felt that way since the moment I left you, and I know it will continue until we are together again."

Not until April 15 could he disclose their destination—Hawaii. "Now it can be told, at least part of it," he wrote. "We are stationed on the island of Oahu. . . . I can't tell you more about the exact location." It was near enough to Pearl Harbor that he went by there as soon as he arrived, looking for Mac. Mac Asbill Jr. by then was an aide to Marine Maj. Gen. Holland M. "Howling Mad" Smith. When Mac, fresh out of Princeton and Marine Corps training, had showed up to interview for the position with General Smith, Howling Mad howled. Mac had a terrific résumé, but he was very young. "I'm not running a G-D kindergarten," the general roared. Mac Asbill won him over and got the job. This proved handy to Sara. Neither Elbert nor Buddy could tell her where he was, but occasionally one of them wrote that he had seen Mac. Sara knew that Mac was with General Smith, and General Smith's movements were often reported in the American press.

In mid-April 1944, when Elbert showed up at General Smith's headquarters at Pearl Harbor, he arranged for Mac to spend Saturday night and Sunday with him. Elbert and Mac visited Elbert's high school pal Francis Cooper for a lunchtime luau. The guests included haole, Hawaiian, and Japanese friends of the Coopers. Old surfing buddies welcomed Elbert warmly, "like a long-lost brother." Elbert and Mac left about 5:00 p.m. and visited another old friend, Jinky Crozier, and his family. They invited Elbert back for dinner, but he had to decline; he had no way of getting there. "I was doubly sorry," he wrote Sara, "because I am just lonesome for a family and home. It does me untold good to step into one for a few minutes."

On April 19 Elbert wrote Sara that he had talked with Gen. Isaac Spalding. The general had told Elbert that he was pleased with his division's organization, and he wanted Elbert to know why he wouldn't be getting a promotion until after they were in a campaign. General Spalding explained that if he lost his executive officer, a Colonel Taylor, he would want Tuttle for his new executive officer, but he needed Tuttle to stay in command of his battalion through the campaign. Taylor, General Spalding feared, might leave before the campaign. Tuttle took this to mean that General Spalding anticipated that Colonel Taylor would be leaving and that Tuttle would be passed over for executive officer and the rank of colonel.

Tuttle had chafed over his inability to earn a promotion. The problem was largely one of logistics. Artillery regiments had been disbanded, and with four artillery battalions assigned to each division there were practically no positions at the rank of colonel in the field artillery. The irony was that stateside officers were moving up; Tuttle calculated that had he remained at a desk, he would be a colonel by now. While still at Fort Sam Houston he had passed up a transfer to the China-Burma-India theater in Southeast Asia that would have carried the rank of brigadier or major general because he wanted to stay in the field artillery. Now he was being passed over. Nonetheless, he wrote Sara, he was content with the situation. "I can't mind," he wrote, "because I want to command my battalion in combat, and I am willing to wait for a promotion until after that. Sweet, I don't feel about it as I did once, so don't feel that I am in the least downhearted. Everything is perfect, and I am as pleased as punch with the entire set-up."

The Seventy-Seventh Division spent three months on Oahu practicing amphibious landings, while the 304th tested their artillery skills. In mid-May Tuttle was made acting division artillery commander. Even so, he was only authorized to use a jeep in emergency situations. Mac, on the other hand, could drive pretty much at will. Together they dined with Tuttle's old friends in their homes. Tuttle's nonresident membership at the Outrigger Club, the surfing club his father had helped found some three decades earlier, enabled him to repay the kindnesses of his friends by taking them to dinners and parties there. Whenever he had a free afternoon, he would stop by for lunch and surfing. "Honestly," he wrote Sara, "I have such a delightful time when I am not working that I have a guilty conscience." The only flaw, he wrote, was missing her.

He missed the rest of the family too. He had Sara send him Buddy's letters to her. Elbert and Sara were now able to write to each other every other day, and the children wrote home every other day. Buddy wrote both his parents with regularity, but his letters to his father, Elbert told Sara, were mostly "soldier talk." His letters to his mother were more introspective. Buddy was, on the one hand, a handsome and daring fighter pilot whose tent boasted a phonograph and became jazz central to his fellow soldiers. He was also intense, sensitive, and serious—a philosopher at heart. The raw realities of war forced him to consider and reconsider how he could lead a meaningful life.

At home, Nicky was about to graduate from Wellesley. On May 5 Elbert wrote Sara that he had ordered two orchid leis to be shipped from Hilo to Wellesley. Near the end of May he got Nicky's letter thanking him for them; they had arrived on time and in good condition. In early June, Sara's letter describing Nicky at commencement with some of the orchids entwined in her hair arrived. Elbert replied, "Sweet, I can really see her." Instead of going back to Atlanta, Sara and Nicky went to Malcolm's home in New Rochelle, New York. Nicky crewed for Malcolm on his sailboat, preparing for a July 4 race. On June 10 Elbert wrote Sara that he was sending sport shirts with a Hawaiian coat of arms. "I think they should *win* the race on July 4th in these new uniforms," he wrote. He added a note for Malcolm: "Yesterday there was a slight Kona wind. . . . Malcolm will recall exactly how the ocean swelled and how the waves sort of fell over themselves as they broke."

Even as he wrote of his regret at missing Nicky's commencement, Elbert insisted that she go ahead with her plans to marry John Harmon. No one should have any concern over whether he could be there, he wrote; his only worry was that Johnny might be sent back overseas. "Darling," he wrote to Sara, "I expect that when Johnny comes home things will move so fast that you can't let me know much. Please don't give any thought to that Sweetheart. Do everything you can to make them happy, and let's give them their wedding trip. Darling, if necessary write to Bill for $250 . . . They will be together so short a time that I want it to be perfect."

John Harmon was, along with Buddy Tuttle and Mac Asbill, in the

Princeton class of 1942. All three wanted to do their part in the war effort, but John had a caveat—he was a pacifist. In the spring of 1942, he joined the British Field Service as an ambulance driver. He had been seeing Nicky since meeting her in the summer of 1941, after her freshman year in college, and by the time he left they were "sort of engaged." John had doggedly read every issue of the *Christian Century*, the topic of his senior thesis, but he hadn't written the paper, so he could not graduate with his class. He went anyway to see Mac and Buddy graduate. Then, on June 22, 1942, he left for the thick of combat. In the fall of 1942, John Harmon ferried wounded and dying men throughout the Battle of El Alamein, where British general Bernard Montgomery went on the offensive, broke through enemy lines, and forced German general Erwin Rommel's troops back toward Tunisia. The bitter fighting at El Alamein marked Hitler's first defeat in North Africa; it proved to be one of the turning points of the war.

In 1944, two years after he first left, John returned for a three-month leave. Nicky and John decided to get married before he returned to the front. Sara and Nicky had stayed with Elbert's brother, Malcolm, and his wife, Aurilla, in New Rochelle, and Nicky and John decided to be married there. Nicky's friend Betty Haverty arrived from Georgia to be Nicky's maid of honor; her cousins, Malcolm's daughters Ellen and Ann, were attendants. On July 25, at Saint John's Episcopal Church in Larchmont, Malcolm stood in for his brother and gave Nicky away; then he and Rilla hosted a reception at their home in neighboring New Rochelle. Nicky was so caught up in the excitement of the wedding that she had no time to keep up with war news. Three days before the wedding, the *New York Times* reported that the Seventy-Seventh Division was participating in the invasion of Guam. Sara knew and was distraught, yet she kept her composure and kept the news from Nicky and John.

Guam had been an American possession until, just after Pearl Harbor, it fell to the Japanese. Taking Guam and nearby Wake Island had given the Japanese control of the line of communications across the Central Pacific and allowed them to isolate the Philippines.[1] In early July 1944, Elbert Tuttle's battalion sailed west from Hawaii. On July 6, he wrote one last letter from Oahu; his next letter begins, "As you might well have guessed, we are on the move again—this time to our first campaign." For the first time, a letter from Elbert had been censored: the day on which it was written had been blacked out. It was a matter of security. Elbert's battalion was en route to Guam. Knowing he was going into battle, he wrote Sara, "I truly hope, darling, that your mind can be as much at peace as mine is." His thoughts went to Nicky: "Darling, the more I think about the important things in life the better satisfied I am with Nicky's common sense. I am so glad she is not interested in the glamour and glitter of 'things.' It is her inner life and Johnny's that counts. She and Johnny both have an inner fire that will drive them and that will sustain them when the going gets tough, and that is worth more than all the material wealth in the world."

He wrote four more letters from shipboard "somewhere over the Pacific," as he put it. There were some pleasures. There was time to read and time to write thank-you notes to his friends in Hawaii. The food was an improvement over the base chow at Oahu, and there was always ice cream. A group started sing-alongs, enhanced by a professional tenor among the soldiers. Elbert enjoyed them, but they made him terribly homesick. On July 20 he wrote, "Sweetheart, I just wish there were some way you could be around the corner so I could talk to you. I've told you not to worry—I mean no matter how long there may be between letters—just know, Darling, that always, everything is alright. I mean Everything!!"

The next day, July 21, 1944, the Seventy-Seventh Division, supporting the First Marine Division, landed on Guam against stiff opposition. To the north, the Third Marine Division had even tougher going because of high ground around the beaches. They managed to establish a beachhead and, with artillery and naval gunfire support, cleared the hills and cliffs. The Third Division was firmly ashore, but it was overextended. On July 26 the Japanese launched a counterattack. The fighting was intense and the outcome uncertain; one battalion suffered 50 percent casualties, but it held. The Japanese attack on July 26 had two prongs. To the south, where the First Marine Division had landed, the Japanese ran headfirst into Marine lines supported by the Statue of Liberty Division artillery. The intense barrage at close quarters took a heavy toll on the Japanese attackers. "Arms and legs flew like snow," read one report.[2] In the two offensives, the Japanese lost some thirty-five hundred men; the losses included 95 percent of the Japanese officers on Guam. The battle for Guam was not over, but the outcome had been determined.

The two Marine divisions, with their army support, moved toward Apra

Harbor, where they met and continued to sweep north. As they moved deeper into Japanese-held territory, Tuttle became increasingly worried about his driver. When Tuttle became battalion commander in 1943, he inherited the battalion commander's driver, Nan Jew (pronounced Chu), a Brooklyn laundryman of Chinese descent. Jew took great pride in his job. Now Tuttle decided to leave him behind. He had heard tales of the army's Japanese interpreters being shot at by American soldiers; then one day he saw it happen. A Japanese interpreter appeared suddenly, and just as quickly a soldier fired. That afternoon, Tuttle told Jew to stay behind. "No," Jew said. "I Chinese, I not Japanese." "I know, and I can tell you apart, but some of these new recruits are apt to shoot first and look afterward," Tuttle explained. "No," Jew said again. "The other boys go up front, I go too." Tuttle was moved but not persuaded; tomorrow, he told Jew, he would use another driver. The next morning, Jew was waiting at Tuttle's jeep. He had found a chalklike rock and carefully lettered "U.S." on his helmet in large block letters. Tuttle tried again. "Jew, most of our men know you, but these Marines—they're different. They're pretty fast on the trigger." "No," Jew said again. "I go."[3] When the Seventy-Seventh reached the north end of Guam on August 8, Nan Jew was driving Lieutenant Colonel Tuttle. Two days later, on August 10, 1944, Guam was declared secure.

The battle for Guam marked the first time the Seventy-Seventh Division saw combat. War-seasoned officers worried about the untested troops, but the Seventy-Seventh proved itself and more. It got high marks, to the surprise of some.[4] Few of the men of the Seventy-Seventh were army regulars, and those who had been drafted were older than the average draftee. "Circumstances were not normal in March, 1942, when the 77th was activated. The Army had to make fighting men, and quickly, out of whatever Selective Service turned up. For the 77th, it happened to turn up mostly older, settled men, averaging thirty-two years of age." Maj. Gen. Robert Eichelberger had pushed them hard, and it paid off. The men of the Seventy-Seventh were disciplined, determined, and extremely well trained. Watching them swarm ashore at Guam, a young combat-tested Marine christened them with a name that stuck—"Lookit those old buzzards go," he exclaimed.[5]

The Seventy-Seventh had been scheduled to go on to Guadalcanal from Guam, but those plans were changed, and the division awaited orders to move. In the flatlands, American forces began an enormous construction effort, building bases and expanding and improving the airfields left by the Japanese. With nowhere else to put them, the Seventy-Seventh was parked in the hills. The soldiers settled in with pup tents and improvised bamboo and palm shacks for shelter and combat rations for food. It was the rainy season; mud and mildew covered everything, and mosquitoes, flies, and rats plagued the men. The men of the Seventy-Seventh spent a long ten weeks in the hills of Guam.

Gen. Harmon "Howling Mad" Smith had temporary headquarters on Guam; as soon as he could, Elbert Tuttle hitched a ride there, where he found Mac Asbill. Mac told Elbert that Buddy's squadron was nearby, some ninety miles away on Tinian Island. Somehow he got word to Buddy, and a few days later, Elbert Tuttle saw his son stride into camp. Buddy was taken aback; as a fighter pilot, he shared a sixteen-by-sixteen-foot wooden-floored tent with his roommate; they had a phonograph and a jazz collection that made them legendary in the squadron, and they were served real meals three times a day. It was a shock to find his father sleeping on the ground, sheltered by a pup tent, and lucky to have it to himself; his men, including junior officers, all shared. A storm came in, so Buddy stayed the night. The next day, he flew his dad to Tinian, then back. Flying into Tinian, Buddy couldn't resist showing off a little. With his dad in the open cockpit behind him, he swept through an Immelmann turn; only a powerful centrifugal force kept his dad safely in his seat. Buddy went back to flying his torpedo bomber patrols. When the rains let up, the Seventy-Seventh Division artillery began intense training. By late October "all battalions had reached the peak of physical and technical proficiency."[6] It was just in time. On October 18 the Japanese decided to make their stand at Leyte, an island in the Philippines.

In October John Harmon had returned to the front with an ambulance unit attached to the British Eighth Army. After John left, Nicky joined her mother in Atlanta, where Sara had taken an apartment in the Georgian Terrace. Nicky took a job with a government nursery for children whose mothers were working in war industries. Together she and her mother took a nurse's aide course at Crawford Long Hospital. Once trained, they signed on for the 3:00 to 11:00 p.m. shift at St. Joseph's Hospital. The nuns welcomed them, and Sara and Nicky welcomed the work. "We ate our dinners at the hospital, which was good," Sara remembered, "and that shift took care of the lonely hours between 5 p.m. and bedtime which were hours that I dreaded." The nurse's aide program and bridge got her through the war, "the first because I was so involved with the troubles of others it left me less time to worry about my own, and the latter because I was with friends who understood if my mind wandered and I trumped my partner's ace." When her mind wandered, it wandered halfway across the world to the Philippines. From 1898 until 1935, when the Philippines became a self-governing commonwealth, the United States had ruled the islands. In 1942 Japanese forces invaded and took control of the islands. Gen. Douglas MacArthur led the American forces defending the islands until March 1942, when Roosevelt ordered him to leave. When he reached Australia, MacArthur made his famous pledge: "I shall return." On October 20, 1944, he did return, landing on Leyte. The stage was set for a defining battle in the Pacific.

In late October the Seventy-Seventh finally left Guam. Transports arrived, and the entire division embarked in thirty-six hours. They sailed on November 3, headed for New Caledonia, a French-held island that had become a strategic foothold for the Americans. The men looked forward to being on a peaceful island devoid of enemy forces; even more, they looked forward to having fresh food. On November 11, four days out from New Caledonia, new orders came through. They were to turn northwest, to Manus, in the Admiralty Islands. From Manus they were ordered to Leyte. Elbert wrote Sara from Manus, where they sat offshore, on Sunday, November 19. It was very hot, he reported, but he had a top bunk near an open porthole and could usually catch a breeze. Thoughts of his family were very much with him. He was reading a biography of Thoreau, he wrote, "because of Buddy's interest in parts of Thoreau's philosophy." That morning he had been to services, where a soldier had sung "The Old Rugged Cross." "He sang it beautifully, and I thought of Nanny [Sara's mother] so poignantly that I found myself very much moved. Of course, then I thought of you, too, and thought how wonderful it is for Nanny to have passed so much of her fineness to you and from you to Buddy and little Nicky and then I got in a really sentimental dither. Life is good, Sweetheart."

In his next letter, written on November 21, he wrote that he would be happy to get moving again. He got his wish. Orders came through to proceed to Leyte. The next day, en route, Elbert got off a short note. He had found a verse that expressed his thoughts:

If I shall find when
All the wars have ceased
The hands of time
Have gently on you lain,
Then all the longing,
All these lonely hours
Are not in vain.

"And so another day passes, Sweetheart, bringing closer the day when we will be together again."

They reached the east coast of Leyte on Thanksgiving Day, November 23, 1944. MacArthur had been struggling for control for over a month. Two weeks later, the Seventy-Seventh boarded ships that would take them around the southern end of Leyte to Ormoc Bay on the western shore. The landing craft leading the convoy carried the 304th. At dusk, Tuttle went to the bridge to watch a tropical sunset over the ocean. Instead, he saw a kamikaze plane dive from the sky into the deck of a destroyer protecting their flotilla. In moments, the destroyer rolled over and sank, desperate men clinging to its sides. Tuttle's transport kept moving; the mission required it.

Trying to slip into Ormoc Bay late that night, the Seventy-Seventh Division found itself in the cross-fire of a naval battle. Evading harm, transports reached the tiny beach, and, under cover of darkness, the division went ashore, behind Japanese lines, on December 7. They drove north, slogging on muddy paths and across rice fields, battling tenacious Japanese soldiers every step of the way, and on December 11 they captured Ormoc. Two weeks later, the capture of Palompon on Christmas Day marked the official end of the battle for Leyte. The Seventy-Seventh stayed on until February 5, clearing the Palompon Road and engaging fighting bands of Japanese left in northeastern Leyte. All told, the Seventy-Seventh lost 543 men at Leyte, and another 1,469 were wounded.[7]

On February 5 the Seventy-Seventh Division was withdrawn and sent back to the east coast of Leyte to regroup and prepare for landings in the Kerama Rotto, a group of small, rocky islands just west of Okinawa. With the fighting over, Tuttle admitted that he had been suffering from dysentery for about three weeks. He was always slim, and the combination of the privations of war and the illness left him too thin. Reluctantly, he went into the hospital; he had never before been a patient in a hospital. After a week's stay in the hospital, the illness subsided. The doctors remained unsure what had caused it, but they discharged him anyway. He got back to his company just in time for a rare occurrence, a dance party. He wasn't very much interested in it, he wrote Sara, and neither were his men. Many of the officers were married, and, he wrote, they were "very married."

The division arrived at Kerama Rotto at dawn on March 26. Now experienced, the division launched five battalion teams onto five islands simultaneously. Tuttle's team, the 306th Marine Infantry supported by the 304th Field Army Artillery, which he commanded, took Geruma quickly. By the 27th, all five of the first islands assaulted were secure; the Seventy-Seventh moved on, taking several more islands, including, on March 31, four low, sandy islands called Keise Shima, just off Naha Harbor. Two battalions of 155 mm guns were quickly emplaced there and provided critical support for the Tenth Army's landing on Okinawa the next day. On April 2 the Seventy-Seventh Division boarded three navy transport divisions and moved 350 miles out to sea to escape Japanese air activity. As the convoy moved away from Kerama Rotto, eight Japanese kamikaze attacked; five ships were hit, and twenty-two men of the Seventy-Seventh were killed in the surprise attack. The Seventy-Seventh steamed around several hundred miles off Okinawa for more than a week. On April 12, the day President Roosevelt died, the Seventy-Seventh was ordered to assault the island of Ie Shima on April 16. Ie Shima, located less than three miles west of Okinawa, was 2.5 miles wide by 5 miles long, slightly bigger than Iwo Jima. The Japanese had constructed a three-strip airbase, with each strip over fifty-five hundred feet long, on the level plateau that covered almost the entire top of the island. The enemy garrison had housed as many as five thousand men, but some believed, on the basis of reconnaissance flights, aerial photographs, and interrogations of captured Japanese soldiers, that Ie Shima had been evacuated. Gen. Andrew D. Bruce looked on those reports with suspicion; similar information about Leyte had simply proven the Japanese to be masters of deception and camouflage. His men estimated some 2,500 enemy troops remained on the island. Even that proved low. When the fighting ended, 4,794 Japanese had been killed and 140 taken prisoner. Nearly half were armed citizens, as opposed to formal military units, but all were, in the battle for Ie Shima, enemy forces. The Japanese had managed to keep some six thousand soldiers and citizens out of sight, making the island look virtually uninhabited.

Because General Bruce had not been fooled, the Americans had taken no chances. Just before dawn, on April 16, 1945, the division convoy plus units of the Fifth Fleet arrived off Ie Shima. Two battleships, two heavy cruisers, two light cruisers, seven destroyers, twenty-four mortar boats, and six gunboats fired round after round. Units from the navy's air force chimed in with bombs and strafing. Elbert Tuttle's field artillery battalion, the 304th, the only field artillery battalion landed at Ie Shima, went ashore in DUKWs ("ducks"), amphibious vehicles that were part boat and part open truck. Tuttle rode in the first duck off the LST (landing ship tank) with members of his staff and his air officer, Ed Laroussini. As they disembarked, Tuttle pointed out a palm tree near the beach. "Steer for that tree," he told the driver. When the duck got some five hundred yards from shore, a Japanese machine gun erupted. Bullets flew past them—narrow misses. The driver veered to the right, away from the fire. "No, don't go to the right," Tuttle ordered, following his own orders to the letter. "Keep heading for that tree." The driver obeyed, but with each burst of fire from the machine gun, he would veer right and then left when Tuttle ordered him back to his course. They were in range of the machine gun and getting closer when the firing suddenly stopped. In air thick with smoke, Tuttle stepped ashore at the center of his battalion's landing area.

The 306th Infantry began a rapid advance across the island. Tuttle's 304th Artillery Battalion made camp near the beach. From the terraced, grass-covered sand dunes the 304th supported the infantry's advance on the town of Ie. Tuttle worried about overextending his men. Dozens had to stay up all night firing their twelve artillery pieces in support of the infantry; others were posted as guards at the perimeter of the camp. On the afternoon of the 18th, when an amphibious tractor ("alligator") company landed and camped between the 304th and the high-water mark, Tuttle sent his executive officer, Maj. Dan Schaeffer, to make a deal. The 304th would protect the alligator company from the land side, and the alligator company could stand guard for the 304th from the ocean side. This let a handful of exhausted men try to get a night's sleep.

As Tuttle's men slept, the guard on the west flank of the amphibious tractor company saw twenty-odd men crossing the beach. He had heard that Japanese soldiers were poorly trained, so, as he told Dan Schaeffer the next day, "Hell, Major, they were marching down the beach in a straight column of twos and I just took them for American soldiers." By then, Tuttle easily slept through artillery fire, but he awoke when he heard men whispering in Japanese. Suddenly, a grenade exploded, sending steel fragments into his back and legs; two more landed with thuds but failed to detonate. Tuttle yelled "Japs, Japs" to alert his men as he struggled with two Japanese soldiers, each armed with a long pole. One attempted to impale Tuttle; the other swung over and over, striking at Tuttle's head. The tent line staking out the front cushioned the blows and probably saved his life. Tuttle grabbed the pole thrusting at him and managed to push his attacker backward. One of his men, Lt. Forney Holt, shot and killed that intruder, and Tuttle managed to scramble downhill to the first aid station.

The medics, Clarence Becker and Joseph Nitowski, had just stabbed and killed a Japanese soldier who had leapt into their foxhole. Nitowski grabbed his rifle, peered out, and saw a tall man running downhill toward them. It was pitch-black dark, but Nitowski thought he recognized Tuttle and held his fire. Becker pulled Tuttle in to safety; seeing he was wounded, they brought out dressings. As they worked, a cap appeared at the edge of the foxhole; Nitowski fired. A dead Japanese soldier tumbled into the foxhole. In the quiet that followed, they heard calls for medics. As Becker treated Tuttle, Nitowski struck out. In the dark, he could hardly find the men, and when he could, he had difficulty seeing well enough to treat them. His first casualty, Sgt. John Haley, assured him he would be okay and sent him on. Others were in worse shape, including the radio operator, Sergeant Echols, whose left hand was nearly severed by a slashing sword. By then, the sun was rising. In the morning light, more than twenty Japanese soldiers lay dead; nine men of the 304th, including Tuttle, were wounded seriously enough to be evacuated to hospital ships that lay a mile offshore. The Japanese, they later learned, were members of a suicide group sent in to blow up the artillery pieces. None had rifles or pistols, but some had mortar shells strapped to their bodies.

At daybreak, Dan Schaeffer found Tuttle in boxer shorts and a T-shirt sitting on a tree stump, bloody from wounds on his head, neck, and back. "Colonel Tuttle," he asked, "how are you; how do you feel?" Rays from the sun shot across the horizon, and Tuttle, aware that he was lucky to see it, told Schaeffer, "I never felt better in my life." His wounds from shrapnel were superficial, and if he suffered a concussion from the blows to his head, it healed itself. The thrusting pole had done the most damage, causing a hernia in his groin that required surgery.

While Tuttle waited to board the LST that would take him to the navy hospital ship, his driver, Nan Jew, showed up with clothes for him. "Colonel," he said, "these Jap, they try very hard to kill you." He showed Tuttle his steel helmet, perforated on both sides. It had been lying by Tuttle as he slept. "They throw three grenades in your tent," he told Tuttle. Only aware of one, Tuttle asked how Jew knew. "One go off," Jew said, "and you got some of that; one blow just the plug and no go off; the other one a dud." "Well, Jew, you saved my life last night." "I don't understand, Colonel; I sleep." But it was Jew who set Tuttle's tent up, and it was Jew who time after time had found a small tree to tie the front line to so that Tuttle didn't bang into a front pole going in and out. It had taken Tuttle all morning to figure out why the Japanese attacker bashing him on the head with his sturdy pole hadn't knocked him out. "I know," Jew said, smiling. "Every time he bang that club down it hit the rope, and when he hit your head it not hit so hard."

On board the hospital ship, Tuttle learned of the death of Ernie Pyle. Pyle had reported the war from London during the Blitz, where he dodged the bombs of the Luftwaffe; from North Africa, where he narrowly escaped the disaster at Kasserine Pass; from Sicily and from Anzio, where he was wounded by fragments from a German five-hundred-pound bomb. The soldiers loved him for telling their stories and for telling them from the front lines. Pyle had gone ashore on the afternoon of April 17, the second day of the invasion. He spent the night at the command post of the 305th Infantry. In the morning, Ernie Pyle left in a jeep with the regimental commander, Lt. Col. Joseph B. Coolidge, driving, to visit the soldiers on the front lines. As they approached the outskirts of Ie Town, a Japanese machine gunner hidden by the side of the road burst into fire; the first blasts missed, and Coolidge and Pyle abandoned the jeep and scrambled into a ditch. They waited there in dead silence. Then they raised their heads carefully, just enough to try to locate the enemy, and another burst of machine gun fire rang out. They both dropped, Coolidge of his own volition. Pyle had been struck in the temple, just below the rim of his steel helmet. Coolidge crawled along the ditch to a safer position; determined to recover Pyle's body, he called for help. Tanks couldn't traverse the difficult terrain, and it took infantry patrols three hours to destroy the machine gun position.[8]

The nation's leading newspapers covered the fighting on Ie Shima. First came banner headlines mourning Ernie Pyle. Then a story about Tuttle by William McGaffin of the Daily News Foreign Service ran across the country; friends sent Sara clippings from California, Chicago, and Hawaii. In Atlanta it ran on the front page on April 25, 1945, under the headline "Atlanta Colonel Victorious in Wild Hand-to-Hand Battle with Japs": "Lieut. Colonel Elbert Tuttle is his battlefield title, but in peace time lawyer Tuttle was one of the smartest attorneys in Atlanta, Ga.," McGaffin wrote. Sara was spared the shock of learning from a headline that her husband had been wounded. One of Nicky's friends worked at the paper and called Sara when she saw the story come over the wire. By the time she actually read the article, Sara had also been contacted by the War Department, and she knew her husband was safe aboard a hospital ship. By May 2 he was back with his men. Intending to reassure her, he wrote: "We are in action now in the Ryukyus and except for the night-long disturbances of artillery firing last night was very quiet, and I expect it will continue to be so for my battalion. I am well dug in in a Jap cave and there will be no infiltration here." The next day he wrote again. The Japanese, he reported, "stick like leeches in these rocky cliffs and caves. My command post is in a cave to avoid artillery fire and I am sleeping there now as well." He worried about her worrying about him, and he worried about keeping her spirits up. "Darling don't deny yourself pretty things," he wrote. "I want you to continue to be the sweetest girl in Atlanta. I haven't sent my check for the last two months, because we haven't been paid, but I guess they'll get around to it when this campaign is over." He worried about Johnny; he had heard good news from Italy and hoped that might mean Johnny would be released, but he didn't expect it.

The one person he wasn't worried about was his best friend, Leckie Mattox. Leckie had been with the Seventy-Seventh Division and, like Tuttle, had been in the thick of things. "I know he will have some big tales to tell," Elbert wrote. "I don't think he slept away from Division Hq. 2 nights— maybe 3." He had been observing the capabilities of different armaments for a report for General Bruce that was now in the general's hands. "I told him goodbye today, Sweetheart. He is through with us."

In his next letter, dated May 5, Elbert's spirits were down: "I don't think I have ever admitted it before, Sweetheart, but I am pretty low tonight—altho all of my affairs are running smoothly and the battalion is doing fine work. Just once in a while all the killing and dying away out here sort of gets you down. Nothing can be as important for the future as our taking whatever steps may be necessary to prevent another war if it is humanly possible." On May 8 he wrote explaining his depression. Leckie had decided to take one final look at the action from an infantry observation post. Japanese machine gun fire caused the small group he was with to duck. After a few moments of quiet, a Japanese artillery shell burst, spraying shrapnel, which hit him in the right side. Although medics on the scene gave him plasma and loaded him into an ambulance, he was dead when the ambulance arrived at the Medical Collecting Company. He had never regained consciousness and was probably beyond all help from the moment he had been hit.

Leckie Mattox's death was a loss that Tuttle took hard. The day it happened another officer, not knowing how close they were, casually said to Tuttle, "Did you hear that Leckie Mattox was killed?" Tuttle protested. "That can't be," he argued. "He was with me only an hour ago." Too quickly he realized that it could be, it was. He wrote Leckie's wife, Gabrielle, a long letter, telling her all that he knew of what had happened, hoping that knowing the truth of Leckie's last moments would be some solace. Then he wrote Sara that he could not "put in words just how bad it made me feel, but I have to put these things out of my mind as quickly as I can." Again he tried to reassure her.

> My normal duties are not in a forward observation post. I have had to go forward occasionally, but the occasions are less and less frequent as I get more and more confidence in my forward observers, and while I hate to have any one else do a more dangerous job than I do, nevertheless, common sense tells me that I should perform my duties where I am most needed, and that is in the battalion area. Casualties there are extremely infrequent, except for a freak accident like Ie Shima.

At home, Sara worried. No amount of reassurance could change the fact that Elbert was on the front lines of a war. She tried to keep busy, because there was no peace of mind: "You never knew, when you laid your head down at night, if your loved ones were safe." Sara had not wanted Elbert to volunteer for overseas duty, but she acquiesced because it meant so much to him. Now he was soldiering on even though he had not fully recovered from the wounds he received at Ie Shima. Sara was not alone in her concern. General Bruce was aware that Tuttle had not fully recovered from the privations and illness incurred in the invasion of Guam. On May 18 Elbert wrote Sara with "a birthday present for myself, and maybe for you." "I have accepted your request . . . and General Bruce's suggestion, contrary to my own personal desires, or rather inclination, but I have done so little you wanted me to in connection with military affairs, I am glad to acquiesce in this most important matter of all. Having made up my mind, I feel fully satisfied." General Bruce had been direct. "The General was highly complimentary and all that, but he felt that with my strength threatened by loss of weight and the strain of repeated battle situations I should be relieved of the responsibilities and strain of the battalion and do staff work. I feel that anything I could do on the staff any of a number of people could do, and so I told him I would accept his suggestion and terminate my service."

As he signed off, Elbert was on his way to the hospital, then home. Things were moving fast, he wrote. Things were moving fast for his son as well. Buddy had finished his year of combat in early February but had stayed on in the Pacific. He wouldn't go home until his father did. The Marines were gearing up for the assault on Iwo Jima. Buddy joined the flotilla, traveling by sea tender, and by the end of February he sat offshore watching the fighting on Iwo Jima. On February 19, 1945, he saw fellow Marines raise the flag on Mount Suribachi. From the beach, Secretary of the Navy James Forrestal saw it too; he turned to Marine general Holland Smith: "Holland, the raising of that flag on Suribachi means a Marine Corps for the next 500 years."[9]

Buddy watched the struggle for Iwo Jima for ten days. As soon as an airstrip had been secured, he flew in—the first American pilot to land on Iwo Jima.[10] The first thing he did was search out his cousin and closest friend, Mac Asbill, who was on Iwo with General Smith. Then he went about the work of setting up a flight operation for bombing caves. The islands of the Pacific were riddled with caves, and the caves were shelter and base to Japanese soldiers. American encampments were subject to sudden attack by enemies who literally arose in their midst. In April he was put in command of an antisubmarine patrol. Once again he was flying his torpedo bomber over the Pacific; once again he was struck by the contrast between the peacefulness of the vast sky and sea and the violence of his mission.

By the end of May, Elbert was in the hospital in the Mariannas, preparing to ship out for home. On May 24 he sent word to Buddy; on May 26 Buddy flew in for two days. When he returned to Iwo, he told his superior officers he was ready to go home. He managed one more flight to see his father in early June, before Elbert was transferred to the hospital on Oahu on June 9. Elbert was happy to be back in Hawaii, he wrote Sara, even if it was as a hospital patient. He hoped to be sent back to the States but was not yet sure what his orders would be. After a long three weeks, on July 1 he wrote Sara from San Francisco. Buddy and Mac were there as well. For two years they had been crossing each other's paths in the war-torn islands of the Pacific; now they were together on American soil, Buddy and Mac unharmed, Elbert recovering. John Harmon had been among the few Americans with the British forces that liberated Bergen-Belsen in April and had shipped home after Germany surrendered in May. Leckie was dead. The Japanese would not surrender until August 15, 1945, but for the Tuttle family, the war was over.

CHAPTER NINE

Building a Republican
Party in Georgia

When Elbert and Sara Tuttle moved to Atlanta in 1923, he was only twenty-six and had not yet affiliated himself with any political party. In Hawaii, where "a high sugar tariff meant prosperity for the Hawaiian sugar indus-try," his parents had been Republicans. Upon arriving in Georgia, Tuttle noticed a singular irony. "I found that whereas I had left a place where all of the dark people were Democrats, I had arrived at a place where all of the dark people were Republicans."[1]

Georgia was a one-party state, and the one party was the white Democratic Party. Because you had to be a member of the Democratic Party to vote in the Democratic primary and because you had to be white to be a member of the party, black voters were excluded from any mean-ingful participation in the political process. They could vote in the general election, but by then their vote meant little. In contests for statewide of-fice, winning the Democratic primary meant winning the election. From 1900 until the white Democratic primary in Georgia was finally held un-constitutional in 1945, every Democratic nominee for statewide office was elected.[2]

For Elbert Tuttle, joining the Democratic Party was not an option. In his eyes, the Democratic Party in Georgia was a "paternalistic at best, and autocratic at worse, group of politicians running the state. Nothing 'demo-cratic' about it at all except the name."[3] If, for the time being, not joining meant forgoing the opportunity to be a player in the political arena, so be it. He had other things to occupy him—a young family, a developing law practice, his service in the National Guard, his involvement in professional and civic affairs. Most of all, he could not abide the wrong. "I could see absolutely no reason to become involved with what I then thought was the most undemocratic form of government of any state in the Union—that is, the white Democratic Party of Georgia, which of course was merely typical of the white Democratic parties of the other Southern States." Instead, he undertook to identify himself, when he could, with the "very small number of liberal thinking white people in Atlanta and environs [working] to improve the lot of the Negro people of Georgia."[4] At first, he was not active in the Republican Party. Until 1932 black members controlled the Republican Party in Georgia, and very few whites were involved. When whites began to express interest in the party, black Republicans welcomed them. By 1932, although blacks still had the votes to control the party, whites dominated the state Republican Committee with two-thirds of the seats. In 1936 black members were thrown off the state committee. Black Republicans stayed the course, and in 1940 twenty-two of the sixty-seven committee members elected were black. That victory was short lived; the majority of the committee voted the black members off.[5]

The battle for control of the Republican Party created two factions. At the 1940 national convention, most of Georgia's black Republicans supported the delegation led by W. R. Tucker. Benjamin J. Davis Sr., the publisher of the *Atlanta Independent* (the black community's weekly newspaper) and the leader of the Republican Party in the 1930s, dubbed the other delegation, headed by Roscoe Pickett, the "lily-white" delegation. The Pickett delegation actually had one black delegate out of fourteen and three black alternates out of thirteen, but when Davis called them lily white, the name stuck.[6] "Lily white" did not mean they were not shrewd enough to include black delegates and alternates; it meant that the black members were mere tokens.

In the 1930s Tuttle attended one or two Republican conventions in Atlanta. They were not inspiring.

At that time they were held, you might say, in a telephone booth, because it was the avowed and open and known practice for certain candidates at upcoming conventions to send 20 to 40 or 50 thousand dollars to a favored person, usually to the United States Attorney, who could then engage in politics, but who subsequently of course under the Hatch Act could no longer do so, or to the collector of Internal Revenue who was also active in politics. He would spend this money wisely retaining such part of it as he thought was appropriate for his services, and get enough people to come to Atlanta to elect a delegation to the upcoming national convention, and of course they would always go there pledged to the person who supplied him money.[7]

In 1940 Elbert Tuttle attended his first national convention in Philadelphia as an observer. His attention to the convention was disrupted when news came that the Germans had stormed through the Ardennes Forest. A commissioned officer in the National Guard, he left for home at once. His unit was called into active duty in September 1940, some eleven months before the Japanese attack at Pearl Harbor resulted in widespread mobilization of American forces. When he finally returned home to Atlanta in 1945, he felt that he owed it to his law partners to focus on the practice. The firm had carried him for five long years, paying him the difference between his military salary and his partner's share. Now it was time for him to help rebuild the practice.

By then, however, Elbert Tuttle was well known to Atlanta's civic leaders. His friend Harry Sommers was the president of the Chamber of Commerce, and he called on Tuttle to help with the problem of housing returning veterans. Serving as chair of the housing committee, Tuttle began by gathering data, which showed that housing problems were particularly acute for the black population of Atlanta: while they comprised some 30 to 40 percent of the population, they had access to only some 10 percent of the residential areas. "We had very difficult problems," Tuttle would recall.[8] Working with Mayor William B. Hartsfield, Tuttle and his committee undertook to open up large areas for additional housing. They didn't solve all the problems, but they made an impressive effort. At year's end, Elbert Tuttle was elected president of the Chamber of Commerce.[9] His inaugural dinner was held on December 7, 1948. It was the anniversary of the Japanese attack on Pearl Harbor, and it was a scant week since Tuttle had attended the reburial at home of Dan Pace, a young flier who had served under him before dying in combat in Germany. In his inaugural speech, Tuttle recalled standing by Dan Pace's grave and thinking "of the obligation that is on those of us who were spared to come home. We build many kinds of memorials, but it seemed to me the best kind of memorial we could build would be a living one: To do, for and in the name of those young men who lost their lives, the things they would want us to do."

Even before he was elected president of the Chamber of Commerce,

Tuttle was elected chairman of the Fulton County Republican Committee. Downtown Atlanta, home to the Georgia capitol, lies in Fulton County. Shortly before the county convention in 1948, party leaders asked Tuttle to run for chairman. He ran and he won, defeating the long-term county chair, Henry H. Turner. Reelected as treasurer, Harry Sommers was the only officer to retain his position. Ben J. Davis, who had earlier been a Republican national committeeman and the "GOP patronage czar for Georgia," was elected as one of eighteen delegates to the state convention. Five of the delegates, including Davis, were black.[10] The fledgling party was beginning to sense the possibility of significance. The postwar influx of "outsiders" to Atlanta had brought a number of Republicans. Most of them, Tuttle recalled, were liberal Republicans, Republicans of the party of Lincoln. Those were the Republicans Tuttle and Sommers actively recruited: "Our efforts were to have a party that would appeal to people who were normally Republicans in their politics but would be wide open to the Negro voters."

Enthusiasm ran so high that on September 11, 1948, the state Republican committee met to consider offering a Republican candidate for governor. The last Republican governor had been Rufus Bullock, elected in 1868. No Republican had stood for the office of governor since 1878, when J. A. Hotzclaw was defeated. Now, with the party resurgent, three men were mentioned as possible candidates for governor: C. J. Hilkie, the retired dean of Emory Law School; Elbert Tuttle; and Harry Sommers. Tuttle and Sommers both opposed offering a candidate in 1948. They thought Thomas E. Dewey, governor of New York, would be the nominee for president, and they thought he would carry Georgia and the country. A Republican national administration would create an opportunity to establish a meaningful Republican Party in Georgia, and both Tuttle and Sommers thought that running a candidate for governor would hurt Dewey.[11] No one thought there was any possibility a Republican could actually be elected governor of Georgia. By the turn of the century, over fifty years later, no Republican had yet been elected governor of Georgia.[12]

Enormous political tension had been engendered by the change in the membership of the Republican Party in Georgia, and it came to a boil at the 1944 national convention when two delegations claimed the right to represent Georgia. The state Republican convention had been tumultuous. Prior to the state convention, county conventions were held to elect delegates. In Fulton County, Georgia's most populous county, three separate county conventions had been held. One was led by Henry H. Turner; after the meeting Turner proudly announced that "for the first time in many years only white delegates were elected to the state and federal district conventions." At a preconvention meeting of the Republican state central committee a week later, Turner took an aggressive step toward creating a lily-white party. When Frank Doughman, state party secretary, called the roll of the state executive committee, he left out the twenty-two black members. They rose to protest, but Turner, as parliamentarian, ruled them out of order.[13]

Although Turner and Doughman appeared to work in concert at the state central committee meeting, they supported rival delegates. The second Fulton County meeting to elect delegates was chaired by Frank Doughman and Harry Sommers. It was attended by "most of Atlanta's well known Republicans. . . . There were 26 men, two white women, and two Negroes present."[14] Ben Davis, who had led the Georgia Republican Party when it had been left to African Americans, served as chair of the third meeting. The Davis meeting was attended by some two hundred African Americans and two or three white men. They selected thirty-one delegates to the state convention.

The Republican state convention was called to order in a courtroom in the Fulton County courthouse on May 23, 1944. Delegates who had been elected in meetings held throughout Georgia filled the courtroom and overflowed into the halls. A motion was made to move the convention to a larger venue, Taft Hall in the municipal auditorium. Ben Davis objected on formal grounds: the notice had stated that the convention would be in the courthouse. He had another, more salient concern: "He . . . feared that Negro delegates might be barred from Taft Hall." Davis's objection was overruled, and a roll-call vote began. When Frank Doughman, who was reading the names of delegates eligible to vote, called the name of a white delegate who had, two days earlier, been unseated by a black delegate, pandemonium broke out. Unable to restore order, the chair managed to call for a voice vote on the motion to move. On hearing a chorus of "ayes," he declared the meeting adjourned, to reconvene in Taft Hall. Ben Davis protested; standing on a chair, he urged the delegates to stay. About half left; about half stayed. The group that remained elected W. R. Tucker chair and Harry Sommers treasurer of the state central committee. The Tucker faction also elected fourteen delegates to the national convention and pledged them to Dewey. The group that had decamped elected Roy Foster as chair, recognized the ten delegates who had been elected by district conventions, and elected four more.[15]

When the Republican national convention convened in Chicago on June 24, 1944, two delegations claimed the right to represent Georgia. W. R. Tucker led a Georgia delegation that was committed to Dewey, Roy Foster led an uninstructed delegation, and both claimed legitimacy. Lines had been drawn on race.[16] The Tucker faction had absorbed the black leaders of the party, while the Foster faction had been engineered by Republicans committed to a lily-white party. In Chicago at the national convention, the Tucker group prevailed and was seated. But Foster didn't take the loss well; in fact, he didn't take it at all. The Foster faction appealed to the Georgia secretary of state, and he certified their electors. The Tucker faction had won where it counted, at the national convention, but the Foster faction refused to die.

Four years later, in 1948, the Foster delegation was formally uncommitted but understood to be for Senator Robert Taft, the conservative son of former president William Howard Taft. Tuttle, to whom the isolationist Taft was anathema, threw his weight in with Republican national committeeman Wilson Williams and joined his friend Harry Sommers as a member of the Williams delegation. Although formally uncommitted, the delegation was widely thought to be for Dewey. It included four black delegates and seven black alternates, a distinguished group led by John Wesley Dobbs, father of opera singer Mattiwilda Dobbs Janzon and grandfather of Maynard Jackson Jr., Atlanta's first black mayor.[17] Another member, Dr. T. H. Brewer from Columbus, Georgia, had "promoted the suit that broke the back of the Georgia 'White Primary.'"[18]

At the national convention, Tuttle fired the opening salvo. Even though the Foster delegation included black members, Tuttle echoed Ben Davis's charge and called the Foster group "lily white republicans." "Since 1920," he wrote in a prepared brief, "there has been an element in the Republican Party in Georgia which has sought to bring about . . . the elimination of all Negroes in participation in party affairs, including the right to vote."[19] He charged the Foster faction with having a secret alliance with the Democratic governor of Georgia, Eugene Talmadge, an alliance directed at preserving the county unit system method of electing public officers, which gave vastly disproportionate power to the rural areas of the state. Tuttle made a strong case for the legitimacy of his delegation. Anticipating a challenge, Tuttle and Harry Sommers had researched the national party rules and regulations and made sure that they complied with them. They had called county meetings, then district meetings, and then a state convention. At every stage they diligently posted notices in the county courthouse of every one of Georgia's 159 counties. Tuttle and Sommers knew that a separate group of Georgia Republicans had ignored their notices and simply called a state convention, where they elected the Taft delegation headed by Roy Foster. Foster had a simple claim to legitimacy. Twice, in 1944 and now in 1948, he had been certified by the Georgia secretary of state as the legally elected Georgia Republican chairman.

Roy Foster and Harry Sommers clashed very publicly. Foster angrily charged that Sommers had sent orchids to the female members of the national committee in an attempt to win them over; the Sommers camp responded that he only sent four, and those to ladies already on his side. Sommers, in his closing remarks before the national committee, disparaged the Foster group's description of one of its delegates, Tobie Grant of Scottdale, as one of the "highest and most influential Negroes in Georgia." Sommers called Grant a "colored fortune-teller" and added, "You can't get people to rally around a standard like that."[20] The formal proceedings were more dignified but no less heated. On Thursday, June 17, Tuttle and John Wesley Dobbs argued the Williams delegation's case before the Republican National Committee.[21] The next day the committee voted 48–44 in their favor. Roscoe Pickett immediately announced that the Foster delegation would appeal to the credentials committee.[22] For the appeal, the pro-Taft Foster committee retained Senator George Wharton Pepper of Pennsylvania. A highly regarded lawyer, Senator Pepper was a formidable opponent. Tuttle, however, responded to Pepper's argument with a simple point: Pepper was an excellent lawyer, but he had the facts wrong. The record bore Tuttle out, and his delegation was seated. The fight, which had nominally been about proper procedure in selecting the delegates, had been punctuated by charges that it had really been about which candidate rival delegations supported and about race. It was about both. It was also about the future of the Georgia Republican Party, which was now far brighter than it had ever been.

The burgeoning Republican Party in Georgia included men like Killian Townsend. Townsend, an attorney who owned an air-conditioning company, had moved to Atlanta after World War II from Nassau County on Long Island, a national center of Republicanism. When he arrived in Georgia, he quickly realized there was no real Republican Party. Most white Republicans seemed to be "post office Republicans," nominal Republicans hanging on in hope of obtaining a patronage job should a Republican be in office. Prominent leaders of the black community were Republicans, but they had no power. In 1947 Townsend met Tuttle at a Lawyers' Club meeting and realized with relief that he had found the real Republican Party in Georgia.[23] Four people, according to Townsend, led the Georgia Republicans: Tuttle and his close friends Harry Sommers, a Chrysler dealer and the president of the Chamber of Commerce ("everyone knew Harry"), and Bob Snodgrass and his wife, owners of a finance company. They gave the effort stature, and they gave it funding. In 1948, with the money they raised and contributed, they rented a storefront on Peachtree Street in the heart of Atlanta and hired a public relations expert. They even prevailed upon Mayor Hartsfield, a dyed-in-the-wool Democrat, to let them hang a Dewey-Warren banner across Peachtree Street.

On election night in 1948, an excited crowd gathered at the headquarters. It was a well-integrated group, a rarity in Georgia at the time. Although you could not prove it by the press, and many white citizens were unaware of it, Atlanta had a sizeable population of well-educated black people. They were almost all Republicans, and many of them were there that night. The Georgia Republicans were ebullient when they arrived and depressed when they finally departed. Dewey had been defeated; Harry Truman would take the oath of office again. Truman's election struck a blow. Nonetheless, by the end of the 1940s, the Republican Party in Georgia was more credible than it had ever been. As the Draft Ike movement grew, the Georgia Republican Party grew along with it. After the credentials battles in 1944 and 1948, the two branches of the party claimed unity, claims that proved to be shallow at best.

CHAPTER TEN

The 1952 Republican National Convention

In the fall of 1951, the big question was whether Dwight D. Eisenhower would accept a Republican nomination. The general remained above the fray. If he ran, he would be challenging Robert Taft, who had lost the nomination to Dewey in 1948. Dewey had suffered a surprising, devastating loss to Harry Truman. Now, four years later, Taft's position was strong. The son of a president and himself a senator, Taft had positioned himself to take the nomination. No party regular was a serious threat to "Mr. Republican." Earl Warren was a candidate, but Warren understood he had little chance unless Eisenhower ran and split the delegates. Harold Stassen had thrown his hat in for the second of nine attempts, but no one expected him to prevail. Dwight Eisenhower represented a very real threat to Taft's ambitions, but Dwight Eisenhower would not commit.

As the 1952 convention approached, of the three white men who were the architects of the effort to build a meaningful Republican Party in Georgia, only Harry Sommers was for Taft. Elbert Tuttle, for his part, pinned his hopes on an Eisenhower candidacy, despite reservations. Eisenhower, he felt, had far too little civic experience. After graduating from West Point, Eisenhower had spent his entire career, except for a short stint as the president of Columbia University, in the army. But it appeared that if Eisenhower didn't win the nomination, Taft would. Recalling a "very strong speech" Taft had made in the Senate in 1940 opposing an extension of the draft, Tuttle thought that Taft, a committed isolationist, presented a real threat. "To my way of thinking," Tuttle explained, "this showed an utter lack by Senator Taft of the realities that the world faced and particularly the United States faced."[1] He would take his chances with the general—that is, if he could. As long as Eisenhower had not entered

86

the race and Taft remained the overwhelmingly likely nominee, Tuttle remained silent.

Eisenhower supporters had little reason for optimism, especially after it was reported that Hugh Scott, the Republican senator from Pennsylvania, had not been able to talk Ike into running. Eisenhower himself remained remote. Then, in October, Killian Townsend got a call from Tuttle. Tuttle explained that he had received a call from "the Rockefeller people." They wanted Eisenhower supporters to form a citizens' committee for Eisenhower; their goal was to establish one in every state. Townsend rounded up fifteen Republican friends, not including Tuttle, who as the Fulton County Republican chair remained officially neutral. Then Townsend took his list to George Goodwin, political reporter for the *Atlanta Journal* and a Pulitzer Prize winner. Goodwin perused the list of Georgia Citizens for Eisenhower for President and told Townsend he wasn't going to give the group any coverage: "No one on here means anything," he explained. Except for James Dorsey, son of former governor Hugh Dorsey, no one had a high public profile. When Townsend pushed for a story, Goodwin's response was direct: "Well, you know who's really for Eisenhower—Mr. Woodruff and Bobby Jones. Get them and you've got a story."[2]

Mr. Woodruff was Robert Woodruff, president of the Coca-Cola Company and a national figure. Bobby Jones, an Atlanta attorney, was better known as the best amateur golfer of his day. Jones had retired from tournament play in 1930 after becoming the only player to win what was then golf's grand slam: the British Amateur, the British Open, the U.S. Amateur, and the U.S. Open. Townsend did not know either of them personally, but he shared space with an attorney who knew Woodruff well enough to have his private number. His colleague agreed to get Woodruff on the phone. Woodruff had a reputation for being extremely difficult to work for; to Townsend he was simply rude. Woodruff made it clear that he did not appreciate being called by a stranger. "No," he told Townsend, "don't use my name." Townsend was demoralized. After that tongue-lashing, it was hard to pick up the phone and make another call, but he did. Bobby Jones could not have been more gracious. He listened to Townsend's explanation for the call and then made a simple request. "Can you give me twenty-four hours?" he asked.

Townsend was beside himself with excitement. He knew that Bobby

Jones was close to Eisenhower. Jones had designed the course at Augusta National Golf Club, where the Masters Tournament is played; his cottage there was one of Eisenhower's favorite retreats. Jones's request for time meant that he was going to check with Eisenhower. If he came back with a yes, it would mean that Eisenhower would run. Two days later, Bobby Jones called Townsend back. "Mr. Townsend," he said, "what do I need to do?" On October 30, 1951, the *Atlanta Journal* carried the story on the front page in the right-hand column. The headline read: "Group for Ike Gets Charter Here: Bobby Jones among 15 Launching State Move to Draft General." Although a number of prominent black men and women, including John Wesley Dobbs, W. J. "Bill" Shaw, and L. B. Toomer, had been the mainstays of the Republican Party in Georgia and were still active in its ranks, none were included in the group of fifteen.

Two months later, on January 7, 1952, Eisenhower finally announced that he would accept the nomination of the Republican Party. Once Eisenhower declared his candidacy, Tuttle announced his support. On January 11, 1952, the *Atlanta Journal* reported that "three top members of the state Republican organization came out firmly for General Eisenhower."[3] They were the chairman of the state party, W. R. Tucker; the national committeewoman, Mrs. Robert Snodgrass; and Elbert Tuttle. A month later, on February 16, state chairman Tucker called for mass meetings to choose delegates in each of Georgia's 159 counties, to be followed by district conventions on April 26 and a state convention on May 31. The laborious work of posting notices and holding meetings all across Georgia, the largest state east of the Mississippi, began. When the state convention ended, it had selected a delegation. Several prominent black Republicans, including John Calhoun, John Wesley Dobbs, L. B. Toomer, and Bill Shaw, were members.[4] Of the seventeen members of the delegation, thirteen were for Eisenhower. Tuttle was among the thirteen; Harry Sommers was still a Taft man.

The rival group, headed by Roy Foster, also put a delegation together. Once again they ignored the protocols established by the national party. They held a meeting, a single meeting, took a vote, and elected a seventeen-member delegation. All seventeen members of the Foster delegation were for Taft. In 1944 and 1948 Foster's strongest claim to legitimacy had been that Georgia's secretary of state had certified his delegation as the official Georgia Republican delegation. By 1952 a new secretary of state, Ben Fortson, had been elected; Fortson indicated that, if asked, he would certify the Tucker group. Foster bypassed Fortson; instead, shortly before the convention, he filed suit in Spalding Superior Court and obtained an order designating his delegation as the legal representative of the Republican Party in Georgia. The *Washington Post* reported: "With 159 counties in Georgia, it is not much of a trick to find a Democratic judge willing to encourage a Republican split."[5]

Planning for the convention, the Eisenhower people saw the importance of the southern delegations. In June General Eisenhower, then president of Columbia University, invited Tuttle to bring his delegation to New York. Eleven Georgians, including two black delegates, accepted the invitation.[6] At the Eisenhowers' Morningside Heights home, Sara sat next to Ike, and they carried on an animated conversation. Across the room, Elbert couldn't hear what they were talking about. When he rejoined Sara, "What were you and the general talking about for so long?" were the first words out of his mouth. "Our grandchildren," she answered with a smile. It became one of Sara Tuttle's favorite stories, matched by one from the 1960s when, as chief judge of the Fifth Circuit, presiding over the federal courts of the Deep South, Elbert Tuttle became a lightning rod. "You had better keep your opinions to yourself," he suggested. "People could say I've prejudged the issue, because when they hear you they could assume you think what I think." "Not if they know me, they won't," she answered.

One week before the 1952 Republican Convention opened Taft led Eisenhower by a slim margin, but he did not have enough votes to win on the first ballot. Taft was counting on capturing most of the delegates from several southern states where rival delegations fought for recognition, including Georgia, Louisiana, and Texas.[7] A preconvention gentlemen's agreement that the preconvention hearings as well as the convention itself would be televised had been made with the nascent television industry. At the time of the 1948 Republican convention, there had been less than 400,000 television sets in America; suddenly, there were 19 million.

At the eleventh hour, the Taft forces realized that they did not want the public to see the credentials battles. On July 1, when the matter came for a vote, the Taft forces opposed television and radio coverage of the preconvention hearings and prevailed by a margin of 60–40. Winning the battle, they lost the war. Every television and radio station in the country was aligned in favor of access, and the country's newspapers supported them. The Taft move, which smacked of an antidemocratic power play, received enormous publicity.[8] All of it was bad. The debate on media coverage took up so much of the credentials committee's time that the committee was able to hear and resolve only one contest. The Florida delegation, headed by the national committeeman for Florida and solidly for Taft, was seated. The hearing on the Georgia delegation was rescheduled for 10:00 the next morning.

Although the Georgia hearing was not broadcast, it was well reported. Before the convention had opened, the national press had recognized that the nomination might well turn on the delegate contests in the southern states. On June 22 the *New York Times* carried a story by Arthur Krock subtitled "Southern Bloc Could Be Sufficient to Swing Nomination." When Krock got down to details, the first three delegations he mentioned were those from Texas, Georgia, and Louisiana.[9] Arguing the case for the Tucker delegation, Tuttle dismissed the lawsuit Foster had filed in a superior court in Georgia as "conniving." He radiated confidence, in part because he knew that his delegation alone had complied with party rules and regulations. Also, his delegation included Harry Sommers, the national committeeman for Georgia. The Taft forces would stop at little, but they would stop at discrediting Sommers, an avowed Taft supporter.

Because Tuttle understood the importance of Sommers's role to his delegation, he reacted immediately when Monte Appel, a Washington attorney arguing for the Foster delegation, remarked that the Foster delegation would, if seated, reelect Harry Sommers as national committeeman. "In other words," as *Time* reported, "if Sommers would scratch the back of the Foster delegation by repudiating his official delegation, Foster & Co. would scratch his back by appointing him for another term." Tuttle was on his feet instantly. He asked Sommers, his closest friend, the man he had worked with so long and so hard to build the Republican Party in Georgia, to either repudiate this offer of a deal or admit the truth of it. Sommers's empty reply was devastating. "In view of all the controversy," he said, "I will not make any comment."[10]

With Sommers's demurral, it was suddenly clear that he would not defend the legitimacy of the delegation. An audible gasp ran through the committee room. At that stage, before the national committee of which he was the Georgia member, Sommers's betrayal was determinative. The national committee voted 62–39 to seat the Foster delegation; Taft supporters dominated it, and they voted for the delegation that supported their candidate. The Foster group was now recognized as the official delegation from Georgia. Adding insult to injury, the Foster group now claimed hotel rooms occupied by Tuttle and his people. Reservations had been made by the party, and just as official badges to enter the floor were at stake, so were accommodations. Chicago hotels were packed, so the Tuttles and the Townsends ended up sharing the only room they could find.[11]

Tuttle appreciated full well that far more than a hotel room was at stake. Furious, he labeled Sommers's act "the most amazing double cross I've ever experienced."[12] Sommers had long been on record as supporting the Tucker delegation. His change of position was stunning but not inexplicable. Ford and General Motors were firmly behind Eisenhower. Chrysler Corporation was for Taft. Sommers had a Chrysler dealership; in fact, he had the oldest continuously operating Chrysler dealership in the South. Some observers felt that Chrysler had simply put the squeeze on Sommers.[13] Sommers had poured a great deal of energy into civic activities, and the one closest to his heart was the Republican Party.[14] To betray his colleagues must have been unthinkable, until it became a reality.

Tuttle announced immediately that he would appeal the decision of the national committee to the credentials committee. The Taft forces had taken a beating over the decision to bar television and radio from preconvention hearings. Now they relented and agreed to televised hearings. When the credentials committee opened hearings on the second day of the convention, they did so in full view of the nation. The Georgia contest was the first significant matter taken up.[15] Arguing for the Tucker delegation, Tuttle pointed out that it had been recognized by the Republican National Convention in both 1944 and 1948. Moreover, he produced a 1948 letter from Roy Foster, leader of the rival delegation, recognizing the Tucker group as the official party in Georgia and purporting to unite with it. Tuttle also produced a letter from Harry Sommers, written in his capacity as national committeeman, that recognized the Tucker group as the legitimate Republican Party in Georgia.

Of the twenty minutes allotted to the delegation to make its case, Tuttle gave five to John Wesley Dobbs. Dobbs delivered an impassioned address, according to Atlanta's black newspaper, the *Atlanta Daily World*.[16] The national press, which covered the Georgia contest intensively, did not report the fact that John Wesley Dobbs appeared for his delegation. Only the *Atlanta Journal* mentioned him, calling him G. W. Dobbs.[17] To the national white press, including the *New York Times*, the *Washington Post*, and the *Chicago Daily Sun-Times*, John Wesley Dobbs was an invisible man. Elbert Tuttle spent a lifetime correcting the record. He never repeated the oft-told tale of the 1952 Chicago convention without stressing the fact that at the critical moment, the argument before the credentials committee, he had shared the microphone with John Wesley Dobbs.

Roscoe Pickett and Monte Appel argued for the Foster group. They contended that the Tucker faction had never been properly organized and relied heavily on the ruling by Judge Byars. The entire hearing was fractious, so much so that Pickett was ruled out of order three times by the committee chair, Ross Rizley, even though Rizley, like Pickett, was a Taft supporter.[18] Despite the strength of Tuttle's case, to no one's surprise, votes on the credentials committee broke down on candidate lines. The committee voted 30–21 in favor of the Foster delegation. Once again, Tuttle and Tucker announced immediately that they would appeal. The matter would be decided on the floor of the convention. For only the second time in its one-hundred-year history, the Republican National Convention would include a floor fight over delegates.[19]

The credentials committee had more work to do before it adjourned. Next on the agenda came the Louisiana delegation. John Minor Wisdom, leader of the Eisenhower delegation, produced a prodigious array of charts and witnesses and made a powerful argument. Charging that John Jackson, leader of the Taft delegation, had rigged the process, Wisdom called the state credentials proceedings worse than a kangaroo court. "A decent, respectable kangaroo wouldn't be caught dead in such meetings," Wisdom declaimed.[20] When he concluded the presentation of his challenge at 3:45 a.m., the exhausted committee went into recess without voting. Wisdom and his group crowed with delight; they had lost their national audience in the early hours of the morning if not before; now they would regain it the next day. In the morning, mindful of the audience and aware of the strength and persuasiveness of Wisdom's presentation, the credentials committee voted unanimously to seat the Eisenhower delegation from Louisiana. The die was cast. That evening the credentials committee's recommendations went to the full convention. As Tuttle and the rest of the Tucker delegation waited outside the hall, Ross Rizley moved adoption of the committee's decision to seat the Taft delegation from Georgia headed by Roy Foster.

Donald Eastvold, a lanky young state senator from Washington, jumped to his feet and objected. A political unknown when he arrived at the convention, Eastvold bore "a resemblance to Jimmy Stewart," and he had made a good impression with an earlier argument in committee.[21] With one eye on the television cameras, Republican strategists decided to use Eastvold in the floor fight. In an impassioned argument, Eastvold attacked the concept that a Georgia judge could decide the legitimacy of a Republican delegation and bind the convention, and he reminded the delegates that they were their "own Supreme Court" on party matters. The ruling of a single trial court judge in Georgia, he argued, was immaterial. He moved the Tucker-led Eisenhower delegation be seated.

Aligned against Eastvold, Senator Everett Dirksen of Illinois argued that the delegates as a whole did not know enough about the Georgia situation to pass on it, so they should affirm the committee. This argument had a signal weakness: the credentials committee proceedings had been televised; not only the delegates but millions of citizens knew the facts underlying the controversy over the Georgia delegation. Aware of this, Dirksen did not tarry on this argument; he launched into a diversionary attack on Dewey, who had wrested the nomination from Taft and then lost to Truman in 1948. Pointing dramatically at Dewey, Dirksen said, "When my friend Tom Dewey was a candidate, I tried to be one of his best campaigners. We followed you before and you took us down the road to defeat. And don't do this to us again."[22] Dirksen's attack on Dewey generated a "loud, ugly boo" from the Taft supporters. As it trailed off, the roll call began. Tension mounted in the great hall as each of four large, pivotal states— California, Michigan, Minnesota, and Pennsylvania—cast a substantial majority of their votes for the Eastvold motion. When the roll call ended, the Georgia delegation that had been so carefully constructed by Elbert Tuttle had prevailed by a vote of 607–531.

Harry Sommers was seated on the stage, one of a group of twenty or so prominent Republicans. When the vote was announced, as Tuttle and the Tucker delegation rushed into the hall triumphantly, Harry Sommers quietly left the stage. The next day, the delegation's first order of business was to replace Sommers as national committeeman with W. R. Tucker. When Harry Sommers walked off the stage, he disappeared. No one saw him, according to Townsend, for at least a month. When Sommers finally resurfaced in Atlanta, he contacted Townsend; in addition to their work with the Republican Party, they shared a commitment to the Atlanta Humane Society, of which they had both been director. Townsend became a go-between for Tuttle and Sommers, and Elbert Tuttle never spoke to Harry Sommers again.

Tuttle had gained a new friend, John Minor Wisdom, a native southerner who, like Tuttle, believed a viable two-party system was critical to the political, economic, and social health of the region. While still a law student at Tulane, in New Orleans, Wisdom had registered as a Republican, in part as a protest against the dictatorial reign of Governor Huey Long. Then he took a bolder step: Huey Long, by then in the Senate, handpicked his successor as governor and advertised a wager: he would put $50,000 up at 2–1 odds against anyone who did not believe his man would win the Democratic primary without a runoff. John Minor Wisdom stepped up and put $15 down against Long. Furious at Wisdom's temerity, Long told the publisher of the *New Orleans States-Item* to run a story that would humiliate Wisdom. The next day, a banner headline read: "Lone GOP Takes $15 of $50,000 Wager." Wisdom rather enjoyed the publicity; Long, unsatisfied, tried to get Wisdom's brother fired.[23] Wisdom's determination to form a viable Republican Party was reinforced.

Henry Cabot Lodge, one of Eisenhower's chief strategists, realized early on that the southern states would be critical in a struggle between Eisenhower and Taft. Lodge had watched Elbert Tuttle manage, and win, the credentials fight for his delegation in 1948. When John Minor Wisdom sought help building an Eisenhower delegation in Louisiana, Lodge offered succinct advice: talk to Elbert Tuttle.[24] On a Saturday morning early in 1951, Wisdom had called Tuttle and introduced himself. Tuttle took the overnight train to New Orleans. Elbert Tuttle and John Minor Wisdom spent that Sunday afternoon in the garden behind Wisdom's elegant Garden District home. As Tuttle and Wisdom talked, the enormity of the task became more and more apparent. "I don't think even [Herbert] Brownell understood the actual mechanics of it," Wisdom recalled; getting up a qualified delegation was "very very hard work."[25] That first night in New Orleans, after the two men mapped out their strategy, Tuttle stayed overnight with the Wisdoms. By the end of the visit, he "had simply fallen in love with the Wisdoms."

Elbert Tuttle and John Minor Wisdom had much in common. Both were seasoned trial attorneys who loved the practice of law; both abhorred the control of the white Democratic Party over their states; and both were long and happily married to women whose intelligence and will matched their own. On the surface, however, they could hardly have been more different. Reserved and formal in manner, Tuttle was a lifelong teetotaler; high spirited and convivial, Wisdom enjoyed imbibing. Friends, law partners, and men who served under Tuttle in World War II often described him as straitlaced, a term never applied to Wisdom. Where Tuttle was succinct in expression of every kind, Wisdom was verbose. They were both, however, men of great ability, and they had shared values and a shared commitment to bringing the South into the mainstream of American political life. They both understood that racial segregation stood in the way.

Like Tuttle, Wisdom was as much against Taft as he was for Eisenhower. He blamed Taft for the lack of a viable Republican Party in the South, and therefore the lack of a vigorous two-party system and any semblance of democracy. The Taft people, Wisdom thought, had deliberately kept the ranks of Republicans in key southern states small to give themselves control over the delegations and power at the national conventions. The internal politics of the southern states, so critical to Tuttle and Wisdom, did not concern them. Tuttle's strategy in Georgia would be essentially the one Wisdom would adopt in Louisiana. The basic plan was simple: find out what the rules are and then comply with them. The devil was in the details. In Georgia, Tuttle had to worry about 159 counties. Wisdom was dealing with all the parishes in Louisiana. He took no chances; every document was notarized, every meeting was attended by a policeman.

Wisdom focused his efforts on both recruiting voters to the Republican Party and getting registered Republicans who were for Eisenhower to the critical meetings. Bonnie Wisdom threw herself into the work. In New Orleans, where they had long lived, Bonnie Wisdom moved easily in the upper echelons of society. Now she learned her way around the black neighborhoods that dotted New Orleans. One of Bonnie Wisdom's great successes occurred in the Fifth Ward, a New Orleans district that included part of the French Quarter and part of a poor black neighborhood. Bonnie learned that the Taft Republicans expected only eight Republicans, who were evenly split between Eisenhower and Taft, to come to the mass meeting. Under party rules, a split vote would allow the chair, a Taft man, to vote again to break the tie. Perusing the list of registered Republicans, she came upon the name of the aunt of a friend, Mrs. Schwartz, a grande dame of New Orleans society who lived in her family home on Esplanade Avenue. Esplanade lies on the other side of the French Quarter from the Garden District, putting it in the Fifth Ward. Bonnie Wisdom called Mrs. Schwartz with a question. "I said, 'Mrs. Schwartz, how would you like to be the most important person in the world for a night?'" All she had to do, Bonnie suggested, was come to the ward meeting and vote for Eisenhower; her vote would carry the ward. The meeting was to be held on Good Friday at the home of a black midwife in one of the poorest areas of the city. When Mrs. Schwartz arrived, the Taft Republicans were nonplussed. They pulled in two passersby off the street—two bums, as Bonnie Wisdom recalled. Adding a manic note, on the first ballot the stooges got confused and voted for Eisenhower. Taftites tore those ballots up and started over. On the second vote, the stooges got their orders right and voted for Taft. Neither was on the list of registered Republicans, but according to the tally turned in by the Taft man who reported for the ward, Taft had carried it.[26]

That summer, at the convention, Wisdom would document incident after incident to illustrate his central contention: the Taft people were trying to steal the nomination. Armed with witnesses and exhibits, he made a compelling presentation, and he made it not just before the Taft-controlled credentials committee but before television cameras as well.[27] "They were stealing them blind. I just couldn't vote for the Taft crowd when my neighbors back home saw it all on television," Bonnie Wisdom overheard one committee member bemoan.[28] In committee meetings, the representative for Rhode Island, a young attorney named Bayard Ewing, made the same point: "The Louisiana Taft delegation is a stolen delegation. We know it is. Is the Republican Party going to swallow it?"[29] John Minor Wisdom's characterization of the Taft people as "stealing" the Louisiana delegation was considerably advanced by the press reaction to the contest over the Texas delegation. In Texas, as in Louisiana, the old guard Taft supporters had always been able to control things, and they came to Chicago expecting to win the credentials battles simply because they had the votes in the credentials committee. They were confounded by two developments: televised proceedings and the Fair Play Amendment. The televised proceedings exposed the chicanery. The Fair Play Amendment, a brainstorm attributed to Herbert Brownell, provided that no disputed delegate could vote unless the delegate's credentials had been approved by two-thirds of the national committee and were disputed only because they were being appealed. This had the practical effect of not allowing the Taft delegations from Texas, Louisiana, and Georgia to vote on the credentials of the mostly Eisenhower delegates who challenged them. In combination with the ability of the Eisenhower forces to claim the high moral ground before the first national audience for a political convention, it gave Eisenhower the advantage and, in the end, the nomination.

Before Wisdom's compelling presentation, the credentials committee was split 29–23 in favor of the Taft delegation. When four members indicated they would switch, the Taft men decided to make it a unanimous vote in favor of Wisdom's delegation. They hoped that by sacrificing the thirteen votes represented by members of the Wisdom delegation who were committed to Ike, they would regain the moral high ground and be able to win the Georgia and Texas floor votes. The strategy did not work. The next day, Tuttle's delegation was seated on a floor vote of the convention. "'Imagine,' said a disgusted Ohio delegate, 'the cotton state of Georgia deciding a Republican convention—especially on a moral issue.'"[30] After the dramatic roll call vote on the Georgia delegation, the Taft forces agreed to seat a Texas delegation that was 33–5 for Eisenhower. For the first time, Eisenhower was ahead of Taft in the delegate count. It was not enough to be ahead; Eisenhower needed 604 votes to win the nomination, and he needed to win on the critical first ballot. The first roll call of the states on the nomination itself ended with 595 votes for Eisenhower, 500 for Taft. "Favorite son" votes held the balance of power. Governor Earl Warren of California held eighty votes; former governor Harold Stassen of Minnesota held twenty; General MacArthur had ten.

Under convention rules, if a candidate did not receive 10 percent of the votes cast on the first ballot, his delegates could be released from their pledge to give him their first-round vote and could recast their ballots. A tearful Stassen released his loyalists, and Senator Thye of Minnesota raised the state's standard, requesting recognition. The chairman of the convention called on Warren E. Burger, an attorney from Saint Paul who led the delegation. Both Tuttle and Wisdom knew Burger from the 1948 convention. Accounts differ on who actually announced the changed votes; some say Thye grabbed the microphone at the critical moment. Whoever uttered the words, they caused pandemonium to break out: Gen. Dwight David Eisenhower had captured the nomination of the Republican Party for president of the United States from "Mr. Republican," Senator Robert Taft. When Eisenhower won the nomination, two of his allies effectively won appointments to the United States Supreme Court. Earl Warren's California delegation, by casting all seventy of its votes for the Fair Play Amendment, had made Eisenhower's victory possible. When Chief Justice Fred Vinson died suddenly of a heart attack in September 1953, Eisenhower nominated Earl Warren to fill his seat.[31] Warren Burger's pivotal role propelled him into a series of federal positions that culminated in 1974 with his appointment as chief justice of the United States. He succeeded Earl Warren.

The evening that Eisenhower's nomination became official, Eisenhower and Brownell dined alone. Brownell asked Eisenhower for a short list of men he found acceptable as a vice president. Eisenhower responded with five names; Richard Nixon topped the list. Nixon met all of Eisenhower's criteria: he was young, offsetting Eisenhower's age; he was a veteran of World War II; he was from California, bringing the ticket needed strength in the West; he had a solid record in Congress; and he was already known as strongly anti-Communist. The next morning, Brownell called a meeting of some twenty key campaign leaders, including Elbert Tuttle and John Wisdom. Eisenhower wanted their recommendation for vice president. Gen. Lucius Clay, who had been Eisenhower's chief of staff and who remained one of his closest advisors, was among the select group invited to the meeting. Clay was a Georgian, and Sutherland & Tuttle had represented his brother in legal matters. When Tuttle arrived, Clay intercepted him with a request: would he present Nixon's name if no one else did? Tuttle agreed, but he was uncomfortable. Having watched Richard Nixon win his Senate seat in 1950 by viciously attacking Helen Gahagan Douglas as soft on Communism (he had attached the label "the Pink Lady" to her), Tuttle was wary of Nixon. Still, he had agreed, and he would have put Nixon's name on the table, had Governor Dewey not spoken first. Once Governor Dewey of New York proposed Nixon, the group unanimously endorsed him.

Tuttle and Wisdom were now part of the inner circle of the Eisenhower campaign. Later in the summer, they were invited to the Brown Palace, the Denver hotel that served as Eisenhower's western headquarters, for a strategy meeting. Tuttle took the opportunity to ask Eisenhower to open his southern campaign in Atlanta. The day after Labor Day, Eisenhower flew into Atlanta on a chartered plane and was met at the airport by his good friend, golf champion Bobby Jones. Elbert Tuttle sat behind Ike on the speaker's platform; Mayor William B. Hartsfield, a friend of Tuttle's, sat beside him. On the other side of Hartsfield sat the governor, Eugene Talmadge, "one of the worst of the South's old line racist, pseudo-Populist demagogues."[32]

CHAPTER ELEVEN

The Washington Years

Tuttle campaigned vigorously for Eisenhower in Georgia, but, to no one's surprise, Adlai Stevenson carried the state. Ike carried the country, however, and he knew he owed his victory in no small part to the southern Republican strategists who had helped him win the nomination. Once elected, Eisenhower delegated the selection of most of his cabinet to his two most trusted advisors: Herbert Brownell and Lucius Clay. He claimed but one firm rule: no one who sought a position would be selected for it. Not a professional politician himself, Ike preferred men from outside government.[1]

For secretary of the treasury, Brownell and Clay recommended George M. Humphrey, president of the Mark M. Hanna Company of Cleveland. The Hanna Company had become, in Humphrey's hands, one of the country's biggest industrial holding companies, with large interests in iron ore, steel, coal, fiber, plastics, copper, petroleum, shipping, and banks. Humphrey had attracted national attention in 1947 when he stunned most observers by negotiating a national miners' wage contract, providing for a fifteen-cent-an-hour raise and an eight-hour day, directly with John L. Lewis. When a congressional committee demanded an explanation, he gave two reasons: "(1) he had observed, he said, that once Government intervened in labor disputes, the unions generally got their demands anyway; and (2) the miners deserved an eight hour day and would probably be more productive for it."[2]

After the war, Humphrey had chaired a committee responsible for the revision of reparations and the dismantling and reorganization of German plants to remove their war-making potential while providing ongoing industrial functions. In this capacity, he had come to know Gen. Lucius Clay, and through Clay he came to Eisenhower's attention.[3] Humphrey had not taken a leadership role in Eisenhower's campaign; before the election, the two men had never met. When they did meet, they formed an instant bond. George Humphrey turned out to be the only member of the cabinet besides John Foster Dulles, the secretary of state, with whom Eisenhower developed a close personal relationship.

Just as Eisenhower had not met George Humphrey before he decided to offer him a position in his cabinet, so had George Humphrey never met Elbert Tuttle. Shortly after January 1, before the inauguration, Tuttle answered the phone to find his friend Bobby Jones on the line. Jones explained that he was calling to introduce Bob Woodruff, and Jones put Robert Woodruff, the CEO of the Coca-Cola Company, on the phone. Woodruff took the phone and said, "I want to introduce you to George M. Humphrey." Tuttle asked, "You mean George M. Humphrey, the designated secretary of the treasury?" Woodruff said yes, that was who he meant, and passed the phone to Humphrey. Humphrey explained that he was calling because he would be coming through Atlanta over the next weekend, and he wondered if Tuttle would meet him at the airport. George Humphrey and Robert Woodruff were neighbors of a sort; both had plantations in southern Georgia. After he was elected, Ike would visit Humphrey when he could. Whenever the three men—Eisenhower, Humphrey, and Woodruff— were together, and when they could get a fourth, often General Clay, they played bridge. Elbert Tuttle, who played bridge only to accommodate his wife, was bemused by the idea of these four powerful men making up a foursome at bridge.

The weekend after Humphrey's call, Tuttle, accompanied by his wife, Sara, drove out to the Atlanta airport. After they exchanged pleasantries, Sara sat to the side, giving the men some privacy. She had already agreed to go to Washington should Elbert be offered a spot he wanted, even though it meant leaving her new home empty. Early in 1949, Sara and Elbert had moved into the home they built in Ansley Park, near downtown Atlanta—an unpretentious two-story frame home painted Colonial yellow. A newspaper article called it a "dream home," but one irate letter writer complained that it did not meet the standards of the neighborhood, where most homes were more palatial. Elbert and Sara were perfectly happy with it. She had been the most involved with planning and building; after all, she pointed out, Elbert had his hands full with "other things." But he was equally pleased, because, as she explained, "If it suits me, it suits him, too."[4]

Humphrey asked Tuttle to serve as general counsel to the Department of the Treasury. Tuttle had become accustomed to being perceived as a tax attorney because he was a founding partner of one of the country's pre-eminent tax firms. He felt obliged to explain to Humphrey that he did not, in fact, have a tax practice. Humphrey fielded that easily. "That's alright," he said, "the IRS handles that." Tuttle accepted, but he told Humphrey he would only commit to staying two years. Eisenhower appointed Tuttle on January 14, six days before his own inauguration, and Tuttle was sworn in on January 30. He and Sara took a furnished apartment at the Wardman Park Hotel. At his confirmation hearing before the Senate Finance Committee, Tuttle explained that he had "divested himself of all stock holdings which might conflict with his duties as head of the Treasury Department's legal department." He had retained about ten thousand dollars' worth of stock in Southern Mills, a Georgia company.[5] Selling the stock was easy for Tuttle; severing his ties with the law firm he had founded was not.

Tuttle did not pretend to sever his personal ties with the law firm. He was a founding partner, and his brother-in-law, Bill Sutherland, was still running the firm. Moreover, his beloved nephew Mac Asbill Jr. was quickly becoming a principal player. When Tuttle left the firm, Mac was one of eight partners.[6] After the war, Mac had attended Harvard Law School, where he did very well, so well that he was offered a spot on the *Harvard Law Review*—which he turned down. Jim Wilson was the president of the *Law Review* that year. Although they both had Atlanta ties, they had first met in Pearl Harbor during the war. When Mac told Jim Wilson he "sure appreciated the honor," but he was going to turn it down, Wilson was as-tounded. "Good Lord," he said, "why are you going to turn it down?" Mac's reason was simple. He had gotten married during the war, just before he shipped out; now he had an infant son. "I just want to see something of my family," he explained.[7] Wilson, also a veteran, thought that was a good rea-son. He didn't try to argue him out of it. After graduating from Harvard, Mac had joined the law firm, bringing his father, Mac Asbill Sr., with him. In 1952, when Tuttle left the firm, Sutherland, Tuttle & Brennan was an eminent firm with national clients; it was also in important ways a fam-ily firm. Elbert Tuttle was happy about his new position, but it was a sad day when he watched his name removed from the firm name on the office doors. It helped that his name was replaced by that of his brother-in-law, Mac Asbill Sr. It also helped that he had every intention of returning to the firm after his stint with the government, and he could expect to be welcomed back with open arms.

When Tuttle went to Washington in January 1953, he did not resign his position as chairman of the Republican Party of Georgia. He felt obligated to continue the work of building the party that he had begun, and, as he pointed out, he was keeping his home in Georgia. From the beginning, he knew that his decision to maintain control would be controversial. John Sibley, chairman of the Trust Company of Georgia, wrote Tuttle a cautionary letter as soon as the appointment was announced.

> I am glad the Treasury will have you to look after its legal affairs. I know you will do an outstanding job.
>
> I hope, however, that you will not control patronage in Georgia but pass it on to some other high class Republican.
>
> If you do relieve yourself of that responsibility, I believe that you will find that you will keep your Government job away from politics and save yourself a lot of headaches.
>
> I have no personal interest in patronage but I have a lot of personal interest in your success.[8]

The next morning, Ralph McGill, legendary editor of the *Atlanta Constitution*, published a front-page editorial applauding Tuttle's appointment. Tuttle wrote to thank him and took the opportunity to preempt criticism.

> I value your good will so much that I want you to understand that the only reason I can't relinquish the chairmanship of the Party at the moment is that I can't imagine anything worse than the scramble that would result if we were to call a State Convention or a State Central Committee meeting to elect a successor on the eve of recommending so many people for jobs in Georgia.
>
> I simply want you to have this background and hope that nothing that develops in the future will cause you to feel that this decision has been a mistake.[9]

At the same time, Tuttle replied to Sibley's letter. He explained that he had asked Bob Snodgrass to stand in for him and handle all patronage matters.

"I am just not relinquishing the office of chairman because we would have a terrible cat and dog fight, with all of this patronage ahead, if we called a State Central Committee meeting to elect a successor," he explained. "I deeply value your judgment as well as your friendship," he went on. "If you feel that this is the wrong approach to it, I would consider it a favor for you to give me your views."[10] Sibley wrote back, signaling that this arrangement would suffice. "I know you have a tight situation here . . . and I am glad that Bob Snodgrass will actively take over your duties regarding patronage while you are in Washington."[11]

Just three weeks after Tuttle was sworn in as general counsel to the Treasury Department, rumors that he would be ousted as chair of the Georgia Republican Party erupted into headlines.[12] At a meeting of the Republican state central committee, called by Tuttle to set policies for the next four years, his control was challenged by a motion that the secretary be designated to act in Tuttle's stead whenever Tuttle was in Washington. The motion was seconded by John Wesley Dobbs, one of the most prominent black Republicans in Georgia. Dobbs and Tuttle had long been allies, but now Dobbs opposed Tuttle. As long as Tuttle retained the chairmanship, he had the last word on doling out many of the jobs with the federal government in Georgia. He was moving too slowly for some, and he was not treating party membership as conclusive in the matter of an applicant's qualifications. "Republicans should be given available jobs only if they are the men 'best qualified by ability and character to hold them,'" Tuttle maintained. Dobbs saw it differently. He spoke bluntly when he seconded the motion to usurp Tuttle's authority. "Maybe some of you aren't interested in patronage," Dobbs said, "but I am." The motion was defeated by a vote of 63–44. Tuttle tried to characterize it as a parliamentary matter, but the press saw it as a struggle for control of the party, and at least one highly placed Tuttle supporter called it "too close for comfort."

Tuttle held on to the state party chairmanship for another year. By then the newspaper was predicting that the upcoming meeting of the state central committee would be "explosive." As Tuttle arrived for it, he announced that he supported William A. "Gus" Bootle for a seat on the federal district court for the Middle District of Georgia.[13] Frank O. Evans of Milledgeville, general counsel to the state central committee and a favorite of many party regulars, also wanted the appointment. The meeting marked a final triumph for Tuttle. He was succeeded by his assistant, Atlanta businessman

W. B. Shartzer, whom he had endorsed, and, after Evans withdrew his name, Bootle got the nod for the nomination. One final gesture marked the day. Although Roy Foster and Harry Sommers had long been Republican loyalists, when they lost the roll call vote at the 1952 National Convention, they lost their positions in the state party as well. Now national committeeman Roscoe Tucker and state chairman Elbert Tuttle put party unity above all else. Tuttle stepped down from the chair to join Tucker in nominating the two men for at-large positions that had been created for them.[14] That gesture aside, Tuttle remained completely estranged from Harry Sommers. On that bittersweet note, Elbert Tuttle ended his work with the Georgia Republican Party. He had plenty to occupy his time in Washington.

As general counsel to the Treasury Department, Tuttle was the chief law officer of the department and the head of the Legal Division, which was composed of some 567 attorneys providing legal service to all offices and bureaus of the department.[15] Treasury included the Comptroller of the Currency; the Internal Revenue Service; the Bureau of Alcohol, Tobacco and Firearms; Customs; and the International Monetary Fund. Many bureaus had their own general counsels, each of whom was a deputy counsel to Tuttle. Tuttle was satisfied with the staff of his office; he could recall making only two changes, although, as he put it, "there'd been a Democratic administration for twenty years and people were mighty hungry." He replaced the chief counsel to the Internal Revenue Service, a presidential appointee who made policy decisions, and he replaced the head of the legislative advisory section of the Treasury Department.[16] He did not select a new man for the tax policy slot because the incumbent was competent and nonpartisan, and his memory bank on tax policy issues would have been hard to replace. Presidents and their appointees come and go, Tuttle realized, and civil service veterans stay on and do much of the essential work of government.

Tuttle was instrumental in the appointment of two Georgia Republicans. Louis B. "Bill" Toomer, the African American president of Carver State Bank in Savannah, was named register of the Department of the Treasury. Toomer had been with Tuttle at the 1944, 1948, and 1952 Republican conventions; he was first put forward for appointment as the head of Customs in Savannah. One of Georgia's Democratic senators, Walter F. George, voiced opposition to that and derailed it.[17] Instead, that post went to Mrs. Jessie Dixon Sayler, whose husband, Maj. Gen. Henry B. Sayler, had graduated from West Point with Eisenhower in 1916. Lifelong friends of the Eisenhowers, the Saylers had organized the Citizens for Eisenhower group in Savannah.[18]

In addition to the Toomer and Sayler appointments, Tuttle took one other immediate action. The press had more than once criticized the Truman administration for intervening in tax matters on behalf of political allies. A number of cases involving substantial disputes had been settled favorably to the taxpayer. On one of his first days in office, Tuttle offered Secretary Humphrey unsolicited advice. The secretary should institute a policy, Tuttle advised, that neither he nor Tuttle would talk with anyone about his personal tax matters; both of them would refer all such matters to the Internal Revenue Service. Humphrey agreed. Within a few days, Tuttle was visited by an attorney for Arthur Summerfield. Tuttle explained that he could not speak with the attorney about Summerfield's tax problems. The attorney demurred; Summerfield, he pointed out to Tuttle, had been a critical player in Eisenhower's campaign for the nomination and the presidency, and he was Eisenhower's newly appointed postmaster general. Tuttle was blunt: "Do you think the Secretary of the Treasury ought to make an exception for a political ally?" The attorney responded even more bluntly: "Of course I do." "Well," said Tuttle, "that's not our policy." Summerfield did not take being rebuffed well; apparently, he complained to the president. A week or so later, Tuttle recalled, Humphrey told him, "You got me in trouble with the chief." Eisenhower, he explained, was upset that Humphrey couldn't talk to Summerfield's attorney about Summerfield's tax case. "Well," Tuttle said, "I can't change my advice, but you don't have to follow it." "I'm going to follow it," Humphrey replied.[19] Later, when Summerfield's difficulties hit the press (he had paid a tax assessed, but under protest), both the president and the secretary were glad they had taken Tuttle's advice, even though in the end Summerfield's position was upheld by the Sixth Circuit.[20]

When Eisenhower took office, Senator Joe McCarthy held sway with his infamous witch hunt for Communists. To preempt McCarthy, Eisenhower promulgated an executive order addressing security requirements for government employees.[21] Section 2 of the order provided that "the head of each department and agency of the Government shall be responsible for establishing and maintaining within his department or agency an effective program to insure that the employment and retention in employment of any civilian officer or employee within the department or agency is clearly consistent with the interests of the national security." Already the general counsel to the Department of the Treasury, Tuttle was also named the chief security officer for the Treasury. In February 1954 he reported to Congress that the Treasury had identified and dismissed 131 employees based on a determination that they represented security risks. Employees could be considered security risks for a number of reasons that did not implicate their patriotism or loyalty. Alcoholism, homosexuality, having a relative behind the iron curtain—all were reasons an employee might be denominated a risk. When Tuttle appeared before Congress, he declined to state how many of the 131 dismissed employees had been deemed "disloyal" or "subversive types." Information would not be forthcoming, he testified, about the number of discharged employees whose removal was "effected for reasons classified as 'subversive,' if by this term is meant some identi-fication with Communist or Soviet causes or interests." Under consider-able pressure from the House Appropriations Committee, Tuttle held his ground. He was called back, however, by a subcommittee, and that time Congressman J. Vaughan Gary would not relent. Finally, Tuttle responded that of all those removed as security risks, in only four cases had a finding of disloyalty been made.[22]

Tuttle had no brief for McCarthy. Fortunately, he had a strong ally in the assistant secretary of the treasury, Chapman "Chappie" Rose. The two men fought off McCarthy when he "was demanding things from the Treasury Department." Once Tuttle had to fight off Richard Nixon as well. Nixon called a meeting of the security chiefs from the various departments, and Tuttle was there for the Treasury. "We each of us reported," Tuttle recalled. "Justice Department found none, State Department found three, Treasury Department—I said, well, we have one case under advisement. The rest of them, we've concluded, there's no real problem." After everyone had re-ported, it was clear that very few problematic employees had been identi-fied. Nixon was not happy. "God damn it, I want numbers! I want num-bers!" Tuttle recalled him saying.[23]

A good deal of Tuttle's work during his years with the Eisenhower administration was on national security issues. In March 1953 President Eisenhower created the Planning Board of the National Security Council. The National Security Council itself was chaired by the president and had five statutory members: the president, the vice president, the secretaries of state and defense, and the director of the Office of Defense Mobilization. The National Security Council Planning Board met Tuesday and Friday afternoons to review and refine recommendations from agencies, including the Department of Defense, before passing them on to the National Security Council. The board consisted of designees at the assistant secretary level from the agencies with permanent or standing representation on the council and advisors from the Joint Chiefs of Staff and the CIA. Secretary Humphrey originally named Chapman Rose as the Treasury designee to the Planning Board. When it became apparent that Rose could not carry out all his responsibilities as an assistant secretary and attend to the business of the Planning Board as well, Humphrey replaced him with Tuttle. He had come to know Tuttle quite well, in large part because they lunched together nearly every day in the private dining room at the Treasury Department. It was Humphrey's practice to have lunch with the deputy secretary, the three assistant secretaries, the general counsel, the commissioner of the Internal Revenue Service, and occasional others whom the secretary would invite.

In his years at Treasury, Tuttle developed a great respect for Secretary Humphrey and for a number of his colleagues, particularly Chappie Rose and Bobby Cutler. Cutler served as chairman of the National Security Council Planning Board for two terms, 1953–55 and 1957–58. During Tuttle's tenure, the Planning Board considered and then advised the National Security Council on a number of critical matters. He recalled the discussion of whether to continue the Berlin airlift begun by Truman and how to deal with Soviet efforts to stop it. He also recalled that the council resisted the proposal by the Joint Chiefs of Staff to drop an atomic bomb on Vietnam and unanimously decided not to recommend sending American troops to Dien Bien Phu.[24]

Tuttle's work as general counsel to the Treasury Department—both the Treasury work and the National Security Council Planning Board work—meant a great deal to him. But he had made only a two-year commitment, and he could not afford to stay longer. He and Sara had kept their Atlanta home and lived in a suite at the Wardman Park Hotel. It was time to go back home. He had come to realize, however, that by being on the inside at Treasury he had created the potential for conflict of interest with many of the firm's most important clients. There was a solution; he would simply recuse himself for a year from any matter that involved the Treasury

Department. Tuttle knew that whatever he did to clarify his lack of participation in Treasury-related matters, clients would come to the firm hoping
for the benefit of an inside track, and that worried him. It did not worry
Bill Sutherland. While he adhered to high professional standards and had
every intention of following the rules on recusal, Sutherland also knew that
no matter how much he disclaimed any special influence in Washington,
clients would come, hoping it was there. Finally, Tuttle would be bringing
in substantial corporate clients.

In February 1954 Congress passed an omnibus federal judgeship bill;
it authorized an additional seat on the Fifth Circuit. Almost immediately,
Walton Hall, president of the Atlanta Bar Association, sent a telegram to
Senator Richard Russell:

> The executive committee of the Atlanta Bar Association having observed
> that the bill creating an additional judgeship on the Fifth Circuit Court of
> Appeals has been passed and sent to the president for signature in regu-
> lar meeting on last evening unanimously voted to urge the appointment
> of honorable Elbert Tuttle general counsel for the Treasury Department of
> the United States as the new member of the Fifth Circuit Court of Appeals.
> Mr Tuttle is an exceedingly capable lawyer and a man of the highest in-
> tegrity. The executive committee of the Atlanta Bar Association urges your
> support.[25]

Senator Russell responded by telegram the next day: "I hold Elbert Tuttle
in the highest regard and in the event the President sees fit to submit his
nomination for the additional judgeship on the Fifth Circuit I shall be glad
to support his confirmation."[26]

At that time there were six states (Alabama, Florida, Georgia, Louisiana,
Mississippi, and Texas) in the Fifth Circuit and six judges, one from each
state. Texas, as the largest state, claimed first rights to the seat, but the
Eisenhower people resisted. They turned to John Minor Wisdom, who
had been so instrumental in Eisenhower's struggle for the nomination.
Wisdom had returned to Louisiana and continued to work on building a
viable Republican Party there. With his love of research and writing and
his scholarly bent, he wanted to be a judge. Still, Wisdom turned the offer down. It came too soon. "I had too many political commitments," he
recalled. "I was in charge of all the political patronage for the state. That
meant everything; that meant even the district judges, because we had

no interference at all from the Democrats."[27] Moreover, with children to send to college, he needed a few more years back in practice to secure his finances.

Tuttle was unaware of the legislation creating a new judgeship, but he had given some thought to the possibility of joining the court after an encounter with Senator Russell in the halls of the Treasury Department. As they exchanged pleasantries, Russell remarked that he had just returned from New York. Tuttle asked what had taken him there, and Russell responded that he was visiting his brother Bob, who sat on the Fifth Circuit and who was undergoing treatment for cancer. The prognosis was not good. Bob, Senator Russell told Tuttle, had told him that if anything happened to him, he hoped Tuttle would take his place on the court. Tuttle responded that he hoped Bob recovered his health. He wasn't interested in the court, he explained. He planned on returning to his practice when his term at the Treasury was over. Soon after that, Wisdom called. He told Tuttle about the new seat on the Fifth Circuit, which was news to Tuttle. He also told Tuttle to expect a call about it and encouraged him to take the job. Tuttle was not entirely uninterested, but when Bill Rogers, deputy attorney general under Herbert Brownell, called, he demurred. He explained to Rogers that he had promised Secretary Humphrey that he would stay at Treasury for two years; scarcely more than a year had passed, and he could not renege. Rogers countered with a reminder that these openings didn't come along often. If Tuttle had any interest in becoming a federal judge, now is the time to act, he advised. Tuttle thanked him but stood his ground; he did not feel he was free to leave the Treasury.

Months passed before Rogers called again. This time he had talked with Secretary Humphrey first and had his blessing. "You would be doing us a favor if you would take this judgeship," Rogers told Tuttle. Tuttle inquired how he could be doing the administration a favor by accepting a much sought after judgeship. Texas lays claim to it, Rogers explained, but the man they want to put on the court "wouldn't make a good postmaster, let alone a judge on the court of appeals."[28] The Texas Republicans based their claim on two points: the extra seat should go to the largest state in the circuit, and they had earned it by helping to give Eisenhower the nomination. Only by giving the nomination to someone he owed as much as he owed the Texans could Eisenhower appease them. Tuttle told Rogers he would give him an answer the next day. Tuttle wanted to accept. He had loved practicing law, but he had spent more than a quarter of a century doing it; also, going on the Fifth Circuit would resolve the conflicted feelings he harbored about returning to the firm. He would be forgoing the opportunity to take home a partner's draw, but his government check would be adequate for himself and Sara, and it would continue through both their lives. He called his children, and both encouraged him to accept. By then, Nicky and John were living in the Roxbury neighborhood of Boston, where John, now an ordained Episcopal priest, was rector of Saint John's Episcopal Church. Buddy had married Virginia "Ginny" Bauer in 1952; they were living in Boston, where Buddy, who had earned his MD at Harvard, was an intern at Massachusetts General Hospital. That left one issue—travel.

The judges of the Fifth Circuit rode the circuit. Panels sat regularly in New Orleans, less regularly in the other states that comprised the circuit. At least once a month, Tuttle could anticipate being away from home for most of a week. Travel appealed to him, but travel without Sara was unthinkable. Elbert loved his wife and treasured his home life. Throughout his career he had put his family first. Even when he was a young attorney building a practice, he often managed to leave the office in time to join the family for dinner. It meant a great deal to him to go home at the end of the day to his wife, so much that he would only accept an appointment on the federal bench if she agreed to travel with him. He knew what this meant. When he traveled, the clerk of the court would set up a temporary office for him. Tuttle would usually take a law clerk and sometimes his secretary with him; his days would be busy, filled with oral argument and conferences with his colleagues. Sara, his enormously intelligent, active, and engaged wife, would be left alone in a hotel room. Most judges' wives did not travel with them, so she could not count on company from that quarter. In Atlanta, Sara had her neighbors, her friends, and her clubs. On the road, she would be a business traveler with no business to attend to. But Elbert was firm; he would not take the appointment unless she would travel with him. Sara agreed, with two conditions. She would only keep one home, and she would live as well on the road as she did at home. Elbert agreed, and the deal was struck. Sara never regretted it. "From a lucrative law practice to a judge at $17,000 a year took some planning," she remembered, "but it was the best decision of our lives."

Tuttle called Bill Rogers and accepted. By then it was July, and he was accepting a position that had been created in February. None of the delay was attributable to getting anyone to pass on Tuttle. Ordinarily, the president would consult with, even defer to, members of Congress from his party from the state concerned, but there were no Republican congressmen from Georgia. After formally accepting the appointment, Tuttle went about informally telling his colleagues about his decision. By then, he spent most of his time on the work of the National Security Council Planning Board. In recent months, they had watched the fall of Dien Bien Phu and fended off suggestions that nuclear weapons be used in Vietnam. Tuttle felt almost as if he were retiring. He didn't anticipate that the work of the court would be anywhere near that stressful. One friend laughed. "You haven't been reading the newspapers," he suggested. In May the Supreme Court had handed down its unanimous opinion in *Brown v. Board of Education* (*Brown I*) and announced that state-imposed segregation of the races in public education violated the equal protection clause of the Constitution. Tuttle was not overly concerned about the reaction to *Brown*; he simply could not imagine that the South's political and civic leaders, many of whom he knew, would encourage defiance of the law. "Oh yes, but they'll fall in line," Tuttle responded.[29]

The subcommittee of the Committee on the Judiciary opened Tuttle's confirmation hearing promptly at 10:15 a.m. on Friday, July 16, 1954. The congenial proceedings lasted such a short time that the transcript is only four pages long. Tuttle had received an enthusiastic supporting letter from the president of the state bar of Georgia and a rating of "exceptionally well qualified" from the American Bar Association. As was customary, both the senators from Georgia, Richard Russell and Walter F. George, had been contacted and asked to return either a yellow slip, indicating an objection, or a blue slip, indicating none. Senator George had returned the blue slip, with the comment that Tuttle "is a lawyer of recognized ability and experience, and is a man of character." Despite his earlier expressions of support to Tuttle himself and in response to the telegram from the Atlanta Bar Association, Senator Russell returned neither slip. Mr. Davis, the staff member for the subcommittee, had checked with Russell's office and been told that "the blue slip on the nomination will not be returned, but that there is no objection known to the nominee."[30]

On July 30 a second, longer, and contentious hearing took place. Mrs. Mary Fahy had written the subcommittee and asked for an opportunity to appear. Mary Fahy was the sister-in-law of Judge Charles Fahy, a former solicitor general of the United States, then sitting on the Court of Appeals for the District of Columbia. Her husband, Judge Fahy's brother, had died, leaving her with three minor sons to support. At the time of his death, he had been a partner in what Tuttle described as "a prosperous family partnership in Rome, Georgia, a mercantile establishment." In confused, almost hysterical testimony, Mary Fahy accused Tuttle of unethical conduct in his handling of the settlement of the estate. She charged Tuttle with ineptness and inattention and with binding her, as guardian for her children, to a ridiculously low settlement figure. "The devil is the father of all liars and the Bible says no liar shall enter into the Kingdom of Heaven. I do not lie," she told the committee. She concluded, "It is your responsibility. He will be called 'Your Honor.' I would hate to have [to go] in there and stand up and call him 'Your Honor.'"[31]

Tuttle spoke in his own defense. He explained the legalities and practicalities that led him to settle the case as he did, and he also explained how he came to be involved. It was against his better judgment because he knew that two good Atlanta law firms had already been involved. He spoke to the attorneys, whom he knew to be honorable men, and "they said they were unable to do what she hoped to be accomplished and therefore it was utterly impossible to help her."[32] He took the case only because Judge Fahy had called Bill Sutherland, who was by then in the Washington office of the firm. Judge Fahy told Sutherland that his sister-in-law desperately needed a Georgia lawyer and asked him to prevail upon Tuttle to take the matter. Tuttle had put 143 hours into the case and incurred out-of-pocket expenses traveling to Rome to investigate the facts, but he had not been able to satisfy his client, so he had collected no fee.

Tuttle concluded by explaining that he had met with Mrs. Fahy at his Washington office and, with her present and the Georgia litigants on the phone, worked out a settlement agreement. Mrs. Fahy erupted: "I never authorized you to accept $40,250. That is what I objected to and Charles Fahy said accept one-half of their education and leave one-twentieth invested both in the partnership and the real estate." Tuttle responded that he had asked Judge Fahy to be there, and he had come and "sat through this whole thing in anticipation that some criticism might come because this lady is so terribly wrought up about this."[33] At that point the chairman put in the record a telegram from Judge Fahy to the Senate Judiciary Committee, dated July 22, 1954:

> Regarding question raised by widow of my brother Joseph A. Fahy as to qualifications of Mr. Tuttle for confirmation as Judge United States Court of Appeals for Fifth Circuit I respectfully advise that when Mr. Tuttle was considering representing the estate of my said brother I urged him to do so because of his fine reputation my conviction of his ability and integrity and my desire that the widow and children have representation of high character. In all respects events justified my position and his advice in re settlement was carefully considered completely honest and conscientious and should in no degree in my opinion be a barrier to your committee's favorable consideration of his nomination.[34]

With that, the committee voted unanimously in favor of Tuttle's appointment, and the hearing was adjourned. It saddened Tuttle that his career at the bar concluded with a harsh attack from a dissatisfied client, but it was a private sorrow. Confirmation hearings, by and large, received little public attention. One month later, on September 1, 1954, at the Supreme Court, Tuttle was sworn in as a judge of the United States Court of Appeals for the Fifth Circuit by Associate Justice Harold Burton. Tuttle knew Chief Justice Earl Warren from their work on the Eisenhower campaign, and he had called to ask him to swear him in. Warren had declined with regrets because his schedule took him out of town on the designated day. As it happened, Warren was in Washington that day after all, and he joined Tuttle's family and friends at the ceremony.

Two years later, on September 7, 1956, Associate Justice Sherman Minton announced his retirement from the United States Supreme Court, effective October 15. *Atlanta Constitution* editor Ralph McGill had telegraphed President Eisenhower in 1953 suggesting that he nominate Tuttle to succeed Chief Justice Fred Vinson. "No man in our state or region enjoys more respect than he," McGill told the president.[35] Earl Warren had garnered that appointment. When the Minton vacancy came up, McGill again put Tuttle's name forward. This time he had company. Atlanta attorney John Sibley, chairman of the board of the Trust Company of Georgia, lost no time in mounting a small campaign by encouraging others to write on Tuttle's behalf; on September 11 he circulated this letter:

I hope that we can get consideration for Judge Tuttle for the Supreme Court of the United States. His experience, his age and his character eminently fit him for this great job. I am enclosing a copy of a letter I have written to the President and also a copy of a letter to the Attorney General.

I am bringing the matter to the attention of some of my friends, who I am sure will send in their endorsements.[36]

Writing the president, Sibley explained: "Judge Tuttle is a profound student of the law. He has had wide experience in the practice and his integrity and ability are respected and recognized by everyone." McGill and Sibley were joined in their endorsement by many prominent attorneys, including Howell Hollis, president of the Georgia Bar Association; Tuttle's good friend Jim Wilson, representing the five-hundred-member-strong Lawyers' Club; Allen Post, president of the Atlanta Bar Association; and Tuttle's brother-in-law Bill Sutherland, all of whom sent letters. That seat went to William J. Brennan. In 1957, when Associate Justice Stanley Reed stepped down, Tuttle's friends and supporters again put his name forward. That seat went to Charles Whittaker. A September 17, 1958, memo from President Eisenhower to Attorney General Bill Rogers indicates that Tuttle was on Eisenhower's short list more than once. Eisenhower had selected three men from a list of possible nominees—Herbert Brownell, Warren Burger, and Elbert Tuttle. Of Tuttle he wrote, "I once considered him for a Court position and for some reason that I cannot now recall, we dropped his name." Eisenhower indicated in his note to Rogers that one reason he chose Tuttle for the short list was that "he is of Southern origin. . . . It is possible that it would be a good idea to have two Southerners on the Court, and I think Black is the only one now who would be in that category." A few weeks later he nominated Potter Stewart. Ironically, Tuttle thought it extremely unlikely he would be nominated because he was from the South; he counted Justice Tom Clark from Texas along with Justice Hugo Black, and he doubted the president would appoint a third southerner.

As his career on the bench progressed, just as he felt fortunate that he owed no political debts to elected southern officials, Tuttle was grateful that any ambition he might have had to sit on the Supreme Court was blunted by political astuteness. The bottom line was that he was never looking over his shoulder, wondering whom he might please or displease. That was, no doubt, more attributable to his character than to his circumstances. As

John Sibley put it in a 1957 letter to Eisenhower's national security advisor, Bobby Cutler: "Judge Tuttle is respected and admired, both by the bar and by the people, for his integrity and his learning as well as his good citizenship. Although born and educated in another section of the country, he has attained great popularity in the South. This is due to the fact that his honesty and sincerity are so well recognized that everyone respects his views, although they are nowise colored by partisanship or local environment."[37]

CHAPTER TWELVE

The Great Writ

Tuttle's confirmation hearings were typical of the times. Seats on the circuit courts of appeals were understood to "belong" to certain states. If that state's senators belonged to the president's party, they would be consulted about appointments and their preferences weighted heavily. If they belonged to the opposition party, civility indicated that their opinion be formally sought by the committee—but it was of little import. Neither of the senators from Georgia was a Republican; for that matter, none of Georgia's representatives in the House were Republican. As time wore on, Tuttle would realize how fortunate that was. In difficult times, and there would be difficult times, no one could claim that Tuttle owed him anything or that Tuttle had let him down. No one could knock on Tuttle's door and attempt to collect on a political debt.

The hearings were also typical in that little about Tuttle's career as an attorney was explored. It was evident that he had been a successful lawyer, and that was enough for the committee. His heroic service in World War II was a bonus. No doubt the committee thought they were considering a fairly typical Ivy League–educated corporate attorney. A closer look might have surprised them and alarmed their southern colleagues in Congress. Tuttle had much closer ties to black professionals than was customary at the time, and these relationships flowed from several sources. His work on behalf of John Downer in the 1930s had served to introduce him to A. T. Walden, the dean of the Atlanta black bar. His work building the Republican Party in Georgia had even broader impact. Barred from the white Democratic Party, black Georgians had joined the only party available to them. In the 1940s Republican Party meetings were a rare instance of interracial gatherings. Through those meetings, Tuttle came to know the leaders of the black community in Atlanta, among them Dr. Benjamin Mays. In 1950 Dr. Mays had invited Tuttle to join the board of trustees of

Morehouse College; Tuttle accepted gratefully, and in short order he also became a member of the board of trustees of Atlanta University, Spelman College, and the Interdenominational Theological Center—all black institutions.[1] In 1982 he publicly thanked Dr. Mays for "attitudes and actions of his that were of untold value to me and I hope to the society we both sought to serve" and for bringing him "in fairly frequent contact with exceptional people whom, under the custom of the times, I would probably never have met."[2]

The members of the Senate Committee on the Judiciary might also have been surprised at the extent to which Tuttle had handled constitutional, not corporate, matters on a pro bono basis. In addition to his mighty efforts on behalf of John Downer, he had handled two major habeas corpus cases, both of which resulted in landmark opinions. In the first, he represented Angelo Herndon, a young black man who when only nineteen years old had helped organize a multiracial protest of the city of Atlanta's decision to cut off relief funding. It was 1932, and the circumstances could not have been more dire. Atlanta, like the rest of the country, suffered mightily in the Great Depression. The Emergency Relief Committee, the only source of support for many of the four thousand families it served, had run out of money. The county government had slashed salaries, some, including those of the district attorney and superior court judges, by as much as 25 percent, but the money saved was pledged to reduce the deficit, not to provide relief. Many wage earners were suffering, albeit not as much as the unemployed; still, the county commission had resisted raising taxes.[3]

Leftists, communists, and other activists in the Atlanta area formed the Unemployed Council. The voice of the dispossessed, they worked hard at assisting the unemployed to find work and assistance. When the Emergency Relief Committee was forced to announce that it was closing its doors, they decided to take direct action. Angelo Herndon and his colleagues prepared and distributed pamphlets calling for a rally at the Fulton County Courthouse. On June 30, 1932, some one thousand desperate people, black and white, gathered. The stunned county commissioners met with a small delegation of unemployed white workers and barred black demonstrators from the meeting. Then they promised an appropriation of $6,000 to buy groceries for families cut off earlier and suggested that the county would pay transportation home for anyone who had family outside Atlanta. The crowd dispersed. A few days later, Atlanta detectives arrested

Angelo Herndon as he picked up mail from a post office box used by the Unemployed Council. He was taken in under a charge of "on suspicion." On the ledger at the police headquarters, the vague charge was clarified; one word, "Communist," was scribbled across from his name.

Herndon was held without bond for investigation until a superior court judge ordered that he be indicted or freed. On July 22, eleven days after his arrest, he was indicted for attempting to incite insurrection. By calling meetings, making speeches, and circulating pamphlets, the indictment charged, he was inciting insurrection, uprisings, and riots and attempting to overthrow the lawful authority of the state of Georgia. Given the temper of the times when Angelo Herndon was tried, his conviction was a foregone conclusion; the only surprise was that the jury took some three hours to return a verdict. The delay, it turned out, had nothing to do with the verdict. The jury had been unable to agree on the sentence because two jurors had held out for the death penalty. In the end, his sentence of eighteen to twenty years to be served on a Georgia chain gang was the equivalent of the death penalty.

Angelo Herndon's attorneys appealed his conviction. While Herndon's appeal was pending, on March 16, 1934, John Downer was executed. Two months later, on May 24, 1934, the Georgia Supreme Court issued its opinion in Herndon's case.[4] His objections to the all-white jury panel and to the constitutionality of the statute were dismissed as not timely raised. The court reached one First Amendment issue. Herndon argued that even if the statute was constitutional, the evidence was insufficient to establish that his speech was so imminently dangerous as to be subject to suppression. The Georgia Supreme Court disagreed.[5] Angelo Herndon's conviction was affirmed.

The case became a cause célèbre, locally and nationally. In mid-June, probably in an effort to deflect criticism, the state agreed to bail. The defense team's sense of victory evaporated when the judge set bail at $15,000. Despite the fact that the figure was almost prohibitive, the International Labor Defense (ILD), which some saw as the legal arm of the Communist Party and which had sponsored Herndon's defense team, raised it.[6] On August 4, Angelo Herndon left his cell in the Fulton Towers prison in the company of two of his attorneys and two detectives sent by the Seaboard Railroad. The day before his release the National Committee for the Defense of Political Prisoners had received a call warning that the Ku Klux

Klan would not let Herndon leave Georgia. Herndon planned to take the train to New York that evening, so the railroad assigned the two detectives to accompany him from the jail to the train and to remain with him on the train until he left the South. Governor Eugene Talmadge took the threats less seriously. When the nationally acclaimed novelist Theodore Dreiser called the governor, Talmadge reassured him. "I get letters and telegrams every day from people worried about the matter, but the people down here don't molest a nigger for any crime except a white woman."[7]

In late September, the Georgia Supreme Court denied Herndon's petition for rehearing. Now his only recourse was the United States Supreme Court. At this juncture, the ILD recognized the need for distinguished counsel. Carol Weiss King, a leftist New York City attorney, began seeking help.[8] She enlisted Whitney North Seymour, a prominent attorney and dedicated civil libertarian who would later become the president of the American Bar Association. Only thirty, he had served as first assistant to the solicitor general. A Republican, an Episcopalian, and a graduate of Columbia Law School, Seymour's credentials were impeccable. His connections matched his credentials; he contacted Harvard Law School graduate and former law clerk to Justice Brandeis William A. Sutherland in Atlanta and sought his help.[9] Sutherland signed on and enlisted his brother-in-law, Elbert Tuttle. The team was rounded out by Walter Gellhorn and Herbert Wechsler, two young Columbia law professors who would be, in time, luminaries of the profession.[10] Herndon could not have had a stronger team.

Nor could Herndon's timing have been better. On February 15, 1935, the Court had heard oral argument in one of the infamous Scottsboro boys cases. On April 1 the Court announced its decision reversing the conviction of Clarence Norris because of the systematic exclusion of black citizens from jury service in Alabama.[11] Herndon's trial counsel had not perfected their challenge to the Fulton County jury panels, so the issue was not before the Court in his case, but everyone knew that he had suffered the same injustice. Moreover, Herndon's case had captured the attention of the national press. On April 10 the *New Republic* carried an editorial that concluded: "Few cases in American jurisprudence have been of greater importance than the appeal of Angelo Herndon."[12] On April 12, 1935, Whitney North Seymour, accompanied by Bill Sutherland at counsels' table, arose and eloquently argued the First Amendment issues presented by the Georgia statute. His brilliance and the weight of the matter notwithstanding, the Court did not reach the issues he argued. On May 20, 1935, a scant six weeks after oral argument, the Court dismissed Herndon's appeal, ruling that because he had failed to raise his constitutional arguments at the first opportunity, there was no federal question on appeal that would give the United States Supreme Court jurisdiction.[13]

At the beginning of the next term, in October, the Court denied Herndon's motion for rehearing. On Monday morning, October 28, accompanied by Elbert Tuttle, his attorney, and by Joseph North, a sympathetic journalist, Angelo Herndon surrendered to Sheriff James Lowry and re-entered the Fulton Towers prison in Atlanta.[14] With his client in jail, Tuttle prepared to file his petition for writ of habeas corpus. The great writ allowed Herndon to challenge his conviction on federal constitutional grounds. The Georgia statute, Tuttle asserted on behalf of his client, was too vague to be enforceable. A plain reading would render criminal speech that was clearly protected by the First Amendment. Jurisdiction for the petition lay in the superior court of Fulton County, the county in which Herndon was incarcerated. At the time, it was possible to file a petition with a particular judge, as opposed to the current practice of filing the petition with the clerk of the court, who then distributes all cases using a random assignment system. Tuttle chose to file it with Judge Hugh M. Dorsey, a former governor of Georgia.

Hugh Dorsey was the district attorney who had, two decades earlier, won the conviction of a young Jewish man, Leo Frank, for the rape and murder of Mary Phagan. Marked by intense anti-Semitism, the Frank trial remains one of the most notorious in American legal history. Leo Frank had been raised in Brooklyn and educated at Pratt and Cornell, where he earned a degree in mechanical engineering in 1906. A year or two later, he moved to Atlanta, where he and his uncle opened a pencil factory. Frank was a part owner of the company and the superintendent of the factory. In the early morning hours of April 27, 1913, the black night watchman, Newt Lee, found the body of a fourteen-year-old employee, Mary Phagan, lying lifeless in the basement. An inept police investigation immediately focused on Newt Lee and on Leo Frank, who had apparently, when she collected her pay, been the last person other than her murderer to see Mary Phagan alive. Frank was arrested for the crime on April 29. The onetime populist Tom Watson led a vituperative anti-Semitic campaign using his weekly newspaper, the *Jeffersonian*, and his magazine, *Watson's Monthly*. Leo Frank was a perfect target, as the pastor of the Phagan family's Baptist Church explained: "My feelings, upon the arrest of the poor old nightwatchman [Newt Lee], were to the effect that this one old negro would be poor atonement for the life of this innocent girl. But, when on the next day, the police arrested a Jew, and a Yankee Jew at that, all of the inborn prejudice against Jews rose up in a feeling of satisfaction, that here would be a victim worthy to pay for the crime."[15]

Frank was convicted and sentenced to die after a trial dominated by an anti-Semitic mob. Nonetheless, the United States Supreme Court denied relief.[16] Frank then sought clemency from the Georgia Prison Commission. By then the attorney for the black janitor, Jim Conley, whose testimony had been used to convict Frank, announced that his client had killed Mary Phagan. He contended that it was his duty to come forward to save the life of an innocent man and that his disclosure could not harm his client because he had been convicted of complicity in the crime (Conley had claimed to have helped Frank move the body to the basement) and could not be retried. Moreover, the trial court judge, who had since died, had written Frank's attorney to state his own lack of certainty in Frank's guilt and to admit that "perhaps he had shown 'undue deference to the opinion of the jury.'" Still, the commission voted 2–1 not to commute Leo Frank's death sentence. Frank's last hope was an appeal for clemency from the governor of Georgia.[17]

Governor John Slayton was by then near the end of his term. Frank's attorneys hastened to get a petition for clemency on Slayton's desk before he left office because his successor, Nathaniel Harris, was a close friend and political associate of Tom Watson. Governor Slayton could have left the matter for his successor to handle; instead, after agonizing deliberation and painstaking review, he commuted Frank's death sentence. Public reaction was swift; angry mobs attacked the capitol and the governor's mansion, forcing Slayton and his wife to leave the state. Two months later, twenty-five community leaders from Mary Phagan's hometown, Marietta, drove the 125 miles from Marietta to the state prison farm at Milledgeville where Frank was held, overcame the two guards on duty, and seized Frank. The cavalcade then drove back to Marietta, where Leo Frank was hanged.

After the lynching of Leo Frank, it would be decades before the Jewish community in Atlanta regained a sense of security.[18] John Slayton, once considered a certain candidate for a seat in the Senate, would never hold political office again. But for the prosecutor, Hugh Dorsey, the episode provided a great political boost. In 1916, the year after the lynching, "the demand for his entrance into the gubernatorial race was so strong 'that it swept the state like a prairie fire, rolling from the mountains to the sea.'"[19] He won overwhelmingly. After his term as governor, and after being defeated by Tom Watson in a three-way race for the Senate, Dorsey became a judge, first on the Atlanta City Court and then on Fulton County Superior Court.[20] Many were startled when Tuttle chose to file Herndon's petition for writ of habeas corpus with Dorsey, but Tuttle had good reason for his choice. He knew Dorsey personally, and he knew that during his term as governor, Dorsey had been a moderate on race.[21] Tuttle thought, he sometimes quietly explained, that Dorsey might be ready to atone.

The hearing on Herndon's petition for a writ of habeas corpus began on November 12, 1935. Herndon, who was still being held in the Fulton Towers, was allowed to attend. Dressed in a suit and tie, Herndon sat at counsels' table with a large book in front of him with lettering so clear that observers could see the title: *The Letters of Sacco and Vanzetti*.

Whitney North Seymour had traveled to Atlanta for the hearing; he shared the time for argument with Bill Sutherland. Elbert Tuttle, who had drafted the petition and handled the legwork, deferred to Seymour and to his brother-in-law. Seymour handled the formal First Amendment argument, contending that the statute violated the principle that speech that did not present a clear and present danger could not be suppressed and that it was too vague to be enforceable. Bill Sutherland, a native Georgian, was blunt. "This conviction," he argued, "places the state of Georgia in a ridiculous position before the people of this country and the world."[22] Three weeks later, Judge Dorsey handed down his opinion: the statute was, he wrote, too vague to be enforceable; it did not set "a sufficiently ascertainable standard of guilt."[23] A valid law protecting against insurrection could be drafted and survive constitutional muster, but this one did not. Dorsey gave the state twenty days to file a notice of appeal and ordered Herndon released on a bond pending appeal of eight thousand dollars.

Tuttle lost no time; before one o'clock that afternoon, he met his client in the sheriff's office at the Fulton Towers. Cliff Mackay, a reporter with Atlanta's black-owned newspaper the *Daily World*, was there as well. Tuttle handed over the bond, and the three men left together. Later that evening, Herndon left Atlanta on a train to New York. As a precautionary measure, Sutherland and Tuttle delegated a young attorney from the firm, Ed Kane, to travel with him. Even though Kane's sole reason for the trip was to accompany Herndon, when they boarded the train, they had to part company; in the 1930s, in the American South, passenger train cars were segregated by race.[24] In time, the Georgia Supreme Court reversed Judge Dorsey's ruling, only to be reversed itself in the United States Supreme Court. The final opinion, *Herndon v. Lowry*, remains a landmark in First Amendment jurisprudence.[25]

When Angelo Herndon boarded the train to leave Atlanta in December 1935, Tuttle's next habeas corpus client had been languishing in the Atlanta Federal Penitentiary for nearly a year. Monroe Bridwell and John Johnson, two young Marines stationed in South Carolina, had been arrested in the fall of 1934 at a Charleston brothel. Frequenting a brothel was not a federal offense, but passing forged bills was. They were indicted for possessing and uttering counterfeit money; unable to raise bail, they stayed in jail until, on January 23, 1935, they were brought to federal district court for arraignment and trial. Exactly what happened that day in the courtroom was never completely resolved. It is clear that when the court proceeded with the arraignment, notifying the defendants of the charges against them and asking how they pleaded, they pleaded not guilty. It is also clear that the court asked if they had counsel but did not ask if they wished to have counsel appointed. On those points, all parties agreed. But Johnson and Bridwell contended that they did want attorneys, that they asked the U. S. attorney to arrange for counsel, and that he told them that in South Carolina counsel was only appointed in capital cases.[26] The U. S. attorney denied that any request was made.

They proceeded to trial without counsel. Johnson and Bridwell contended that they told the judge they were ready to proceed because the U. S. attorney told them it was too late to subpoena witnesses. The U. S. attorney denied having said that as well. At any rate, having just learned of the charges against them, they acquiesced in having the proceeding go forward. By the end of the day, they stood convicted. Both were sentenced to four years and six months' imprisonment. Two days later, they were transported to the Atlanta Federal Penitentiary and placed, as was the custom with new prisoners, in isolation for sixteen days. Not until May 15, nearly four months later, did they file notices of appeal, which were quickly dismissed as untimely.

Johnson and Bridwell then filed petitions for writs of habeas corpus. Because they were incarcerated in Atlanta, jurisdiction lay in the federal district court in Atlanta. When they appeared, Judge Emory Marvin Underwood, noting that they "were men of little education and without counsel or funds to procure same," offered to appoint counsel to represent them. They accepted.[27] Judge Underwood appointed Frank Doughman, who proceeded to investigate, to take depositions, and to prepare for the hearing. Doughman won on a critical point—Judge Underwood ruled that the defendants had a constitutional right to have counsel appointed before they were tried for felonies in federal court. But he also ruled that it was too late to raise that claim; it should have been asserted on appeal. Judge Underwood did not think that he had jurisdiction. His opinion clarified the unfairness of the result; his own dissatisfaction seemed apparent. On the one hand, that gave ammunition to Bridwell and Johnson. On the other hand, it strengthened the order that even a sympathetic judge could not find a way to rule for them. Judge Underwood's description of the defendants conveyed his concerns. "Both petitioners," he wrote, "lived in distant cities of other states and had neither relatives, friends, nor acquaintances in Charleston. Both had little education and were without funds."[28] And both stood convicted.

At that point Judge Underwood contacted Elbert Tuttle.[29] For a federal judge to seek pro bono counsel to defend a criminal prosecution or to file a petition for habeas corpus was not unusual, but seeking out an attorney to handle an appeal from his own order was unusual. Tuttle went to the Atlanta Federal Penitentiary to meet Johnson, who explained that he would be happy to have Tuttle represent him, but he could not afford to pay him.[30] Tuttle took the case pro bono, and the ACLU agreed to pay for the printing costs in the court of appeals. The three-judge panel unanimously affirmed in a brisk opinion, and further appeal seemed futile, especially because there was no further appeal of right. If the matter were to go forward, it would be on writ of certiorari. Moreover, the ACLU could not continue financial support. That meant Tuttle himself would have to pay court costs, printing costs, and his own travel expenses. With the support of the firm, he decided to go on. His petition for writ of certiorari was granted, and the case was set for oral argument. It would turn out to be the only case he ever argued in the United States Supreme Court. "I quit while I was ahead," he often noted. It would also prove to be one of the most significant cases ever decided in the area of constitutional criminal procedure.[31]

Tuttle had to win on two grounds to secure a real victory for his client. First, he had to convince the court that a defendant in a federal felony trial had a constitutional right to appointed counsel.[32] At that time, it was not uncommon for federal judges to appoint counsel; it may have been more common than not.[33] Had either Bridwell or Johnson asked the federal district court judge before whom they were tried for counsel, an attorney may well have been provided. But the Constitution, as it was then understood, did not require it. In only one case had the Supreme Court found a right to appointed counsel. A few years earlier, in 1932, in *Powell v. Alabama*, one of the Scottsboro boys cases, the Supreme Court had for the first time found a constitutional right to appointed counsel.[34] But *Powell* was a death penalty case. It was a long step from a rule applying only in capital cases to a rule applying in all federal felonies. The second ground on which Tuttle had to prevail was more intractable. It was the point that had bedeviled Judge Underwood, who had been sympathetic to Bridwell and Johnson on the appointment of counsel issue. Even if one assumed that they did have a right to counsel, how could one get around the fact that they had waived it? The judge asked them if they were ready to proceed, and they had said yes. By not raising the issue with the court, by simply going forward, they had waived any right they might have. The waiver issue had enormous ramifications, and the members of the Supreme Court could be expected to be sensitive to them.

Justice Hugo Black wrote the opinion for the Court, and four other justices joined it.[35] That was enough. On behalf of his client, John Johnson, Tuttle had won a sweeping victory. The Sixth Amendment, Justice Black wrote, required that before a defendant could be tried in federal court for a felony, he or she must be provided with the assistance of counsel, unless it had been waived. It had already been established that the due process clause required waivers to be voluntary.[36] Justice Black went considerably further by ruling that a defendant could not be considered to have waived a right he did not know he had—a waiver would only be effective if it was knowing and intelligent.[37] Both rulings made by the Court in *Johnson v. Zerbst* were important, but the ruling on the right to counsel applied only in federal felony proceedings. The waiver rule, on the other hand, applied to the waiver of most federal constitutional rights.[38] Over the next few decades, *Johnson v. Zerbst* became the most often cited opinion in American jurisprudence.

By the time the Supreme Court ruled, Johnson had been imprisoned for three years. Tuttle went back to the penitentiary to tell him the good news. Tuttle had not yet had the order releasing Johnson signed, because the Supreme Court had ordered the matter remanded for determination of whether there had been a knowing, intelligent, and voluntary waiver of the right to counsel. If Tuttle had the order signed, and if on remand the lower court found there had been no waiver, the original conviction would be set aside, and Johnson could be tried again. That was unlikely but possible. It gave Johnson pause. He was getting out anyway, within days, on good behavior. He could just let things be, but then he would have a felony conviction on his record. Johnson decided to take the chance; he directed Tuttle to have the order signed.

Before Tuttle left, Johnson asked him a question: "You must have put up some money?" Tuttle responded that he had spent a couple of hundred dollars. "Well," Johnson said, "I'll send you a check someday." Someday never came. Tuttle didn't mind. He had never expected to be paid. Besides, in addition to the honor of having argued and won in the Supreme Court, he took home an anecdote he loved to tell. During his argument, Chief Justice Charles Evans Hughes had interrupted to remark, "Mr. Tuttle, the next thing you'll be arguing is that before a man pleads guilty he'll be entitled to have a lawyer." Keeping the focus on the point he was making, Tuttle ducked. "Fortunately, Mr. Chief Justice," he responded, "that's not the issue before the court today."[39]

CHAPTER THIRTEEN

Forming the Historic
Fifth Circuit: Nine Men

When Elbert Tuttle returned to Atlanta to assume his seat on the United
States Court of Appeals for the Fifth Circuit, he expected to serve out his
years in peace and quiet. The Fifth Circuit had long been one of the busi-
est federal circuits in the nation. The work of the judges was steady, but it
was not heavy, and it was carried out at the judge's pace in the isolation of
his chambers. Tuttle joked to friends in D.C. that he was going home "to
retire" to the court. Instead, he found himself at the epicenter of one of
the greatest social upheavals in history. The men he served with, especially
during his term as chief judge, from 1960 to 1967, would be called upon to
make the great majority of the critical judicial decisions during the determinative years of the civil rights revolution. They would decide whether
Jim Crow lived or died.

Tuttle moved into chambers on the third floor of the federal courthouse
in Atlanta, a six-story building with massive stone walls that occupied an
entire city block. A door from Tuttle's secretary's office led to a small robing room that itself led directly into the impressively appointed third-floor
courtroom. His first day on the bench, Monday, October 4, 1954, did not
begin auspiciously. Just before 10:00, Tuttle joined the chief judge of the
circuit, Joseph C. Hutcheson Jr. of Texas, and Judge Richard Rives in the
robing room. Judge Hutcheson had been in Atlanta for arguments the week
before, but he had confined his interaction with Tuttle to the briefest of in-
troductions. In the robing room, Hutcheson had nothing to say to Tuttle
until, as they prepared to enter the courtroom, he tossed a curt direction
over his shoulder. "Tuttle," he called back, "you go last."[1]

Chief Judge Hutcheson had been first appointed to the federal district
court in 1918 by President Wilson and then elevated to the Fifth Circuit in

1931 by President Hoover. He had become chief judge in 1948. A dyed-in-
the-wool Texas Democrat, Hutcheson was proud of having been appointed
by a Republican president, but that was the extent of his appreciation of the
Republican Party. He loved the court, and he wasn't particularly impressed
by the new judge. Hutcheson had authored books and law review articles,
had barely missed out on an appointment to the Supreme Court (which
went to Hugo Black), and was highly regarded as a legal scholar.[2] He saw
in Tuttle the highly political Republican appointment of a tax lawyer, a
specialization that to Hutcheson did not indicate intellectual breadth or
depth.

As chief, Judge Hutcheson ran things his way. "He didn't pay all that
much attention to formalities," Tuttle recalled. "No one did." Once when
the court had been sitting en banc in New Orleans, the judges adjourned
to lunch together at a local eatery, Mike's on the Avenue. As they left the
restaurant, Chief Judge Hutcheson, referring to the requirement that the
circuit hold a judicial council meeting twice a year, announced, "Well, the
law requires us to hold two meetings a year. That was one of them."[3] For his
part, Tuttle found Hutcheson to be "an interesting judge, very bright, well
read." Tuttle brushed aside Hutcheson's lack of warmth, even after an incident later that week, when Tuttle suggested to Hutcheson that he call him
Elbert or Tut. "I wouldn't think of it," Judge Hutcheson replied. "First thing
I know, you'll be calling me Joe."[4] Presumably, Hutcheson held everyone at
arm's length. Two years later, in 1956, he sent a thoughtful and affectionate
three-page handwritten note thanking the Tuttles for their part in a fiftieth-
anniversary gift the judges and their wives had given the Hutchesons. The
salutation is "Dear Judge and Mrs. Tuttle," and he closes with: "I take the
greatest pleasure in signing myself Most sincerely your friend, Joseph C.
Hutcheson."

Remembering those early days, Sara Tuttle was less circumspect than
her husband. "Judge Hutcheson was ugly to us when we came on the court,"
she remembered. "He thought the Eisenhower appointees were ruining his
court and he didn't like anything about us." Nor was Mrs. Hutcheson wel-
coming, Sara felt. High spirited and outgoing, Sara thought good social relations were important to good working relations, and she was determined
to make her husband's job easier. When she attended a luncheon for the
judges' wives, she enjoyed herself enormously, chatting and laughing and
humorously recounting her experiences. "Mrs. Hutcheson," Sara recalled,

"looked at me, very straight faced, and she said, 'Well you certainly have had a good time since you came on this court.' I looked her in the eye and I said, 'Mrs. Hutcheson, I didn't wait until I came on this court to have a good time; I've been having a good time ALL of my life.'"[5] Sara had made her point, and after that the two women became good friends.

Elbert Tuttle and Joseph Hutcheson never became good friends, but they did become stalwart colleagues, with great respect for each other. After Judge Hutcheson had a stroke in 1961, he still went to his office, but he was unable to travel to sit on the court.[6] The Fifth Circuit had never held oral arguments in Houston; in Texas they sat in Fort Worth. By then Tuttle was chief judge, and he called Judge Hutcheson and suggested that the court sit in Houston. Judge Hutcheson's first reaction was hesitant. "Do you think the Court can sit here?" he asked. "Of course we can," Tuttle responded. "Well then I would be happy to have you come to Houston and hold court here," Judge Hutcheson said.[7] The court sat in Houston, and Tuttle presided over the three-judge panel, with Judge Hutcheson sitting to his right. Every day of that first week of oral arguments, some member of Judge Hutcheson's family attended court. Tuttle took almost as much pleasure as Hutcheson did in their presence. Sara Tuttle was in Houston as well; she kept her promise to always travel with her husband. One evening, the judges and their spouses gathered for some light socializing. She was chatting with Judge Hutcheson, by then in his eighties, when he gripped her arm. "Sara," he said, staring into her eyes, "remember that Browning poem, 'come grow old along with me, the best is yet to be'?" She remembered it, and she tossed off the first verse from memory. As she finished, he tightened his grip on her arm. "Sara," he said, "don't believe it; it's a damn lie."[8] They shared a bittersweet laugh. In her own decline, in her nineties, recalling the story could always bring Sara laughter again.

There were five judges in addition to Hutcheson on the Fifth Circuit when Tuttle was nominated for a seat on the court. Two died within a year. Judge Louie Willard Strum, a Democrat from Florida, died on July 26, 1954, and Judge Robert Russell, a Democrat from Georgia and Senator Richard Russell's brother, died on January 18, 1955. Two others took senior status within Tuttle's first two years on the court. Judge Edwin Holmes, a Democrat from Mississippi, took senior status on November 30, 1954; he died on December 10, 1961. Judge Wayne Borah, a Democrat from Louisiana, took senior status on December 31, 1956, continued to sit only through 1958, and died on February 6, 1966. The fifth, a Truman appointee, Richard Rives of Alabama, became one of Tuttle's most steadfast allies and closest friends. With two judges dying and two taking senior status, President Eisenhower suddenly had four appointments to make. By June 27, 1957, when John Minor Wisdom received his commission, of seven judges on the Fifth Circuit, five were Republicans, and of the five Republicans, only two had been raised in the South. Change was overtaking the court and the country.

Had Tuttle known what lay ahead for the Fifth Circuit as the civil rights revolution played out in the federal courts of the Deep South, he might have been concerned by Richard Rives's background. Unlike Tuttle, Rives was a southerner through and through. He was born in Montgomery in 1895; decades earlier, his maternal great-great-grandfather had been the first Baptist minister in Montgomery County. Richard Rives's grandparents on both sides had been raised in Alabama. His father's family had been well-off plantation owners before the Civil War; after it, they were economically devastated. Valedictorian of his high school class, Richard Rives won a tuition scholarship to Tulane and spent one year there with the help of a loan from one of his sisters. At the end of the year, instead of borrowing more, he decided to stay home and work to repay her. His father, a deputy sheriff, knew that his son belonged in college. He couldn't afford to send him, but Rives's father did the next best thing. He called on Wiley Hill, a Montgomery lawyer whose family had been neighbors of the Rives family before the Civil War. Wiley Hill agreed to let young Richard Rives study law in his office; apparently, he was a good teacher. In 1914, at the age of nineteen, Richard Rives passed the Alabama bar examination.

Rives only practiced law for about a year before being sent to the Mexican border; from 1918 to 1919, during World War I, he served as a first lieutenant in the Signal Corps of the American Expeditionary Forces. When he returned to Alabama, he steadily built a practice and a reputation. In 1926 he directed Hugo Black's successful campaign for the Senate; in 1939–40 he served as president of the Alabama State Bar; and many credited him with "guid[ing] Chauncy Sparks into the governor's chair in 1942."[9] Many also thought he could have been governor himself, but in 1951, while arguing a case before the United States Supreme Court, Richard Rives was handed a note telling him that President Truman had nominated him to the Fifth Circuit. He won the case, and he accepted the nomination.

The nomination had not entirely been a surprise to Rives. A few years earlier, Judge Leon McCord of the Fifth Circuit had encouraged Rives to consider going on the court. Rives had talked it over with his son, Richard Rives Jr. "Dick thought that on the beliefs we had and things that mattered to us, I would have a much wider effect as a judge," Rives told an interviewer years later.[10] What his son had thought was of critical importance to Richard Rives. A graduate of Exeter and Harvard, young Dick Rives had enjoyed the formal education his father never had. While on active duty with the navy in the Pacific during World War II, he fell seriously ill. In the weeks he spent recuperating in a military hospital, with black servicemen lying alongside him, he found himself reflecting on the injustice of segregation. After the war, as a law student at the University of Michigan, he read Gunnar Myrdal's 1944 study of race relations, *An American Dilemma: The Negro Problem and Modern Democracy*. He recommended it to his father, who was deeply influenced by Myrdal's work and by the progressive views of his own son. The two men, father and son, looked forward to practicing law together. Then came the great tragedy of Richard Rives's life. In the summer of 1949, his son, riding with a friend to his parents' beach home at Mary Esther, Florida, died in an automobile accident.

Two years later, Judge McCord announced his retirement. He may well have waited for Rives's most intense grief to subside. At any rate, he encouraged Rives to talk to Senator Lister Hill. Lister Hill was an old friend who had relied on Rives for political support and advice; he assured him that he was behind him and sent him on to Senator John Sparkman. Rives knew Sparkman but was not close to him; still, Sparkman told Rives "he would make a fine judge, was well qualified, and he would give him 'every consideration.'" Rives recounted Sparkman's remarks to McCord, who did not like what he heard. Had he ever walked a certain foot trail by the Alabama River, McCord asked Rives? "Of course," Rives said. "Well," McCord said, "I made that trail walking back from being sold down the river so many times. You go back to see Senator Sparkman." Rives took Senator Hill's advice, went back to Senator Sparkman, and told him what Hill had said. With more force and clarity, Senator Sparkman again assured Rives of his support.[11] In short order, the nomination came through.

Richard Rives was very much a son of Alabama, and the way in which he dealt with racial issues early in his career reflected that. When black voters began a voting drive in Montgomery, the Board of Registrars sought Rives's advice. A line of blacks stretched around the park, board members explained; they had all come to register to vote. "Well, the only thing to do is go on and let them come in, take their application, let them sign up and you all pass on it after they leave," he recalls advising them. He didn't tell them how to pass on it; "they didn't need any advice on that." His strategy worked, and the voting drive campaign failed. Likewise, he recalled, when he was judge advocate of the Montgomery American Legion, blacks tried to join. The rules provided that all applicants would be voted upon. They were. No black applicant was ever told he could not apply, and no black applicant ever received a positive vote or an offer of membership.[12] But Richard Rives was a thoughtful, fair-minded man, and his attitude toward segregation evolved as he matured. Rank injustice unsettled him. As a young attorney, he was retained by the family of a young black woman who had died in a "gruesome" elevator accident. He proved the liability of the company that had installed the elevator easily, and because the plaintiff had been a young, healthy woman, he expected a substantial verdict. But as the insurance adjuster who had tried to settle it with him had pointed out, no black death in Alabama had ever brought in a verdict over $1,000. True to form, the jury awarded $1,000. Rives was shocked. The episode marked a turning point in his awareness of the pervasive and corrosive effects of segregation.

By 1946 Richard Rives was openly splitting with the old guard. For decades, southern states had effectively denied suffrage to black voters by use of the white primary. In the Deep South, the Democratic candidate always won the important statewide elections—the race for governor or for the state supreme court. In other words, whoever won the Democratic primary won the general election. Not all registered voters could vote in the Democratic primary, only registered Democrats, only, that is, members of the white Democratic Party. The Democratic Party itself was segregated, no blacks allowed. Black citizens could vote in the general election, but by then the contest had been decided. In 1944, in *Smith v. Allwright*, the United States Supreme Court upset that applecart.[13] In a case that arose in Texas, the Court rejected the Democratic Party's argument that it was a private organization and the primary was a private function; therefore, the equal protection clause of the Constitution did not apply. The primary, the Court noted, was provided for and operated pursuant to Texas statutes,

and it was inextricably linked to the general election. Under those conditions, the right to vote in the primary could not be restricted to white
voters. The Alabama Democratic Executive Committee reacted with alac-
rity. With the support of the committee, the chairman recommended to
the legislature "changes he deemed advisable in Alabama's election laws
to meet the 'Texas case,' under which Democratic primaries could no longer be limited to white voters." The emblem of the party, the chairman
reminded his constituency, was a crowing rooster, with the words "White
Supremacy" emblazoned above it and the words "For the Right" below
it. "It is entirely proper that the State Democratic Executive Committee
should lead the fight to maintain the traditions of our Party in this state by
adopting the proposed amendment to our Constitution and endeavoring,
as far as it can legally be done, to make the Democratic Party in Alabama
the 'White Man's Party.'"[14]

The proposed amendment was deceptively simple: it provided that
only those persons who could "understand and explain" any article of the
U.S. Constitution could be registered to vote. Its mechanics were ruthless:
registrars had complete discretion, pursuant to which they could choose
to query only black voters and could reject out of hand their answers. It
was too much for Richard Rives. He opposed the amendment in a public debate, where his opponents were, as described by the *Montgomery
Advertiser*, "a prominent Birmingham lawyer who was Grand Cyclops of
the Ku Klux Klan and the very conservative Gov. Frank Dixon."[15] Speaking
to the public, in 1946 in Alabama, Richard Rives made a calculated appeal
to his audience's better instincts.

> When we use arbitrary law as the basis for white supremacy, we are build-
> ing on quicksand. But when we assert the white man's leadership in terms
> of intelligence, character and sense of justice, we are building upon a solid
> foundation of rock. . . . The chains we forge to shackle qualified Negroes can
> be used to keep white voters of Alabama from walking to the polls. These
> chains would not only breed resistance in the Negro, but, far worse, would
> rub a moral cancer on the character of the white man.[16]

In his appeal to the members of the bar, he was more direct. "Let us be
frank and honest with ourselves. You and I know that the people of our
State are expected to adopt this Amendment in order to give the Registrars
arbitrary power to exclude Negroes from voting."[17] An opponent, also a

prominent attorney, conceded the point: "I earnestly favor a law that will make it impossible for a Negro to qualify." Richard Rives lost the battle but won the war. The Boswell Amendment passed handily, but, as Rives had predicted over and over, it was immediately challenged and held unconstitutional.[18]

In 1951, the year before *Brown v. Board of Education* was docketed, Richard Rives's opposition to the Boswell Amendment did not become an issue that thwarted his chance to sit on the Fifth Circuit. Nominations were still relatively uncontroversial, and organized opposition on the basis of a nominee's political views was rare. When the note confirming his nomination by President Truman was passed to him, only one barrier remained: his own integrity. Richard Rives needed advice and support, and the one person who could best provide both was at hand. After Rives left the courtroom, he went by the office of his old friend from Alabama, Hugo Black. Careful not to speak of the case he had argued, he reminded Justice Black of what Black already knew: Rives had "never seen the inside of a law school." He had a practice he enjoyed and more than three decades of lawyering under his belt, but there were important areas of federal law of which he knew nothing. With Hugo Black he could be candid; he wasn't sure he was up to the job. Black was reassuring. Cases that reached the court of appeals, like those that reached the Supreme Court, were often very close, he pointed out. They could legitimately go either way. Then he delivered his punch line: "You can't do any real harm," he told his old friend.[19]

Richard Rives took his seat in 1951. On August 4, 1954, he was joined on the court by President Eisenhower's first appointment, Elbert Tuttle. Before year's end, on November 11, 1954, Judge Edwin Holmes took senior status, opening up a seat. That sent the Eisenhower team on a search for a qualified Republican in Holmes's home state, Mississippi. There was no one like Elbert Tuttle or John Minor Wisdom in Mississippi, no one who had seen the crippling effect of the state's white Democratic Party and devoted himself to creating a strong Republican Party, no one who had committed himself to Eisenhower and made a difference in the nomination process. Eisenhower turned to Ben F. Cameron of Meridian, Mississippi. In 1928 Cameron identified himself with the Republican Party when he campaigned for Herbert Hoover because he was unhappy with Al Smith's stand against Prohibition. In return, Hoover appointed Cameron as U.S. attorney for the Southern District of Mississippi, an office Cameron held from 1929 to 1933. Since then, Cameron had not been active in either political party.

In 1955 federal judicial nominations were not subject to the scrutiny that accompanies them now, but they were vetted through the American Bar Association (ABA) and, in the case of southern judges, the NAACP. Cameron was deemed acceptable by both. Nonetheless, Herbert Brownell was wary. Senator James O. Eastland warmly supported Cameron, and that raised red flags. On the other hand, John Minor Wisdom, a Republican colleague of whom Brownell thought very highly, put in a call on Cameron's behalf. Wisdom called because Blanc Monroe, a New Orleans attorney and chief counsel for the Southern Railroad, asked him to. From what Wisdom knew of Cameron, he was well read, intelligent, and a highly respected trial attorney. "At Blanc Monroe's urging," he recalled, "I gave a very strong recommendation of Cameron."[20] Even with Wisdom's call and the NAACP's approval on the record, Brownell remained concerned. He had Deputy Attorney General Bill Rogers call Cameron, but in an hour-long conversation Rogers did not find out anything disqualifying. Cameron did not, for example, belong to the local Citizens' Council, a middle- and upper-class version of the Klan that enjoyed great popularity across the South.[21] Cameron finally suggested to Rogers, "I think you will find I'm just a nice old gentleman." In many ways he was. Like Tuttle, Cameron neither drank nor smoked; he was "a somewhat scholarly man who shunned an active social life."[22] Cameron was devoted to his two sons and to his wife, to whom he wrote a love letter each year on her birthday. As a young man, he volunteered to coach football at the local high school; later, he fearlessly led a struggle to shut down a red light district. As a member of the court, however, Ben Cameron was an obstructionist, in one infamous instance entering four stays in an attempt to block James Meredith from enrolling at the University of Mississippi.[23] His endorsement by the NAACP remains a mystery, although Cameron had once made a one-hundred-dollar gift to Piney Woods College, a black college in Mississippi; he himself was said to have thought that accounted for the NAACP's position.[24] It was one they would regret. Judge Cameron turned out to be the NAACP's nemesis and Tuttle's as well.

The Cameron appointment had moved quickly; Judge Holmes did not vacate his seat until November 30, 1954, and Cameron was sworn in on March 16, 1955. Meanwhile, Judge Strum, who sat in the Northern District of Florida, had died in July 1954, and although Warren Jones's name surfaced almost immediately, he had not been nominated. Tuttle was frustrated by the delay. He didn't know Warren Jones well, but he liked his record. Jones had moved to Jacksonville, Florida, in 1926. Like Tuttle in Atlanta, he arrived with little besides his education and his ability; as they did with Tuttle, they served him well. Jones had enjoyed a successful practice, founded a prominent law firm, and served as president of the Chamber of Commerce and of the local and state bar associations.[25]

Jones was also like Tuttle in that he was not a native of the Deep South. Born and raised in Gordon, Nebraska, Jones was a 1924 honors graduate of the University of Denver Law School. Gordon lies in the Sand Hills, in northwestern Nebraska. Pine Ridge Indian Reservation, home to the Oglala Sioux and site of the 1890 massacre at Wounded Knee, lies just over the state line in southwestern South Dakota. As a child, Jones was highly aware of the nearby reservation; his own community would occasionally take precautions in fear of conflict with the Indians. He had positive associations as well. Buffalo Bill Cody used Pine Ridge Sioux in his Wild West Show, and Jones's father, an occasional physician, performed medical exams of the performers. Jones could recall seeing Buffalo Bill consulting with Red Cloud and watching the Sioux perform their traditional dances. More history came his way through stories told by his grandfather Marlow Jones. As a young man, Marlow worked in a livery stable in Springfield, Illinois, at a time when Abraham Lincoln was riding the circuit as an Illinois state judge. Marlow Jones sometimes drove Lincoln's buggy, and he could recount a number of conversations with the Great Emancipator. Warren Jones could remember his grandfather recounting his tales, but he couldn't recall the substance of them. Nonetheless, the stories contributed to Jones's lifelong interest in Lincoln. By his death, he had collected some thirty-two hundred volumes about Lincoln.[26]

After serving stateside during World War I, Jones used his veterans' benefits to enroll in law school at the University of Denver. He graduated cum laude in 1924. Like Tuttle, by the time he graduated he had a wife and a child to support. Lured by the "Florida Boom," he wrote law firms in Jacksonville and received an offer from Fleming, Hamilton, Diver & Lichliter; the senior partner, Francis Fleming, was chairman of the State Board of Bar Examiners and the son of a former governor. Jones started in title work, but he soon moved to commercial and banking law and developed a specialty in trusts and estates.[27] Sutherland and Tuttle handled a good deal of trust work; it may be in that connection that Tuttle met Jones.

Before Tuttle left Washington to assume his own seat on the court, he had dinner with the Brownells and the Humphreys. Herbert Brownell, Eisenhower's attorney general, had been instrumental in Tuttle's appointment; George Humphrey, the secretary of the treasury and Tuttle's boss in Washington, had enthusiastically endorsed him. Brownell was sensitive to civil rights, some thought more sensitive than Eisenhower himself.[28] As an attorney, he understood the importance of the federal judges in the South. It was Brownell who vetted the Eisenhower nominees with an eye to nominating only men who could be expected to carry out the mandate of *Brown*.[29] Brownell was considering Warren Jones to fill the seat on the Fifth Circuit created by Judge Strum's death. At dinner, he asked Tuttle if he knew Jones well enough to appraise him. Tuttle responded that he "had met Mr. Jones several times in a business way, was very favorably impressed with him and knew that he had a fine reputation among the lawyers of the bar."[30]

Tuttle did not let the matter rest there. Upon his return to Georgia, he made discreet inquiries of a few Jacksonville attorneys as well as a few trusted personal friends who lived in Jacksonville. In early November he wrote Brownell to report the result of his inquiries. "The answer is uniformly to the effect that Warren would be an excellent choice for a judicial appointment. My own conclusion, based on all I have heard as well as on my personal observation, is that I would be very glad to sit with Warren as a member of this Court." Tuttle concluded the letter to Brownell with a personal note. "I can't tell you how appreciative I am of your thoughtfulness in the consideration you have given me in this appointment. I can only wish for you the same degree of relaxed and professional leisure for the next two years that I anticipate for myself."[31] *Brown I* had been decided the previous May; *Brown II*, with its temporizing formula of "all deliberate speed," would be handed down the next May. Judge Elbert Tuttle sat in the eye of the storm but did not yet realize it; he did not foresee the outright defiance of the rule of law that so many of the South's political and civic leaders would engage in.

Brownell answered Tuttle's letter warmly and promptly. "Many thanks for your letter about Mr. Warren Jones, which will be most helpful. I am delighted to know that you are enjoying your new activities. We hope to see you here from time to time."[32] Other than that, Tuttle heard nothing about Jones's proposed nomination. Sometime that spring, after Cameron joined the court, Tuttle called friends in Washington. "Why in the world don't you go ahead with Warren Jones' appointment," he asked. "You can't get a better lawyer in the state of Florida." It was good that he called. It seemed that there was some concern about Jones being closely related to a national committeeman from Florida. Tuttle thought that was a nonissue. The matter moved forward; on March 4, 1955, the president nominated Jones for a seat on the Fifth Circuit, and he was sworn in on May 6, 1955. With Jones's appointment, in less than two years President Eisenhower had put three judges on the United States Court of Appeals for the Fifth Circuit. There were more to come.

Robert Russell of Georgia, brother of Senator Richard Russell, died on January 18, 1955. In 1955 there were six states in the Fifth Circuit: Alabama, Florida, Georgia, Louisiana, Mississippi, and Texas. After Robert Russell's death, there were six judges in active service, one from each state. In 1954, when Congress created a seventh seat, Texas felt entitled to it, but that seat had gone to Tuttle, giving Georgia, for a brief time, two judges of the seven. When Robert Russell died, Eisenhower acceded to his Texas supporters and agreed to replace Russell with a judge from Texas. As soon as it became apparent that the seat would go to Texas, John R. Brown got in line.[33]

Brown had been a member of a contested Eisenhower delegation at the 1952 convention, but, unlike Tuttle and Wisdom, he had not played a pivotal role. Born in Nebraska in 1909, he was younger than Tuttle (born in 1897) and Wisdom (1905). John Brown had attended the University of Nebraska and then gone on to the University of Michigan for law school. He graduated with honors, drove to Texas, and, as he liked in later years to remind law clerks who were courted by firms, pounded the pavement looking for a job. He found one with a Houston firm, Royster & Rayzor, that specialized in admiralty work. Brown mastered admiralty law, an unlikely specialty for a boy from Nebraska, but it was the Great Depression, and bright young attorneys learned what they needed to know. As he learned about admiralty law in the port city of Houston, he learned about racism in the American South. Only one black man had lived in Holdrege, Nebraska, where Brown grew up; he shined shoes at a barber shop, and Brown was casually friendly with him. Black Americans were not much in evidence at either the University of Nebraska or the University of Michigan. Those he did encounter seemed to blend in. Thus, it came as a shock to John Brown to see the judge and jurors in a Houston trial visibly react when his partner addressed a black witness as "Mister."

During World War II Brown served as a port administrator in the Philippines; at war's end he returned to Houston and to the firm. In 1947 one of the largest disasters in American history occurred in Texas City, near Galveston, when two ships loaded with the fertilizer ammonium nitrate exploded at a dock. Much of Texas City was destroyed, 565 people were killed, and more than 2,000 people were injured. As fallout, some 273 suits were filed against the United States under the Federal Tort Claims Act by the hundred or so attorneys involved. The parties agreed to consolidate the cases and agreed on a working committee of attorneys who would try the consolidated suit. John Brown was on the working committee. The court tried the issue of liability first and found for the plaintiffs. Brown and his colleagues had won a tremendous victory. Damages had not been ruled upon, but claims totaled some $70 million. The government appealed; John Brown was one of only seven attorneys on the brief for the plaintiffs. They lost their verdict in 1952 when the Fifth Circuit, sitting en banc, reversed the trial court's ruling on liability.[34] Judge Rives wrote the opinion for the court; Chief Judge Hutcheson, the only judge from Texas, dissented. The case was settled when the government paid out $16 million. Despite the loss on appeal, John Brown had burnished his reputation by emerging as a lead attorney in the complex litigation for the Texas City case. It would, however, return to haunt him.

John Brown's confirmation hearing opened on May 25, 1955, before a special subcommittee of the Senate Judiciary Committee. Senator Lyndon Johnson of Texas indicated by a blue slip, according to committee rules, that he had no objection to the nomination. Letters from the committees on the Federal Judiciary of the State Bar of Texas and of the American Bar Association recommending confirmation were introduced. The third member of the special subcommittee, Senator Daniel, a former attorney general of Texas, presented Brown as "one of the outstanding attorneys of the State Bar of Texas." Brown, Daniel went on, "has had wide experience in the federal courts, [is] a man of high character, of experience and ability, which I think will fit him to make an excellent member of the United States Circuit Court. I highly recommend him to the committee."[35]

At that point, Senator Butler noted that he had a request from Senator Kefauver to hold the record open for a few days. The committee adjourned. Then the storm broke. Muckraking Washington columnist Drew Pearson published charges that Brown had altered bills of lading in the Texas City disaster litigation. On June 4, 1955, Brown sent a wire to the members of the court: "I want to assure each of you that there is no basis whatsoever to the charges being made against me by some unidentified source. I am confident that these baseless charges will be rejected."[36] Tuttle had successfully headed off untrue criticism by Pearson prior to his own confirmation as general counsel to the Treasury Department.[37] He immediately took Brown's side, responding by letter the same day:

> Receipt of your telegram reminded me that I had failed to carry out an immediate impulse that came to me when I first saw this scurrilous matter. I intended then to write you a note of encouragement, but the rush of leaving for New Orleans for the last time this year caused me to overlook it.
>
> Please know that we have almost all had our bouts with this type of yellow journalism, and my feelings are first sympathy for the victim, and second a feeling of outrage that such a thing is possible.
>
> I hope you are not too greatly embarrassed by the delay inevitably caused by the throwing of this stink bomb.[38]

The special subcommittee reconvened on July 15. The first witness, Charles E. Goodell, an assistant attorney general, explained that questions about Brown's conduct in the Texas City disaster litigation had surfaced in the course of his background check. After a thorough investigation, Goodell reported, "We were . . . convinced that there was nothing in here which was in any way blameworthy of Mr. Brown and that convinced us that it should not be a smudge upon his record in any way."[39]

The next witness, Joseph Cash, did not agree. Cash had come into the litigation some fifteen months after the explosion. Appointed as a special assistant attorney general, he joined George John on the trial team; in the Washington office, Assistant Attorney General Graham Morrison, chief of the Claims Division, oversaw the litigation. Cash accused John Brown of having fraudulently manipulated the evidence by altering the bills of lading.

After Cash testified, Assistant Attorney General Morrison appeared before the committee. Morrison did not support Cash's charge.[40] He had, however, been infuriated by what he termed the "unreasonable harassment" of the government's attorneys by the working committee of attorneys, of which John Brown had been a member. Morrison had considered their litigation strategy so unacceptably aggressive that he had referred the matter for investigation as to whether a criminal indictment should issue. According to him, that matter was dropped because the government feared charges that it was using criminal processes to harass plaintiffs' attorneys.[41]

Finally, John Brown addressed the committee. He explained that when he had heard about the disaster, he had driven straight to Galveston: "I knew we lost two ships and many men had been killed and I knew I would be needed when I got down there."[42] Brown reached Galveston in time for a hurried investigatory hearing held by the Coast Guard the morning after the *High Flyer*, his client's vessel, exploded. At that meeting he was stunned to learn that the material that had blown up—ammonium nitrate fertilizer—had been produced in government ordnance plants and shipped by rail to Texas City. That meant the U.S. government might be the negligent party. As an admiralty lawyer, Brown knew that the official bill of lading could not be issued until loading was complete because it described what had actually been loaded. It was customary for the carrier who delivered the goods to prepare a bill prior to delivery and for the carrier who received the goods to issue it to confirm delivery. John Brown told his client, the Lykes Brothers Steamship Company, not to issue bills of lading until he could approve them. Before approving them, he had the designations on the documents—"Ammonium Nitrate Fertilizer" and "Ammonium Nitrate" and, in one instance, "Fertilizer Compound"—changed to the officially recognized designation "Ammonium Nitrate-Oxidating Material."

After Brown testified, one final witness appeared—George John, Cash's cocounsel at trial.[43] John had sent a telegram strongly endorsing Brown to the committee in early June, when the scandal erupted; he reiterated his support in a short statement. Only one matter remained. Senator O'Mahoney, the chair of the subcommittee, introduced into the record the telegram that John Brown had sent to the members of the court after Drew Pearson printed his attack as well as responses from the three judges who had been on the panel that heard the Texas City appeal, Chief Judge

Hutcheson and Judges Borah and Rives. Judge Rives's reply was typical of that of his colleagues: "The baseless attacks have not altered my high opinion of you as a lawyer and as a man," he wrote Brown. "I am confident of your confirmation and will be proud to serve on the Court with you."[44] The Senate was satisfied, and John Brown was confirmed on July 27, 1955.[45] He took his seat that September.

Another year passed before the last vacancy President Eisenhower filled occurred. On December 31, 1956, Judge Wayne Borah of Louisiana took senior status. John Minor Wisdom, who had deferred to Tuttle in 1954, was now ready to fulfill his long-held ambition and join the court. Wisdom's ability was unquestioned and his political claim strong—he had played a critical role in garnering the nomination for Eisenhower in 1952, and, in the intervening years, he had continued to build the party as the Republican national committeeman from Louisiana. Nonetheless, Wisdom ran into stormy weather, first in securing the nomination, then in obtaining confirmation.

Years earlier, Wisdom had passed up a sure nomination, certain his time would come again. Now a Louisiana seat had opened, but former governor Robert F. Kennon wanted it too. Kennon was a Democrat, but he had been the first southern Democratic governor to endorse Eisenhower. Kennon had other Republican allies; in particular, he was close to Sherman Adams, Eisenhower's chief of staff.[46] Wisdom knew Adams too—"Adams was friendly with me, but he may have been more friendly with Kennon."[47] In the end, according to Herbert Brownell, Eisenhower himself made the choice, "in part because of [Wisdom's] 'better record as a lawyer.'"[48] Moreover, according to Brownell, appointing Wisdom "was especially significant in signaling the administration's commitment to enforcing desegregation." Kennon had supported Eisenhower for president, but he "remained a staunch segregationist."[49]

Nomination in hand, Wisdom proceeded to his confirmation hearing before the special subcommittee on nominations. The hearing opened on April 29, 1957, in Washington, with Senator James O. Eastland of Mississippi presiding. Eastland was chair of the special subcommittee as well as of the Senate Judiciary Committee itself. Elected to the Senate in 1942, Eastland became chair of the Judiciary Committee in 1956. He held that chairmanship an unprecedented twenty-two years, until his resignation from the Senate at the end of 1978. Prior to Eastland's election to the Senate, he held a seat vacated by the death of Senator Pat Harrison. In those few months, from June 30 to September 28, 1941, he rose to the Senate floor more than once to complain about possible "mongrelization" of the races. Running for the Senate for the first time, in 1942, he promised to stop blacks and whites from eating together—in Washington. They did not eat together in Mississippi. If Eastland had his way, they never would.

Wisdom's nomination unsettled Eastland. By 1956 it had become clear that the southern states would not comply with the mandate of *Brown v. Board of Education* voluntarily. All but three southern senators, Lyndon Johnson, Estes Kefauver, and Albert Gore, had signed the Southern Manifesto, which denounced *Brown*, denounced the Court for overstepping its bounds and issuing *Brown*, and approved resistance to integration by any lawful means.[50] If desegregation occurred, it would be under court order—federal court order. Who sat on the Fifth Circuit had become critical.

In Senator Allen J. Ellender's introductory remarks, he declared himself neutral. Attorneys, by and large, gave Wisdom high marks, Ellender reported, but he had received a number of letters from constituents who objected because of Wisdom's "contacts in Louisiana with the Urban League and participation in matters which they thought were below the dignity of the person aspiring for the position of Judge."[51] Six witnesses showed up, four against Wisdom and two in favor. The two in favor were Harry McCall, a New Orleans attorney who was president elect of the Louisiana State Bar Association, and Payne Breazeale, a Baton Rouge attorney who was a past president of the Louisiana State Bar. The four opposed were Dr. Emmet Irwin, a New Orleans surgeon; Robert Chandler, a Shreveport attorney; Cecil Pettepher, a New Orleans businessman; and William Dane, a Taft Republican. Pettepher and Dane were political opponents from within the Republican Party. Chandler allowed that Wisdom had a good reputation as an attorney but argued that he had no judicial experience and that he was too political. Dr. Irwin leveled a plethora of charges, some quite serious, but all based on hearsay at best. On that first day, none of the opponents mentioned race.

Wisdom himself brought up his membership on the board of the New Orleans Urban League.

WISDOM: There is only one other point I would like to make, and that is in regard to the Urban League. There may have been a good many—not a good many, but there may have been some objections to me because of my membership on the Board of the New Orleans League. I became interested in civic affairs, particularly Juvenile Court work and adoptions, and have served for a good many years on the Board of the Protestant Home for Babies, and was later Chairman and President of the Children's Bureau, and later of the Council of Social Agencies.

In that work I was drawn into work for the Urban League. The Urban League is an organization designed to procure better racial relations between the races, particularly in the field of employment, and particularly using the technique of moderation and conciliation and persuasion; it has never gone into court, never had a legislative lobby, never exerted any undue pressure.

I feel strongly that if conditions deteriorate between the two races, it is important to maintain channels of communication, and that an agency with a proven experience of moderation and persuasion is performing a worthwhile function.

SENATOR EASTLAND: Moderate and persuade what? What is the object now?

WISDOM: The object is to—when a friction comes up, to seek to adjust the situation so that there will be not—so that you can overcome the friction, No. 1.

SENATOR EASTLAND: Is the Urban League in New Orleans interested in the segregation question, the school integration question?

WISDOM: Not the Urban League in New Orleans.[52]

The committee adjourned but reconvened in New Orleans on May 11 and again on May 21 and 22. Dr. Irwin was back; on May 11 he was the first witness. This time he did raise race. The Urban League, he told the committee, "works hand in hand with the NAACP, which, as they say, the NAACP is like the Army—the militant branch and the Urban League works like the State Department, quietly, underhandedly and smoothly . . . like termites."[53] The political opponents were back too, with added force. New witnesses included Republican Party operatives who had been displaced by Wisdom when he took over as president of the Republican Club of Louisiana after the 1952 convention and supporters of John E. Jackson, the longtime head of the Louisiana Republican Party whom Wisdom had deposed. In their anger over Wisdom's control of the Louisiana Republican Party, they disparaged him personally with charges of cursing and drinking to excess and one insinuation of an inappropriate overture to a young woman at a party.

The serious charges of inappropriate use of influence, of accepting kickbacks, and of insisting that any post office employee seeking a promotion change his or her party registration to Republican were based on hearsay and innuendo and were, in the end, unconvincing. Wisdom conceded his control of patronage, remarking that "there is precious little of it, I may say." One serious charge, that he had used political leverage to intercede with the U.S. Customs on behalf of a client accused of smuggling cattle, had been published by Drew Pearson. Dr. Irwin had introduced that column. Wisdom pointed out that Dr. Irwin had not introduced the second column Pearson wrote, exonerating Wisdom. "I am very proud of the fact that I am one of the few people who got what is in the nature of a retraction by Mr. Pearson. . . . He said that there was no political pull and no political pressure."[54] At the end of the day, there were no serious, supported allegations that would derail a nomination. There was the matter of Wisdom's attitudes on race. Observers expected Senator Eastland to oppose Wisdom's confirmation. There were too many red flags, from the Urban League to the fact that he had a Jewish law partner. The largest red flag—the fact that he had spent so much of his adult life building a viable Republican Party in order to challenge the stranglehold of the white Democratic Party of Louisiana—was the most provocative and the most telling. Yet Senator Eastland announced himself "satisfied" with the nomination, and on June 24, 1956, the Judiciary Committee voted unanimously in Wisdom's favor.

Many tales have been told to explain Eastland's action. One version has it that he simply made "one of his 'famous' arrangements" with Attorney General Bill Rogers.[55] As powerful as he was, Senator Eastland could not generate a nomination to the federal bench; that power lay with the president. If the administration "owed" Eastland, he could arrange for a name to go forward that would not otherwise be deemed acceptable. Another version has it that Eastland felt indebted to John Wisdom for his help earlier with Judge Ben Cameron of Mississippi. Eisenhower had hesitated to nominate Cameron, in part because Eastland supported him. It had helped Cameron considerably that John Minor Wisdom had given Cameron a "very strong recommendation."[56] A third version had Wisdom calling Cameron and asking him to tell Eastland that Wisdom "would go no further in his civil rights opinions than Cameron would."[57] Wisdom denied making any call. "I didn't have to ask Cameron for any help, I knew he would help me without any request, and I never did ask him for any help, but I felt certain in my own mind that he would help me."[58] Wisdom's own explanation for Eastland's compliance in his confirmation was that he and Eastland "were both Southerners from the same social and economic class and . . . I was precisely the kind of guy he was comfortable dealing with." Moreover, Wisdom had not yet "developed any public position on controversial civil rights issues such as school segregation."[59]

If Eastland did feel comfortable that Wisdom was a conservative southerner of the ilk of himself and Cameron, he was quickly disabused of that notion. Wisdom was sworn in on July 13, 1957. In September he granted a stay of execution to Edgar Labat, a black man who had been convicted of aggravated rape of a white woman. Labat's attorneys argued that he had been denied a fair trial because black citizens were systematically excluded from grand and petit juries in Louisiana. Nine years later, after "tortuous ascents and descents through the courts," including three orders by the United States Supreme Court and nine stays of execution, Wisdom wrote an opinion that is a classic of civil rights jurisprudence, ruling for Labat.[60] Eastland did not have to wait that long to realize he had made a mistake; Wisdom's granting the stay told the tale.

Eisenhower had two full years of his second term left, but Wisdom proved to be Eisenhower's last appointment to the Fifth Circuit. It was enough. Of seven active judges, Eisenhower had appointed five: Tuttle, Cameron, Jones, Brown, and Wisdom. When Tuttle became chief judge in late 1960, these men, plus Judges Hutcheson and Rives, made up the United States Court of Appeals for the Fifth Circuit, the federal appellate court with jurisdiction over most of the critical litigation of the civil rights revolution.[61] Many federal trial court judges in the South were obstructionists, but in a remarkable turn of history, at that point in time only one of the seven judges of the Fifth Circuit, Judge Ben F. Cameron of Mississippi, was committed to preserving Jim Crow segregation.

In 1961 the Omnibus Judgeship Bill created seventy-one new judge-ships, including two seats on the Fifth Circuit Court of Appeals and several district court judgeships. Chief Judge Tuttle traveled to Washington to speak to Attorney General Robert Kennedy about the judgeships. He wanted to make sure that Kennedy recognized the import of membership in a Citizens' Council, the white-collar Ku Klux Klan. As the *Montgomery Advertiser* editorialized on November 30, 1954, "The manicured Kluxism of these White Citizens Councils is rash, indecent and vicious." Still, many prominent lawyers throughout the South belonged. As Citizens' Councils gained in power, few resisted the pressure to join, and most voices against them were muted.[62] Tuttle considered membership in a Citizens' Council as disqualifying as membership in the Klan, and he wanted to be sure Kennedy understood that. While Tuttle was there, Kennedy asked him whom the president should nominate for the Fifth Circuit. That was easy for Tuttle—Skelly Wright.

Even before the Omnibus Judgeship Bill was signed by President Kennedy on May 20, 1961, speculation soared that Judge Skelly Wright of New Orleans might move up. He had been serving as a district court judge in New Orleans since 1950, and in the eyes of many, his service had been exemplary, in large part because he had stayed the course in the school desegregation cases despite enormous pressure. Both Judge Tuttle and Judge Wisdom had commended him to Burke Marshall, chief of the Justice Department's Civil Rights Division. They told Marshall that if Wright were to be "passed over, it would be regarded by all judges as a punishment for his unflinching enforcement of *Brown v. Board of Education.*"[63] Everyone who was paying attention knew that if Wright were passed over, it would be because of his stalwart implementation of *Brown.* Louisiana senator Russell Long made that clear when he vowed that Wright would be appointed "over my dead body." Senator James O. Eastland of Mississippi, the powerful chair of the Senate Judiciary Committee, was among Judge Wright's sworn enemies. Complicating matters for the president, Eastland took credit for holding up the bill until a Democratic administration was in office, and Senator Long told President Kennedy that appointing Wright would cost the Democrats his Senate seat. He would not be reelected in 1962, he explained, if Wright were appointed.[64] He was likely right about that. Just a year before, on November 23, 1960, an extraordinary session of the Louisiana legislature had been interrupted by a "mourners' march" commemorating November 14, 1960, when a handful of African American children had first attended white public schools in New Orleans. The pa-raders carried a coffin in which lay a blackened doll dressed in judicial robes and labeled "Smelly Wright." Louisiana lawmakers gave the march-ers a standing ovation.[65] In the fall of 1961 Judge Wright received a phone call from the attorney general. Robert Kennedy told Wright he had been holding up the two appointments to the Fifth Circuit, hoping he could get Wright confirmed. Now Kennedy had given up. Adding that he had "checked again with the Senators," he told Wright what he had told Tuttle months earlier: "It's impossible."[66]

With Judge Wright out of the way, the Kennedy administration moved quickly to fill the new seats. The president's nominees, Griffin Bell of Georgia and Walter Gewin of Alabama, received their commissions on October 5, 1961, and began to sit at once. No confirmation hearings slowed up their initial appointments; with Congress in recess, Kennedy could and did put them right to work. Their recess appointments were good until the end of the next term of the Senate; confirmation hearings for both men would open in January. Walter Pettus Gewin's hearing came first. On Wednesday, January 24, Senator Olin Johnston opened the hearing before the subcommittee on nominations of the Judiciary Committee, composed of Senator Olin Johnston (D-S.C.), Senator James O. Eastland (D-Miss.), and Senator Roman Hruska (R-Neb.). Both the senators from Alabama, Lister Hill and John Sparkman, knew Gewin, and each had returned a blue slip indicating he approved the nomination. Not only that, both showed up to testify. The ABA had found the nominee "exceptionally well qualified," and the senators joined in fulsome praise. The double-spaced transcript of the hearing covers a mere eight pages; no one objected to the nominee.

The subcommittee convened again on Tuesday, January 30, to take up the nomination of Griffin Boyette Bell. Both of Georgia's senators, Richard Russell and Herman Talmadge, had returned blue slips indicating approval. The ABA had found Bell "well qualified." Senator Talmadge appeared and spoke; he had, he said, known Bell some fifteen years. "He is a man of character, honor, integrity, ability, capacity, and, in my judgement, he is well qualified for the appointment," he told the committee. Senator Russell could not appear because of a conflict, but he sent his executive secretary to express his regrets and to report that he joined in Senator Talmadge's remarks. Noting that "there is no opposition to [this] appointment whatsoever," Senator Johnston adjourned the hearing. The transcript is a scant four and one-half pages long. Less than a week later, on February 5, 1962, both Bell's and Gewin's nominations, along with a long list of others, were approved by the Senate in a unanimous consent agreement.[67]

Tuttle was not heartened. Sailing through Senator Eastland's Judiciary Committee and then through the Senate with the enthusiastic support of the senators of Alabama and Georgia did not bode well. He did not know Walter Gewin, who did not have much of a political biography. Although Gewin had been president of the Alabama Bar Association and had served a four-year term in the state legislature, his nomination was an accident of history. Gewin's law partner, Marc Ray "Foots" Clement, an advisor to Senator Lister Hill, had served as Kennedy's campaign manager in Alabama; it was Clement who was in line for the nomination. Clement unexpectedly fell gravely ill; before he died, he made it clear he wanted the judgeship to go to his partner, and that wish was honored.[68] Tuttle could take heart from the fact that his friend and colleague on the court, Richard Rives, supported Gewin's nomination. Also, Clement had been known for mentoring progressive, politically ambitious young men. Gewin, however, was steeped in the Jim Crow culture of Alabama, and he believed firmly in the good faith of state officials. Senator Eastland could see that, and he was counting on it.[69]

Griffin Bell was another matter. Tuttle knew Bell's political history too well. Tuttle had watched Ernest Vandiver's 1958 campaign for governor of Georgia move from a moderate (for the times) position on race to one dominated by the demagogic slogan "No, not one." No, not one Georgia child would attend an integrated school during his administration, he would thunder, and the crowd would thunder back.[70] Griffin Bell had been Vandiver's chief of staff. At that time in Georgia, the governor's chief of staff was an unpaid position. The holder had enormous prestige and significant political power by virtue of the office; that was pay enough. Bell was a trusted confidant and a valued advisor. That he had been part of Vandiver's campaign, which had been premised on defiance of *Brown*, was unsettling. On the other hand, Griffin Bell's major contribution to the Vandiver administration was the concept that led to the Sibley Commission. With public school desegregation litigation pending, Bell suggested to Vandiver that he "create a committee composed of outstanding citizens who would be required to hold one hearing in each of the state's ten congressional districts.

These hearings would allow any person who desired to be heard on this issue to give testimony." Vandiver lined up John Sibley, one of Georgia's most prominent citizens, to chair the committee.[71]

Valedictorian of his law school class at the University of Georgia in 1911, Sibley and his brother won their first case in the Georgia Supreme Court in 1913. Soon he formed a friendship with Robert Woodruff and became general counsel to the Coca-Cola Company. In 1946, when his good friend T. K. Glenn died, Sibley took over as chairman of the board of the Trust Company Bank. Although his standing could hardly be overstated, Sibley, somewhat disingenuously, attributed his selection to a simpler reason: he had been born and raised in rural Georgia, so he knew how the country people thought, but he had made his way in Atlanta, and he knew how the city people thought too.[72]

John Sibley combined a commanding presence with a human touch. He believed in segregation, and he made no bones about it, but he also believed in the importance of stability. He did not support *Brown v. Topeka*; in a 1960 speech he called it "clearly erroneous" and an invasion of "the function of the law-making branch of government." Still, he recognized, "the decision . . . is binding upon the courts and upon the people and will be enforced and must be obeyed."[73] He opened each hearing with a dramatic statement: "Although that decision [Brown] is devoid of legal reasoning and sociological validity, and sets in motion racial tensions, hatred, and violence, it is binding upon the lower federal courts and will be enforced by them, notwithstanding the evil effect that such enforcement will entail[,] that is certain."[74] Those who appeared were asked to select between two options: close down all the schools rather than integrate any, or allow for a local option so that communities could decide whether to integrate or to close. Speakers at the hearings were allowed to make brief statements; those who rambled on would be politely but firmly asked by Chairman Sibley to select an option. It was a remarkable undertaking. It let people vent, and vent they did. Some hard-line segregationists wanted to maintain segregation at any cost, even the cost of lives. Others wanted to maintain it at great cost, but perhaps not at the cost of all public education. Black people were often eloquent in their simple expressions of frustration and hurt. Not all wanted integrated schools, but none wanted the unequal system that existed, and true equality of two separate systems, as one speaker noted, would bankrupt the state overnight. Across the state the Sibley

Commission let people say their piece but at the same time forced them to think about the consequences of digging in their heels. Not many Georgia communities could fund a school system without state support. Not many families could afford private schools, even if they existed in sufficient numbers. In the end, John Sibley reported that a majority of Georgians did not want to close the public schools. He chose not to emphasize the fact that some 60 percent wanted the schools to remain completely segregated. The Sibley Commission recommended grudging compliance with the court's desegregation order; that is, it counseled against outright defiance but proffered strategies to minimize desegregation.[75]

The creation of the Sibley Commission was Griffin Bell's political legacy when he joined the court. Griffin Bell and Walter Gewin were President Kennedy's only appointments to the Fifth Circuit. They brought the number of judges to nine.[76]

CHAPTER FOURTEEN

Justice Is Never Simple: *Brown I* and *II*

Despite all of his years in Georgia and despite his considerable political insight, Elbert Tuttle badly misread the effect that the Supreme Court's decision in *Brown v. Board of Education* would have. When he casually told a friend, "they'll fall in line," meaning the southern states would accept the mandate laid down by the court, he meant it.[1] In later years, he understood the miscalculation he had made. He had not anticipated that the political and social leaders of the South would defer to the demagogues, even join them. He thought responsible, thoughtful politicians would stand up and be counted—that at a minimum, they would say, this is the law, this is what the Supreme Court has determined our Constitution provides, and we will comply. He was not alone in his optimism. At least one "discerning southern journalist," Jonathan Daniels, editor of the *Raleigh News and Observer,* in a speech in the spring of 1954, "optimistically predicted that the South would respond to any decision the Court might make 'with the good sense and goodwill of the people of both races in a manner which will serve the children and honor America.'"[2] Shortly after the opinion was announced, John Popham reported in the *New York Times* on May 18, 1954, that "the South's reaction . . . appeared to be tempered considerably today."[3] Senator Russell B. Long of Louisiana, while making it clear that he deplored the ruling and completely disagreed with it, called for compliance. "My oath of office requires me to accept it as the law. Every citizen is likewise bound by his oath of allegiance to his country. I urge all Southern officials to avoid any sort of rash or hasty action."[4]

On the other hand, at least some of the writing was on the wall. Even before the decision in *Brown,* ardent segregationists like Herman Talmadge in Georgia had taken preemptive steps. In 1953 Talmadge proposed a short but sweeping amendment to the Georgia Constitution. It authorized using public money to provide grants directly to state citizens "for educational purposes, in discharge of all obligations of the State to provide adequate education for its citizens."[5] In other words, the amendment allowed the state to abandon the public school system and instead provide "tuition grants" that could be used at private schools, which would be beyond the reach of any Supreme Court ruling. Talmadge staked his reputation on passing the amendment, so much so that some thought its passage "essential to Talmadge's prestige." The General Assembly created the Georgia Commission on Education, "a segregationist strategy group." Talmadge himself chaired the commission; swearing in the other members in January 1954, he announced his readiness to use the state militia in the service of preserving segregation in education.[6]

Talmadge had reacted to a line of cases that culminated in two cases, decided in 1950, that presaged Brown: *Sweatt v. Painter* and *McLaurin v. Oklahoma State Regents*. Heman Marion Sweatt had applied to the law school of the University of Texas and been rejected because of his race. Texas realized that if it were to exclude citizens from state-operated schools because of race, it would have to provide "separate but equal" accommodations—that was the lesson of the Supreme Court's approval of segregated, separate but equal railroad cars in *Plessy v. Ferguson* in 1896. While several states did so by paying out-of-state tuition for black students, Texas decided to take a different route; Texas created a black law school. Without overruling the concept that separate but equal facilities satisfied the mandate of the equal protection clause, the Court found that Texas's alternative did not meet the test.

At the turn of the century, in *Plessy* itself, a majority of the justices had put blinders on and ruled that relegating black train passengers to segregated cars did not create, or bespeak, a badge of inferiority. As long as the accommodations were equal, it was not discriminatory to force black passengers into them—to forbid them passage in the white-only cars. After all, whites were forbidden access to the black cars by the same law. The only member of the Court who had been a slaveholder, Justice John Marshall Harlan of Kentucky, dissented. No justice joined him, even though he pointed out the obvious. The law did bespeak and enforce a badge of inferiority, and to pretend otherwise was to do just that—to pretend. In *Plessy* the majority articulated an absurd concept, but it was just that, a concept.

There was no contention that the accommodations provided were not, in fact, equal. In *Sweatt* the Court was asked to find an absurd fact, to find that the hastily conceived and constructed law school for blacks provided by Texas was equal to its white counterpart, the prestigious University of Texas Law School. That the Court could not, and did not, do.[7]

On the same day that the Court announced its decision in *Sweatt*, it also handed down its ruling in *McLaurin v. Oklahoma State Regents*.[8] Oklahoma had taken a different tack. After George W. McLaurin won a challenge to the Oklahoma statutes that enforced segregation by making it a misdemeanor to provide or receive an education in integrated facilities, he was admitted to the Graduate School of Education of the University of Oklahoma. The state provided him with separate accommodations. McLaurin had his own table in the cafeteria and his own table in the library; he even had his own classroom. "He was required to sit apart at a designated desk in an anteroom adjoining the classroom; to sit at a designated desk on the mezzanine floor of the library, but not to use the desks in the regular reading room; and to sit at a designated table and to eat at a different time from the other students in the school cafeteria."[9]

McLaurin went back to the three-judge district court that had struck down the Jim Crow laws and asked for an injunction requiring the university to provide "equal" facilities. The court denied relief; "while conceivable the same facilities might be afforded under conditions so odious as to amount to a denial of equal protection of the law," the lower court ruled, "we cannot find any justifiable legal basis for the mental discomfiture which the plaintiff says deprives him of equal educational facilities here."[10] While the case was on its way back to the Supreme Court, Oklahoma relented, a little. Previously, McLaurin had sat behind a rail with a sign that said "Reserved for Colored"; now he sat in a row specified for colored students—but there was no rail and no sign. He still had an assigned table in the library, but it was now on the main floor. He still had an assigned table in the cafeteria, but now he could eat at the same time as other students did. The United States Supreme Court was unimpressed. As had been the case in *Sweatt*, the Court could not regurgitate the Oklahoma position and pretend it made sense: McLaurin was not receiving the same educational opportunity as his fellow students were, and his right to equal protection under the Constitution was being violated.

Southern leaders intent on preserving segregation were concerned about *Sweatt* and *McLaurin*. They went on high alert two years later, in 1952, when the Court set for oral argument five cases challenging segregation in public school systems in Kansas, South Carolina, Virginia, Delaware, and the District of Columbia.[11] For the NAACP, having the five school cases before the Court was the culmination of decades of work under the visionary leadership of Charles Hamilton Houston. A 1922 graduate of Harvard Law School, he had been the first African American student to be elected as an editor of the *Law Review*; moreover, he had been a protégé of one of Harvard's leading faculty members, Felix Frankfurter. Under Frankfurter's tutelage, Houston had come to understand law as "social engineering" and lawyers as social engineers who "had to decide what sort of society they wanted to construct."[12] Houston knew what kind of society he wanted to construct—one that honored the promise of the equal protection clause. It was that simple, and that hard.

After practicing law with his father, Houston joined the Howard Law School faculty and became academic dean in 1929. Houston brought high standards and the rigor necessary to accomplish them. Under his guidance, the Howard University School of Law earned accreditation from the Association of American Law Schools, considerably improved its library, and attracted prominent attorneys and serious scholars, Clarence Darrow and Roscoe Pound among them, to address the students. The students could not all rise to the challenge; of the class that entered with Thurgood Marshall, only a quarter graduated with him in 1933.[13] Of that quarter, more than a few were committed to Houston's vision. By 1930 the vision had a focus—creating the best legal strategy to deal with *Plessy v. Ferguson*. When it legitimated Jim Crow seating on train cars, *Plessy* legitimated all manner of legally enforceable segregation. Houston and the NAACP understood that nothing stood more in the way of racial equality than the Supreme Court's decision in *Plessy*.

Charles Hamilton Houston served as NAACP legal counsel from 1935 to 1940; in 1936 he hired his protégé, Howard Law School graduate Thurgood Marshall, as associate counsel. When Houston died of a heart attack in 1950 at the age of fifty-four, his friends thought he had simply worked himself to death. Thurgood Marshall was a worthy heir. He built the office until by the end of 1949 he had five attorneys on staff: himself, Constance Baker Motley, Robert Carter, Jack Greenberg, and Franklin Williams. Beginning in the 1930s, the NAACP had managed to actively litigate on many fronts, including salary equalization for black teachers, jury discrimination, and voting discrimination. If there was a focus, however, it was the school cases. Marshall and his colleagues understood that if *Plessy* was to be overcome, it would happen in the schools.[14] Now, finally, in 1952 they were poised for a frontal assault on the concept of separate but equal.

The cases known collectively and colloquially as *Brown v. Board of Education* were argued from December 9 through December 12, 1952.[15] On December 13 the justices discussed the cases in conference. The conference is, by highly respected tradition, confidential. *Brown*, however, has drawn such intensive scrutiny that historians have penetrated the veil of confidentiality.[16] While there appears to have been a consensus that *Plessy* had been wrong, there was not a consensus as to why, as a constitutional matter, it was wrong or as to how to proceed. Ordinarily, the opinion would have been delivered by July, before the court went into recess. Instead, on June 8, 1953, the court ordered reargument and directed counsel to address five questions, three of which had subparts. Some of the questions sought an articulation of the constitutional theory determinative of the substantive question, Is segregation in public schools inconsistent with the Fourteenth Amendment? The last two questions strongly suggested the direction the Court was taking; they asked how the Court should effectuate its opinion if it ruled that segregation was unconstitutional.

On September 8, 1953, Chief Justice Fred M. Vinson died. On September 30, President Eisenhower nominated Earl Warren to succeed Vinson as chief justice; on October 5 Warren took his seat as a recess appointment. He had not yet been confirmed by the Senate; that confirmation would come on March 1, 1954. Because of the rise in political contentiousness over nominees, recess appointments are no longer used. It is an interesting quirk of history that when Chief Justice Earl Warren presided over the reargument of *Brown* between December 7 and 9, 1953, and presided over the Court's conferences, he had not yet been confirmed by the Senate.

Earl Warren had the political wisdom to see the importance of the Court speaking with one voice and the political skill necessary to bring it about, and he is widely credited with moving the Court to unanimity in *Brown*, although not all scholars agree. Justice Byron White's biographer, Dennis Hutchinson, calls that theory a "persistent myth" and argues that "unanimity in 1954 was the ultimate step in a gradual process that had begun with the 1950 Trilogy [*Sweatt v. Painter, McLaurin v. Oklahoma State Regents*, and *Henderson v. United States*].["17] On May 17, 1954, in an opinion written by Chief Justice Earl Warren and joined by every other justice, the Supreme Court found that segregation in public schools violated the equal protection clause of the Fourteenth Amendment. A year later, on May 31, 1955, the Court issued *Brown II* with its infamous mandate: desegregation should proceed "with all deliberate speed." The ambiguity of *Brown II* would plague the country for the next two decades. Half a century later, civil rights historian Michael Klarman concluded that it "seems to have encouraged defiance and undermined those moderates who were already taking preliminary steps toward desegregation."[18]

Elbert Tuttle found the decision disappointing from the beginning. He had thought the southern states would comply with a direct order from the Supreme Court, an order that said, for instance, that at a minimum either one grade or a certain percentage of schools in a district must be desegregated by the end of each year. "All deliberate speed" allowed segregationists to deliberately fail to comply and then to argue that they were not in noncompliance. After all, who could say how long it would take to desegregate with all deliberate speed? A federal judge could, but only after costly, laborious, time-consuming litigation.

Tuttle first sat as a judge of the Fifth Circuit the week of October 4, 1955. The court sat in panels of three and heard oral arguments in morning and afternoon sessions. After the last argument of the day, the judges held a confidential conference in which they would vote on how to decide the cases and assign the task of writing the opinion to one of their number. Tuttle took his fair share of cases from the conference and went to work. By October 22 his first three opinions had been issued: he had written them, circulated them to the other members of the court, and delivered them to West Publishing Company in time to allow them to be printed and circulated on the 22nd.[19] None of the three cases was particularly notable, nor was the way in which Tuttle handled them, except that they exemplified his approach to his work. He was decisive; once he understood the facts and the law, he made a decision and moved forward. He wrote spare, lucid opinions. Concerned with getting the job done, he did not labor over rhetorical devices or sophisticated allusions. Finally, he worked hard and efficiently. The very first opinion issued under his name involved a commercial dispute over electric motors; decades later, the court's deputy clerk,

Gilbert Ganucheau, quipped that Tuttle had been going like an electric motor ever since.

One other thing distinguished those first opinions. Of the three, one was per curiam, that is, it did not carry Tuttle's name as author. By agreement among the judges, if an opinion was less than three double-spaced pages, it was not signed. Charles Hornsbrook had filed a petition for writ of habeas corpus seeking to vacate a conviction. He had raised some seven grounds. Tuttle recited them in crisp phrases, rejected them in one paragraph, and affirmed the trial court's dismissal of the petition. It would have been a very simple matter to stretch the opinion enough to allow him to sign it. Tuttle wanted only to decide the case as fairly and quickly as possible. He took that approach with all matters before the court, including desegregation litigation. If any area demanded quick resolution, in Tuttle's mind it was civil rights. Justice—basic constitutional rights—had been long delayed, and justice delayed was justice denied. Yet in the first school desegregation case he sat on, he joined with Judge Rives in an opinion that would come to haunt the court, an opinion that, some judges felt, "held us back for years."[20]

Tuttle did not sit on the panel that issued the first desegregation order in the Fifth Circuit; that fell to Judges Hutcheson, Rives, and Brown. On October 7, 1955, three black high school students filed a complaint seeking an injunction against the Mansfield, Texas, Independent School District. All twelve of the black high school students who lived in Mansfield were bused to Fort Worth, allowing the Mansfield school to remain segregated. After a hearing, the trial court judge, Joe Ewing Estes, an Eisenhower appointee who had taken office on August 1, denied the request for an injunction. The school year had already begun, he noted, and transferring students midyear would be awkward on many levels. Moreover, in his opinion, the farmers who sat on the school board were "making the start toward 'obeying the law' which their abilities dictated."[21]

On appeal, writing for the panel, Chief Judge Hutcheson disagreed with Judge Estes's estimation of the situation. The only decision the board had made, he noted, was not to desegregate during the 1955–56 academic year. Cowed by—or perhaps in agreement with—the community sentiment against desegregation, the board had no plan to move forward. "We are going to try to desegregate as soon as we think it is practical at all," a member of the subcommittee working on the issue testified. No one knew when that might be. Where Judge Estes had found "good faith efforts toward integration," Judge Hutcheson saw stalling. The panel reversed and remanded the case to Judge Estes with instruction that an injunction declaring the plaintiffs' right to enter Mansfield High School issue forthwith. On August 27, 1956, in time to allow the students to register and attend the first day of classes, Judge Estes entered the injunction.

Like many towns in the South, Mansfield had a white Citizens' Council, a suit-and-tie Ku Klux Klan. Council members flooded the town's newspaper with letters denouncing integration of the high school; the newspaper published the letters as well as "editorials expressing extreme prosegregationist views." When a group of local ministers tried to disperse hostile crowds, the paper called them "'pin-head preachers who preach the brotherhood of man.'"[22] Moderate civil and political leaders remained silent as crosses burned in black neighborhoods and crowds gathered at the school to protest. A black effigy was hung on Main Street, another from the school itself. Finally, on August 31 Governor Allan Shivers sent in the Texas Rangers. By then, there was no need to protect black students who wanted to attend Mansfield High. No black student tried to register. They had gotten the message, and they got back on the bus to Fort Worth.

One hundred miles or so away, in Wichita Falls, Texas, in January 1956, twenty black students filed a class-action lawsuit, asking the court to certify students discriminated against by the Wichita Falls Independent School District as a class and to enjoin the district from denying them the right to attend the public school nearest their home. The district served some thirteen thousand students, of whom slightly over a thousand were black. Virtually all of the black families in Wichita Falls lived in what the court called one single concentrated area, but they did not all live in one school district. About 140 black children, including the 20 plaintiffs, lived in the Barwise School District; about 17 lived in other school districts. Yet all black children in Wichita Falls, with the exception of 14 to 16 who attended school on Sheppard Air Force Base, were assigned to one school—Booker T. Washington.

After the complaint was filed but before it was decided, the district opened a new school in Sunnyside Heights, a white section of town. All of the white students who had previously attended Barwise transferred to Sunnyside. Barwise, renamed the A. E. Holland School after a black principal at the Booker T. Washington School, reopened as a nominally desegregated school in which only black students enrolled. The result was that the schools were still segregated, but the students who had applied to Barwise and been rejected were now enrolled there. On motion of the school district, the trial court dismissed the complaint because the defendant school district said it was going "to carry out desegregation in the schools of the District during the next school term."[23] At that moment, the district argued, it could not be charged with doing anything wrong—the black students who had applied to Barwise were going to Barwise, so the lawsuit should be dismissed. The plaintiffs did not want it dismissed because they did not anticipate that the district would spontaneously desegregate the schools, and they did not want to have to start over with the time-consuming, expensive process of filing a complaint and getting a lawsuit off the ground.

On appeal, Judge Rives and Judge Tuttle, with Judge Rives writing, reversed. They agreed with the attorneys for the children, Thurgood Marshall among them, who had argued that "voluntary cessation of illegal conduct" does not make a case moot. Dismissal is only appropriate, Rives wrote, when "the court finds that there is no reasonable probability of a return to the illegal conduct[,] . . . that no disputed question of law or fact remains to be determined, [and] that no controversy remains to be settled."[24] The trial court should not have dismissed this case, Rives and Tuttle held. Rather, it should hold evidentiary hearings on the matter of the district's good-faith compliance with the mandate of *Brown v. Board of Education*, and it should retain jurisdiction so that it could ascertain or, if necessary, require good-faith compliance.

The holding in the Wichita Falls case presages the Fifth Circuit's approach to school desegregation cases. School board platitudes would not be taken at face value; technical ploys would not suffice; and the court would not be dissuaded from seeing the matter through. The opinion would be remembered, however, not for its ruling but for its dictum—material included in the opinion that was not necessary to its resolution. Judge Rives quoted a substantial chunk of the opinion of a three-judge court in South Carolina that was issued in one of the five cases decided under the rubric of *Brown v. Board of Education* after its remand. The *Briggs* court, expounding on the meaning of *Brown*, articulated in several different ways the notion that the Constitution does not require integration; rather, it forbids discrimination. Moreover, the Constitution does not forbid voluntary segregation, only segregation enforced by governmental power.[25] In isolation, the *Briggs* dictum simply sets forth important constitutional principles. In the context of dismantling state-enforced segregation that had been put into place during a century of apartheid, the *Briggs* dictum all too often wreaked havoc.

Not burdened by the distorted perception of those who had been raised in the Deep South, Elbert Tuttle did not foresee the harm the *Briggs* dictum would wreak. To his eye, governmental involvement in the continued segregation in Wichita Falls was apparent. The government of Texas, from the school board through the governor, was committed to maintaining segregation in public education and in much else of life. The school board had shown its hand when it assigned students to Holland and Sunnyside so that each school was totally segregated by race—this in the year after *Brown II* was decided. The governor had shown his hand in Mansfield first by dragging his feet and then by explaining that he was sending the Texas Rangers to Mansfield not to facilitate desegregation but to protect against the outbreak of violence.[26] The *Briggs* dictum—the recognition that the Constitution did not require integration but instead forbade segregation caused by governmental discrimination—was accurate as a matter of constitutional theory, but it was also irrelevant in most of the South. Throughout the southern states, the "government," from lowly clerks in voter registration offices to the governors themselves, was committed to enforcing racial segregation.

Judge Ben Cameron of Mississippi did not see it that way. In a lengthy dissent in the Wichita Falls case, he took Rives and Tuttle to task for not supporting the federal district court judge who had dismissed the lawsuit and who had credited the school district with having made good-faith efforts toward desegregation. Judge Cameron insisted that the court was required to defer to the trial court judge. He wrote learnedly about equity jurisdiction and movingly about the superiority of an approach that relies not on force but on persuasion, not on power but on trust. The fundamental difference between his approach and that of Rives and Tuttle has, in the end, precious little to do with legal analysis. The difference between them is the gulf of perception. Rives had come to understand what Tuttle had always known—that segregation enforced by custom and reinforced by law, that is, the way the South treated its black citizens, was a great and pernicious evil. Rives and Tuttle also understood that in many cases nothing would change unless the federal courts made it change. A deadly silence emanated from the White House, the Southern Manifesto staked out Congress's position, and state governments and local communities were increasingly held hostage by demagogues. Tuttle and Rives did not, however, foresee that the *Briggs* dictum would become a sword wielded in the service of segregation. Nor did they foresee how intransigent many school boards would prove to be.

Dallas, Texas, was a case in point. The Dallas public schools had been segregated as long as they had existed, some ninety years, when *Brown II* was decided on May 31, 1955. On September 5, 1955, twenty-seven black children applied to white schools. Not one was admitted. They filed suit, and Judge William H. Atwell was assigned to hear the case. Atwell, at eighty-six, was one of the oldest federal judges still sitting. He was also an "avowed segregationist" who apparently thought *Brown v. Board of Education* was simply wrong.[27] Twice the black Dallas schoolchildren's complaint came before him, and twice he summarily dismissed it; the first hearing took only thirty minutes. After Atwell dismissed the complaint for the second time, the Fifth Circuit panel hearing the appeal took no chances. In a brief opinion, Judges Rives, joined by Judges John Brown and Warren Jones, directed that an injunction be entered.[28] The plaintiffs, they pointed out, had been moderate in their request: "They do not pray for any immediate or en masse desegregation." Their prayer was that an order be entered requiring that the district be desegregated "with all deliberate speed." At the next hearing on the matter, Judge Atwell told counsel, "It is difficult, gentlemen, for me to approve this order, but this is a land of the law and it is my duty." He then entered an order that, instead of requiring desegregation with all deliberate speed, required that it be instantaneous. His order restrained the defendants from "requiring or permitting segregation of the races in any school under their supervision, beginning and not before the mid-Winter school term of 1957–58 [which was some four months away]."[29] Even the plaintiffs had not sought the utterly impracticable remedy of immediate desegregation of the entire Dallas school system. The school board appealed. Counsel for the school board conceded that over the two years since the suit had first been filed the school board had done virtually nothing. Not only had no steps toward desegregation been taken, no plan to manage desegregation of the huge Dallas school system was in place. The Fifth Circuit, which had been pushing Judge Atwell to move the matter forward, now found itself applying the brakes. "In our opinion on the last appeal," Judge Rives wrote, "we noted that the then appellants prayed for no more stringent order than one requiring appellees to desegregate the schools under their jurisdiction 'with all deliberate speed.'"[30] The district court should give the school authorities "a reasonable further opportunity to meet their primary responsibility," and if the plaintiffs claimed that they failed to perform their duty, they should be accorded "a full and fair hearing."[31] If the judges harbored the hope that their forbearance would generate cooperation, they were quickly disabused. Over the next two years, the only thing the Dallas Independent School District did was file a frivolous lawsuit, apparently for purposes of delay.[32]

Among the major cities in the Fifth Circuit, during the mid-1950s New Orleans, "the Big Easy," was relatively "easy" about race. New Orleans had black policemen and integrated buses, and it had opened to all races its public libraries and public recreation facilities—but not its schools.[33] The public schools had been segregated since their inception in 1877, and the schools for black children were "grossly inferior." By 1950 the black community had had enough. The NAACP Legal Defense Fund, Inc., the "Inc. Fund," was ready to support them. At a meeting at the Macarty School, an overcrowded, dilapidated frame building, the president of the PTA stepped forward. Oliver Bush, a salesman for a black-owned insurance company, had thirteen children; his son Earl Benjamin Bush became the lead plaintiff in the New Orleans school desegregation cases. *Bush v. Orleans Parish School Board* was filed on September 5, 1952.[34] In negotiations with the attorney for the school board, the plaintiffs agreed not to move forward with the lawsuit until the segregation cases, as *Brown* and its companion cases were called, were decided by the Supreme Court. After *Brown I* was decided, Louisiana amended its constitution to require segregation by race in the public schools, and the legislature passed a statute requiring pupil assignment by race. Still the Bush plaintiffs did not press forward; the NAACP was simply stretched too thin. In 1955, after *Brown II* was decided, the NAACP attorneys representing the Bush plaintiffs again petitioned the school board for relief, but they did not go back to court. The school board did, however, moving for dismissal of the lawsuit. In response, the plaintiffs asked for a declaratory judgment that the constitutional provision and the statute were invalid and an injunction ending segregation.

When it was filed, the Bush case had been assigned to Judge Skelly Wright. Now the school board asked that it be reassigned to a three-judge district court because the constitutionality of a state statute and a state constitutional provision were in question. Although the Louisiana provisions were so patently unconstitutional after *Brown I* that a three-judge court was not required, in an abundance of caution Judge Wright referred the request to Chief Judge Hutcheson, and Judge Hutcheson appointed Judges Wright, Wayne Borah, and Herbert Christenberry to a three-judge panel. On February 15, 1956, in just three paragraphs, they noted that insofar "as the provisions of the Louisiana Constitution and subordinate statutes . . . require or permit segregation of the races in public schools, they are invalid under . . . *Brown*."[35] The panel sent the case back to Judge Wright, who ruled for the plaintiffs. The school board appealed.

On appeal, Judge Tuttle wrote for the panel, joined in his opinion by Judges Rives and Brown. He affirmed Judge Wright on every ground. Tuttle addressed head-on the twin theories that segregationists promulgated in defiance of *Brown I*. Both arguments—one factual, one theoretical—were embodied in the Louisiana constitutional provision, which required mandatory segregation of the public schools "in the exercise of the state police power to promote and protect public health, morals, better education and the peace and good order of the State, and not because of race." Louisiana had introduced affidavits reciting statistics that allegedly showed blacks were inferior to whites "as to intelligence ratings, school progress, incidence of certain diseases, and percentage of illegitimate births." The state was not really discriminating on the basis of race, attorneys for the state argued; it was using race as a proxy in order to appropriately classify students with undesirable traits. Tuttle was furious. "Strangely enough," he observed, Louisiana had not tried to classify students by these traits before. A reasonable classification on the basis of the traits themselves might be legitimate, he wrote, but "*it is unthinkable* that an arbitrary classification by race because of a more frequent identification of one race than another with certain undesirable qualities would be such reasonable classification."[36]

In Louisiana's view it did not matter what Tuttle or any other federal judge thought about the constitutionality of what it was doing. In the exercise of its police power, to protect the health and welfare of its citizens, it was sovereign. This argument articulated the doctrines of interposition and nullification, the battle cries of the states' rights movement. Proponents asserted that a state can interpose itself between its citizens and the federal government and declare federal law null and void within its boundaries. As political theory, this is at odds with the central tenets of our system of government. As political rhetoric, it had considerable appeal, and demagogues who knew better did not hesitate to trumpet its legitimacy. It became important enough that Martin Luther King Jr. addressed these theories directly in his "I Have a Dream" speech: "I have a dream that one day, down in Alabama, with its vicious racists, with its governor having his lips dripping with the words of interposition and nullification, that one day right there in Alabama, little black boys and black girls will be able to join hands with little white boys and white girls as sisters and brothers."[37] In *Bush* Tuttle made short shrift of these theories. "The use of the term police power works no magic in itself. Undeniably, the States retain an extremely broad police power. This power, however, as everyone knows, is itself limited by the protective shield of the Federal Constitution." "As everyone knows": Tuttle took aim, with that phrase, at the multitude of educated people who aggressively touted this indefensible position. He cited a Supreme Court opinion that held that police power could not justify a law that conflicted with the United States Constitution, and he noted that "that principle has been so frequently affirmed in this court that we need not stop to cite the cases."[38]

Tuttle concluded the opinion with a passage that provides insight into his steely determination throughout the civil rights era: "The vindication of rights guaranteed by the Constitution cannot be conditioned on the absence of practical difficulties . . . [The adoption of the Fourteenth Amendment] implies that there are matters of fundamental justice that the citizens of the United States consider so essentially an ingredient of human rights as to require a restraint on action on behalf of any state that appears to ignore them."[39] At that point, in 1958, the *Bush* litigation should have been all but over. It wasn't. By 1962 forty-one judicial decisions had issued, forty-four statutes enacted by the Louisiana legislature had been invalidated, two state officials had been convicted of contempt, and injunctions had been issued against a state court, all state executives, and the entire Louisiana legislature.[40] Through it all, the Supreme Court never issued a full written opinion; it never had to. Judge Skelly Wright and his colleague on the federal district court for the Eastern District of Louisiana, Judge Herbert Christenberry, backed up by the judges of the Fifth Circuit, had invariably gotten it right. The federal court had stood virtually alone, but it had held its ground. Without support from the city government, the school board, the local police, or even the local bar, the court could not control the screaming mobs who came to symbolize New Orleans. Judge Skelly Wright, to whom most of the litigation fell because he sat in New Orleans, could and did insist on implementation of the mandate of *Brown*. He did it at considerable personal cost—from the loss of old friends to threats that at one time forced him out of his home. Judge Wright was one of two district court judges assigned to the Eastern District of Louisiana. His colleague Herbert Christenberry sat in Baton Rouge. When called upon, Judge Christenberry, like Judge Wright, was stalwart in his fair-handed adherence to the mandate of *Brown*. At one rally a marshal asked a protester holding a placard reading soc what it meant. "It's supposed to mean Save our Children," she replied, "but it really means Shit on Christenberry."[41]

In 1954 there were forty-eight federal district court judges in eleven southern states: the six states in the Fifth Circuit (Alabama, Georgia, Florida, Louisiana, Mississippi, and Texas) and the five in the Fourth Circuit (Maryland, North Carolina, South Carolina, Virginia, and West Virginia). Those forty-eight men were the front lines of the federal judicial system. Along with the ten judges who sat on the Fourth and Fifth Circuit courts of appeals, they are the 58 *Lonely Men* of Jack W. Pelatson's classic study of southern federal judges and school desegregation.[42] Federal judgeships traditionally went to successful attorneys with good political connections; the men who held them were leaders in their communities, with social prestige that facilitated a gracious lifestyle. Until *Brown*, to be a federal judge was to be highly regarded. In the South, for many federal judges, *Brown* changed all that. For more than a decade after *Brown I* was decided, desegregation litigation was overwhelmingly one-sided on the merits. Most of the time, black Americans were seeking to enforce long-denied basic constitutional rights, and they were entitled to prevail. Even so, when they did prevail, the judge was often castigated, even threatened. All too often, no matter the merits of the claim, they did not prevail. Several federal judges were ardent segregationists and active obstructionists—they disagreed with *Brown*, and they would play no role in implementing it. As Tuttle would come to know too well, in the Fifth Circuit, a troubling number of the federal judges could not be counted on to fulfill their oath of office. Others were nothing short of heroic.

CHAPTER FIFTEEN

From *Plessy* to *Brown* to Buses

On May 17, 1954, many observers thought that the decision in *Brown I* sounded the death knell of Jim Crow segregation. As it would turn out, they were correct, but *Brown* itself did not make that clear. Just as Charles Hamilton Houston and his colleagues at the NAACP had carefully honed in on education as the area where separate but equal was least defensible, the Supreme Court also carefully constricted the opinion to what had been argued. "Today," the Court pointed out, "education is perhaps the most important function of state and local governments." Because of the importance of public education, and because the plaintiffs had made a record that established that harm did flow from segregation in education, the Court concluded that "in the field of public education the doctrine of 'separate but equal' has no place."[1] Over the decade after *Brown* was decided, the judges of the Fifth Circuit would be called on to implement it in education cases—and to extend it to other areas. No case more dramatically highlighted what was at stake than the litigation that followed Rosa Parks's simple refusal to relinquish her seat on a Montgomery, Alabama, city bus. Ironically, although *Browder v. Gayle* is known colloquially as the Rosa Parks case, Mrs. Parks was not a party.[2]

When Rosa Parks refused to give up her seat on December 1, 1955, the arresting officer charged her with violating the Montgomery ordinance that prescribed racial segregation in public transportation. Before trial, the city attorney changed the charge to recite a violation of the state law instead of the city ordinance. At her bench trial on December 5, her attorney, Fred Gray, raised constitutional issues, which were summarily denied. Given that she had in fact violated the state law, it was not surprising that she was convicted. To add insult to injury, Rosa Parks, whom the world came to know as one of its most dignified, pacific citizens, was also convicted of disorderly conduct. She was fined ten dollars and costs.[3] Fred Gray was ready to handle Rosa Parks's case in part because in March 1955 he had represented fifteen-year-old Claudette Colvin, who, like Mrs. Parks, had refused to relinquish her seat on a bus. Colvin was convicted in Juvenile Court and put on indefinite, unsupervised probation. Gray thought Colvin's case a good platform from which to challenge the law; his elders in Montgomery's black community disagreed. With so much at stake, they were wary of going forward with litigation, especially with a feisty teenage plaintiff.[4] Everyone counseled against a lawsuit, even Professor JoAnn Robinson of Alabama State, who recalled with shame and anger a day when she had given up her seat, too afraid of being beaten to resist. In response to Claudette Colvin's arrest, Professor Robinson mobilized the Women's Political Council, arranged a meeting with the mayor and representatives of the city council and the bus company, and threatened to start a public protest. She yielded when both city and bus company officials apologized and promised that "bus drivers would be more courteous in the future."[5]

By the time Rosa Parks was arrested, black leaders like Professor Robinson and their white supporters (notably, local attorney and Rhodes scholar Clifford Durr and his wife, Virginia, who was Hugo Black's sister-in-law) were ready to formally and publicly challenge the city and state laws that required racial segregation on Montgomery buses. The first meeting of what would become the Montgomery Improvement Association took place on December 3 at the Dexter Avenue Baptist Church, where a newcomer to town, Dr. Martin Luther King Jr., was pastor. By the next day, December 4, with the help of Alabama State students, JoAnn Robinson had mimeographed thirty thousand leaflets calling for people to stay off the buses on Monday, December 5, the day of Rosa Parks's trial.

For Rosa Parks to challenge the city and state laws that required segregation on Montgomery buses would seem appropriate, except that she was still appealing her conviction. If she were to join a lawsuit challenging the segregation laws, the defendants could argue that she was attempting to mount a collateral attack on a state conviction, opening up complex issues related only to her standing. Fred Gray and his cocounsel wanted to bring a straightforward attack on Jim Crow segregation in public transportation in federal court, so they did not include Rosa Parks as a plaintiff. Three African American women (Aurelia Browder, Susie McDonald, and Jeanetta Reese), joined by two teenage girls (Claudette Colvin by her father, Q. P. Colvin, and Mary Louise Smith by her father, Frank Smith), were the named plaintiffs in the class-action lawsuit.

Martin Luther King Jr.'s home, the parsonage at Dexter Avenue Baptist Church, was bombed on January 30, 1956. Three days later, on February 2, Fred Gray filed the complaint in the federal district court in Montgomery. Gray began receiving calls from white men asking him or telling him to dismiss the lawsuit. Proceeding would give him a bad reputation, some suggested; others offered to make letting it go worth his while by assuring him of referrals that would bring him substantial fees. When he turned a deaf ear, they tried another tack. In March Gray was indicted for representing Jeanetta Reese without her consent. Mrs. Reese, it seemed, worked in the home of a "high-ranking Montgomery police official." Under pressure, she claimed not to know anything about the lawsuit. Gray, however, had her signed retainer, pictures taken for *Jet* magazine, and tape recordings of conversations in which she spoke of "her desire to be a part of the lawsuit and to obtain justice."[6]

Meanwhile, *Browder v. Gayle* (W. A. Gayle was the mayor of Montgomery) moved forward. Because the plaintiffs were challenging the constitutionality of a state statute, it was assigned to a three-judge court. Judge Richard Rives of the Fifth Circuit presided, joined by two federal district court judges, Frank Johnson and Seybourn Lynne. All three judges were natives of Alabama. Judge Lynne, a Truman appointee, had joined the district court for the Northern District of Alabama on January 3, 1946, and had become chief judge in 1953. Lynne, while not an out-and-out obstructionist, would stand his ground as a member of the old guard, both in 1956 and as matters progressed. Frank Johnson, on the other hand, would become one of the heroic figures of the civil rights revolution. When *Browder* was filed, however, he had just become a district court judge. Sworn in on February 1, 1956, at thirty-seven he was the youngest federal judge in the country. Now, on May 11, 1956, just three months later, he sat on the bench in a Montgomery courtroom as the court heard the matter of *Browder v. Gayle*.

In the months since Frank Johnson had been sworn in, the civil rights movement had suffered two major setbacks. On Monday, February 6, Autherine Lucy, a young black woman who had the audacity to apply to the University of Alabama, had been driven off campus by rioters and then expelled by the trustees. Even more ominously, on March 12, 101 of the 128 members of Congress from the eleven former Confederate states signed the Southern Manifesto, excoriating the Supreme Court, deploring the decision in *Brown*, and commending "the motives of those states which have declared their intention to resist integration by any lawful means." Everyone knew about the Southern Manifesto; no one knew about a recent conversation between Senator Lister Hill and Judge Richard Rives. Rives was close to both of the senators from Alabama, Democrats Lister Hill and John Sparkman. Sparkman, who had run for vice president alongside Adlai Stevenson in 1952, and Hill had positioned themselves as moderates and avoided engaging in the politics of race. At the time, Hill's Alabama office was in the federal courthouse in Montgomery, so when he returned for a visit that spring, Rives stopped in to visit, as was his custom. Their conversation turned to the Southern Manifesto, and Hill explained that he and Sparkman "reluctantly went along because changed political realities forced them to." Rives heard his old friend out. "Well Lister," he responded, "I think I understand it now. You fellows have just risen above principle."[7]

The *Browder* hearing started at 9:00 a.m. and took all day. The four named plaintiffs each took the stand, explaining on direct examination how they had been injured by the laws they were challenging. The city's attorneys tried to erode that testimony and establish that each plaintiff had been "put up to it" by Fred Gray or by the new young pastor who had taken a leadership role in the Montgomery Improvement Association, Dr. Martin Luther King Jr. When they took the stand, defendants Mayor W. A. Gayle and Commissioner Clyde Sellers expressed their belief that if segregation on the buses was ended, violence would ensue. At one point Judge Rives wondered out loud, "Can you command one man to surrender his constitutional rights—if they are his constitutional rights—to prevent another man from committing a crime?"[8]

At the end of the hearing, Judge Rives led his colleagues to Judge Johnson's conference room. At the conference, as the junior judge, Johnson was expected to speak first—a rule developed to avoid having new judges simply accede to the views of their elders. At the time, Judge Johnson later recalled, none of them knew what the others thought. When Judge Rives turned to him for his opinion, Johnson was succinct and direct. "Judge," he said, "as far as I'm concerned, state-imposed segregation on public facilities violates the Constitution. I'm going to run with the plaintiffs here."

Judge Lynne shook his head no but remained silent. Rives spoke next. "You know, I feel the same way as you do," he told Johnson.[9]

Lynne disagreed, pointing out that the Supreme Court had approved racial segregation in public transportation in *Plessy*, and it had not, in *Brown* or otherwise, overruled *Plessy*.[10] Johnson and Rives understood his point, but they both believed that *Plessy* could not be reconciled with *Brown*.[11] Moreover, although the Supreme Court had not overruled *Plessy* in *Brown*, it seemed to have done so in *Dawson v. Mayor and City Council of Baltimore*. *Dawson* raised precisely the issue raised in *Browder* in the context of public beaches and bathhouses. A panel of Fourth Circuit judges had held, on March 15, 1955, that the authority of cases decided pursuant to *Plessy* had been "swept away by the subsequent decisions of the Supreme Court," including *Brown*. "It is now obvious," the court held, "that segregation cannot be justified as a means to preserve the public peace merely because the tangible facilities furnished to one race are equal to those furnished to the other."[12] On November 7 the Supreme Court had affirmed, without commenting, in a per curiam order. That was a strange way in which to overrule *Plessy*, but there was no other plausible reading of the Court's action. Writing the opinion for himself and Judge Johnson in *Browder*, Judge Rives relied on *Dawson*. Judge Lynne wrote the first dissent of his judicial career.

When the opinion in *Browder* was issued on June 19, 1956, the black citizens of Montgomery had won a tremendous victory, but they could not celebrate yet. The city appealed. In a per curiam, one-sentence opinion, on November 13, 1956, the Supreme Court affirmed. Still, it was not over—the city petitioned for clarification and rehearing. Those petitions were denied on December 17. Finally, more than a year after it had started, the Montgomery bus boycott ended. On Friday, December 21, Martin Luther King Jr. and Fred Gray, joined by Ralph Abernathy and Glenn Smiley, were the first to board a desegregated bus; the driver politely told them, "We are glad to have you."[13] Throughout the morning, "groups of well dressed Negroes" and sympathetic whites rode the buses; a couple of cars with white men in leather jackets watched for a while, then left.[14] Peace reigned. It lasted until Sunday morning, when someone fired a shotgun into Dr. King's home. No one was hurt, but the message was clear. The struggle was far from over.

One other thing was clear—black people in the American South had precious few allies. Their own state governments—the executive, legislative, and judicial branches—repeatedly betrayed them. Their white neighbors were for the most part unified against them—the lower class with bats and bricks, shotguns and bombs; the upper class with Citizens' Councils, the suit-and-tie Ku Klux Klan, wielding pernicious theories like interposition and using sophisticated weapons like lawsuits and arrests. The federal government offered limited recourse. National politicians needed the southern vote; because black voters had been totally disenfranchised, that meant politicians needed the southern white vote. In that political climate, even though President Eisenhower had been stalwart in standing up to Governor Faubus in Little Rock, for the most part Eisenhower's administration was silent on the matter of civil rights. Under Robert Kennedy as attorney general, the Civil Rights Division of the Justice Department, led by Burke Marshall and John Doar, took to the field and struggled to secure the right to vote for black Americans in the Deep South. At the same time, President Kennedy found it politically necessary to defer to Senator James O. Eastland of Mississippi, chair of the Senate Judiciary Committee and a virulent racist intent on putting like-minded men on the federal bench. The Southern Manifesto, which went so far as to commend "the motives of those states which have declared their intention to resist integration by any lawful means," sent a stunning message of defiance of *Brown* directly from the halls of Congress.

With *Brown*, the Supreme Court had taken the first bold step toward recognizing the long-denied constitutional rights of black Americans. Going forward would depend on the tenacious, courageous work of those very citizens and, in large part, on their ability to call on the federal courts to help them realize the promise of *Brown*.

CHAPTER SIXTEEN

The Desegregation of the University of Georgia

Richard Rives was sworn in as chief judge of the Fifth Circuit in 1959 at the age of sixty-four. A year later, he resigned, and Tuttle took his place. Although tradition indicated that he would serve until he reached the age of seventy, Rives explained that he had found the administrative work burdensome, more so because his wife suffered from poor health. Years later, Rives would admit another motivation—he admired Tuttle and thought him a likely candidate for the United States Supreme Court. Being chief judge, Rives calculated, would increase Tuttle's chances of appointment.[1] Elbert Tuttle took office as chief judge of the Fifth Circuit on December 5, 1960. The decision in *Brown II* was more than five years old, and all deliberate speed had turned out to be "little deliberation and no speed."[2] Not only did most elementary and high schools throughout the South remain segregated, so did most of the undergraduate colleges of the Deep South's public universities.[3]

The South was terribly cruel to its black citizens, and by 1960 *Brown v. Board of Education* had made barely a dent. At the undergraduate level, one of the first challenges to systematic exclusion had occurred in Alabama. Autherine Lucy had first applied to the University of Alabama in 1952.[4] Rejected by university officials because of her race, she took her cause to federal court. In August 1955 Judge Harlan J. Grooms of the Northern District of Alabama ruled for her; as the year ended, his order was affirmed by a panel of the Fifth Circuit.[5] Autherine Lucy finally attended classes in 1956, only to be suspended after three days for causing a disruption—a campus mob had attacked her. Judge Grooms ordered her readmitted. Her petition seeking readmission, however, alleged that officers of the university had been part of a conspiracy to create "the air of riot and disorder and

174

rebellion on campus" in order to create cause to suspend her. Her attorneys tried to withdraw that allegation, but the damage had been done. In a resolution accusing Lucy of falsely defaming the university, the board of trustees expelled her.[6] The next day, finally worn down, she left the state. Elbert Tuttle had been aware of Autherine Lucy's struggle but uninvolved in it. In 1952, when she first applied, Tuttle was living in Washington and serving as general counsel to the Treasury. In the first two years he sat on the court, Autherine Lucy's attorneys would turn to the Fifth Circuit more than once. Tuttle never sat on a panel that heard her case, but he knew her story, and he understood the lessons it taught. In very short order, he would put that understanding into play.

Hoping to attend the University of Georgia, Charlayne Hunter and Hamilton Holmes applied to enter with the freshman class in the fall of 1959. Their applications were in part the result of a long campaign by Jesse Hill Jr., then chief actuary of the Atlanta Life Insurance Company, one of the most successful black enterprises in the country. Hill and other black leaders in Atlanta had been actively recruiting applicants to integrate Georgia's university system since 1957. In 1958 they compiled a list of outstanding black high school students and began interviewing them. Many were interested in attending UGA, Georgia State, or Georgia Tech, but for one reason or another, all faltered. In some cases, the mentors realized their young charges' vulnerability to the kinds of attacks the state was sure to mount; in others, the black students and their parents lacked the will to go forward, knowing too well what they faced. Some of Atlanta's black leaders warned Hill that he would generate reprisals in the community and chastised him with a frightening thought: "You're going to mess up some kids."[7] A suit filed in 1956 on behalf of three female applicants to the Georgia State College of Business Administration (now Georgia State University) had resulted in an order that found all three academically qualified but also held that two of the three, who had each borne a child conceived out of wedlock, were not of good moral character. The third was in her forties; before she could enroll, the General Assembly passed a law providing that no one over twenty-one could enroll in a Georgia college.[8]

In June 1959, when the committee found Charlayne Hunter and Hamilton Holmes, they knew they had their candidates. Jesse Hill recalled, "I really didn't have to recruit those kids; they almost recruited me."[9] Charlayne Hunter had been third in her class at Atlanta's Turner High

School, president of the Honor Society, and editor in chief of the school newspaper for two years. Her classmate Hamilton Holmes was cocaptain of both the football and the basketball teams, president of his class his junior and senior years, and valedictorian. Charlayne wanted to go to the University of Georgia for the journalism school. Hamilton wanted to go because he followed the football team and because he had already decided on a career in medicine, and he understood that the University of Georgia could give him the undergraduate education he needed.

Hamilton Holmes at seventeen also understood firsthand the principle that had driven so much, in the early years, of what would become the civil rights revolution: the victories would not come from the political process, not in a country where most black citizens had been disenfranchised. They would come, if at all, in the federal courts. Hamilton's grandfather, father, and uncle had already proven that, winning one of Atlanta's first civil rights lawsuits. The subject was golf. According to Holmes, his grandfather was not political, he was "just a good, old time country doctor." His father and his uncle, on the other hand, were political. Uncle Oliver, a civil rights leader and a minister, had moved to Atlanta to direct his church's civil rights activities nationally, and Hamilton's father, Albert, had graduated from college, worked for a time in Detroit, and "wouldn't take a back seat to anyone."[10] All three men loved golf. They filed suit because they wanted to play golf and they didn't have a decent course; it was as simple as that.

Dr. Holmes did not start playing until he was in his fifties, but he was something of a natural; at eighty, he could shoot his age. His son Albert, too old to try out for the pro tour when golf finally integrated, was the national Negro champion for about ten years in the 1940s.[11] At Lincoln Golf Course, the nine short holes were littered with rocks and bricks. No other Atlanta course was open to black players, although approximately 30 percent of the city's population was black and the city operated seven golf courses. In 1951 Dr. Holmes and his sons asked the city to be allowed to play at Bobby Jones Golf Course and the city's other public courses. The answer was no. No other recourse at hand, they filed suit in federal district court.[12] On November 7, 1955, they won, by order of the United States Supreme Court.[13]

On Christmas Eve Dr. Holmes and his sons went to play Bobby Jones Golf Course for the first time. Scores of their friends traveled in a convoy with them in case of trouble. The mood was tense, but the day was uneventful, except for its fundamental significance. Black Americans had taken another step in the long, slow, arduous march away from slavery and toward equality. Hamilton Holmes would carry on that tradition. He would become one of the first two black students to attend the University of Georgia. And he would do it the same way: first, he would ask, politely; then, he would file suit in federal court.

In the fall of 1958, Ernest Vandiver was waging a campaign for governor. A protégé of Herman Talmadge, Vandiver ran under the slogan "No, not one." In that charged atmosphere, no one was surprised that Hamilton Holmes and Charlayne Hunter, despite outstanding records, were not admitted to the University of Georgia. They had been prepared for this rebuff; and they went on with their promising lives and began college elsewhere, Charlayne at Wayne State, Hamilton at Morehouse College. But they also pressed on with their applications to UGA. Using one ruse after another, the university kept them at bay. Simply keeping them at bay was enough. Soon the issue would be moot.

On the state's side, the fight was waged at the highest levels. The governor, Ernest Vandiver, had been elected on his stand of defiance of the Supreme Court. In 1956, as lieutenant governor, in an address at the annual meeting of the State Bar Association, he had invoked the doctrine of interposition and called *Brown* "utterly impossible of enforcement."[14] Now he repeated the slogan on which he had campaigned: "No, not one." To buttress the state's position, the General Assembly in 1956 had passed a law cutting off all state funding for any school or college providing education to members of both "the white and colored races."[15] In 1960 the Board of Regents passed a new rule restricting the right to transfer into the system or within it.[16]

The university system, for its part, had created an internal appeal process in November 1950, six weeks after Horace Ward applied to the University of Georgia College of Law, thereby becoming the first black applicant to the university. Delay worked in Ward's case. By the time the matter came on for trial in December 1956, Ward had completed his first semester of law school at Northwestern. Federal District Court Judge Frank A. Hooper dismissed Ward's suit, in part on mootness grounds. By 1960 Ward had earned his law degree, had passed the Georgia bar, and was assisting his former attorney, Donald Hollowell, in the Holmes and Hunter litigation.[17]

The procedure adopted in 1950 to stymie Horace Ward required students appealing the denial of admission to appeal first to the president of the institution applied to, then to the chancellor of the University System, and finally to the board of regents. This process never proved to be a stumbling block for Charlayne Hunter because she never had occasion to appeal; when the matter came on for trial in January 1961, the university had yet to act on her application; it had simply repeatedly written, quarter after quarter, that she could not be considered for admission because the dormitories for female students were full. Hamilton Holmes, on the other hand, had finally been denied admission in November 1960. His internal appeal, which the university argued was a predicate to litigation, had not been resolved because the board of regents found it impossible to convene to hear the appeal.

In the fall of 1960 both Holmes and Hunter had completed their first year of college. Either they were admitted soon, or their case would be moot. On September 2, 1960, they filed suit. They and their attorneys were sure of their legal position, sure that they would prevail if the matter ever reached the United States Supreme Court. But first there would be a trial before Federal District Court Judge William A. "Gus" Bootle. Decades later, Hamilton Holmes would recall that Bootle tried it fairly and that "the proceedings were dignified."[18] Even so, he was not optimistic about the outcome. The matter was in the hands of the judge, and Judge Bootle was an unknown quantity. Although federal judges provided much of the leadership on race issues that was so sorely lacking in elected officials, their ranks included many die-hard segregationists and obstructionists.

Bootle, like Tuttle, was a Republican appointee, which gave the plaintiffs some grounds for optimism. In 1960 the Georgia Republican Party was one of the very few integrated organizations in the state. Unlike Tuttle, however, Bootle had never been active in state party politics. Born in South Carolina, Bootle attended both undergraduate school and law school at Mercer University in Macon, Georgia. In 1928 he became an assistant in the office of Scott Russell, the federal district attorney (now known as the U.S. attorney) for the Middle District of Georgia. In 1929, when Russell announced his resignation, Bootle was appointed to succeed him. He held the office until 1933, when the Democrats regained the White House.[19] Bootle spent the next two decades in practice as well as teaching and even serving as acting dean at his alma mater. Then, on May 20, 1954, three days after the historic decision in *Brown v. Board of Education*, Walter A. Bootle was appointed a federal district judge for the Middle District of Georgia.

Despite all the sound and fury over the *Brown* decision, some six years later, when Hamilton Holmes and Charlayne Hunter filed suit, relatively little had changed in the South. In addition to Georgia, where Governor Vandiver led the resistance, four other southern states had held out altogether; in August 1960, no integration at all had occurred in public elementary and secondary schools in Alabama, Georgia, Louisiana, Mississippi, and South Carolina. "Token integration" had occurred in Arkansas, Florida, North Carolina, Tennessee, Texas, and Virginia.[20] Token meant in Virginia, for instance, that 169 black children spread among ten communities attended school with white children; the other 211,000 black children remained in segregated schools. In North Carolina the numbers were even worse; after four years of a "pupil placement plan" meant to appease the federal courts without actually integrating the schools, fewer than 60 black students attended mixed schools, leaving 319,000 in segregated schools.[21] The nation had followed the token integration in Arkansas. "Integration"— nine students attended Central High School in Little Rock during the 1957–58 school year—had been accomplished in Arkansas only by virtue of President Eisenhower's decision to send federal troops to enforce the court's desegregation order. Resistance, in the streets and in the legislature, continued, and in the summer of 1958, Judge Harry J. Lemley granted a petition by the school board to suspend compliance until 1960–61.[22] The order served to "renew the determination of states which plan to resist desegregation."[23] In an expedited appeal, the Eighth Circuit reversed Judge Lemley's June 23 order on August 18.[24] The U.S. Supreme Court, in turn, expedited its review and affirmed the circuit court ruling on September 12. The clearly frustrated court seized the opportunity to announce that the three justices who had joined the court since *Brown* was first decided "are at one with the Justices still on the Court who participated in that basic decision as to its correctness." That decision, the court announced firmly, "is now unanimously reaffirmed."[25]

Despite the Supreme Court's resolve, in the hands of obstructionists the standard of deliberateness became the strategy of delay. Over and over again, it worked. Delay gave the demagogues time to rouse the rabble and gave the legislatures time to invent creative legislation to ensure segregation. Because the education of children was at issue, delay sometimes took the contestants out of the field by allowing them to grow up as their claims for fairness languished in the courts. Delay was threatening to render the applications of Hamilton Holmes and Charlayne Hunter moot. Of five hard-core states where schools were still, six years after *Brown*, totally segregated, four had managed to forestall integration at the college and postgraduate levels as well. Only in Louisiana had black students sued, won, and actually attended state colleges and universities.[26] In Alabama, Georgia, Mississippi, and South Carolina, not one black student attended a publicly supported institution of higher education with white students.[27]

When Hamilton Holmes and Charlayne Hunter filed suit on September 2, 1960, their attorneys asked for a speedy hearing of their motion for a preliminary injunction; Judge Bootle set the matter down for September 9. Counsel for the university appeared and asked for an extension; Judge Bootle granted their motion, but gave them only five days. The September 14 hearing lasted all day. On September 25 Judge Bootle issued his opinion. He set forth in precise detail the tortuous path the plaintiffs' applications had taken, the laborious correspondence, the continuous stream of deferrals and rejections proffered by the university, even the board of regents' transparent excuse of being unable to convene a quorum for failing to act on Hamilton Holmes's appeal—but he nonetheless denied relief. An interlocutory injunction was not appropriate for two reasons, he wrote. First, because the board of regents had not acted, the applicants had not exhausted their administrative appeals. In the face of the university's mighty intransigence, Judge Bootle carefully gave it yet another chance to admit the two students. Second, the issue was too important for decision after only a preliminary hearing; a full trial was warranted and appropriate. Judge Bootle set the matter for trial in December.

The issue was grave and important; on the other hand, its appropriate constitutional resolution was painfully obvious. The only real question was whether the university had refused to admit Hamilton Holmes and Charlayne Hunter because they were black. Although everyone knew the answer, the plaintiffs had the burden of proving it. In a state where the governor had pledged that not one black student would attend school with whites and the legislature had passed a plethora of laws aimed at preventing that from happening, determining the answer to that question would nonetheless require a full-scale trial. The trial began on December 12 and ended on December 16. Holmes and Hunter were represented by an impressive team of black attorneys: Constance Baker Motley, an NAACP attorney from New York who was by then a veteran of innumerable civil rights trials in southern courtrooms; Donald L. Hollowell, an Atlanta NAACP attorney who would represent Martin Luther King Jr. at critical junctures in future years; and Horace Ward, who had been the first black student to apply to the University of Georgia. They were assisted by Hollowell's law clerk, Vernon Jordan, a recent graduate of Howard University School of Law. Motley and Ward went on to become federal judges. Hollowell became the first African American regional director of a major federal agency.[28] Jordan became a trusted advisor to President Clinton. In 1960 they were working very hard with paltry resources against a foe enormously superior in size and strength, and the state and its officers were willing to go to virtually any length to defeat them, including lying under oath. In a sad spectacle, the chancellor of the university system, the chairman of the board of regents, the president of the University of Georgia, and the registrar all testified to the effect that race played no part in admissions decisions at the University of Georgia.[29]

On January 6, 1961, Judge Bootle issued a lengthy opinion.[30] One by one he dealt with the state's contentions and found them wanting. The students could not be denied access to federal court until they had exhausted their state law remedy, the appeal to the board of regents, because the board of regents had neglected to impose any time limit on its action. If Holmes and Hunter couldn't sue until after the board acted, it would simply never act. As Judge Bootle noted, the university had not yet, over a year and a half later, acted on Hunter's application. Moreover, because a vote in either applicant's favor would cause the university to lose all state funding, the right to appeal did not really create a remedy. Moving to the core question, armed with evidence that the plaintiffs' legal team had discovered in a laborious search of university records, Judge Bootle found that the inadequate facilities argument used to defer Hunter's application had been but a pretext.[31] Holmes's case was different; he had been rejected, a decision made "from a review of [his] records and on the basis of [his] personal interview." Unlike most applicants, who were briefly interviewed during college days, or in the admissions office, or by neighboring alumni, Hamilton Holmes underwent a forty-five-minute interview conducted by the registrar himself, Walter Danner; the assistant dean of admissions, Paul Kea; and another admissions staff member, Dr. Morris Phelps. Holmes was asked a number of questions, the court found, that "had probably never been asked of any applicant before," including whether he had ever attended interracial parties. "Apparently," Bootle wrote, "the interview was conducted with the purpose in mind of finding a basis for rejecting Holmes."[32] The committee evaluated Hamilton Holmes, who for over a year and a half had struggled to obtain admission to the university, average on seriousness of purpose; they also found him to be poor in verbal expression.[33] Judge Bootle, however, had his own opportunity to observe the young man who would go on to become an associate dean at Emory and the medical director of one of Atlanta's largest hospitals. "From the evidence as a whole and particularly from Holmes' appearance as a witness at the trial," he wrote, "it is evident that, had the interview of Holmes been conducted and evaluated in the same manner as the interview of white applicants, Holmes would have been found to be an acceptable candidate for admission to the university."[34]

Judge Bootle's order represented a tremendous victory for the plaintiffs and for the entire civil rights movement, but problems remained—timing, for one. Judge Bootle ruled on Friday, January 6, only three days before registration for the winter quarter closed.[35] Nothing about this litigation had been easy, beginning with the simple matter of obtaining applications. Donald Hollowell had solved that problem with the help of black janitors at the university. Now he needed registration packets, and there was no time for subterfuge. Early the next morning, Dr. Samuel Williams, head of the Atlanta chapter of the NAACP, Hollowell, Holmes and his father, and Julian Bond, traveling as a reporter for the *Atlanta Inquirer*, left for Athens. Athens, where the night before hundreds of students had burned crosses and shouted epithets, and where the dean of men, William "Bill" Tate, alone among prominent administrators, had struggled to stop the disorder, putting out one flaming cross after another and pulling down an effigy of Hamilton Holmes erected by a student mob at the university arch while he confiscated student ID cards for use in disciplinary proceedings.[36] Undaunted, the next morning the Holmes party walked onto campus and into the administration building shortly before it closed at noon. Hollowell, who had so recently cross-examined Walter Danner, now laid Judge Bootle's order before him. Danner handed over the registration materials. Meanwhile, Georgia

Attorney General Eugene Cook drove toward Macon to deliver a motion for a stay.

Judge Bootle set the motion for hearing in the federal court in Macon at 9:30 a.m. on Monday. That Sunday, Governor Vandiver and his advisors holed up in strategy sessions. Charlayne Hunter flew back to Atlanta from Detroit, and Constance Baker Motley arrived from New York. Hamilton Holmes and his family celebrated a private triumph: Dr. Hamilton Holmes Sr. shot his first hole in one at the Adams Park golf course. In Macon, Judge Bootle, who had been hanged in effigy in his hometown's Tattnall Square, passed the afternoon at home, joined by a few close friends and, to his surprise, several doctors whom he did not know well.[37] There was no discussion of the events of the day, of why they had come. The afternoon passed quietly; when dusk fell and no threats had materialized, the stalwart group disbanded, taking their leave as unobtrusively as they had arrived.

Promptly at 9:30 the next morning, Judge Bootle convened court. Constance Baker Motley and Donald Hollowell appeared for the plaintiffs. On this day they were alone at counsels' table. Vernon Jordan and Horace Ward were in Athens, where Holmes and Hunter were prepared to register. Accompanied by his father and her mother and their attorneys, they walked onto the campus through the arch where Holmes had so recently been hanged in effigy, past groups of students, some merely curious, some threatening, past the now ubiquitous press to the administration building. As they began the registration process, a cheer rang out. The six-foot-five Vernon Jordan heard a student who was peering into the office call to others outside, "That big nigger lawyer's not smiling now." In moments the phone rang with the official news: Judge Bootle had stayed his order.[38]

In Athens, Jordan and Ward, Holmes and Hunter, and their parents repaired to the home of a local black businessman, Ray Ware, who had offered them sanctuary before, during the December trial. In Macon, Motley and Hollowell went in search of a telephone. This had become a custom for Motley. The mother of a young son, after every hearing she went directly to the clerk's office and borrowed a phone to call home, reversing the charges; that simple act had created a surprising bond between the white southern clerk and the black woman lawyer from New York.[39] This call, however, was different. Motley wasn't calling home; she was calling Judge Elbert Tuttle in Atlanta. She and Hollowell found a pay phone in the courthouse and made the call.[40] How soon, she asked, could Tuttle hear an appeal of Judge Bootle's order granting the stay? How soon, Tuttle responded, could she be in Atlanta? They agreed on 2:30 p.m., Tuttle asking Motley to give notice to the state's attorneys. Before they hung up, he pointed out one more thing: he would not have jurisdiction until a notice of appeal was filed with the clerk of the court of appeals. Had one been filed? Not yet, but it would be, she assured him.[41]

Tuttle knew about Bootle's order that Holmes and Hunter be admitted; the whole state, in fact, much of the country, knew of that. Nonetheless, his chambers at the federal courthouse in Atlanta had been quiet that morning until Motley's call.[42] In moments, after Tuttle spoke with Constance Motley, the work of the day had been put aside and his law clerk had his marching orders: find whatever authority there was on reversing stays prior to full appeals. Most critically, find authority that a single appellate judge, sitting alone, could do it. Tuttle set himself to the task as well. For the very judge who had entered an order to impose a stay pending appeal ordinarily indicated that the judge felt the ultimate outcome of the matter was questionable enough that the status quo should be maintained until the appellate court ruled. The trial judge's determination would usually be honored. Judge Bootle, however, indicated that he harbored no uncertainty about his decision. "As the Court sees it," he wrote, "the particular problem is not difficult; it is not complicated. At the same time," he continued, "every litigant has the right of appeal."[43]

The particular problem that now faced Tuttle was not difficult either, in one regard. The court of appeals could lift the stay; no one disputed that. Autherine Lucy, for example, had faced exactly the same situation Charlayne Hunter and Hamilton Holmes now faced. In 1955 she sought recourse in federal court when the University of Alabama rejected her application for admission. Judge Grooms of the federal district court in Alabama ruled in her favor in an order dated August 26, 1955, but he stayed his order pending full appeal.[44] Lucy, like Holmes and Hunter, asked a judge of the Fifth Circuit (whose identity is unrecorded) to vacate the stay.[45] When he denied her motion, she appealed to the United States Supreme Court. In a per curiam opinion, the Court vacated the stay.[46] By the time the Court ruled on October 10, more than six weeks had elapsed. The fall term was well under way, so Lucy waited and finally began classes in 1956. All of the delay allowed hatemongers to fan the flames and passions to rise; her arrival on campus precipitated serious unrest, including an attack by a campus mob. The trustees promptly expelled her for causing a disruption.

In one sense, with the *Lucy* case in hand, Tuttle had his authority. On almost identical facts, the United States Supreme Court had vacated a stay pending full appeal. Even without the *Lucy* case, it was clear that on the merits, Holmes and Hunter were entitled to have the stay lifted. But did Tuttle, sitting alone, have the power to lift it? As a judge of a federal circuit court of appeals, Tuttle was a creature of statute. The laws that created his position also established his jurisdiction, his power. Under those laws, the court sat in three-judge panels. In 1961, however, Tuttle was the only Fifth Circuit judge who resided in Georgia. Bringing in two colleagues would take time, and time was of the essence. Because registration for the winter semester closed in a few hours, this was a case in which justice delayed would likely be justice denied. Like Autherine Lucy, Holmes and Hunter were in danger of winning the battle but losing the war. Moreover, the distressing end to Autherine Lucy's long, courageous battle to study at the University of Alabama had been a serious blow to the rule of law itself. When Lucy was suspended because of student rioting, "the message flashed across the South that violence still works."[47]

Tuttle could have appointed two of the federal district court judges who sat in Atlanta to sit with him. Instead, certain of the correct ruling on the merits, Tuttle searched for the authority to act alone. He found it in the very rule that had authorized Judge Bootle to grant the stay. The power given the district court judge to issue a stay pending appeal did "not limit any power of an appellate court *or of a judge or justice thereof . . .* to suspend, modify, restore, or grant an injunction during the pendency of an appeal."[48] Although this provision had apparently never been used by a single circuit court judge to reverse a district court order granting a stay, it was enough for Tuttle. Comfortable with his power to hear the matter sitting alone, precisely at 2:30 p.m. he took the bench.

Before the bailiff's gavel fell, the Atlanta courtroom was swarming; members of the local and national press mixed with curious onlookers. The central figures in the drama, Hamilton Holmes and Charlayne Hunter, were not there; they were in Athens anxiously awaiting news. Nor were their attorneys. It had been a frantic morning. Constance Motley and Donald Hollowell had raced back to Atlanta from Macon and gone directly to Hollowell's Hunter Street office. There they prepared the notice of appeal and other papers to present to the court. The NAACP regional office, headed by Ruby Hurley, was next door; Hurley's secretary, using a typewriter with a blue ribbon, helped Hollowell's secretary, using a black ribbon, with the work. Time permitting, the fastidious Hollowell would not have submitted multicolored papers; even so, the symbolism was not lost on him.[49]

Hollowell and Motley arrived in court at 2:32. It was not a good feeling, Donald Hollowell would recall, to see Tuttle, legendary for his punctuality, already on the bench.[50] Tuttle simply continued to announce the case as they took their places at counsels' table. Across the aisle, Eugene Cook, the attorney general of the state of Georgia, ostentatiously turned his chair and presented his back to the bench.[51] B. D. "Buck" Murphy, a prominent Atlanta attorney who had been retained by the state on civil rights matters, argued for the state. The arguments were brief; Judge Tuttle did not brook delay. Nor could he be distracted from the matter at hand; he simply ignored Gene Cook's insulting gesture. Constance Baker Motley no doubt took particular pleasure in that small victory; in 1954, when she rose to argue for the NAACP in the Mobile school case, Fifth Circuit Judge Louis Strum had turned his chair and sat with his back to her.[52]

After the attorneys had concluded their arguments, Tuttle announced that he would have a written opinion in a short time. Back in his chambers, Tuttle reflected on the arguments. Then he dictated an order and issued it in less than an hour. Many in the courtroom had waited for the order; Tuttle's secretary, Lillian Klaiss, handed out copies.[53] Short, spare, and to the point, the opinion was quintessential Tuttle. He began by citing Rule 62(g) for his authority to act, proceeded through a summary of the proceedings to date, and concluded with the reasons for his reversal. No showing was made, Tuttle noted, that there was any likelihood that the order would be reversed when it was appealed in the fullness of time. Meanwhile, the stay effectuated the ongoing denial of a constitutional right. That was not tolerable, Tuttle explained, and in that explanation lay much of the jurisprudence he would bring to bear on critical civil rights cases through the next decades:

> The denial of a constitutional right, for whatever reason, cannot be said
> to be wanting in serious damage merely because the damage cannot be mea-
> sured by money. Irreparable injury results in the denial of a constitutional

right, largely because it cannot be measured by any known scale of value. I do not believe that the courts can deny relief when asked to prevent a continued denial of constitutional rights merely on the ground that the grant of relief will produce difficult or unpopular results. See *Bush vs. Orleans Parish School Board*, 263 F.2d 78. Nor can a court refuse to enforce rights guaranteed under the 14th Amendment because the State has taken such action as to make its problems of compliance more difficult or even impossible.

I am of the opinion that the quickest disposition that can be made of this case, so far as granting these plaintiffs their right to an education in a State institution, as the trial court has clearly found that they are entitled to, is the best solution not only for them but for all others concerned.

Finding no basis for the grant of the stay by the trial court other than its recognition of the right of every litigant to appeal from an adverse decision, I have concluded that the stay was improvidently granted.[54]

The order ended with a cite to *Lucy v. Adams*, the case in which the United States Supreme Court had vacated the district court judge's stay of his own order desegregating the University of Alabama. That petition had been denied by a judge of the Fifth Circuit and then presented to Justice Black. Justice Black, who could have ruled alone, took the petition to each member of the court, which then issued a per curiam opinion lifting the stay.[55] Tuttle boldly took the opposite course; sitting alone, he lifted the stay, thereby reinstating Judge Bootle's order on the merits.

Earlier in the morning, Donald Hollowell and Constance Motley had been stunned and disappointed. Now it was the state's attorneys who were stunned. Tuttle had lifted the stay. He had not waited for a record of the proceedings below; he had not convened a three-judge panel. Sitting alone, the chief judge of the United States Court of Appeals for the Fifth Circuit issued a simple order. The plaintiffs' right to relief was clear, he stated, and Judge Bootle's order indicated that the state had been granted a stay for no reason other than the fact that the state had asked for it. That was not reason enough, not when the effectuation of the plaintiffs' constitutional rights was at stake. He had the power to act, so he did. Once again, Donald Hollowell raced to a phone. He called Vernon Jordan at the Ware house in Athens and gave his law clerk the news and his marching orders. Jordan and Ware took Holmes and Hunter back to the UGA campus; this time, the school completed the registration process. Holmes and Hunter left the registrar's office with their academic schedules in hand.[56]

At 1:00 p.m. that day, between the time Bootle issued his stay and Tuttle set it aside, the governor had taken the floor to address a joint session of the General Assembly. On Friday, upon learning of Bootle's ruling in favor of Holmes and Hunter, Governor Vandiver had invited fifty to sixty political allies to a meeting at the governor's mansion. They gathered on Sunday afternoon, and they all knew that the critical moment had come.[57] The state had two choices: it could allow the two black students to enroll, or it could close the university. While the Constitution did not allow states to condition admission to public schools on race, it also did not require states to operate public schools in the first place. The same choice would confront the legislature when the inevitable orders to desegregate elementary and secondary school systems became effective, and an order requiring desegregation of Atlanta schools to begin in September 1961 had already been entered.[58] The costs of defiance were extraordinary, and they would be paid, for the most part, by the children. Nonetheless, man by man, the assembled power brokers voted to stay the course until the governor's floor leader in the House, Frank Twitty, stunned them by dissenting. "You can't close the schools," he told the governor. State Senator Carl Sanders, later elected governor, stood with Twitty.[59] Both made public statements that Sunday afternoon; they believed in segregation, they insisted, but not at the cost of closing the university or the public schools.[60] When Governor Vandiver addressed a joint session of the legislature at 1:00 p.m. on Monday, January 9, he continued his strident support of segregation. But along with the racist rhetoric, he uttered a critical phrase: "We cannot abandon public education."[61]

Governor Vandiver described Bootle's original order as "a sweeping edict, the harsh and vicious terms of which threaten to destroy or disrupt the University of Georgia."[62] With Bootle's stay in hand, he claimed victory. When Tuttle set the stay aside, reinstituting the desegregation order, Vandiver was not ready to concede; he directed the attorney general to appeal Tuttle's action to the Supreme Court and at midnight that night issued a public statement reaffirming his pledge to uphold segregation. The university, he announced, would close for at least one week, beginning at noon the next day. He was, he said, simply complying with the state law that ordered all state appropriations cut off to any school that educated both black and white students, and he added, "It is the saddest day of my life."[63]

Although Vandiver was "a protégé of Senator Herman Talmadge," he had begun his political career as what passed for a moderate on race in Georgia in the 1950s.[64] Like every other Democratic candidate for a major office, he vigorously supported segregation, but he had largely avoided race-baiting and inflammatory rhetoric. That could not be said of the Reverend William T. Bodenhamer, the Baptist minister who opposed Vandiver for the 1958 Democratic nomination for governor.[65] When Vandiver made a speech in 1957 in which he tried to lower the tone of racial rhetoric, the newspaper headlined its coverage "Vandiver Urges Middle of Road." Bodenhamer seized on that as proof that Vandiver was "weak on segregation." Vandiver responded by heating up his own rhetoric, in particular, by using the fateful phrase "No, not one" in the speech that opened his campaign for governor.[66] Now, with the decisive moment at hand, he reverted to his earlier posture. He concluded his letter informing the president of the Senate and the Speaker of the House that he was closing the university with a recommendation that the 1956 statute that prohibited state funding of schools that educated both black and white students be repealed and with a clarification of his own position: "I will not be a party to defiance of law, as a few would wish, or do anything which might foment strife and violence in an explosive situation."[67] Ernest Vandiver, the governor of Georgia, would not stand in the schoolhouse door.

Vandiver would carry on the fight in the courts, however. Constance Motley and Donald Hollowell had foreseen that the state would press on and take the matter to the United States Supreme Court. Before they left the courthouse in Macon that morning, they had called Jack Greenberg at the NAACP's New York office. Motley had brought Greenberg up to date, urging him to draft a response to the petition she anticipated the state would file and get it to the Supreme Court. They talked throughout the day, and early the next morning Greenberg was waiting at the Supreme Court when the clerk opened his office. There was just one problem, the clerk dryly noted: Greenberg couldn't file a response until the state had filed its petition. About two hours later, the Georgia delegation, which had the advantage of traveling on a state plane, reached the Supreme Court with a seven-page petition.

Meanwhile, Motley and Hollowell were back in Judge Bootle's Macon courtroom alleging the immediate danger of irreparable harm and seeking a temporary restraining order against the governor as well as the state's auditor. Judge Bootle recognized the enormous import of what he was asked to do. Sensitive to the implications of a federal court controlling a state's policy decisions, he had given the governor and the board of regents every opportunity to retain control and act in compliance with the U.S. Constitution. Stubbornly defiant, they had refused. Now, his original order having been backed up by Tuttle, Bootle unhesitatingly issued a temporary restraining order that restrained the governor from cutting off funds.[68] The university stayed open.[69] Governor Vandiver fired off a telegram to Bootle protesting the temporary restraining order but conceding that he would not defy it.[70] When he was served by a federal marshal at the governor's mansion that evening, he raged at the insult. In truth, he was in all likelihood relieved. He had, figuratively, stood in the schoolhouse door: he had fought for segregation till the bitter end, and he could now concede with a semblance of dignity and, more important, with the people of the state largely behind him. Georgians did not want their flagship university desegregated, but they wanted it closed even less. Even if the parents would choose that ultimate form of resistance, few of their children would. Roy McCracken, a Vandiver ally and longtime legislator, had told Vandiver he was going to Athens to retrieve his daughter. He came back to Atlanta alone. "She wouldn't leave," the surprised father told the governor.[71] She was not alone. On Monday morning, January 9, the *Atlanta Constitution* reported that "lights burned late in the University of Georgia's old chapel Sunday night as it became the rallying point for students who want to keep the university open." By 9:00 p.m., the paper reported, they had accumulated some two thousand signatures, and they expected to gather hundreds more.[72]

After Tuttle's order lifting Bootle's stay had been affirmed by the Supreme Court, after Bootle had enjoined the governor from closing the university, Bootle entered another critical injunction. Holmes's and Hunter's first day of classes, Wednesday, January 11, ended in student rioting protesting their presence. The mayor of Athens charged that Vandiver delayed deploying the state police to help quell the rioting, a charge Vandiver bitterly denied. When the state police did arrive at around midnight, they transported Holmes and Hunter back to their homes in Atlanta.[73] Both were suspended "for their own protection and that of other students."[74] Their attorneys went back to Bootle, and he ordered them readmitted by 8:00 a.m. Monday.[75] Holmes and Hunter went back to Athens. The University of Georgia had been desegregated. The next year, the University of Mississippi would be desegregated, and the year after that, the University of Alabama. The tide had turned. At the *Atlanta Constitution*, longtime political cartoonist Clifford "Baldy" Baldowski sketched out three black-robed men on a baseball diamond. Playing on the phrase "Tinker to Evers to Chance" with which sports writer Franklin P. Adams had immortalized the 1910 Chicago Cubs infielders, Baldowski captioned his drawing "Bootle to Tuttle to Black."[76] A baseball fan since his summer job writing up games for the *Honolulu Advertiser*, Tuttle prized the cartoon.

The state continued to fight about details. Judge Bootle recalled attorneys for both sides appearing one day when he was sitting in Columbus. Something about the swimming pool had come up, they said; could he hear them out? When he left the bench for lunch, he called them into his chambers, where Attorney General Cook explained what had come up: were the two students allowed to use the swimming pool under Bootle's order? "Well," the judge asked, "is the swimming pool there for the students?" "Yes," replied the attorney general. "And aren't they students?" "Yes," again. "Take an order," the judge told Hollowell, indicating that he should draft an order for the judge's signature providing that his clients could use the swimming pool. As Hollowell left the office, Cook lingered. Bootle recalled him averting his gaze, glancing out the window as he said, "Judge, we're sorry to have to trouble you with all this, but you know how it is."[77] Bootle knew exactly what he meant. The political leaders in the South were not going to provide leadership on this issue. They were not going to take the heat, they were going to deflect it onto the federal bench. They would comply with the law, if at all, only under court order. As was often the case throughout the South, the district court judge, Walter "Gus" Bootle, had borne much of the load. The trial court judges were the frontline troops. Nonetheless, it was Tuttle's decisive and virtually unprecedented intervention that carried the day. The newly installed chief judge of the United States Court of Appeals for the Fifth Circuit had made himself abundantly clear. On his watch, the constitutional rights of black citizens of the Fifth Circuit would not be honored in the breach. In the matter of the desegregation of the university, Georgia had been disarmed of its most potent weapon: delay. Tuttle's conduct would prove to be a harbinger of things to come; under his leadership, the Fifth Circuit would take the lead not simply in effectuating the mandate of *Brown v. Board of Education* but in giving vibrant life to the equal protection clause of the Constitution and the landmark Civil Rights Act of 1964. Years later, Burke Marshall, who had served as assistant attorney general in charge of the Civil Rights Division of the Justice Department in the Kennedy administration, remarked, "If it hadn't been for judges like that on the Fifth Circuit, I think *Brown* would have failed in the end."[78]

Tuttle's order in the UGA case was characteristic—swift, decisive, well grounded in the law, and brooking no interference with constitutional rights. A new message flashed across the South: in the states of the Fifth Circuit—Alabama, Georgia, Florida, Louisiana, Mississippi, and Texas— justice would no longer be denied or delayed. Not a month had passed since Elbert Tuttle became the chief judge, and he had already become a lightning rod for the aspirations of civil rights plaintiffs and the anger of southern political leaders. Thanks to his decisive intervention, Charlayne Hunter and Hamilton Holmes would earn their undergraduate degrees at the University of Georgia. Both would go on to distinguished careers, hers in journalism, his in medicine. More than thirty years later Hunter published a memoir, *In My Place*. Remembering when word reached them that they had won, that Tuttle had reversed Judge Bootle's stay, she wrote, "At that moment, we all loved Judge Tuttle."[79]

CHAPTER SEVENTEEN

The Costs of Conscience

When Charlayne Hunter and Hamilton Holmes registered for classes at the University of Georgia in 1961, *Brown* had been on the books for more than six years. Precious little had changed in three key areas of civic life—education, public accommodations, and voting—but the pace was quickening. As prevalent as civil rights litigation was, it represented only a small fraction of the work of the circuit. Ironically, for a man who so often found himself explaining that he was not a tax attorney, the first opinion Tuttle authored as chief involved a corporate income tax question, specifically, how much the St. Joe Paper Company could deduct for attorney's fees paid in its legal struggle over ownership of the Florida East Coast Railway. The second involved fraud in a transaction wherein stock was exchanged for real property, and the third arose under the Miller Act, a federal law requiring contract surety bonds on federal construction projects.[1] And on the list goes. Still, by February, Tuttle was writing in the ubiquitous Louisiana school desegregation cases.[2]

Tuttle's tenure as chief judge coincided with what are arguably the most critical years of the civil rights revolution. The Fifth Circuit would oversee the desegregation of another icon of the American South, Ole Miss, and it would lock itself into an unprecedented struggle with the governor of Mississippi. The "Children's Crusade," the Freedom Rides, Selma, and the Atlanta sit-ins—all would occur on Tuttle's watch. Perhaps most significantly, attorneys from the Justice Department, led by Burke Marshall and, in the field, by John Doar, would expose the massive illegalities that kept black Americans disenfranchised. Judges of the district courts of the Fifth Circuit, Frank Johnson of Alabama first and foremost, would develop the remedies later codified in the 1965 Voting Rights Act, and the long-denied constitutional right to vote would grudgingly begin to be restored. Throughout this period, as throughout his life, Tuttle's natural reserve stood him in good stead. He could not be quoted as having made the occasional inappropriate comment or as having belittled a colleague, because he didn't engage in small talk. To the extent that his reserved manner could be off-putting, it was softened by his wife's convivial, yet determined, nature. Sara thought it her role to grease the social wheels, and she took that responsibility seriously. Unlike her husband, she enjoyed a drink—an old-fashioned if someone were mixing cocktails.

If Sara Tuttle had not agreed to travel with Elbert when he sat with the court in other cities, he would not have accepted the nomination. He loved his wife, and he loved the life they shared. He was not willing to give it up again; the war years had been enough. What he asked, he realized, was no small thing. In Atlanta, Sara had a full life. She had friends who would visit her at home or invite her to their homes for afternoons of bridge and conversation. She enjoyed her book club, her needlepoint group, and, for a while, her investment club. After they moved back in 1956, Buddy and Ginny lived just around the corner, the grandchildren were in and out constantly, and at least once a week the whole family came to dinner. Friends of the grandchildren often came too; Sara included anyone who was around. "You would invite all the stray dogs and cats!" her housekeeper, Bessie Mayfield, sometimes teased. On the road, during the day while Elbert sat hearing oral argument or in conference with his colleagues, Sara was often at loose ends. Very few of the other wives traveled with their husbands; no one else took every trip. Other judges' wives, in particular, Bonnie Wisdom in New Orleans, regularly invited Sara for lunch and for afternoons of bridge; still, she was left with a lot of spare time. She filled the hours with her books and her needlepoint, with watching television, and with writing letters to her children and to Bessie.

At home, Sara was always ready to entertain friends. That did not change just because she and Elbert were on the road. Sara Tuttle understood that the more cordial the judges' relationships were, the easier her husband's job would be, and she was determined to ease his burden in any way she could. Traveling to a sitting, she packed cheese biscuits, peanut butter straws, toast points, dips, and caviar mousse as well as bourbon, scotch, sherry, and a half dozen cocktail glasses. Decades before minibars appeared in hotel rooms, her careful preparations allowed Elbert to invite the other judges in for a drink before dinner. Her efforts did not go unappreciated. "The common court view," according to Judge Paul

Roney, "is that the Fifth Circuit became a collegial court when Elbert Parr Tuttle became Chief Judge in 1960. . . . He and his wife, Sara, are the traditional founders of the spirit of collegiality maintained on the Fifth Circuit."[3]

The cheese biscuits and peanut butter straws, made by Sara's housekeeper, Bessie Mayfield, were particular favorites; everyone loved them. Bessie had gone to work for the Tuttles soon after they moved back to Atlanta from Washington in 1953 or 1954. Sara Tuttle had a full-time housekeeper, but she needed extra help for the summer; Nicky and John were coming with their children. The master bedroom was on the first floor of the home the Tuttles had built in 1949 on Peachtree Circle; upstairs there were two bedrooms connected by a full bath—just enough room for the Harmon family. By 1953 Nicky and John had four daughters: Betsy, born in 1946, Cappy in 1948, Sara in 1951, and Peggy, an infant. For several summers, Bessie went along when the whole family (Elbert and Sara, Nicky and John and their children, and Buddy and Ginny and their children) vacationed on Saint Simons Island off the Georgia coast. In 1959 she began working for them full-time. It was often Bessie who answered the phone when the hate calls came. However harassing or vulgar the callers were, they did not bother her much. Like Sara Tuttle, she thanked the caller for having called and hung up. It was more unnerving when for days on end there would be an occupied car parked near the house. No one ever accosted Bessie, but Sara, worried that they might, never failed to stand watch at her window as Bessie arrived and left.

When Sara Tuttle didn't lunch at home or at the nearby Piedmont Driving Club, she might well be at the Magnolia Room at Rich's Department Store. Opened in 1867, Rich's thrived under family control for more than a century. During the Great Depression, when the city was broke, Mayor James Key used scrip to pay the city's workers, including schoolteachers, with the promise that when the city became solvent, holders would be able to redeem the scrip for face value. Most merchants, even those selling essentials, either would not take it or imposed a surcharge—as much as 25 percent. Rich's not only took scrip for payment but also simply cashed it.[4] Rich's "had been the favorite store for black Atlantans for a generation. It had been the first to extend credit to all races and subsequently the first to have desegregated water fountains."[5] It was also the first store to allow black shoppers to try on clothes, albeit in segregated dressing rooms.[6] But black shoppers could not eat in Rich's famed Magnolia Room or at any of the other store restaurants.

That policy came under pressure after the sit-in by four young black men at a Woolworth's in Greensboro, North Carolina, on February 1, 1960—not the first demonstration of its kind, but the one that kindled a nationwide flame. Atlanta, home of Martin Luther King Sr. and his son and home to a handful of distinguished black colleges and universities, including Atlanta University and Morehouse and Spelman Colleges, was a natural target. The elders of the black community and of the colleges cautioned restraint, and Mayor Hartsfield met with student leaders in early March and urged that they open negotiations with white business owners before beginning protests, but on March 15 the students forged ahead. Some two hundred students participated in sit-ins at ten carefully chosen locations: lunch counters at the state capitol, the Fulton County courthouse, city hall, the Trailways and Greyhound bus stations, the Union and Terminal Railway stations, an S. H. Kress five-and-dime, and two cafeterias in federal buildings. Seventy-seven students were arrested on charges of breach of the peace, intimidating restaurant owners, refusing to leave the premises, and conspiracy. Probably due to the intervention of Mayor Hartsfield, no one was brought to trial.[7]

The students regrouped in the fall, and on October 19, 1960, Martin Luther King Jr. joined fifty-one other demonstrators at Rich's.[8] They were denied service at a snack bar but not arrested. When King led the group to the Magnolia Room, store officials called for their arrest; protestors at simultaneous sit-ins across the city were also arrested and taken to jail. On October 24 everyone was released except King; police told Donald Hollowell that they were holding King on a bench warrant from De Kalb County. In the spring, King had been stopped while driving the white writer Lillian Smith to Emory University Hospital. The stop was simply harassment by a policeman who reacted to seeing a white woman in a car driven by a black man; King, however, had been living in Atlanta some three months and had not yet obtained a Georgia driver's license. For that offense, De Kalb County judge Oscar Mitchell imposed a fine and a twelve-month sentence, suspended on the condition that King not break any state laws. Based on the arrest at Rich's, Judge Mitchell revoked probation and sentenced King to four months on a chain gang. Donald Hollowell called the De Kalb County sheriff the next morning to let him know that he would be coming by with a writ of habeas corpus; one of the deputies told Hollowell, "He ain't here." The sheriff had not waited for daybreak; in the middle of the night, he drove King to the state penitentiary at Reidsville. The news shook King's family and friends to the core; his wife, Coretta, then six months pregnant, feared he would be killed, and she was not alone. As it happened, King was not killed; he was released the next day after a series of events in and out of court, the most famous of which is presidential candidate Jack Kennedy's call to Coretta to express his concern. That led Dr. Martin Luther King Sr. ("Daddy King") to openly endorse Kennedy. Martin Luther King Jr., who thought a partisan endorsement would be improper because he was the head of the Southern Christian Leadership Conference, simply expressed his deep gratitude for Kennedy's "genuine concern." Black voters got the message, and many commentators credit Kennedy's victory over Nixon to Kennedy's having secured so much of the traditionally Republican black vote.

Throughout this episode, Dick Rich, long thought of as moderate on racial matters, had been a stumbling block. When the students attempted to negotiate with him in June, he refused to make any concessions and angrily walked out of the meeting. It took "much pleading" by Mayor Hartsfield to convince Rich to let the charges be dropped.[9] Once King was freed and the crisis had passed, Hartsfield brokered a thirty-day moratorium on protests while he attempted to negotiate a desegregation agreement. His first efforts were unsuccessful, and in January 1961, the sit-ins started again. A few weeks earlier, the Tuttles had attended a holiday party at the home of Edith and Herbert Elsas. Dick Rich was there too. Some ten years earlier, Dick Rich had succeeded Tuttle as president of the Atlanta Chamber of Commerce. As they stood in a buffet line, Rich brought up the sit-ins. He knew they were right, he told Tuttle, and he should serve black patrons, but he refused to change the store's policy under pressure. Tuttle's response was blunt. "Dick," he asked, "when has there ever been progress without pressure?" Tuttle never knew how much impact their brief conversation had, but Rich did join other white business leaders in telling Ivan Allen Jr., president of the Chamber of Commerce, "Go ahead and work something out. Get us off the hook, even if it means desegregating the stores."[10]

A plan developed that tied desegregation of mercantile establishments to desegregation of the Atlanta school system. On September 29, 1961, a headline on page 1 of the *New York Times* reported: "Atlanta Integrates

Restaurants Calmly." "Probably the most symbolic single victory today for Atlanta Negroes was the ending of discrimination in the Magnolia Room, a restaurant at Rich's," the story explained, recalling that the restaurant had been the scene of Martin Luther King Jr.'s arrest a year earlier.[11] The victory that day was largely symbolic; much of Atlanta remained segregated and would stay that way until another round of sit-ins in 1963, followed by passage of the landmark Civil Rights Act of 1964.

Looking back on those years, Sara emphatically maintained that the Tuttles never lost a friend, and Elbert would agree. They did not suffer the kind of open rudeness and hostility from longtime friends and neighbors that befell others, like Judge Richard Rives and Judge Frank Johnson in Montgomery and Judge Skelly Wright in New Orleans. Tuttle thought that the fact that he was not a southerner helped to insulate him. "They didn't expect much of me," he explained with a wry smile. His partner, Herbert Elsas, confirmed that. In Atlanta's close-knit society, "everyone knew," Elsas explained, "that Elbert had gone to an integrated school."[12] At the time, that was a shocking fact and one that explained his difference. It also meant that while many in Tuttle's circle may have felt anger toward him, they did not feel they had been betrayed. Still, Sara's sister Ginny Asbill qualified her sister's recollection. "If she said they never lost a friend, it's true," she said. "But I will tell you this: there were years when their appearance in the door to a room would bring all conversation to a halt." Many of those rooms were at the Piedmont Driving Club. Elbert and Sara had belonged since 1925. The driving club was only blocks from their home in Ansley Park, and it was without question Atlanta's most exclusive club. Only white males could be members; only their white friends and family were welcome as guests.

When Elbert Tuttle joined the Fifth Circuit in 1954, he relinquished his membership in the Lawyers' Club, an elite association of white Atlanta attorneys of which he had served as president. To his dismay, not until 1971 did the Lawyers' Club elect a black attorney, Horace Ward, to membership, and even then members blackballed Maynard Jackson, who would two years later become the mayor of Atlanta.[13] Tuttle did not resign from the Piedmont Driving Club, which was nominally a social organization. As late as 1973, neither blacks nor Jews could be members of the Piedmont Driving Club, and blacks were not even welcome as the guests of members.[14] After Griffin Bell, who had been Tuttle's colleague on the Fifth Circuit, was nominated as attorney general by President Carter in 1976, Bell's membership in the Piedmont Driving Club was cited by the NAACP in its resolution urging the Senate to reject the nomination. Effective January 18, 1977, Bell resigned his memberships in private clubs.[15] Still, Tuttle did not resign. In later years, he candidly recalled that when he first joined in 1925, the fact that blacks and Jews were excluded was so ordinary and so universal that he didn't give it any thought, but he would not speak of why he contin-ued his membership. Almost certainly a major factor, if not the sole rea-son, was that Sara wanted him to. She enjoyed meeting her friends there for lunch and going with Elbert and sometimes the rest of the family for dinner. Moreover, the social standing membership conferred meant a lot to her.

Elbert Tuttle realized that agreeing that he would go on the court had been a sacrifice for Sara. There was the matter of the travel, not a small thing. Then there was the matter of money. When he left the firm to go to the Treasury Department, the arrangement with the firm was that he was "to be compensated for his share of work in process by the equivalent of 2 years' earnings at current rate less his expected salary for such 2 years from the Government." Tuttle's share at the firm for 1953 was projected at $39,375, while his expected government salary was $15,000.[16] For 1953 and 1954, the two years he spent at Treasury, the firm paid him the difference, or $24,375 per year. When he decided to join the court instead of returning to the firm, his salary as a judge, $17,500, represented all of his earnings. Then, before a year was out, he sat on a case involving a patent for a device used in refining petroleum and separating crude oil into gasoline.[17] As he listened to the argument, it troubled him that he owned a few shares of Texaco; Texaco wasn't involved in the litigation, but it could be affected by the outcome. He could have retained the stock and recused himself from related cases, but he decided instead to sell the Texaco stock along with some AT&T stock he held. He also asked Sara to resign from a ladies' in-vestment club she belonged to and enjoyed. Later, when his stepmother died and left more Texaco stock (1,050 shares) to him in her will, he sold it quickly.

Tuttle's salary as a federal judge paid all the bills; per diem allowances paid for their extensive travel for his work; and, most important, if he died, Sara would continue to receive his salary, so he was secure in knowing she was well provided for. They had a comfortable home in a very good neigh-

borhood; they had a full-time housekeeper; they drove a new car. Still, decades later, when the press started reporting the extent of federal judges'
assets, Tuttle had the least. His decision to divest himself and Sara of any
stock investments so that he could always sit when called upon was an
expensive one for his family. He never minded that cost. In 1975 Tuttle was
asked to sit on a Fourth Circuit case involving almost every major player in
the telecommunications industry as well as the FCC and other regulators.[18]
Only one judge in the entire Fourth Circuit, Judge H. Emory Widener, did
not hold disqualifying investments. Tuttle and Widener were joined on the
panel by Judge William Hastie of the Third Circuit. Explaining his avail-
ability to another judge, Tuttle wrote: "You can chalk it down on your book
that neither I nor my wife will ever be disqualified by virtue of ownership
of securities. . . . The same goes for my son who lives in Atlanta and my
daughter who lives in Rochester. It just happens that we all happily live
from hand-to-mouth."[19]

While his decision to divest himself and his wife of all stock investments
had long-term consequences, it had little impact on their lives at the time.
Another ethical decision hurt more at the time, so much so that he deferred it. Tuttle had been on the board of Larkin Coils since the mid-1920s,
when he had represented Jack Simms, a friend from church who bought
the company out of bankruptcy and became president of the company.
Serving on the board carried with it a perquisite that Elbert and Sara especially enjoyed. Each spring they would take the company yacht, complete
with captain and chef, for a weeklong cruise. Tuttle had not been on the
Fifth Circuit a full year when he sat on an appeal by taxpayers from a finding that the compensation of two officers of a corporation was too high to
be deductible as a "reasonable allowance for salaries."[20] As a member of
the board of Larkin Coils, he participated in setting the officers' salaries.
Ruling in the case caused him to question the propriety of remaining on
the board. There was no real conflict, however, and no rule in place, so he
temporized. In the fall of 1963, Judge Tuttle and Judge Bryan Simpson represented the Fifth Circuit at the Judicial Conference of the United States.
At that meeting, the conference adopted a formal resolution that provided
that "no justice or judge appointed under the authority of the United States
shall serve in the capacity of an officer, director, or employee of a corporation organized for profit."[21] Despite considerable controversy about the au-

thority of the Judicial Conference to regulate the activity of federal judges, Tuttle promptly resigned from the Larkin Coils board.[22] It was hard, he recalled, because he hated to give that association up, but it was easy because he knew what he had to do.

Tuttle's reputation for rectitude led Chief Justice Warren Burger in 1969 to name him as the first chairman of the Advisory Committee on Judicial Activities, known among the judges as the "Dear Abby" committee. Members included Harry Blackmun, then a judge on the Eighth Circuit. Before leaving office in 1969, Chief Justice Earl Warren had asked the Judicial Conference Committee on Court Administration "to consider what might be done to offset the growing apprehension [that untoward conflicts existed] about the federal judiciary."[23] That committee made a number of recommendations, including a recommendation that judges not accept compensation of any kind (e.g., loans, gifts, gratuities, or honoraria) absent approval by the judicial council of the circuit and a recommendation that each judge submit an annual financial statement to the Judicial Conference. In late 1969 Chief Justice Burger implemented these recommendations by creating a review committee, chaired by Judge Edward Tamm of the District of Columbia Circuit, to receive the annual financial statements and the Advisory Committee on Judicial Conduct, with Tuttle as chair, to receive and respond to queries from federal judges as to the ethical appropriateness of any conduct. Redacted responses were published as opinions. Selected because of his reputation for fastidious attention to ethical questions and his unswerving integrity, or, as Tuttle wryly put it, because he was known to be "persnickety," Tuttle chaired the Dear Abby committee until 1976. For Judge Cornelia Kennedy of the Sixth Circuit, who served on the committee, Tuttle set the standard by which she "judged all committee chairs since. . . . [H]e always seemed relaxed, yet he never wasted time with irrelevant issues or small talk but proceeded directly to the agenda items. Nor did he cut debate prematurely. He gave all the members of the committee an opportunity to speak, even multiple times where necessary." Tuttle blended "a commanding presence" with courtesy and patience; moreover, his ability to maintain his position as chair when dealing with a colleague of "very strong personality" who "was used to presiding . . . was diplomacy at its best."[24] The Dear Abby committee worked hard to provide the needed guidance to judges; by 1973, when the

Judicial Conference adopted *The Code of Conduct for United States Judges*, most of the common, recurring situations had been addressed by Tuttle's committee.

On November 18, 1976, Chief Justice Burger wrote Tuttle that he had noted while reviewing committee assignments that Tuttle was chair of both the Advisory Committee on Judicial Activities and the Civil Rules Committee. That was a heavy load. He relieved Tuttle of the chair of the Dear Abby committee but asked him to remain as chair of the Civil Rules Committee, one of the most important and at times most burdensome committees of the conference. Tuttle agreed to remain as a member of the Dear Abby committee and chair of the Civil Rules Committee. "Thank you," he wrote back, "for your generous remarks concerning the Committee work I have engaged in. As you know, it is a blessing to one of my age to be thought useful for extracurricular activities."[25] At seventy-nine, Tuttle was vigorous and healthy. His friend Irving Kaufman, chief judge of the Second Circuit, wrote of his disappointment that Tuttle would no longer be chair of the Advisory Committee. "The federal judiciary has always known that you are a judge dedicated to the maintenance of those high standards without which respect for the law is impossible, but only those who have enjoyed the good fortune of collaboration with you can appreciate the sensitive wit and Solomonic wisdom you have always brought to the task." He would miss him as chair, Kaufman wrote. "Nevertheless, I know it must be a relief to you that the burden of these many years as the 'conscience' of the federal judiciary will at last be lifted from your shoulders."[26]

CHAPTER EIGHTEEN

Oxford, Mississippi: The Battleground

On January 20, 1961, the day after John F. Kennedy was inaugurated president, James Meredith wrote the registrar of the University of Mississippi, requesting an application, a copy of the catalog, and "any other information that might be helpful to me."[1] On January 26 he mailed his completed application. A twenty-seven-year-old native of Kosciusko, Mississippi, Meredith enclosed five certificates from residents of Attala County attesting to his good moral character. He explained that he could not provide five certificates from alumni of the university, as required, because "I am a Negro and all graduates of the school are white. Further, I do not know any graduate personally." On February 4 the registrar sent Meredith a wire telling him he would not be admitted. It seemed that, due to overcrowding, the university was not considering applications received after January 25. On February 20 Meredith wrote the registrar, asked whether his application was complete, and he requested that his application be considered "a continuing application for admission during the summer session beginning June 8, 1961."[2] By this time, Meredith was being advised by Constance Baker Motley, who worked for Thurgood Marshall at the office of the NAACP Legal Defense Fund, Incorporated (the Inc. Fund), in New York. On January 29 he had visited Medgar Evers, the Mississippi field secretary for the NAACP, and Evers had directed him to Marshall and the Inc. Fund.[3]

Over the next few months, the correspondence continued. Finally, on May 25 the registrar informed Meredith that he would not be admitted. On May 31 Meredith filed suit in the United States District Court for the Southern District of Mississippi, seeking to enjoin the University of Mississippi and other state-supported institutions of higher education from continuing to limit admission to white persons. He also asked the court to enjoin the registrar from denying his admission for the summer term on the basis of race. Judge Sidney Mize set the hearing for June 12, four days after the summer term began. On June 12 he continued the case until July 10 because his docket was so crowded that he had only set aside one day, and the hearing could not be completed in that time. Constance Baker Motley realized that a hearing on July 10 would conflict with the scheduled trial of a three-judge court case, which meant that the first summer term would be over before Meredith's case would be heard. She filed a motion asking the court to grant a preliminary injunction before commencement of the second term on July 17. A hearing date—July 11, 1961— was set. On July 10 an assistant attorney general for the state said that he was ill and could not appear. The matter was continued until August 10. On August 10 the hearing began but again was continued, this time to let the assistant attorney general appear in another case. Finally, the hearing resumed on August 15 and concluded the next day. In his order, entered on December 12, 1961, Judge Mize found that denial of Meredith's admission in February 1961 was based on overcrowding at the university. "There was a good deal of testimony introduced in the case," he noted, "but very little conflict, and the overwhelming weight of the testimony is that the plaintiff was not denied admission because of his color or race. The Registrar swore emphatically and unequivocally that the race of plaintiff or his color had nothing in the world to do with the action of the Registrar in denying his application."[4]

The appellate panel, Tuttle, Wisdom, and Rives, was far less credulous. Writing for the panel, Judge Wisdom first provided a detailed and straightforward summary of the facts. When he began his analysis, he could no longer contain himself. "This case," he noted, "was tried below and argued here in the eerie atmosphere of never-never land." Wisdom made short shrift of Mississippi's argument that the state did not have a policy of maintaining segregated institutions of higher learning. Counsel for the state had argued that "appellant's counsel should have examined the genealogical records of all the students and alumni of the University and should have offered these records in evidence in order to prove the University's alleged policy of restricting admissions to white students." On the contrary, Wisdom wrote, the court could, and would, "take judicial notice of this plain fact known to everyone." Likewise, he wrote, the requirement of certificates from five alumni attesting to an applicant's good moral character (adopted, he noted, shortly after *Brown* was decided) was plainly unconstitutional. All that said, however, the record was "muddy," so much so that it was "impossible to determine whether there were valid, non-discriminatory grounds for the University's refusing Meredith's admission." Wisdom recognized that time was of the essence. "A man should be able to find an education by taking the broad highway. He should not have to take by-roads through the woods and follow winding trails through sharp thickets, in constant tension because of pitfalls and traps, and, after years of effort, perhaps attain the threshold of his goal when he is past caring about it," Wisdom wrote. Still, the matter would be remanded for trial. Writing on January 12 and noting that the next semester began on February 6, the court "suggested that the district judge proceed promptly with a full trial on the merits and that judgment be rendered promptly."[5]

Before the trial began on January 17, a Mississippi assistant attorney general met with the five African Americans from Meredith's hometown who had attested to his good character. Four withdrew their letters of recommendation; they had not, they said, understood why he had asked for the recommendations. They thought he was only asking for a job. The registrar relied on the retractions to support the denial of Meredith's application: "This fellow is a troublemaker," he testified.[6] More important, several members of the board of trustees and high-level university administrators testified. All swore, and Judge Mize found as a fact, that "there is no custom or policy now, nor was there any at the time Plaintiff's application was rejected, which excluded qualified Negroes from entering the University." "The proof shows," Judge Mize wrote, "and I find as a fact, that the University is not a racially segregated institution."[7] That Ole Miss was not segregated, Judge Wisdom reportedly quipped, was going to come as a great shock to the people of Mississippi.

Judge Mize's dismal handling of the Meredith litigation stands in sharp contrast to Judge Bootle's forthright handling of the Hunter/Holmes litigation. Where Mize parroted patently absurd and deceptive responses in his findings of fact, Bootle called the testimony that UGA had no policy regarding the race of students what it was—ridiculous—and found as a fact that Charlayne Hunter and Hamilton Holmes had been denied admission because of their race. He had stayed his order pending appeal not, as he wrote, out of any concern that he had erred but only because he believed that the right to an appeal should be protected absent compelling circumstances to the contrary. When Tuttle lifted the stay, Bootle's order was reinstated. If Meredith were to prevail, however, it would be necessary to reverse the order of the trial court denying a preliminary injunction. That, Judges Wisdom and Rives thought, required a review of the record (a transcript of the proceedings and copies of all evidence introduced). The trial had taken ten days, from January 17 until January 27; Judge Mize entered his order on February 3. Meredith's motion seeking an injunction pending appeal was argued on Saturday, February 10. Under ordinary protocols, no one could be admitted to the February term after February 15. There was no possibility that the record would be prepared and a full appeal could be decided by then. Meredith asked the court to order the university to allow him to enroll in the interim, while the appeal was being decided. If, instead, Meredith continued his studies at Jackson State, he would graduate in June, and his application for admission to the undergraduate program at Ole Miss would be moot. In other words, if the court did not order the university to enroll Meredith by February 15, in order to preserve his appeal Meredith would have to drop out of college. Wisdom and Rives saw that as a necessary evil and denied relief.

Tuttle disagreed. Everything indicated that Meredith would, in the end, prevail in his claim that he had been denied admission because of his race. He should not, Tuttle wrote, be forced to sit out of college for a semester in order to maintain his claim. In the last sentence of his brief dissent, his impatience with his colleagues broke through. Responding, apparently, to concern that Meredith might lose credits when he transferred, Tuttle wrote: "I do not think this Court ought to concern itself with any possible damage to the appellant by granting his motion for injunction. He does not need for us to help him decide whether he really wants what he is here fighting so hard to get."[8]

Wisdom and Rives did order that the trial be expedited so that it could be resolved before the beginning of the next college term. After a full-blown trial, Judge Mize again ruled that race had not played a role in the registrar's decision not to admit James Meredith to the University of Mississippi. Meredith appealed; this time, the panel that heard the appeal was composed of Judge Wisdom and Judge John Brown of the Fifth Circuit and Judge Dozier Aldophus DeVane, a senior district court judge from Florida. A Roosevelt appointee, Judge DeVane was seventy-nine at the time of the trial; he was considered "a staunch supporter of states' rights" who had "demonstrated his preference for segregation."[9] Writing for the panel, Judge Wisdom opened his opinion, which would prove to be a masterly if exhaustive review of the history of the litigation, with his conclusion: "A full review of the record leads the Court inescapably to the conclusion that from the moment the defendants discovered Meredith was a Negro they engaged in a carefully calculated campaign of delay, harassment, and masterly inactivity. It was a defense designed to discourage and to defeat by evasive tactics which would have been a credit to Quintus Fabius Maximus."[10] After recounting the procedural history of the case, which had begun when Meredith applied to attend the fall 1961 term, Judge Wisdom summarized the effect of the Fifth Circuit's forbearance:

> The net effect of all these delays was that the February 1961 term, the two summer terms of 1961, and the two regular terms of 1961–62 slipped by before the parties litigant actually came to a showdown fight. . . . We draw the inference that not a few of the continuances and the requests for time in which to write briefs were part of the defendants' delaying action designed to defeat the plaintiff by discouragingly high obstacles that would result in the case carrying through his senior year. It almost worked.[11]

Having reviewed the 1,350-page record, Judge Wisdom, joined by Judge Brown, concluded that Meredith's application had been turned down "solely because he was a Negro. We see no valid, non-discriminatory reason for the University's not accepting Meredith." Judge DeVane dissented; the record, he wrote, supported Judge Mize's finding that Meredith "bore all the characteristics of becoming a troublemaker if permitted to enter the University of Mississippi."[12] After a year and a half of litigation, the Fifth Circuit had finally held that Meredith had proven what everyone knew to be true, that the University of Mississippi had rejected him because of his race. Now, it would seem, all that remained was for him to enroll. Instead, the litigation took a bizarre turn, unprecedented in American jurisprudence.

The panel's opinion was dated June 25, 1962.[13] On July 17 the mandate went down to the trial court judge, Judge Mize. The next morning, Charles Clark, a special assistant attorney general who had briefed and argued the case on behalf of the university, appeared at the office of the clerk of the Fifth Circuit with an order that purported to stay the execution and enforcement of the mandate. It was signed by Judge Ben F. Cameron of the

United States Court of Appeals for the Fifth Circuit. That Judge Cameron, the sole member of the Fifth Circuit from Mississippi, would disagree with the opinion ordering Meredith admitted was no surprise. He had expressed his profound disagreement with *Brown* in *Boman v. Birmingham Transit Company.*[14]

After the decision in *Browder* (the Montgomery bus boycott/"Rosa Parks" case) that the laws that mandated racial segregation on city buses were unconstitutional because the Fourteenth Amendment forbids state action that deprives citizens of equal protection, the city fathers in Birmingham tried to avoid triggering the Fourteenth Amendment by taking state action out of the equation.[15] They repealed the ordinances that required segregation and authorized the bus company "to formulate and promulgate such rules and regulations for the seating of passengers on public conveyances in their charge as are reasonably necessary to assure the speedy, orderly, convenient, safe and peaceful handling of passengers." They went on to provide that "a willful refusal to obey a reasonable request of an operator or driver of such a public conveyance in relation to the seating of passengers thereon shall constitute a breach of the peace."[16]

In short order, nine black people convicted of violating this ordinance filed suit in federal district court seeking to enjoin the enforcement of segregated seating. Judge Hobart Grooms held that because declining to move from one part of a bus to another was not a breach of the peace, the arrests were illegal. Even though the plaintiffs won that battle, under Judge Grooms's order, they lost the war. He also held that the segregated seating mandated by the bus company was not unconstitutional because there was no state action: "The seating arrangement was a matter between the Negroes and the Transit Company."[17] In other words, while black citizens could not be arrested for peaceably sitting in the front of the bus, the bus company could refuse to let them sit there. On appeal, Judge Tuttle, joined by Judge Wisdom, reversed, holding that the bus company had acted under color of law; the effect of the new ordinance, they ruled, was to delegate the authority of the city to the bus company. Moreover, as a common carrier, a type of public utility, the bus company acted as an agent of the state.[18]

Judge Cameron dissented. Ordinarily, a dissent is published at the same time as the majority opinion; in this case, Tuttle was ready to publish the opinion, and Cameron was not. Some seven months had elapsed since the trial court ruling, and Tuttle would not countenance further delay; he announced the opinion of the court on July 12, 1960; Judge Cameron simply wrote "I dissent."[19] Ten months later, on April 14, 1961, Cameron filed his dissent, a thirty-two-page treatise in which he extols states' rights and decries *Brown*.[20] Some months later, he repeated part of his dissent in *United States v. Wood*, a voting rights case. Judge Cameron was blunt. In his view, outsiders were coming to Mississippi and stirring up trouble, and the court was taking their side. Public officials in Mississippi were being unfairly characterized as untrustworthy. In fact, he argued, because of the benevolence of the white citizens of Mississippi, who had forged "close and compassionate contacts" with black citizens, "the progress made by the Negroes . . . has exceeded that achieved by them anywhere else in any country at any time." Outside agitators put that progress at risk; the "rank and file" of Mississippi blacks "resent the efforts of agitators who do not understand." Whites, blacks, and Judge Cameron all resented the judges of the Fifth Circuit who were not "perform[ing] their duties with a sympathetic understanding of the true facts."[21]

Tuttle saw in Judge Cameron's dissents a brief against *Brown*. Because Cameron was convinced *Brown* was wrong, he had no intention of following it. He was, nonetheless, a member of the court. Tuttle did not have the authority to strip Cameron of his office; that would take impeachment. In one critically important circumstance, however, Tuttle believed he did have discretion. In the federal judicial system, the district courts are the trial court; most petitions for relief are heard by a single district court judge, and most trials are held before a single district court judge. At that time, however, a federal statute first enacted in 1910 provided that if a plaintiff wanted to enjoin the enforcement of a state statute on the ground that it violated the U.S. Constitution, that suit would be heard by a three-judge panel.[22] The critical cases of the civil rights revolution often involved challenges to state statutes; witness the seminal case *Browder v. Gayle*. When a three-judge district court was requested, the district court judge with whom the petition was filed would notify the chief judge, who would "designate two other judges, at least one of whom shall be a circuit judge." From 1952 until his death in 1964, Judge Cameron was the only member of the court from Mississippi. It was conventional for the chief judge to appoint as one of the members of each three-judge court a circuit court judge from the state whose statute was being challenged. If Tuttle followed that protocol, each time a Mississippi statute was challenged, he would designate Judge Cameron as a member of the court. Instead, after Cameron's dissents in *Boman* and *Wood*, Tuttle stopped appointing Cameron.

The *Meredith* litigation had not involved a three-judge district court because it had not involved a challenge to a state statute. The case had gone on appeal to a panel of the Fifth Circuit, and Cameron was not a member of the panel. Unlike three-judge district courts, which convened to hear one particular case, appellate panels sat for several days of oral argument in a number of cases. With seven judges and a six-state circuit, it could easily happen that a case of some importance to the law of a particular state might be heard by a panel that did not include the judge from that state. That Judge Cameron was not on the *Meredith* appellate panel was unexceptional, but to Cameron, it was unacceptable.

Cameron issued his order purporting to stay the mandate on July 18, 1962. The panel—Circuit Judges Brown and Wisdom and District Judge DeVane—immediately instructed the clerk of the court to telegraph the parties, "requesting that they exchange and file, within five days, statements of their positions with memorandum briefs for or against the granting of any stays, including the vacating of the stay entered by Judge Cameron, the issuance by this Court of injunctions pending further appeal, or other appropriate action."[23] The telegram was dated July 20; on July 27 a unanimous court issued its opinion. Judge Wisdom opened with a comment on the passage of time: "In this case time is now of the quintessence. Time has been of the essence since January 1961 when James Meredith, in the middle of his junior year at Jackson State College (for Negroes), applied for admission to the University of Mississippi." Tuttle had thought time was of the essence five months earlier, when he could not prevail upon his colleagues to issue an injunction pending appeal and order Meredith admitted. Now, as the state of Mississippi, assisted by Judge Cameron, tried desperately to frustrate the order of the court, the panel was unified in support of its decision. Even Judge DeVane, who had dissented, agreed wholeheartedly that a single judge could not stay the order of a panel after the period during which a judge could move for rehearing had passed. The court vacated the stay and again ordered Judge Mize to enter an injunction directing the university to admit Meredith. Tuttle pointed out that there was another way the court's order could be frustrated: Judge Mize could neglect to enter the injunction. Simply doing nothing would soon mean that it was too late for James Meredith to register for yet another term. So Wisdom added a protocol that Tuttle had pioneered: the Fifth Circuit issued its own preliminary injunction, effectively requiring that Meredith be registered and allowed to attend classes. That injunction stayed in effect until the district court judge entered the final injunction in compliance with the order of the court.[24]

Judge Cameron was undeterred. The next day, July 28, he declared the order of the panel void and issued another stay. The panel set it aside that same day. On July 31 he issued a third stay. On August 4 the panel issued an order holding that all three stays had been set aside and calling them "unauthorized, erroneous and improvident." Judge Cameron promptly signed his fourth stay on August 6, 1962.[25] At that point, Meredith's attorney, Constance Baker Motley, filed a motion with Justice Hugo Black in the United States Supreme Court, asking him to vacate Judge Cameron's orders attempting to stay the order of the panel. She went to Justice Black because he was the member of the court assigned to handle matters in the nature of requests for stays arising from the Fifth Circuit. On September 10 Justice Black issued an order in which he affirmed the orders of the panel vacating Judge Cameron's attempts to stay its judgment. The stays, he noted, harmed Meredith by delaying relief; on the other hand, the university was not harmed by having to enforce the order pending the resolution of a petition for writ of certiorari filed by the university because there was "very little likelihood that [the] Court [would] grant certiorari." Justice Black then added this note: "Although convinced that I have the power to act alone in this matter, I have submitted it to each of my Brethren, and I am authorized to state that each of them agrees that the case is properly before this Court, that I have power to act, and that under the circumstances I should exercise that power as I have done here."[26] On September 13 Judge Mize, as directed, entered the order that should have secured Meredith's admission. That evening, Governor Ross Barnett, a white supremacist who had come into office with the endorsement of the white Citizens' Council, addressed the citizens of Mississippi on television. "We will not drink from the cup of genocide by submitting to the tyranny of judicial oppression," he declaimed as he invoked the doctrine of interposition, the idea that a state could interpose its own sovereignty between its citizens and the Constitution of the United States.[27] In 1956, during the term of Barnett's predecessor in office, Governor James P. Coleman, who later became a member of the Fifth

Circuit, Mississippi had passed an interposition resolution by a vote of 137 to 0 and created the State Sovereignty Commission to enforce it.[28] Barnett relied on the doctrine of interposition for the proposition that the federal government was powerless to enforce the constitutional rights of black citizens. If Mississippi didn't want "race mixing," Mississippi would not have "race mixing." For Barnett, Meredith was a godsend. Barnett's popularity had plummeted when he put gold-plated faucets in the bathroom of the governor's mansion to the point that he was booed at an Ole Miss football game. Now he was hailed as a hero; both the *Jackson Daily News* and the *Clarion-Ledger* headlined their coverage "Ross Risks Jail to Halt Mixing."[29]

One week later, on September 20, Meredith made his first attempt to register pursuant to the order of the Fifth Circuit Court of Appeals. Governor Barnett was there to rebuff him; the board of trustees of the university had delegated the registrar's power to enroll Meredith to Barnett.[30] That gave Barnett the platform from which to grandstand when Meredith showed up to enroll, and he did, repeatedly. On September 25 the court entered a temporary restraining order restraining the governor from "interfering with or obstructing in any manner or by any means the enjoyment of rights" under the court's earlier orders.[31] At 4:30 that afternoon, Meredith again appeared to register, and Governor Barnett again rebuffed him. At that point, the court entered an order requiring Barnett to appear before the court at the Fifth Circuit headquarters in New Orleans at 10:00 a.m. on September 28 and show cause why he should not be held in civil contempt.[32] When the court convened at 10:00 a.m., Tuttle presiding, Barnett was not there. All the members of the court were there, except for Judge Cameron; poor health prevented his attendance. Seven Mississippi attorneys, led by John Satterfield, an avowed segregationist who was the immediate past president of the American Bar Association, had moved that they be allowed to appear as amici curiae and argue on behalf of Mississippi. Tuttle informed them that their motion had been granted. Satterfield then asked to file a motion to dismiss the complaint. Tuttle informed Satterfield that the only motion the court had granted was that asking to appear as amici, and that did not encompass the right to file pleadings in the case. As the clerk of the court, Edward Wadsworth, began to testify, Satterfield asked about the right of amici to participate. Tuttle told him he had no right to object to evidence introduced. Satterfield immediately said, "To which we except," meaning that he objected to that ruling. Tuttle responded, "You have no right to except, I might add."[33] Tuttle's point was that because amici curiae are not parties to the litigation, they have no role in how it proceeds—no right to introduce or object to evidence, to examine witnesses, to make procedural motions such as motions to dismiss. The parties to the litigation, those whose legal rights it will affect, are the only persons who can participate in that manner. Amici can simply submit briefs addressing the position they wish to support. Ordinarily, the parties want to retain control; in this case, Governor Barnett did not want to concede that the court had jurisdiction over him, so he did not appear or authorize anyone to appear for him. On the other hand, he wanted to be represented. Tuttle was telling Satterfield that the governor could not have it both ways.

Wadsworth testified that as soon as he received the notice to show cause on the evening of September 25, he made certified copies of the notice and of the federal government's application to appear as amicus, wrote the governor a cover letter, drove to the post office, and mailed the papers to the governor, airmail, special delivery, return receipt requested. He then went to the Western Union office and sent a night letter to the governor. Wadsworth had not received the return receipt or any other correspondence from the governor.[34] U.S. marshals Warren Emerton and James McShane testified as to their failed efforts to serve the governor with the orders restraining interference with Meredith's admission. Governor Barnett had instructed everyone around him not to let service be made upon him and not to accept service for him. When Emerton tried to simply leave the papers at the governor's office, threats from state troopers warded him off. McShane actually handed the orders to Barnett, repeatedly brushing his hand with them, but Barnett would not take them.[35]

The purpose of personal service is to ensure that the party being served knows of the proceedings against him or her. In this case, there was no doubt about that. The governor's stratagems were transparent, and the court held that it did have jurisdiction of the person of the governor, that he was in contempt of the temporary restraining orders entered on September 25, and that the contempt was continuing. He was committed to the custody of the attorney general of the United States and ordered to pay a fine of ten thousand dollars per day unless, on or before Tuesday, October 2, 1962, at 11:00 a.m., he complied with the court orders and notified all officers under his command and jurisdiction to do so as well; that is, until James Meredith was allowed to register and remain a student at the university. Judges Jones, Gewin, and Bell dissented from the portion of the judgment imposing a fine.[36]

Before closing the hearing, Tuttle, who was presiding, addressed Assistant Attorney General Burke Marshall on the matter of enforcement. "The Court has practically exhausted its powers," Tuttle pointed out, and "the burden now falls on the Executive Branch of the Government."[37] When Marshall responded, "There is no question that the order of the Court is going to be enforced. . . . [T]he executive branch . . . will use whatever force, physical force, is required," Tuttle pressed on with one more point: "I do hope and I assume the executive department has in mind the fact that an order of this kind may be frustrated by delays as well as by failure to act." Other judges chimed in, including Judge Hutcheson, who advised Marshall, referring to the earlier attempt to register Meredith, "if you had one good Texas Ranger, it would have been all right. You could have gotten the job done."[38] Judge Hutcheson's quip aside, the members of the court were deeply concerned.

The Barnett contempt proceedings were only a part of the overarching drama surrounding Meredith. The court also held contempt proceedings against the board of trustees of the University of Mississippi and against Lieutenant Governor Paul Johnson. Governor Barnett hatched a plan to have Meredith arrested for an alleged voter registration fraud that Judge Wisdom had already found to be a spurious charge. The legislature passed a bill directed at preventing Meredith's enrollment. Even a local court, a Jones County chancery court, got in on the action by issuing a temporary injunction forbidding everyone from Meredith through the attorney general of the United States from assisting in Meredith's registration. In the background, Attorney General Robert Kennedy had opened a dialogue with Governor Barnett; between September 15 and September 28 they spoke twenty times.[39] Barnett wanted to yield only to a show of overwhelming force; he wanted to face down rifles and bayonets and then dramatically yield on principle. President Kennedy, on the other hand, wanted to avoid the use of federal troops or a federalized National Guard. They reached a tentative agreement that Meredith would be allowed to register on Monday, October 1. By this point, both Barnett's irresponsibility and the potential for violence had become apparent.

Meredith arrived on campus on Sunday afternoon, accompanied only by several hundred federal law enforcement officers, most of them marshals. A crowd gathered and grew exponentially in menace and size. By 7:30 the crowd had become "nasty and violent, and it would continue getting worse."[40] Journalists and particularly photographers (their cameras gave them away) were targeted, threatened, and roughed up. Kennedy had scheduled a presidential address at 8:00 p.m.; his staff was trying to hold back the use of tear gas, but shortly before 8:00, they could wait no longer. In the end, Kennedy used 16,000 fully armed army troops—including 7,600 men pulled from airborne and infantry divisions in Georgia, Kentucky, and North Carolina; 2,000 men from military police battalions at Fort Bragg, Fort Dix, and Fort Hood; and 2,700 Mississippi National Guard men federalized by the president—to restore order in Oxford, a town of 6,000, and that did not happen until daybreak.[41] By then, 2 people had been killed; hundreds, including 160 marshals and 16 national guardsmen, had been injured; and 200 people had been arrested.

On Monday, October 1, 1962, James Meredith walked to the Lyceum and registered. Had Tuttle's position prevailed in Meredith's first appeal, when Tuttle alone voted to reverse Judge Mize and order Meredith admitted, Meredith would have been in his last term, about to graduate. Instead, he was finally registering. Even then, it was not over. It was not over for James Meredith, who passed an uneasy year at Ole Miss. He persevered and graduated after the summer 1963 session, his final term marred by the assassination of his first mentor, Medgar Evers. It was not over for the Fifth Circuit, either. Governor Ross Barnett and his lieutenant governor, Paul Johnson, were obviously and proudly in contempt of court, but obtaining a judgment finding contempt would require a trial. There would be no trial unless someone moved to show cause why they should not be held in contempt. President Kennedy wanted no part of it. Putting a sitting governor in jail, he thought, would not do any good and might do considerable political harm.[42] Still, when the Fifth Circuit ordered the United States to file a motion to show cause, Attorney General Robert Kennedy complied.[43]

The Fifth Circuit itself created the next roadblock; the court split 4–4 over whether Barnett was entitled to a jury trial. Tuttle, Brown, Rives, and Wisdom expressed their opinion that even though the criminal contempt charges against Barnett and Johnson could result in substantial jail sentences, the court had "no duty or power to accord the defendants a trial by jury, but [was] under the duty to proceed without unnecessary delay to try the defendants for the criminal contempt itself."[44] The remaining four judges—Cameron, Bell, Gewin, and Jones—disagreed. Because of the even split on the question of the right to a jury trial in criminal contempt proceedings, the Supreme Court decided the case by answering a question certified to it by the Fifth Circuit. On April 6, 1964, the court ruled 6–3 that criminal contempt of court proceedings do not trigger a right to a jury trial under the Sixth Amendment. Tuttle's position had prevailed.[45]

Now that the court had the power to try Barnett and Johnson for criminal contempt, it declined to do so. On May 5, 1965, the seven-member court—Judge Cameron had died a little over a year earlier, and Judge Hutcheson had taken senior status—split 4–3. In an unsigned opinion, four of the judges—Bell, Gewin, Jones, and Rives—agreed that "the lapse of time since this Court ordered the criminal contempt proceedings to be instituted, and the changed circumstances and conditions have rendered the further prosecution of criminal contempt proceedings unnecessary."[46] It is unclear what changed circumstances they were referring to, but President Kennedy had been assassinated; Robert Kennedy was no longer attorney general; Ross Barnett was no longer governor, having been succeeded in office by Paul Johnson; and the Civil Rights Act of 1964 had passed the House and on July 2 would pass the Senate and promptly be signed into law by President Lyndon Johnson.

The three dissenting judges—Tuttle, Brown, and Wisdom—each wrote. Tuttle's spare, concise dissent spoke to the importance of proceeding. "The gravity of the charges was enhanced," he wrote, "not lessened, by the fact that they were against a governor and lieutenant governor of a state." Brown wrote at greater length, stressing the high level of public interest in highly placed public officials being held accountable. Wisdom, as was his custom, wrote at even greater length. Like Brown, he pointed out that Barnett's contempt was contempt not just of the court but rather "against American federalism, as established in the Constitution and as defined by the federal courts." Where Tuttle had said that he fully respected the judgment of his colleagues, although he did not share it, Wisdom wrote that he saw "no justification whatever for relieving Barnett of his obligation to comply with the judgment against him for civil contempt." But Wisdom did find some cause for solace as well as an opportunity to pen one of his most eloquent assessments: "There is an unedifying moral to be drawn from this case of The Man in High Office Who Defied the Nation: The mills of the law grind slowly—but not inexorably. If they grind slowly enough, they may even come, unaccountably, to a gradual stop, short of the trial and judgment an ordinary citizen expects when accused of criminal contempt. There is just one compensating thought: Hubris is grist for other mills, which grind exceeding small and sure."[47]

CHAPTER NINETEEN

The Fight for the Right to Vote

The Fifteenth Amendment to the Constitution, ratified in 1870, was a hard-won result of the Civil War: "The right of citizens of the United States to vote shall not be denied or abridged by the United States or by any State on account of race, color, or previous condition of servitude." Its clarity not-withstanding, just as virtually no progress had been made on the education front in 1960, when Elbert Tuttle became chief judge of the circuit, no progress had been made on the voting rights front. Post-Reconstruction, from 1890 to 1900, seven southern states had adopted methods aimed at depriving black people of the right to vote.[1] The two most common statutory methods came to be known as the understanding clauses and the grandfather clauses. Grandfather clauses created property and literacy qualifications and then exempted citizens eligible to vote on January 1, 1866, or some other date prior to adoption of the Fifteenth Amendment, or whose ancestors were eligible at that time. Despite their appellation, grandfather clauses enjoyed only a short life; in 1915 the United States Supreme Court found a typical one unconstitutional, recognizing it for what it was—a blatant attempt to avoid the command of the Fifteenth Amendment.[2]

Understanding clauses persisted; on the face of it, they simply established a reasonable standard that all citizens had to meet before qualifying to vote. In fact, these clauses provided a simple, foolproof mechanism for refusing to register black voters. After all, the standard was the ability to explain some provision of law "to the satisfaction of the registrar." The patently discriminatory use of these clauses gave rise to a joke among civil rights activists. A black man with a doctorate in political science went to his precinct in Mississippi to register to vote. He was given the First Amendment to the Constitution and asked to explain what it meant, and he did, with such eloquence that, despite themselves, everyone in the office was impressed. Somewhat taken aback, the registrar gave him a complex paragraph about taxation by the state; again, he explained it with such clarity that the listeners were spellbound. The registrar then pulled a piece of paper from his desk drawer; on it was a paragraph written in Chinese. "That's Article 3, Section 2 of the State Constitution," he told the applicant. "Can you tell me what that means?" "Certainly," replied the applicant. "You can?!?" the registrar exclaimed. "Of course I can. It means no Negro is going to register to vote in this precinct."

Black applicants faced not only the imperious disdain of the registrar; they faced brazen violence. When Claude Sitton, who was covering voter registration efforts led by the Student Nonviolent Coordinating Committee (SNCC) in Tylertown, Mississippi, in 1961, heard that a "registrar had taken a .38 revolver out of his desk and taken about a half a pound of skin off this SNCC worker's head," he went to interview the registrar, who readily admitted it. "Yeah," he said, "that nigger came in here and I told him to get out and he was a little slow and so I pistol whipped him."[3]

Death was the highest price paid for seeking to exercise the right to vote. It was paid by numbers of black citizens who had the temerity to go to a voting rights class, or to encourage others to register and vote, or to register themselves. In Mississippi in 1955 it was paid by the Reverend George W. Lee of Belzoni, who was shot and killed while driving, and by Lamar Smith, who was assassinated on the courthouse steps in Brookhaven.[4] Six years later, in 1961, Herbert Lee was shot point-blank on a public street in Amite County in southern Mississippi by a member of the state legislature who admitted hounding Lee down but claimed self-defense; two years after that the only witness, Louis Allen, was assassinated.[5] No one was ever prosecuted. In the Deep South, white men who killed black men did so with impunity. The terrorism of night riders (a misnomer, given that they were free to operate in broad daylight) notwithstanding, public officials throughout the South posed the greatest hurdles to enfranchisement.

The Civil Rights Act of 1957 was a modest step in the right direction, but it had no teeth. By 1959 the six-member Commission on Civil Rights created by the legislation had realized it was no match for the multitude of registrars throughout the South who were armed with great discretion and who were often cavalier at best about record keeping, making a charge of discrimination all but impossible to establish. The commission recommended that federal registrars be appointed to handle voter registration for federal elections. This idea provoked a firestorm of reaction among southern senators, from Democrats William Fulbright of Arkansas to Herman Talmadge of Georgia. The Voting Rights Act of 1960 emerged with provisions so watered down that it had little effect. It did provide that once an individual citizen proved a deprivation of the right to vote "on account of race or color," the attorney general of the United States could ask the court to determine if the deprivation was "pursuant to a pattern or practice." If the judge found a pattern or practice of racial discrimination, he could appoint voting referees to investigate and make an initial determination of voter eligibility when a rejected citizen complained.[6] At both junctures in this protocol, black citizens were often stymied: all too many federal district court judges declined to find discrimination even when the facts were egregious, and even if a litigant did establish discrimination, each affected citizen had to then come forward and establish eligibility, which customarily meant passing an understanding test.[7] It would take the Voting Rights Act of 1965 to make a real difference.

In the meantime, Elbert Tuttle took the lead in recognizing the gravity of the issue and in recognizing racial discrimination—in being willing to infer bias from the facts, the disavowals of the principal players notwithstanding. Of course, the registrar who purged black voters from the rolls would deny that race played any part in her decision. That was the stand taken by Mrs. Mae Lucky, voting registrar for Ouchita County, Louisiana, in 1956, after she struck some twenty-five hundred black voters from the rolls in the weeks before a May 22 election for the mayor of the city of Monroe. The matter came to light because Dr. John Reddix brought suit in federal court. Dr. Reddix alleged that between April 1 and May 12, 1956, with an election for the mayor of the city of Monroe scheduled for May 22, the registrar for Ouachita County accepted challenges to the voter registration of some three thousand blacks and subsequently struck some twenty-five hundred registered black voters from the rolls. Like most others, he had been unable to reregister in time to vote. Dr. Reddix alleged that the only purpose of the purge was to deprive blacks of their right to vote. Summary judgment can only be granted when there are no contested issues of material fact, and Dr. Reddix and Mrs. Lucky both filed affidavits in which they contested the truth of the other's declarations so that almost every fact was contested. Still, Judge Benjamin Dawkins Jr. granted summary judgment to the registrar. Judge Dawkins reasoned in part that Dr. Reddix should have simply reregistered to vote instead of coming to court. The judge characterized Dr. Reddix's failure to do so as "bad faith . . . [and] sheer stubborn vindictiveness."[8]

Judge Tuttle did not see it that way. He saw egregious conduct working great harm to black citizens: "It is clear from this abbreviated record that the occurrences during late April and early May, 1956, in which some 3,000 Negro voters and perhaps some white voters were summarily challenged within 30 days of an election under circumstances which concededly made it impossible for them all to be heard, resulting in striking some 2500 Negro voters from the rolls, was a shockingly unfair act by someone." Moreover, he held, it was a violation that demanded redress. "Whatever area of doubt remains as to the identification of other civil rights, there can be no doubt that the right to vote in any state election is guaranteed to every qualified citizen without regard to race or color," Tuttle wrote. Joined by Judge Borah, he reversed the order of District Court Judge Dawkins and remanded the case "for further proceedings not inconsistent with this opinion." In the opinion he had pointed out that the registrar's own affidavit indicated that she had not complied with the statutory requirement that she publish notice of the challenge within five days of mailing notice to the challenged voter. "We think," he wrote, "that Mrs. Lucky's failure to comply with the statute . . . made her subsequent action of striking his name from the rolls a nullity."[9] Dr. Reddix had won.

Tuttle, however, stopped short of giving Dr. Reddix all the relief he requested. Dr. Reddix had filed his complaint "on behalf of himself and all other Negro voters of Ouachita Parish." Unless the matter could proceed as a class action, each disenfranchised black voter would have to file a separate lawsuit. Nonetheless, Tuttle found it not to be "a proper case for a class action. . . . The fact that each voter must allege and prove the circumstances that might add up to an illegal purge, makes it inappropriate, if not impossible, for a single plaintiff to represent them in a class action."[10] It was only 1958, early in the struggle, and it was classic Tuttle. Although he knew to a moral certainty that a racially motivated purge had occurred, he also knew that was not proven by the record in the case—albeit in large part because the district court judge had refused to require the registrar to answer interrogatories. Outraged by what had happened, Tuttle declined to override neutral principles of law—here the rules governing class-action litigation—to reach a particular result. Part of that calculus may have been that he thought he had done enough. Time would challenge and change that perception. Another part may have been that, as shocking as the facts were and as limited as the relief he ordered, he was only able to get one of the two judges he sat with to join in his opinion. Judge Ben F. Cameron of Mississippi dissented.

Cameron argued that the federal court did not have jurisdiction because Reddix had acknowledged that some white voters may have been swept up in the purge; therefore, black and white voters had been treated alike, and no discrimination on the basis of race had occurred. He challenged Tuttle's explanation of the facts, stating: "I am not able to follow this portion of the opinion."[11] With that comment, he became perhaps the sole person ever to question Tuttle's lucidity. Throughout his decades-long career on the bench, Tuttle was known by allies and enemies alike for the clarity of his opinions. Disputes about style were the least of the differences between Judge Cameron and Judge Tuttle. Cameron openly disagreed with the mandate of *Brown*, and he used his judicial power to try to block its implementation at every opportunity. Tuttle saw that as an abdication of duty, and, as chief judge, he refused to assign Cameron to three-judge courts, although custom would have indicated that he be a member when a Mississippi statute was challenged.[12] In time, the conflict between the two men would become public in an explosive manner that threatened the legitimacy of the court.[13]

The seeds were sown in 1958. Not only did Cameron dissent in Dr. Reddix's case, he dissented in a companion case that had been filed by Reddix's attorney, James Sharp Jr. Acting as his own attorney, Sharp sued Mrs. Lucky, alleging that when he went to her office with a client whose registration had been challenged, Mrs. Lucky told him that he and his client would have to go to the police jury room, where her assistant would help them, because "only white persons were waited on in her office."[14] Sharp asked for an injunction ordering Mrs. Lucky to cease discriminating against black voters in her office and for damages. Judge Dawkins read the complaint as alleging only that Sharp had been excluded from the right to practice law, found that not cognizable as a deprivation of civil rights, and dismissed the lawsuit. Writing for himself and Judge Borah, Tuttle reversed. It was plain, Tuttle wrote, that Sharp's complaint was that he and his client were entitled to have access to the voter registrar's office on a nonsegregated basis, and he was correct. "Moreover," Tuttle wrote, "we think it quite clear that the complaint alleged a proper case for a class action" because Sharp and the other black citizens of the parish in the class "all have an identity of interest in having access to the public offices of the Parish on a non-segregated basis."[15] Again, Judge Cameron dissented. In his view, Sharp had not suffered any discrimination on the basis of his race; if there was discrimination, it was against his client, not against him. Moreover, this was a matter for the states, not for the federal government. In Cameron's view, the "so-called Civil Rights statutes," 42 U.S.C. §§ 1981–85, were only constitutional if they were narrowly applied, especially in the context of challenges to "executive action of state officials." As he saw it, neither Dr. Reddix's nor James Sharp's complaint stated a claim over which the federal court had jurisdiction.

Tuttle was infuriated by Cameron's dissents. That Cameron would not recognize the right of black citizens to seek recourse in federal court when they suffered discrimination in the fundamental matter of voting indicated to Tuttle that Cameron would not follow the law faithfully when the civil rights of black citizens were involved. Cameron was waving the flag of states' rights, and he was very close to spouting the doctrine of interposition, the theory that the states could assert their own sovereignty and "interpose" themselves between their citizens and the federal government. In other words, states did not have to follow the mandate of Brown or apply the due process and equal protection clauses of the Fifth and Fourteenth Amendments if their leaders said they did not. Bruited about widely by James Kilpatrick, the editor of the Richmond (Va.) News Leader, interposition became a rallying call across the Deep South. At the urging of Kilpatrick and others, several states passed interposition resolutions—resolutions that simply declared, for example, that the decision in Brown did not apply to that state. The doctrine was so ridiculous and the resolutions so patently meaningless that the NAACP rarely bothered to litigate them. Like the Southern Manifesto, however, by encouraging defiance, including the defiance of thugs, the promulgation of the doctrine of interposition did enormous harm even though it lacked legal effect.[16]

Tuttle was angered and saddened by both the Southern Manifesto and the development of the doctrine of interposition, but a greater disappointment lay ahead, in the penultimate resolution of the litigation surrounding Mrs. Lucky, the voting registrar for Ouachita County, Louisiana.

James Sharp, the black attorney whose case had been dismissed by Judge Dawkins and then reinstated pursuant to Tuttle's opinion, went back to Judge Dawkins's courtroom to try the matter. Dawkins was at least a second-generation Louisianan. His father had been born in Ouachita City in 1881; he too had been a federal district court judge. In fact, the son had been appointed to his father's seat when the father took senior status in 1953. Judge Dawkins had attended college (Tulane) and law school (LSU) in Louisiana and practiced law in Monroe and Shreveport. He did not like the way Tuttle had handled the appeal, and he made that very clear in his order denying any relief to Sharp.

> On appeal, plaintiff completely changed his position by asserting that he sought relief, not as an attorney, but as a Negro. Notwithstanding its own prior rulings . . . holding that such an about-face will not be permitted, two members of a three-judge panel of the Fifth Circuit Court of Appeals reversed our ruling. . . .
>
> As soon as our Calendar permitted . . . we tried the case on its merits . . . and now have arrived at our Findings of Fact . . . and our Conclusions of Law, as follows:
>
> In early August, 1956, in keeping with her duty under the State law . . . defendant proceeded to "purge" the voter registration rolls. . . . On August 13, 1956, defendant sent out approximately 1,500 challenges, of which about 1,000 went to white voters and 500 to Negroes.
>
> Soon after the challenges were issued, voters of both races began pouring into defendant's office. . . . Of their own volition . . . most Negroes stood back and allowed white persons to go ahead of them, with the result that the Negroes were not being fairly and adequately served.
>
> Because of this, defendant made arrangements with Police Jury officials to use its room to handle the overflow. . . .
>
> This method of operation gave the challenged Negro registrants better physical facilities than the whites. . . .
>
> The crucial, undisputed truth is that what was done so obviously was not intended as a discrimination—a designedly malicious segregation of Negroes—but was for their advantage and convenience.[17]

Judge Dawkins's view of race relations in Ouachita County was bizarre in its rosiness; nonetheless, it was enthusiastically endorsed by the three-judge panel of the Fifth Circuit, which heard it on appeal. Judges Hutcheson and

Wisdom signed a per curiam opinion affirming the order denying Sharp relief. Judge Brown concurred in the result, but he did not join the opinion.[18] "We are of the opinion," Judges Wisdom and Hutcheson wrote,

> that the record furnishes full support for the findings of fact and conclusions drawn therefrom by the district judge. . . . Indeed, we are of the opinion that the issuance, on this minuscule claim, of an injunction against the defendant would have been to tithe mint, anise and cumin, and to overlook the weightier matters controlling here, the fair and just administration by the registrar of the duties of her office, in good faith, with good manners, and with good will.[19]

The opinion was issued on April 30, 1959. Tuttle had to have been dismayed. Judge Dawkins's findings of fact had made it difficult for the appellate court to reach any other resolution because he had resolved all credibility issues in favor of Mrs. Lucky, but the court did not have to swallow the opinion whole or to mock the seriousness of the allegations of racial discrimination. Given the overall record of the three judges on the panel, this opinion is hard to understand. Perhaps a clue lies in the controversy around Judge Wisdom's confirmation hearings. Senator Eastland, the entrenched segregationist chair of the Judiciary Committee, had been suspicious of Wisdom, and his confirmation was uncertain.[20] Judge Dawkins, like Wisdom a Louisiana Republican and an Eisenhower nominee, had written Senator Eastland in support of Wisdom, describing him as "supremely qualified, in native ability, education, experience, temperament and integrity."[21] Wisdom presumably held similar opinions about Judge Dawkins; it is not surprising that he would be inclined to defer to his judgment. Moreover, this was one of the first voting rights cases to reach the court; in other words, the judges had not yet been educated in the recalcitrance and the dissembling of registrars that they would come to be familiar with.

Four years later, Tuttle's view was vindicated by Wisdom's landmark opinion in *United States v. Louisiana*.[22] The United States, represented by the heroic assistant attorney general John Doar and his supervisor, Burke Marshall, brought suit against the state of Louisiana, challenging the interpretation test, the provision in the Louisiana Constitution that allowed a registrar to decline to register any person who could not explain a selected passage of the Constitution of the United States or of the state of Louisiana.

In the course of finding the provision unconstitutional, Wisdom, as was his custom, wrote a treatise tracing the long-standing history of disfranchisement of black voters in Louisiana. Mrs. Lucky, it turns out, was almost certainly carrying out directions promulgated by the Citizens' Council of Louisiana in a 1956 pamphlet entitled *Voter Qualifications in Louisiana— The Key to Victory in the Segregation Struggle*. The state of Louisiana sent the pamphlet to its registrars and sponsored meetings to explain the strategy: purge the rolls of "the great numbers of unqualified voters who have been illegally registered," to wit, "the colored bloc," and also some white voters as a cover; then use the interpretation test to deny the colored voters the ability to reregister.[23] Ouachita Parish was one of eight parishes where the Citizens' Council directed special efforts in 1956–58; they challenged all 5,782 registered black voters, and all but 595 were stricken from the record. Twenty years after he issued his opinion commending Mrs. Lucky, Judge Dawkins presided over a class-action filed by all black citizens of Monroe, challenging the at-large election of the city council as an unconstitutional effort to dilute the impact of black voters. This time he ruled with the black plaintiffs, noting with approval the Fifth Circuit finding a year earlier that "open, flagrant, unsophisticated, purposeful discrimination has been the long time pattern in Ouachita County."[24]

The problems in Louisiana were severe; still, as Tuttle was keenly aware, Georgia was second to no state in the magnitude of its voting rights issues. Not only was Georgia home to "Terrible Terrell" County, which John Doar of the Justice Department focused on as being one of the two most promising areas for voter registration litigation (the other was Dallas County, Alabama, home to Selma), but Georgia citizens labored under the county unit system, an antidemocratic method of counting votes in the primaries and allocating representatives and senators in the General Assembly that mocked the concept of equal representation. The largest state east of the Mississippi, Georgia is divided into 159 counties. Several counties are rural and sparsely populated. At the other end of the spectrum, several include large dense metropolitan areas. According to the 1960 United States Census, Fulton County, which includes part of Atlanta, had a population of 556,326, while the least populous county in the state, Echols, had a population of 1,876. Prior to a 1962 amendment to the controlling statute (a last-ditch effort to avoid an adverse federal court ruling), the county unit system used in the Democratic primaries allocated 6 unit votes to each of the

8 largest counties by population, 4 unit votes to each of the 30 next largest by population, and 2 each to the remaining 121 counties. Thus, in Fulton County, each cohort of 92,721 voters had 1 county unit; in Echols County, each cohort of 938 voters had 1 county unit. This rendered it possible to lose the popular vote by a wide margin but still win the office. The county unit system gave control of statewide offices to the rural sectors; it was the source of the Talmadge family's entrenched control.[25] A formula that constituted a variation on this theme was used to determine the composition of both the House and the Senate in Georgia, so that a small fraction of voters controlled the legislative process as well. The eight most populous counties held approximately 41 percent of the population and furnished more than 41 percent of the total state revenue but were represented in the House by 11.7 percent of the representatives and in the Senate by 13 percent of the senators.[26]

In the postwar years, even as Tuttle struggled to build the fledgling Republican Party, he became heavily involved in Atlanta's affairs, culminating in his election in December 1948 as president of the Chamber of Commerce.[27] He joined a few other hardy souls in actively opposing the county unit method. Despite the intensity of the years of the civil rights revolution, Sara Tuttle would later recall that her husband's work in the late 1940s opposing the county unit system had generated the only threat she took seriously.[28] They had arrived home about midnight from Columbus, Georgia, where Tuttle had given a speech criticizing the county unit system. When the phone rang, Sara answered. The caller told her that her husband had better stop "or we'll kill both of you." "Well, I think that's a little extreme," she responded. Her polite, albeit steely, reply aside, Sara was frightened. Both Elbert and Sara thought their house was being watched. Moreover, they understood that because of the threat it posed to the Talmadge political empire, Tuttle's stance was inflammatory—and Herman Talmadge's supporters were easily inflamed. Sara called the police and reported the threat. Before retiring, she wrote a brief note to her adult children, Nicky and Buddy, describing the call. In later years she made the story entertaining; she would explain that had they been found dead in their bed, she didn't want the children to think they had killed each other.

Tuttle went on the bench in 1954. In 1962 he sat on the three-judge district court that held the county unit system unconstitutional.[29] In contemporary times, he no doubt would have recused himself; in 1962 that apparently did not occur to Tuttle or to anyone else involved in the litigation. Part of the reason may have been that by then the United States Supreme Court had, for all practical purposes, already decided the matter. Prior to the landmark decision earlier that year in *Baker v. Carr*, a Tennessee case, the county unit system had been thought to be insulated by the political question doctrine—the concept that apportionment matters were political questions delegated to legislatures that were not subject to judicial review.[30] When the Supreme Court held, in *Baker v. Carr*, that an equal protection challenge to alleged malapportionment of the Tennessee legislature was justiciable, the vulnerability of the county unit system in Georgia was apparent. *Baker v. Carr* had sounded the death knell; the later cases were merely the coups de grâce.

In 1966 Judge Tuttle was invited to deliver the seventh annual James Madison Lecture at NYU. He chose for his topic equality and the vote, and he began with a startling statistic. According to the 1960 census, in Lowndes County, Alabama, 5,322 black and 1,900 white residents were over twenty-one. As of early 1965, not one black person was registered to vote—not one. After the Voting Rights Act of 1965 passed, that changed dramatically: now a majority of the registered voters were black. Also in the news, the Democratic Party had decided to change the design of its primary ballot used in Alabama; the crowing rooster under the legend "White Supremacy" was coming off. Tuttle spoke on March 16, 1966, nine days after the first anniversary of Bloody Sunday.

March 7, 1965, was the day John Lewis and Hosea Williams and the hundreds of marchers they led were brutally beaten by state troopers and local police, many on horseback, as they tried to cross the Edmund Pettus Bridge in Selma, Alabama. They were on their way to Montgomery, the state capital, but that day they got no farther than the bridge. Martin Luther King Jr. rushed to Selma, prepared to march again. But there was a problem: the day after Bloody Sunday, King and his people had asked federal district court judge Frank Johnson to enjoin state and local officials from interfering with their march; instead, Johnson entered an order prohibiting the march until after a hearing, which he scheduled for Thursday, March 11. The issues were not insubstantial: the protestors wanted permission to utilize state and federal highways for a four-day journey. For a federal court to intervene in state and local affairs in order to permit a protest of that scale was unprecedented. Many in King's camp wanted to march in defiance of

Judge Johnson's order. King hesitated. While he had encouraged civil disobedience of nakedly unconstitutional laws, the movement depended on
the rule of law—on the evenhanded enforcement of constitutional rights.
It was the federal courts that had given the movement many of its victories,
and no single district court judge had been more important than Frank
Johnson. King did not want to defy any federal court order and particularly not one authored by Judge Johnson. Still, the pressure was enormous.
Inside the movement, which was increasingly populated by the young activists of the SNCC, almost everyone wanted King to lead a march right
away—but the lawyers cautioned restraint, and King took their advice.

On the first day of the hearing, Judge Johnson reviewed the television
news footage of the police assault on the marchers on Bloody Sunday. John
Lewis had seen the events in person; he watched the judge as the judge
watched the film. Lewis left the courtroom certain the judge would rule
with them. Johnson did rule with them, but he did not rely solely on the
film or on the events of Bloody Sunday. Instead, he put it in context:

> The evidence in this case reflects . . . an almost continuous pattern of con-
> duct . . . on the part of Sheriff Clark, his deputies, and his auxiliary depu-
> ties known as "possemen" of harassment, intimidation, coercion, threaten-
> ing conduct, and sometimes brutal mistreatment [that] reached a climax on
> Sunday, March 7, 1965. . . .
>
> . . . It seems basic to our constitutional principles that the extent of the
> right to assemble, demonstrate and march peaceably along the highways and
> streets in an orderly manner should be commensurate with the enormity of
> the wrongs that are being protested and petitioned against. In this case, the
> wrongs are enormous.[31]

Judge Johnson wrote his order the evening the hearing ended, Tuesday,
March 16. Then he called John Doar, who had appeared as counsel for the
government at the hearing. He told Doar what he proposed to rule, but before he did, he wanted assurance that the federal government would back
him up. When Attorney General Katzenbach called Judge Johnson early
the next morning to give that assurance, Johnson explained that he didn't
want it from Katzenbach, he wanted it from President Lyndon Johnson
himself. Two weeks later, on March 21, 1965, a federalized national guard
protected thirty-two hundred marchers as they left Selma. By the time
they got to Montgomery, four days later, having walked through Lowndes

County, they would be twenty-five thousand strong. As important as Judge Johnson's Selma order was, it stands only first among equals among his opinions. More than once he showed Congress the way forward, as he did, for example, when he pointed out that if Congress really intended "to give full and complete authority to the Attorney General of the United States to enforce the constitutional rights here involved [voting rights]," it would give the United States the power to name a state as a defendant.[32] The Civil Rights Act of 1960 includes a provision that allows the attorney general to name the state as a defendant.

Judge Johnson did not stop at enjoining future discrimination; in a remarkable manner, he corrected past discrimination. Thanks to the extraordinary work of a team of lawyers headed by John Doar, who led the voting rights effort for the Civil Rights Division of the Justice Department, in *United States v. Alabama*, Judge Johnson had reviewed applications of whites who were registered and blacks whose applications had been rejected, and they told the tale: whether applicants were deemed qualified to register depended not on how they filled out their application or performed on the test, it depended on which race they belonged to.[33] He created a list of blacks whose applications had been rejected but would have been accepted had they been white, and he entered a mandatory injunction requiring they be registered. He stopped short, however, of appointing federal referees to take over the work of the Board of Registrars. He wanted to give them a chance, he wrote, to "regain for Macon County and for the State of Alabama the integrity that . . . has been lost in this field of voting rights."[34]

In his next voting rights case, Judge Johnson expanded on the concept he had addressed with his list in the Macon County case. After hearing the testimony of over 175 witnesses and reviewing some 13,000 exhibits, he ruled that the qualifications demanded of black applicants could not be more stringent than those that had historically been used to qualify white applicants. If illiterate white people were qualified to vote, so were illiterate blacks. If mistakes in the application did not disqualify whites, they did not disqualify blacks either. The standards were frozen.[35] The freezing principle came directly from the Civil Rights Act of 1960.[36] Forceful implementation of it came first from Judge Frank Johnson.[37] Freezing was critical because in 1962 almost all whites in several of the states of the Fifth Circuit were registered, and almost no blacks were. The evidence laboriously pulled together and presented to the court by John Doar and his team of attorneys from the Justice Department established that at the same time that black applicants who held doctorates routinely failed voter registration tests, white applicants never did. The test for white applicants was simple: "If you could breathe, you voted."[38]

Like Tuttle, Johnson was labeled an activist, a term meant to degrade. He took that issue on in a 1979 speech: "If federal judges appear more activist, it is not because they have appointed themselves roving commissioners to do good. Rather it is because new procedures have opened the door of the federal courthouse to new interests." Moreover, he noted, "the surest curb on judicial activism, for those who fear it, is executive and legislative activism in defense of constitutional liberties. The courts possess only so much power as the other branches relinquish."[39] Judge Johnson never faltered in his commitment to the defense of constitutional liberties, even when he was vilified, even when he stood virtually alone. He credited the Fifth Circuit in the Tuttle years with providing reinforcement. "It meant that what I said about it was the last word for all practical purposes. The litigants and the people knew it. It . . . [made me] confident that I'm not going to be emasculated if I decide this case like it ought to be. I'm going to be affirmed."[40]

Judge Harold Cox of Mississippi could not have been more different from Judge Johnson when it came to enforcing the constitutional rights of black citizens. Cox owed his seat on the Federal District Court to his friend Senator James O. Eastland. Eastland first proposed Cox's name to the Eisenhower administration in 1955. Deputy Attorney General Bill Rogers shrugged it off, precisely because Senator Eastland, who had characterized Brown as the corrupt decision of a political court and told a cheering crowd that it was "obligated to defy" Brown, supported Cox so strongly.[41] Six years later, Eastland tried again. Now he was dealing with a president of his own party, and he could lay claim to some deference on the matter because of his role in deferring passage of the Omnibus Judgeship Act of 1961 until Kennedy was in office, thereby giving him seventy-one judicial appointments. If Eastland had his way, the very first would be Harold Cox. Once the ABA rated Cox, who had no public record on civil rights, "Extremely Well Qualified," the nomination was firmly on track. Even so, Bobby Kennedy insisted on a private interview. He came away reassured that Cox would, as he had promised, comply with the decisions of

the Supreme Court and the Fifth Circuit in civil rights matters. The problem, Tuttle later quipped in a rare aside, was that they were speaking different languages. When Cox promised to uphold the law of the land, he
didn't mean the Constitution, he meant lynching. And when he agreed that
blacks should have the right to vote, he didn't mean all blacks, he meant
two.[42] When Bobby Kennedy gave Harold Cox his stamp of approval, some
attributed it to deference to Senator Eastland; others said it was simply political poker. President Kennedy wanted to put Thurgood Marshall on the
United States Court of Appeals for the Second Circuit; Eastland reportedly
told Kennedy that he'd "give him the nigger" if Kennedy would nominate
Cox.[43] True to Tuttle's concerns, Cox turned out to be among the most racist federal judges in the circuit. Notoriously, he once called blacks seeking
to register to vote "chimpanzees," and, referring to black teachers seeking
to protect their jobs, he spoke of "colored people's antics."[44] Cox was determined to thwart the implementation of *Brown*, and he did much damage.
The rule of law prevailed in large part due to Tuttle's firm leadership, and
the Theron Lynd litigation is a case in point.

On August 11, 1960, pursuant to Title III of the Civil Rights Act of 1960,
Assistant U.S. Attorney John Doar formally requested that Theron Lynd,
the registrar for Forrest County, Mississippi, make his registration records
available for copying and inspection. Lynd did nothing. On January 19,
1961, Doar filed an enforcement proceeding with the federal district court
judge for the Southern District of Mississippi, Harold Cox. Under the law,
Cox should have entered an order granting Doar's request as a matter of
course; instead, he did nothing. After waiting six months, on July 6, 1961,
Doar filed suit seeking an injunction allowing inspection of the records,
relying on an alternate ground for relief—Rule 34 of the Federal Rules of
Civil Procedure. The next month, on February 15, 1962, Judge Cox dismissed the enforcement proceeding, calling it "abandoned."[45]

Various dilatory motions ensued. Judge Cox granted the motion of the
defendants, Theron Lynd and the state of Mississippi, that Doar allege in
detail the registration experience of each black applicant who had been
turned down and any whites alleged to have been registered without having better qualifications than the rejected blacks, but Judge Cox refused to
require the defendants to allow Doar access to registration records. The
near impossibility of accumulating the relevant evidence notwithstanding,
Doar produced an impressive set of facts. Theron Lynd had taken office

on February 26, 1959; on his watch, not one black had been registered, although Doar could prove that some forty had tried, several on more than one occasion. On the other hand, most if not all white applicants had been permitted to register without even filling out an application form. Judge Cox finally scheduled a hearing on the motion for a temporary injunction, and from March 5 until March 7, 1962, John Doar presented his case. When the government rested, the state of Mississippi and Theron Lynd reserved the right of cross-examination and indicated they needed thirty days to be ready to produce defense witnesses. Judge Cox ordered a recess of thirty days. Fourteen months had passed since the government had first sought access to the registration records pursuant to the Voting Rights Act. Without ever getting those records, to which he was clearly entitled, Doar had made his case. Now he wanted his temporary injunction granted; he wanted the discrimination to stop. Doar filed an appeal with the Fifth Circuit. In response, Lynd pointed out that Judge Cox had never ruled on any of Doar's claims—not on the request for records, nor on the complaint seeking a temporary injunction—so there was nothing to appeal from; moreover, the request for an injunction pending appeal was premature.

On April 10, 1962, Tuttle wrote the opinion for a panel that included Hutcheson and Wisdom. He made short shrift of the argument that the government could not appeal because Judge Cox had never ruled. The government had made out its case that it was entitled to a preliminary injunction. Judge Cox's refusal to rule was equivalent to refusing to grant the injunction, and refusing to grant an injunction is an appealable order.[46] In response to Lynd's argument that no injunction against him could issue until he had put up his case, Tuttle clarified the role of the temporary injunction, which is to protect the rights of the person seeking it until a full adjudication can be had. Not only was the failure of Judge Cox to rule the equivalent of denying relief, denying relief on these facts appeared to be an abuse of discretion. Because the record established a substantial likelihood that the plaintiffs would prevail on the merits in the end, the court would act now to protect their constitutional rights in the interim.[47]

Obtaining appellate jurisdiction by holding that failure to rule was the equivalent of denying the relief sought was bold; Tuttle's next step was breathtaking. He realized that if he followed the ordinary protocol of reversing and remanding with instructions to the trial court to enter an order consistent with the appellate panel's opinion, Judge Cox could once again simply do nothing. It might take him an inordinately long time to draft an appropriate order and even longer to decide to enter it. Tuttle would not give him that opening. Instead, he drafted the terms of the injunction himself and included them in the opinion of the court; it was, he wrote, effective immediately. Moreover, the clerk of the district court for the Southern District of Mississippi was directed to send a certified copy to each party defendant.[48]

The case had languished fourteen months on Judge Cox's docket. Tuttle filed his opinion for the panel on April 10, only four days after oral argument. There would be no more delay, unless the clerk of the court and the registrar were ready to commit contempt of court—and it would not be contempt of the district court, it would be contempt of the United States Court of Appeals for the Fifth Circuit.

Elbert Parr Tuttle. From *The Ties that Bind* by Joe Renouard; courtesy of Sutherland, Asbill & Brennan LLP.

Randolph W. Thrower, Herbert R. Elsas, and Elbert Parr Tuttle. From *The Ties that Bind* by Joe Renouard; courtesy of Sutherland, Asbill & Brennan LLP.

William A. Sutherland,
Mac Asbill, and Joseph
B. Brennan. From *The
Ties that Bind* by Joe
Renouard; courtesy of
Sutherland, Asbill &
Brennan LLP.

Elbert Tuttle introducing
Dwight Eisenhower in
Atlanta, September 1952,
as Eisenhower opens
his Dixie Campaign
and becomes the first
Republican presidential
candidate to speak in
Georgia. Courtesy of
the Tuttle and Harmon
families.

Elbert watching the removal of his name from the firm office, Atlanta, 1952. Courtesy of the Tuttle and Harmon families.

Chief Justice Earl Warren, Justice Harold Burton, and Sara and Elbert Tuttle, September 1, 1954, Supreme Court, Washington, D.C., following Elbert's swearing in by Justice Burton. Courtesy of the Tuttle and Harmon families.

Left: Elbert and Sara Tuttle, Washington, D.C., circa 1954. Courtesy of the Tuttle and Harmon Families. *Right:* Elbert and Sara Tuttle at his fiftieth Cornell University reunion, 1958. Courtesy of the Tuttle and Harmon families.

Sara and Elbert (left) with Malcolm and Rilla Tuttle (right), Hawaii, 1956. Courtesy of the Tuttle and Harmon families.

Left: A. T. Walden, Horace Ward, and Donald Hollowell. Courtesy of Horace T. Ward Personal Archives from *Horace T. Ward: Foot Soldier for Equal Justice* Documentary, Foot Soldier Project for Civil Rights Studies Collection, Richard B. Russell Library for Political Research and Studies, University of Georgia, Athens, Ga.

Below: Hamilton Holmes with his father, Alfred. Copyright Atlanta Journal-Constitution; courtesy of Georgia State University.

Top: Donald Hollowell
with Charlayne Hunter;
Hamilton Holmes;
and Holmes's mother,
Athea Hunter, 1961.
Courtesy of Marilyn
Holmes Personal
Archives from the
*Hamilton Earl Holmes:
The Legacy Continues*
Documentary, Foot
Soldier Project
for Civil Rights
Studies Collection,
Richard B. Russell
Library for Political
Research and Studies,
University of Georgia,
Athens, Ga.

Bottom: Dr. Benjamin
Mays with Judge
Horace Ward on the
occasion of Ward's
appointment to
the Superior Court
bench, 1977. Courtesy
of Horace T. Ward
Personal Archives
from *Horace T. Ward:
Foot Soldier for Equal
Justice* Documentary,
Foot Soldier Project
for Civil Rights
Studies Collection,
Richard B. Russell
Library for Political
Research and Studies,
University of Georgia,
Athens, Ga.

Top left: Hamilton Holmes, leaving through the Arch at the University of Georgia, accompanied by his lawyer Donald L. Hollowell (right) and Rev. Sam Williams, Athens, Georgia, January 1961. Photograph by Dwight Ross Jr.; copyright Atlanta Journal-Constitution; courtesy of Georgia State University.

Above: Federal judge Elbert P. Tuttle (right), and attorney for Hamilton Holmes, Constance Motley (being interviewed), Atlanta, Georgia, January 10, 1961. Photograph by Bob Dendy; copyright Atlanta Journal-Constitution; courtesy of Georgia State University.

Bottom left: Editorial cartoon, by Clifford H. "Baldy" Baldowski, *Atlanta Journal-Constitution*, January 11, 1961. Courtesy of Richard B. Russell Library for Political Research and Studies, University of Georgia Libraries.

U.S. Court of Appeals for the Fifth Circuit, 1965. Bottom row from left to right: John R. Brown (Tex.), Richard T. Rives (Ala.), Elbert P. Tuttle (Ga.), Warren L. Jones (Fla.). Back row from left to right: Homer Thornberry (Tex.), Walter P. Gewin (Ala.), John Minor Wisdom (La.), Griffin Bell (Ga.), James P. Coleman (Miss.). Courtesy of the library of the United States Court of Appeals for the Fifth Circuit, New Orleans, La.

Julian Bond being denied his seat in the Georgia General Assembly. Photograph by Bill Wilson; copyright Atlanta Journal-Constitution; courtesy of Georgia State University.

Supreme Court of the United States
Washington, D. C. 20543

CHAMBERS OF
THE CHIEF JUSTICE

June 21, 1967

Honorable Elbert P. Tuttle,
Chief Judge,
United States Court of Appeals,
Atlanta, Georgia 30301.

My dear Judge Tuttle:

      While I have been painfully conscious of the fact that you are to re-linquish your Chief Judgeship in July in accordance with the statute, you are still the Chief Judge, and for that reason I sent the notification of the meeting of the Judicial Conference to you. When the transfer becomes effective, we will, of course, notify Judge Brown, and will be happy to have him at the September meeting.

      I take this opportunity to express my profound admiration for the manner in which you have administered your court during the trying years of your Chief Judgeship. No court in the country has had the problems which yours has had, and no court has met its problems with greater fidelity. I feel certain that history will record that, under your leadership, the Court of Appeals for the Fifth Circuit has done more to make the Fourteenth Amendment meaningful than any of the others.

      You have certainly earned a respite from your heavy administrative burdens, and I hope it will redound to your good health and well being.

      With every good wish, I am

Sincerely,

Earl Warren

Chief Justice Earl Warren's letter to Chief Judge Elbert Tuttle, June 21, 1967.
Courtesy of the Tuttle and Harmon families.

The two handwritten notes found in Elbert Tuttle's desk at his death. *Above:* "It is said that when Solon was asked in ancient Greece how justice could be secured in Athens, he replied, 'If those who are not injured feel as indignant as those who are.'" *Below:* "Tom Payne. Those who would enjoy the blessings of freedom must, like men, undergo the fatigue of supporting it." Both notes courtesy of the Tuttle and Harmon families.

President James Earl Carter awarding the Presidential Medal of Freedom to Judge Elbert Parr Tuttle, January 16, 1981. Courtesy of the Jimmy Carter Library.

Left: Elbert and Sara Tuttle at the closing ceremony for the Fifth Circuit. Courtesy of the Eleventh Circuit Historical Society. *Right:* Elbert Tuttle receiving an honorary degree from Atlanta University president Kofi B. Bota, June 1984. Courtesy of the Tuttle and Harmon families.

Elbert Parr Tuttle U.S. Court of Appeals Building, Atlanta. From *The Ties that Bind* by Joe Renouard; courtesy of Sutherland, Asbill & Brennan LLP.

Congressman John Lewis presenting Judge Elbert Parr Tuttle with a plaque at a ceremony renaming the Eleventh District United States Circuit Court of Appeals building in his name, Atlanta, Georgia, June 7, 1990. Photograph by Michael A. Schwarz; copyright Atlanta Journal-Constitution; courtesy of Georgia State University.

Judge Elbert Parr Tuttle and his wife Sara Sutherland Tuttle at the renaming, in his honor, of the Eleventh District United States Circuit Court of Appeals building, Atlanta, Georgia, June 7, 1990. Photograph by Michael A. Schwarz; copyright Atlanta Journal-Constitution; courtesy of Georgia State University.

Sara and Elbert Tuttle in front of the Elbert Parr Tuttle Courthouse, headquarters of the United States Court of Appeals for the Eleventh Circuit, Atlanta. Courtesy of the Tuttle and Harmon families.

CHAPTER TWENTY

But for Birmingham

Late in his life, when Elbert Tuttle was asked to name the most significant cases he had decided, two always made the list: *Holmes v. Danner*, in
which he ordered the desegregation of the University of Georgia, and the
Birmingham schoolchildren case. They had two great themes in common:
civil rights and access to education. But those were not the only reasons
he singled them out. It was also because they were cases in which he acted
alone. He was masterful at keeping channels of communication open and
moving a group toward consensus, but he trusted his own judgment, and
he was happy to exercise it unconstrained.[1] Several opinions of the era vie
for the distinction of having proven absolutely critical to the success of the
campaign to eradicate the vestiges of slavery and admit black Americans
to full citizenship. The 1960s were perilous times in which everything
mattered. Nothing mattered more than the resolution of the Birmingham
schoolchildren's case.

In the early months of 1963, when the civil rights movement moved
into Birmingham, it was beset by threats on all sides. Part of the problem
was that the leaders had come from Albany, Georgia, and in Albany they
had been bested. The plight of black Americans was as severe in Albany
as it was in the rest of the Deep South, but the success of the movement
had come from exposing the evils, the brutality, and the utter injustice
of Jim Crow segregation, and in Albany the curtain stayed down. When
Laurie Pritchett, Albany's chief of police, learned that leaders of the Albany
Movement had invited Dr. Martin Luther King Jr. to come to Albany to
deliver a speech, instead of lining up his troops and handing out the billy
clubs, Pritchett read Dr. King's book, *Stride toward Freedom*, in which
King explained nonviolent protest. Pritchett understood that the success
of the movement depended on exposing the brutality of the regime it confronted.[2] Recognizing that King was well served by a violent response to

his nonviolent protest as well as by mass arrests that filled the jails, giving the movement focus and hampering the ability of the police to make more arrests, Pritchett trained his officers to respond nonviolently: "no violence, no dogs, no show of force." He surveyed the area around Albany up to a sixty-mile radius, contacted other local authorities, and was assured he could use their jails. At one time, he recalled, his force had arrested some two thousand marchers—but not one was held in an Albany city jail.[3] One Albany organizer ruefully noted, "We ran out of people before he ran out of jails."[4]

Some gave Pritchett credit for being less brutal than his counterparts; others disagreed. John Lewis thought it was not that Pritchett's men were less violent—after all, they clubbed a pregnant woman, causing a miscarriage; dragged another woman into court by her hair and a man by his testicles; and hanged one jailed man by his thumbs. Rather, it was that "on the whole, they were much more careful than the police had been in Birmingham or Montgomery."[5] When Pritchett did overreach, he quickly corrected. In midwinter he arrested Martin Luther King Jr. and Ralph Abernathy for "parading without a permit." In July they were tried, convicted, and sentenced to either pay a fine of $178 or spend forty-five days in jail. They picked jail. In mid-June, as the press began to descend on the jail, Pritchett recognized his error. Against their wishes, an anonymous donor paid their bail, and they were released.

Perhaps the biggest asset Pritchett possessed he had no part in creating. On January 23, 1962, President Kennedy had nominated J. Robert Elliott for a federal district court judgeship in Albany. Elliott took office on February 17. The Kennedy team had been wary of Elliott, who had served as a floor leader in the Georgia House of Representatives for both governors Eugene and Herman Talmadge. As late as 1952, in an election campaign Elliott said, "I don't want those pinks, radicals and black voters to outvote those who are trying to preserve our own segregation laws and other traditions."[6] When Elliott's name surfaced, Attorney General Robert Kennedy had Burke Marshall call Tuttle for an opinion. Tuttle, who did not know Elliott, called Bootle, who had handled the UGA case at the trial level. For Tuttle and for Bootle, one problem in evaluating Elliott was that virtually every successful politician in Georgia was a Democrat and a Talmadge man. Bootle told Tuttle he thought Elliott would be fair. Tuttle passed that appraisal on. Elliott had somehow garnered the support of the local NAACP and of A. T. Walden, the dean of Georgia's black attorneys; that, combined with Tuttle's report of Bootle's assessment, was enough to allay the Kennedys' concerns.[7] Unfortunately, it was all misguided at best. Elliott turned out to be among the most obstructionist judges on the bench; in those early years, he ruled against blacks in over 90 percent of the civil rights cases that came before him. He caused enormous damage to the movement—not only in terms of the immediate results of his rulings but also because to have a federal judge blatantly ignore the law and wield power unjustly caused the movement to become "increasingly frustrated, fragmented, and radicalized."[8]

Never was that more true than in the summer of 1962, when Judge Elliott enjoined Dr. King and his followers in Albany from walking from church to city hall on Sunday morning. Judge Elliott granted a temporary restraining order (TRO) on the application of the city fathers and without notice to the defendants. At that time, a TRO was valid for ten days unless it was vacated by the judge who had issued it. As soon as Judge Elliott entered his order, he left town, ostensibly for a vacation in Florida. Local counsel C. B. King and Constance Baker Motley turned to Tuttle. They filed a motion asking Tuttle to sit in for Judge Elliott and hear their motion to vacate the TRO. Tuttle took a different tack. Because a TRO can be granted without notice to the parties restrained, they have a right to move to vacate it. Judge Elliott's absence made that impossible. Tuttle ruled that Elliott's absence indicated that he meant his order to be a preliminary injunction, not a TRO. Essentially, Tuttle reasoned that since a judge would not deliberately frustrate a statutory right, Elliott must have mislabeled his order.

Now Tuttle had to take another unusual step: a preliminary injunction could be appealed to the circuit court of appeals—but the appeal would ordinarily be heard by a three-judge panel. Once again, as he had in the litigation around the desegregation of the University of Georgia, Tuttle turned to the All Writs Act, found in it the power to act alone, and vacated Judge Elliott's order.[9] When Constance Baker Motley turned to leave the courtroom, to her surprise she saw that Martin Luther King Jr. and his wife, Coretta, were sitting in the first row. At that moment, she met her client for the first time.[10] She had won an important victory for Dr. King, but she could not undo all of the damage. Elliott's order, and Dr. King's decision to comply with it until he could get it reversed in court, had dealt a body blow to his leadership. The movement had expanded, and not all the new members were committed to the patient process King was orchestrating. Just as Albany left King's leadership challenged, Tuttle's decisive intervention opened the door to challenges to his leadership of the court. For the time being, his decision to sit alone as an appellate judge would merely rankle, but in the tense days following the Birmingham Children's Crusade, he would do it again—and that would be too much for Judge Ben Cameron of Meridian, Mississippi.

Before Dr. King arrived in Birmingham, there was the Reverend Fred Shuttlesworth, the pastor at Bethel Baptist Church. In 1956 Shuttlesworth was also the membership chairman of the Alabama NAACP, until he was relieved of those duties by court order. On June 1 an Alabama judge granted the state attorney general's petition for an injunction against the NAACP and ordered it to "refrain from conducting further activities" in Alabama.[11] In time—to be precise, eight years later—the United States Supreme Court lifted the injunction, holding that it "is beyond debate that freedom to engage in association for the advancement of beliefs and ideas is an inseparable aspect of the 'liberty' assured by the Due Process Clause of the Fourteenth Amendment, which embraces freedom of speech."[12] Shuttlesworth did not wait. Within days of the order, he met with other NAACP leaders and decided to form a new organization along the lines of the Montgomery Improvement Association, which was several months into its historic bus boycott. They scheduled a mass meeting for Tuesday, June 5, to be held at the Sardis Baptist Church in Ensley. That day, Birmingham radio stations announced the meeting hourly, specifying that it had been called by "Fred Shuttlesworth, Negro minister, of 3191 North 29th Avenue"; they gave the church address, Shuttlesworth thought, "so that the Klan would know where to put the bomb."[13] Some 500 brave souls attended the meeting. Another 250 or so could not be crowded into the church. By the end of the evening, the Alabama Christian Movement for Human Rights (ACMHR) had been created, and Fred Shuttlesworth had been elected president by acclamation.

Shuttlesworth's concerns about a bomb were not casual. Birmingham had earned the nickname Bombingham in the late 1940s. After a federal judge ruled Jim Crow zoning unconstitutional, members of the Klan bombed the house the black plaintiff had hoped to move into. College Hills suffered so many bombings that by 1949 it was commonly called

Dynamite Hills. On Christmas Day, 1956, Reverend Shuttlesworth spoke to his congregation about the dangers of the movement. "If it takes being killed to get integration, I'll do just that thing, for God is with me all the way."[14] That evening, a bomb ripped through the parsonage, which shared a common wall with the church. Six sticks of dynamite exploded behind Shuttlesworth's bed, blowing the wall and floor out and collapsing the front porch. Shuttlesworth and his wife and children survived with only minor injuries. Twice in later years, in 1958 and 1962, the church was bombed again.

In 1957 Shuttlesworth joined other movement activists, most notably Dr. King, at a meeting in Atlanta, where the Southern Christian Leadership Conference was founded. By 1963, in addition to the SCLC, both the Student Nonviolent Coordinating Committee (SNCC) and the Congress of Racial Equality (CORE) were engaged in protests in the South. The SNCC had been formed in 1960 at a conference called by Ella Baker, a founding member of the SCLC, at Shaw University in North Carolina. Baker had realized the need to organize and train in nonviolent protest the students who had begun independent sit-ins at lunch counters across the South. Most of the SCLC leadership, King included, would have preferred the formation of a student chapter of the SCLC, but Baker supported the students' drive toward autonomy and independence.[15] James Farmer had founded CORE in Chicago in 1942. Working with a pacifist group called the Fellowship of Reconciliation, Farmer traveled in the Midwest speaking on pacifism and racial equality. Initially a committee of the Fellowship of Reconciliation, CORE soon evolved into an independent organization. Farmer, like King, was a student of Gandhi; in the 1940s CORE successfully pioneered restaurant sit-ins in the Midwest. In the 1960s CORE members organized the Freedom Rides that would galvanize the movement and the nation. Neither the SNCC nor CORE was involved in the SCLC planning for Birmingham, nor did either group have projects pending there. King and the SCLC had been invited to Birmingham by Shuttlesworth and the ACMHR; both men were keenly aware of the need to avoid factions and stay unified. Everyone realized that more than Birmingham was at stake; after being stymied in Albany, if the movement led by Dr. King failed again, the potential consequences were unthinkable.

King arrived in Birmingham on April 2, 1963, the day that a "moderate," Albert Boutwell, won a runoff in the mayor's race against Bull Connor, who remained commissioner of public safety. The plan had four stages. The organizers would begin with small sit-ins and nightly mass meetings; then they would organize a boycott of downtown businesses and slightly larger demonstrations; then would come mass marches to fill the jails; finally, if necessary, they would call on supporters across the country to join them in protest.[16] Although nonviolence was the order of the day, the plan was called Project Confrontation. King and the SCLC understood the role of economic pressure and bad publicity in attaining their goals. On April 3 some sixty-five volunteers fanned out to sit in at five lunch counters that had been targeted. Four of the stores simply closed. At the fifth, management called the police, and twenty demonstrators were carted off to jail.[17] Police Chief Laurie Pritchett came over from Albany to provide advice, but Bull Connor did not heed his counsel. Connor was ready to fill the jails with the demonstrators. In the absence of a permit, anyone who marched would be arrested. King had planned to take the lead, but that would have meant abandoning his essential work on community building and on raising the funds necessary to support the protests. On April 6 Shuttlesworth, joined by the Reverend Charles Billups, led some forty-five well-dressed men and women on a march down Fifth Avenue North. Bull Connor let them walk two and a half blocks before calling for the wagons. The next day, Palm Sunday, three local black ministers, one of them King's younger brother, A. D. King, led marchers along Sixth Avenue North. Although fewer than thirty people joined the march, as many as a thousand, mostly black, watched. Many in the crowd grew angry when the police laid hands on the ministers, directing them to the wagons. But the police were armed and accompanied by their dogs; the bystanders remained, for the most part, subdued.

Fred Shuttlesworth and the Reverend John Porter, a native of Birmingham and the pastor of Sixth Avenue Baptist who had been Dr. King's assistant pastor in Montgomery, had welcomed King and the movement, but much of Birmingham's black establishment, including, most notably, A. G. Gaston, did not. Gaston, son of a sharecropper and grandson of slaves, had made an astounding success out of every commercial venture he touched. He owned the Booker T. Washington Insurance Company, a bank, a funeral home, and the Gaston Motel (where King and his associates stayed). Gaston was close to Shuttlesworth, but he was also close to the white power structure; he favored moderate action over street protest. Those views were shared by "the politically conservative, gradualist Scott Newspaper Syndicate of Atlanta," which owned the twice weekly black newspaper, the *Birmingham World*. Emory Jackson, the editor of the *Birmingham World*, was both brave and progressive, but he was under the thumb of the more conservative Scotts—all of his copy went to Atlanta for final editorial decisions.[18] Jackson may also have been heavily influenced by Gaston and by the Reverend J. L. Ware, president of the Birmingham Baptist Ministers Association and, like Gaston, very much a gradualist.

King needed to convince these men and other conservative black leaders of the need for direct action. The timing could hardly have been worse. Boutwell had, after all, defeated Bull Connor. A virulent racist had been upset by what passed for a moderate in Alabama—a man who was completely committed to Jim Crow segregation but who, one could hope, would rule with a lighter hand. Motivated by both fear and hope, Birmingham's black citizens were not flocking to King's side. Bull Connor, on the other hand, was always by his side, if not with informers, then with microphones. Within moments of King's announcement to those gathered at St. James AME Church on Wednesday, April 10, that "everyone in the movement must have a sacrificial life" and that he would march on Good Friday, Connor sent two city attorneys to a state court judge's home seeking an injunction restraining King, Shuttlesworth, Ralph Abernathy, and more than 130 others from "any further plans or projects commonly called 'sit-in' demonstrations, 'kneel-in' demonstrations, mass street parades, etc." Deputy Ray Belcher served the order on King, Shuttlesworth, and Abernathy in the restaurant at the Gaston Motel at 1:15 a.m. Alerted by the SCLC, the press was there. The significance of the moment was not lost on seasoned movement reporters. Karl Fleming of *Newsweek* called it "an electric event. One knew that people were going to get hurt, possibly killed."[19]

For all the blunt force of his approach, Bull Connor had managed to create real conflict in the movement. King had deliberately violated state trespass laws in other to challenge them, but he had not, until this point, violated a court order. Shuttlesworth was adamant: King had to challenge this sweeping injunction prohibiting the exercise of First Amendment rights by marching. Gaston took the other side: King should not defy a court order but instead let things cool off. Martin Luther King Sr. ("Daddy King") flew in to urge his son to obey the injunction. King himself seemed troubled, but, after prayer, he had made up his mind. He would march. Ralph Abernathy by his side, King led fifty marchers three blocks east and then, finding their way blocked by the police, four blocks south, to- ward downtown, before Bull Connor told his men to stop them. King and Abernathy were hauled into a patrol wagon; the rest of the demonstrators waited patiently for their arrests—all except for Fred Shuttlesworth. He had started the march but dropped out; it didn't seem wise for all three of the leaders to be in jail at the same time.

While he was free, Shuttlesworth called Constance Baker Motley at NAACP headquarters in New York; she dispatched a young attorney, Norman Amaker. Connor refused to let Amaker speak with his clients. About 11:00 p.m. Amaker gave up; the most he could do was fire off tele- grams to President Kennedy and his brother the attorney general. They declined to intervene. Many of the marchers were quickly bailed out, but King and Abernathy were not. It was important that Martin Luther King Jr. stay imprisoned in an Alabama jail. Only by doing so could he become a symbol of the oppression faced by black Americans in the South; only then would the rest of the country notice. Besides, he was busy; he was writing his *Letter from Birmingham Jail*; relatively unnoticed at the time, it was not published in full for nearly two months after it was finished on April 16, 1963. Since then it has been recognized as "probably the most elo- quent statement of the nexus between law and injustice since Henry David Thoreau's essay 'Civil Disobedience.'"[20]

On Saturday, April 20, King and Abernathy bonded out of jail. That Monday they appeared with nine others, including Shuttlesworth, for trial on the charge of contempt of court for violating the injunction; on Friday, April 26, Judge W. A. Jenkins Jr. found them guilty.[21] The movement leaders knew they needed to take decisive action; the Birmingham Movement was in danger of dying. That very day, Fred Shuttlesworth filed a petition for permission to stage a mass protest march on Thursday, May 2. Even if the permit were granted (and it was not), the movement faced a considerable hurdle. A mass protest demanded a volume of protestors. In Birmingham the movement was running out of bodies. The black middle class had been lukewarm at best from the beginning. Despite all the injustice and indig- nity they suffered, things could be worse—and things rapidly got worse for those who joined the protest marches. At a minimum, most could count on losing their job. As time wore on, fewer and fewer participated in the mass meetings held every evening, and few of those who did volunteered to march. For individuals and for the movement, the stakes were very high.

The solution was apparent. Younger SCLC strategists, James Bevel and Wyatt Tee Walker, saw it first: use young people. In the beginning, the focus was on older teenagers. Moderate black leaders—A. G. Gaston and the Reverend John Porter among them—drew the line at college-age students. Walker and Bevel were comfortable with older high school students. When the permit was denied on Tuesday, those who had been the subject of Judge Jenkins's injunction realized that marching would again put them in violation of it. Now, they realized, the state might add "contributing to the delinquency of a minor" to the charges. Still they pressed on. With King's nervous approval, Bevel announced that "a special march of high school students" would go on "with or without a permit." The greatest concern was for the young marchers. They faced the possibility of violence unleashed by Bull Connor and his police forces and the likelihood of arrest and whatever privations and injuries might accompany it. At a minimum, they would emerge with police records, a far from trivial concern. All of this notwithstanding, Bevel had been courting the teenagers since at least April 24. Two young local black disc jockeys had announced a "hot luncheon," really a strategy meeting, at the Gaston Motel, with the invitation going out to high school standouts—football stars and beauty queens— they had gotten to know playing school dances. Twenty to thirty of the "big shots" and church youth leaders showed up. Bevel assigned them to spread the word about the afternoon meetings at Sixteenth Street Baptist, where he encouraged the students to stand up for themselves and lightly schooled them in nonviolence.[22]

By the end of April, the word was out to Birmingham's black children, high school and elementary students alike. Bevel was comfortable with younger and younger children: he even proposed that the standard should be that any child old enough to be a member of a church—to make a conscious affirmation of Christian faith—should be old enough to protest. Under Baptist doctrine, that would mean six-year-olds. King never expressly agreed, yet he went forward. Nine years had passed since *Brown* had been decided, eight years since he had answered the call and led the Montgomery bus boycott. He had given a great deal, risked all, and gained very little. His people were not free of the shackles of enslavement, and somehow he had to expose that. So many efforts, mounted at such great cost, had failed. Now, in a desperate move, "he committed his cause to the witness of schoolchildren."[23]

When the doors to Sixteenth Street Baptist opened about 1:00 p.m. on May 2 and fifty teenagers marched out singing "We Shall Overcome," Bull Connor and his men were ready, they thought. Officers quickly stopped the marchers, reminded them of the injunction, and began shepherding them into paddy wagons. The goals were to arrest them and to keep them from evading police blockades and reaching the downtown business district. Then the door opened again and another group emerged, and another, and yet another. A surprised police officer saw Fred Shuttlesworth outside the church and called over to him, "Hey Fred, how many more have you got?" "At least a thousand," Shuttlesworth called back. "God almighty" was the officer's response.[24] Seasoned officers were stunned not only by the number of students but by their ages. One small girl, asked her age by a police captain as she climbed into a paddy wagon, said she was six. Some of the marchers managed to evade the blockade and move out of the "colored district" and toward downtown; one group of twenty even reached city hall. Still, the police were able to maintain control. By calling in all patrol cars, asking the county sheriff for help, and using school buses to transport the students, they managed to clear the streets by about 4:00 p.m. Out of sight, as many as seventy-five students were packed into cells built for eight.[25] On Friday at noon, May 3, Bull Connor barricaded the area around the Sixteenth Street Church with police lines, fire trucks, squad cars, and school buses. The goal was to confine but not to arrest; city and county jails were crammed past capacity. The first weapon of choice was fire hoses, their force amplified by "monitor guns that forced water from two hoses through a single nozzle mounted on a tripod. The fire department advertised [them] as . . . capable of knocking bricks loose from mortar, or stripping bark off trees at a distance of one hundred feet."[26] The ads did not overstate the power of the monitors; turned on people, they were devastating. One little girl was rolled down the street "like a leaf." Others had their clothes stripped off. Screams of pain and fear filled the air. Student protestors continued to pour into the street from the church. Connor and his forces were losing control of the boundaries; for reinforcement, Bull Connor called in the dogs. Eight K-9 units were brought to the scene. The sight of the dogs terrified most of the marchers and spectators. A few brave if foolhardy teenage boys waved wet shirts like matadors' capes. Most people tried to get away, but the crowd was dense and move-ment constrained.

The images that came out of Birmingham that day transfixed the na-tion. Young people brutally pummeled by high-pressure hoses; a police-man holding a well-dressed fifteen-year-old boy by his shirt while a police dog bit into the boy's abdomen; an officer knocking a demonstrator to the ground with a kick to the knee so a dog could maul him; a well-dressed, distinguished black man attacked by two dogs as he crossed the street. Two disparate groups watched; both came away changed. Black moderates from Birmingham and around the South and the country who had been reluc-tant to support Martin Luther King Jr. and the SCLC, preferring instead to put their faith and their fate in the hands of apparently well-meaning white people, now were unified in the cause. White people who had been able to ignore the South's brutality to its black citizens and to harbor a stereotype of black people as slovenly and no-account were forced to discard those illusions.

The demonstrations went on. Every day the police tried to confine the demonstrators to the black community; every day the marchers tried to slip past. As new people flocked to the protests, the movement leaders tee-tered on the edge of losing control. In the streets they insisted on non-violence, and a delicate balance was maintained. On May 7 as many as three thousand demonstrators were able to gather in the downtown busi-ness district. Birmingham had been shut down. Again the water cannons came out, along with a tanklike armored car. Burke Marshall, head of the Civil Rights Division of the Justice Department, was on the scene, pressur-ing white leaders to negotiate; President Kennedy and the attorney general were on the phones at the same task. Finally, late that evening white lead-ers named a negotiating committee and at midnight sought out Dr. King. By early morning they had an outline; by May 10 they had an agreement. Fitting rooms at stores would be integrated first, by May 13; public rest-rooms and water fountains within thirty days; and lunch counters within sixty days. A biracial committee to discuss desegregating the schools, hir-ing black city employees, and reopening parks would be appointed within fifteen days; black sales clerks would be hired within sixty days.[27]

The fragility of any truce became apparent at once. Until midnight, Saturday, May 11, had been a quiet day in Birmingham. Then the first bomb went off at A. D. King's home and church; another at the Gaston Motel followed quickly. A. D. King led his deacons in calming the crowd that gathered at his church. He may have been able to maintain control, but then the news came that the Gaston Motel had been bombed. The crowd swelled to two thousand; even working together, the black preachers and white police could not completely contain them. A grocery store burned, and bricks flew through the air.

Things were worse at the motel, which had as its neighbors pool halls and bars. This was not the movement's trained corps or the quickly but carefully taught schoolchildren; this was angry adults responding to violence with violence. First a grocery store and then houses were set on fire; by the time the fire department showed up, an entire block had lit up. As firemen hosed down the area, people milled in the street, but most of the drunks and hoodlums had been taken to jail. Movement leaders, including A. D. King and Walker Tee Wyatt, were on the scene, trying to restore order. Chief of Police Jamie Moore and outgoing mayor Art Hames stood at the corner. About 2:30 a.m. Colonel Al Lingo, Alabama's director of public safety, appointed by Governor Wallace, drove up with reinforcements. Lingo had no training in law enforcement; he had piloted Wallace's campaign plane. Some thought his main qualification for his job was "the vulgarity with which he expressed his views of Negroes."[28]

Lingo carried a repeater shotgun. His bodyguards carried Thompson submachine guns. Sensing disaster, Chief Moore politely asked Lingo to leave. "Get your cowardly ass back to your office or your house because I'm in charge now and my orders are to put those black bastards to bed," Lingo answered.[29] In short order, the state troopers charged down the street, wielding billy clubs and rifle butts. Behind them came troops on horseback led by Sheriff Jim Clark of Selma wearing GI helmets and carrying rifles. Journalists at the scene, including Claude Sitton of the New York Times and Karl Fleming of Newsweek, were marched at gunpoint into the motel lobby after Lingo himself shoved his shotgun in Fleming's stomach and threatened to blow him away. Angry crowds driven away from the motel by Lingo and Clark and their men rampaged through the streets. Not until dawn was order restored. Once order was restored, it was critical that it be maintained. Martin Luther King Jr. and his colleagues in the movement knew they would lose control if the city fathers of Birmingham reneged on the negotiated deal they had struck. They feared what that would mean, and they were not alone in that fear.

Members of the Kennedy administration called colleagues in the middle
of the night to report the rioting in Birmingham: Burke Marshall was called
at 2:00 a.m., Attorney General Robert Kennedy at 3:00 a.m. The president
was told when he awoke, at Camp David. He returned to Washington and
went into meetings with the secretary of defense (Robert McNamara), secretary of the army (Cyrus Vance), army chief of staff (Earl Wheeler), and
special counsel (Theodore "Ted" Sorenson). Later they were joined by the
attorney general and two deputy attorneys general (Burke Marshall and
Nicholas Katzenbach). At 8:48 p.m. President Kennedy addressed the nation on television. His manner was grave as he began by expressing his
deep concern over the events that had transpired the night before, beginning with the two bombings. They had led to rioting, he noted, and rioting
had to be contained. He praised the Birmingham agreement as "fair and
just"—"It recognized the fundamental right of all citizens to be accorded
equal treatment and opportunity"—and he called on all the citizens of
Birmingham, black and white, to live up to it.[30] He stopped short of either
dispatching federal troops to Birmingham or federalizing the Alabama
National Guard, but he had directed Secretary of Defense McNamara
to send units of the armed forces trained in riot control to bases near
Birmingham.

On Monday morning, May 13, 1963, the *New York Times* ran a front-
page story headlined "U.S. Sends Troops into Alabama after Riots Sweep
Birmingham; Kennedy Alerts State's Guard." Another front-page story,
"50 Hurt in Negro Rioting after Birmingham Blasts," reported that "riots
raged out of control for more than three hours early today, after bomb-
ings of a motel and an integration leader's home had enraged Negroes."
Yet a third front-page story bore the headline "Wallace Decries Kennedy
Action: Says Birmingham Can Cope with Crisis—Doubts Move Is Legal."
Governor Wallace had fired off a telegram pointing out that neither he nor
the Alabama legislature had asked for federal help. "May I ask," he wrote,
"by what authority you would send Federal troops into this state?"

Martin Luther King Jr. took to the streets of Birmingham. Monday afternoon and evening found him visiting the pool halls and bars pleading for
peace and preaching nonviolence. Birmingham stayed quiet. On Thursday
several members of the Justice Department left Birmingham, heading back
to Washington. Their talk while they traveled was sober. The fragile peace
in Birmingham had held so far, but it was tenuous. Moreover, there were

"Birminghams" near the breaking point all over the country. Any patch-work response would be inadequate; federal civil rights legislation with substance and teeth was called for. They went straight to Attorney General Kennedy's office to say so; a memo from Deputy Attorney General Ramsey Clark to the same effect was already on Kennedy's desk. By Friday an out-line of the proposed bill was on the president's desk. On Saturday, as fate would have it, President Kennedy joined Governor Wallace for a ceremony marking the thirtieth anniversary of the Tennessee Valley Authority (TVA) held at Muscle Shoals, Alabama. Wallace assured the president that all the trouble was due to outsiders, like that "faker" King.

In Birmingham a week had passed without incident since the bomb-ings and the rioting they unleashed; then the most incendiary issue still on the table exploded. As commissioner of public safety, Bull Connor con-trolled not only the Police and Fire Departments but also the schools.[31] On Monday, May 20, the Birmingham School Board expelled for the balance of the term more than a thousand students who had been arrested for parad-ing without a permit.[32] The NAACP Legal Defense Fund's leading attorney in the South, Constance Baker Motley, was already in Birmingham, work-ing on the University of Alabama case. Dr. King's representatives reached out to her for help. She hastily drafted a request for a temporary restrain-ing order against the Birmingham School Board. The named plaintiff was "Linda Cal Woods, a minor, by her father and next friend, the Reverend Calvin Woods." Calvin Woods's three oldest children, Jeanette (eleven), Linda (ten), and Judy (nine), and the three elementary school daughters of his brother, Reverend Abraham Woods, had been arrested. Neither of the brothers had known beforehand that the small girls would be among the marchers; Calvin recalled being "appalled" that they were there. "I thought me being out there would be sufficient," he recalled decades later.[33] Calvin Woods's recollection was that his daughters had gone to school and then left school to join the marchers without his consent.[34] His brother Abraham's daughters had been brought to the protest by their mother. Abraham was surprised to see them there, but he had "been getting other folks' children to go to jail," so he could hardly resist letting his own chil-dren march.[35] Their mother, Marion, watched the arrests, "every bit of it." It hurt, she recalled, "but I was proud of them because I felt they were doing what adults were afraid to do, or wouldn't do, or maybe couldn't do."[36]

The complaint, filed on behalf of ten-year-old Linda Cal Woods and all similarly situated students, noted that time was of the essence—the term ended in just ten days. If relief (reinstatement in school) were not immediate, it would be meaningless. Motley argued that the expulsions and suspensions violated due process because the students had not been accorded a hearing; they had not had the opportunity "to defend against 'the right not to be arbitrarily expelled from public school.'"[37] Motley went directly to the district court and filed her complaint; in short order, she found herself in District Court Judge Clarence Allgood's chambers. Because preventing imminent harm is the essence of a request for a temporary restraining order (TRO), they are heard immediately, even in the absence of those who will be restrained. Once a TRO issues, it is followed quickly by a hearing on whether or not a preliminary injunction should issue; the TRO maintains the status quo until full and fair debate can be had on the question. Because TROs are of brief duration, they are not appealable.

Motley cast her petition as one seeking a TRO perhaps so that she did not have to worry about securing the appearance of the defendant. She had enough to worry about; Judge Allgood she considered to be "another hostile Kennedy appointment."[38] President Kennedy's good work in the civil rights area notwithstanding, several of his appointments to the federal bench were dreadful. It was a Democratic administration; the chair of the Judiciary Committee, James Eastland of Mississippi, was both a senior Democratic senator and an avowed white supremacist, and most successful Democratic politicians in the South were firmly committed to segregation. That combination, along with Kennedy's considerable deference to Eastland, meant that the federal judges appointed in the South during the Kennedy years all too often were segregationists at best, obstructionist white supremacists at worst.

Judge Allgood heard the petition for a TRO and denied it, but not until he had lectured Constance Baker Motley on the evils of using children in demonstrations.[39] As soon as Judge Allgood ruled orally, Motley made her way to a pay phone and called Judge Tuttle in Atlanta. Assuming the parties would catch a midafternoon plane that would get them to Atlanta around 4:00 p.m., Tuttle agreed to hear an appeal at 5:00. Allgood's order, however, could not be appealed until he signed it, and he did not get around to that until after 2:00. Motley thought he delayed on purpose to frustrate the chance that the parties could reach Atlanta during business hours.[40] There was a later plane, however, and when Motley called Tuttle

and explained, he simply pushed the time back to 7:00. Although the letter to students and their parents had indicated they were being disciplined
because of their arrests for "parading without a license," Judge Allgood
changed the focus in his order. After complaining about having to hear the
matter at all ("the court has had to interrupt a heavy docket which has been
set for some months"), he noted that students had been told not to miss
school. Their truancy justified their expulsion, he wrote. While some, he
thought, stayed away out of their own free will, others, he conceded, may
have stayed away out of fear of violence, or they may have been persuaded
"by those who wish to exploit them." In any case, he was "shocked to see
hundreds of school children . . . running loose and wild over the streets of
Birmingham."[41]

At 7:00 p.m. Judge Tuttle took the bench to hear oral argument. Motley
was there for the plaintiff children along with two black colleagues, Arthur
Shores and Orzell Billingsley of Alabama.[42] John Doar, assistant attorney
general in the Civil Rights Division of the Justice Department, appeared
as amicus curiae (friend of the court) on the side of the plaintiffs. Linda
Woods's father, the Reverend Calvin Woods, was there too; he had been
unhappy about the trip both because he didn't even have time to let his wife
know he was going and because he had never flown and never wanted to.
Because his signature was needed on an affidavit not yet drafted when they
took to the air, he soldiered on. Finally, the attorneys for the Birmingham
school system were there; Tuttle had asked Motley to notify them of the
hearing as soon as he scheduled it.

Tuttle announced from the bench that Judge Allgood had called him
to amend his order by adding "the plaintiffs' motion for preliminary injunction will be taken under consideration by the court . . . at the earliest
possible date."[43] Allgood was apparently reminding Tuttle that TROs are not
appealable. There is an exception to that rule, however. When "rights might
be irreparably lost and the cause mooted" in the absence of an appeal, an
otherwise unappealable order such as a TRO could be appealed.[44] Tuttle
moved on to the merits. After hearing argument of counsel, he announced
that he was reversing Judge Allgood and holding that Allgood should have
restrained the school board from suspending or expelling the students.
Noting that Allgood had included personal comments in his order, Tuttle
said he felt free to do so as well. "It appears shocking," he said, "that a
board of education interested in the education of the children committed

to its care, should . . . destroy the value of one term of school for so many children."[45] His expression and tone, wrote Claude Sitton of the *New York Times*, "reflected anger and distress over the treatment of the students." When an attorney for the school board "indicated doubt over whether the board could comply with [Tuttle's] ruling, 'What's that?' he shot at the lawyer, who quickly amended his remarks to say that compliance would be forthcoming." "That's better," observed the judge.[46] But he took no chances with it: before the hearing ended, he directed the attorneys for the school system to contact the radio stations in Birmingham that the schools used for school announcements and to have them broadcast that evening the direction that all students should attend school in the morning.[47]

In overruling Judge Allgood and issuing a restraining order, Tuttle relied on the opinions in four cases decided by the United States Supreme Court just two days earlier, on Monday, May 20. The Court had voided the convictions of four groups of students arrested after peaceful sit-ins at lunch counters.[48] Although the sit-in demonstrators were convicted of violating trespass laws that were race neutral on their face, the facts established (and everyone knew) that the states and the cities were using the law to maintain segregation—to facilitate the continuing deprivation of equal protection to black citizens. Likewise, Tuttle ruled, although the parading without a permit ordinance was race neutral on its face, in this case it was being used by the state and the city to deprive black students of basic constitutional rights. He closed by noting that his order did "not affect the right of . . . the Board of Education to discipline any of said students for acts of actual violence or actual breaches of the peace . . . after a hearing is afforded to any student who is charged with such conduct."[49]

At a 4:00 p.m. press conference on the day Tuttle ruled, Wednesday, May 22, 1963, President Kennedy indicated for the first time that he might propose a broad civil rights act. Asked if, given recent developments, he was considering new civil rights legislation, he responded:

> As you know, we have several proposals up there now, dealing with voting, extension of the Civil Rights Commission, and the Conciliation Service. But I think there may be other things that we could do which would provide a legal outlet for a desire for a remedy other than having to engage in demonstrations which bring them into conflict with the forces of law and order in the community.

I would hope that we would be able to develop some formulas so that those who feel themselves, or who are, as a matter of fact, denied equal rights, would have a remedy. As it is today, in many cases they do not have a remedy, and therefore they take to the streets and we have the kind of incidents that we have in Birmingham. We hope to see if we can develop a legal remedy.[50]

Kennedy had seized the moment; much of the nation was still reeling from the images of violence against black men, women, and children in Birmingham. For the first time, the barbarity of Jim Crow segregation had been exposed on a large stage, and the dignity of its victims had been apparent. Public opinion had turned. Had the expulsion orders stood, had Martin Luther King Jr. and his colleagues not been able to maintain control over the response of their people, public opinion might well have turned again. Instead, on June 11, 1963, on the same day that Vivian Malone and James Hood, backed up by federalized Alabama National Guard troops, registered at the University of Alabama, President Kennedy addressed the nation. "We are confronted primarily with a moral issue," he said. "It is as old as the scriptures and as clear as the American Constitution." Announcing that he would go to Congress in the next week and propose civil rights legislation that would guarantee all citizens the full rights of citizenship, he explained: "Now the time has come for this Nation to fulfill its promise. The events in Birmingham and elsewhere have so increased the cries for equality that no city or State or legislative body can prudently choose to ignore them."[51]

In Birmingham, with the support of Tuttle's decisive intervention, the center held. The SCLC emerged stronger politically and financially. After Birmingham, donations poured in, and the rest of the movement coalesced around King's leadership, which facilitated planning the March on Washington for the fall of 1963. Among those who filled the National Mall on August 28, 1963, were Elbert and Sara Tuttle's daughter, Jane, her husband, John, and their four young daughters.

But the most dramatic and the most tragic event in Birmingham had not yet transpired. It occurred two and a half weeks later, on Sunday, September 15, 1963, when yet another bomb exploded at the Sixteenth Street Baptist Church, claiming the lives of four young girls: Addie Mae Collins, Denise McNair, Carole Robertson, and Cynthia Wesley.

The Houston Conference

On Tuttle's court, the Fifth Circuit, Birmingham festered.

Earlier in the week, Tuttle had sent all members of the court a letter enclosing the agenda for the judicial council meeting scheduled for May 29. Judge Griffin Bell received his copy on the morning of May 23, the day after Tuttle's ruling in the Birmingham school case. Later that day Bell sent his colleagues an eight-page letter in which he argued that Tuttle was wrong in his assertion that a single circuit court judge could vacate an injunction (the Albany case), or reinstate one after the district court judge had stayed it (the desegregation of the University of Georgia), or enter an injunction that a district court judge had declined to enter (Birmingham). He thought the matter should be discussed, and he informed his colleagues that he would, at the Wednesday meeting, make the following motion: "That the order entered by Judge Tuttle in the Birmingham case be vacated and set aside on the basis that it was improvidently granted, a single circuit judge not having the power under the law appertaining to enter such an order; without prejudice however, to the right of appellants in that case to apply for similar relief to a panel of this court consisting of three judges."[1] The next day Judge Walter Gewin weighed in on Judge Bell's side: "First, let me say that I think Judge Bell has raised a vital question in his excellent letter of May 23, 1963."[2] He went on to note that his own office in Tuscaloosa was only 58 miles from the federal courthouse in Birmingham, and Judge Rives's office in Montgomery was only 100 miles away. Tuttle's office in Atlanta, in contrast, was approximately 170 miles away, and in another state. This looked like judge shopping, he suggested, and could only erode regard for the court.

At the conference, Judge Bell's motion did not pass, and Tuttle's ruling stood undisturbed, pending the full appeal to a panel of the court. Nor did the court articulate a position on the power of a single judge to act.

There was no consensus, as a note in the minutes explained: "The power of a single Circuit Judge to act in certain instances, including the power to grant injunctive relief, was next discussed. It was not possible to resolve the question of power by rule or otherwise due to an even division among the members of the Council as to the presence or absence of such power, and because some felt that it was not the appropriate subject matter of a rule."[3] The even division consisted of Brown, Rives, Tuttle, and Wisdom on one side and Bell, Cameron, Gewin, and Jones on the other. Judge Hutcheson did not attend due to poor health.[4] In time, the Birmingham School Board's appeal was heard by Judges Jones and Rives of the Fifth Circuit and Judge Bootle of the Middle District of Georgia. On July 24, 1964, the panel, Jones writing, unanimously affirmed Tuttle's ruling that the plaintiff children had been entitled to an injunction restraining the school board from expelling them.[5] No mention was made of the controversy over whether Tuttle had acted correctly in acting alone.[6]

From a jurisprudential point of view, the Birmingham case raises the most serious questions. In the University of Georgia litigation, Tuttle's action, vacating a stay entered by Judge Bootle to allow a full appeal before his order took effect, simply reinstated the order. In the Albany litigation, when Tuttle vacated an order entered by Judge Elliott, he restored the status quo. But in Birmingham, Tuttle sitting alone entered an injunction that Judge Allgood had declined to enter; in other words, he granted positive relief, sitting alone, where the trial court judge had found that relief was not warranted. Judge Bell's point was not insignificant. Under ordinary protocols, federal judges on circuit courts of appeal sit either in panels of three or en banc.[7] Appellate judges rarely enter individual orders, with the exception of stays or injunctions pending appeal.[8] They do have the power to act unilaterally, however, under Federal Rule of Civil Procedure 62 (g) (1): "This rule does not limit the power of the appellate court or one of its judges or justices . . . to stay proceedings—or suspend, modify, restore, or grant an injunction—while an appeal is pending . . . or (2) to issue an order to preserve the status quo or the effectiveness of the judgment to be entered." In the Birmingham schoolchildren's case, absent immediate relief, scores of children would have lost the opportunity to be promoted to the next grade or to graduate. A judgment in their favor months later could not fix that.

Judge Bell's challenge to Judge Tuttle resonated, however, with Judge Ben Cameron of Mississippi. Cameron was furious at Tuttle's refusal to assign him to three-judge district courts. On that question, Tuttle held firm: the relevant statute directed the chief judge of the circuit to select two of the three judges (one would be the judge before whom the matter was pending). He could not in the good-faith discharge of his duties appoint a judge who would not faithfully apply the law, and Judge Cameron had indicated that in the area of race relations he would not follow *Brown* because he thought it wrong.[9] Because Cameron was the only judge from Mississippi on the Fifth Circuit from the time of his appointment in 1955 until his death in 1964, this meant that when Mississippi statutes were challenged on constitutional grounds, no circuit court judge from Mississippi would sit.

Like virtually all southerners who were opposed to full civil rights for black people, Judge Cameron believed deeply in states' rights. In other words, he wanted to let Mississippi chart its own course and make its own rules. Cameron's antipathy toward the federal government intensified during the civil rights era, but it predated it. Early in their relationship, he told Tuttle that he would never vote to confirm a conviction for income tax evasion. Tuttle said, "Well Ben, that wasn't in my oath of office." Cameron responded, "Well, it was in mine. I kept my fingers crossed."[10]

Tuttle's determination to recognize and enforce the constitutional rights of black plaintiffs and to dismantle state-sponsored segregation—in public transportation, in the voting booth, and in the schools—infuriated Cameron. In July 1963 it all boiled over. The triggering event for Cameron's attack on Tuttle was the Birmingham school desegregation case, *Armstrong v. Board of Education*.[11] When Judge Lynne entered his order on May 28, 1963, nine years had passed since *Brown v. Topeka* had been decided.[12] Despite a black population of about 40 percent and despite overlapping school districts, there had been no integration in Birmingham, not among the students, not among the teachers. Dr. Theo Wright, superintendent of schools, testified that he and the school board had always operated a segregated school system, and they had no plans to change that, but they did stand ready to accept applications for transfer. Judge Lynne approved of that plan; the fault, he ruled, lay not with the school board but with the black families of Birmingham. The court would retain jurisdiction to oversee how applications for transfer were handled.

James Armstrong appealed on behalf of his minor children. As soon as he filed his appeal, he filed a motion seeking an injunction pending appeal, asking for immediate relief. Judges Gewin, Rives, and Tuttle were on the appellate panel. Writing for himself and Judge Tuttle, Judge Rives granted the motion and explained to Judge Lynne that he had simply gotten the law wrong. The Fifth Circuit had consistently held that "the burden of initiating desegregation does not rest on Negro children or parents or on whites, but on the School Board." Moreover, Rives noted, the court had already explained that the plaintiffs need not exhaust state remedies: "It is no answer that the State has a law which if enforced would give relief. The federal remedy is supplementary to the state remedy, and the latter need not be first sought and refused before the federal one is invoked."[13] Still, even though the case had now been pending for three years, Judge Rives worried that a direct order to desegregate even one grade would be precipitate and cause undue and unnecessary confusion. Instead, he ordered that the school board create a plan to make an immediate start on desegregation and submit it to the court by August 19. Tuttle went along, but he wrote separately to say that he would have required that at least one grade of the public schools be desegregated before fall classes began.

Judge Gewin disagreed with both of them. In due time, after oral argument, the panel could enter an opinion; in the meantime, the case presented no urgency. Nor, in his view, did a handful of other civil rights cases the court had expedited. Because he disagreed with the relief afforded in the ruling on the merits (that the board should proceed immediately to draft and produce a plan for desegregation) as well as with what he saw as an unjustified procedural irregularity (granting injunctive relief pending the full appeal), Judge Gewin moved to have the case decided en banc—to have Judge Rives's opinion, which Tuttle had joined, reconsidered by all the members of the Fifth Circuit. Pursuant to the court protocol, Chief Judge Tuttle polled all of the judges in active service. A majority voted against hearing the matter en banc. Then all hell broke loose.

On July 30, 1963, Judge Cameron published an angry dissent. Technically dissenting from the court's denial of en banc review, he used that platform to take aim at the use of injunctions pending appeal and other "unorthodox procedures [that] have arisen in cases involving racial problems."[14] Cameron singled out Tuttle's order in the Birmingham Children's Crusade case, arguing that he did not have jurisdiction to act alone and that he was wrong on the merits (a panel of the Fifth Circuit later affirmed Tuttle's order).[15] By far Cameron's most explosive charges involved how Tuttle allegedly managed the court's docket.

Cameron began his diatribe with quotes from "a feature article . . . appearing in the public press of July 20, 1963," that described the circuit's determination to implement *Brown* and spoke of a split among the judges. "The split was exemplified," the article posited, "by the Court's recent 4–4 deadlock over the issue of a jury trial for Governor Ross Barnett on criminal contempt charges growing out of his defiance of its orders to integrate Ole Miss." The four judges who had stood together in opposition to a jury trial had also consistently stood together in civil rights cases, the article noted, listing Chief Judge Tuttle and Judges Rives, Wisdom, and Brown.[16] Cameron turned the article's praise into a condemnation: Tuttle, Rives, Wisdom, and Brown became "The Four." Cameron purported to have collected all "racial cases" decided by the Fifth Circuit in the previous two years. He listed twenty-five separate cases; on twenty-two of the twenty-five, two members of "The Four" were on the panel.[17] Because of the use of visiting judges, the other five judges (Cameron, Bell, Gewin, Jones, and Hutcheson) only made up the two-man majority on two panels. Cameron went on to charge that "Chief Judge Tuttle's [handling] of three judge district courts in the State of Mississippi is a part of the picture of the crusading spirit which I think has been largely responsible for the errors here discussed."[18] His accusations were reported by newspapers across the country. On July 31, 1963, the *New York Times* referred to "bitter infighting in the United States Court of Appeals for the Fifth Circuit over desegregation cases." Cameron, the *Times* reported, had charged Tuttle with "stacking the deck in hearings involving racial cases."[19]

Cameron's inflammatory dissent was exacerbated by an August 4 article in the *Houston Chronicle* that quoted Judge Rives as explaining that Tuttle had an obligation to appoint judges "who will follow the law honestly and fully and without prejudice." The article quoted a "source close to the court" who was described as "eager" to talk (generally presumed to have been Judge John Brown) as opining that "the chief judge wants honest judges to decide according to law. Some of the cases in which Judge Cameron dissented were cut and dry."[20] Judge Brown, who sat in Houston, circulated copies of the article to his colleagues.[21] Even though Rives's comment was described as "casting a sharp barb in the general direction of Cameron and the federal judiciary of Mississippi" and the anonymous remarks were clearly directed at Judge Cameron, the article insulted and alarmed Judges Bell, Gewin, and Jones.

Shortly after his copy of the article arrived in the morning mail on August 7, Judge Jones received a phone call from Judge Bell. As a member of the court, Bell knew what would not be made public for another fifteen years: except for the three-judge district courts, Judge Brown was making the assignments.[22] Brown's offer when he joined the court in 1955 to help with administrative matters had been gratefully accepted by Chief Judge Hutcheson, who turned over docketing decisions to him. Brown had continued in that role ever since. Cameron had named Tuttle as the target of his ire, however, and outsiders assumed the chief judge managed the calendar. Because Tuttle and his colleagues felt strongly about maintaining the confidentiality of the work of the court, no one disclosed that he did not. The judges knew, however, and Bell suspected it was at the heart of the problem; he told Jones he was drafting a letter to his colleagues "suggesting that the Chief Judge resume the function of assigning judges."[23]

After talking with Bell, Judge Jones decided to call the clerk of the court, Ed Wadsworth. Wadsworth declined to answer direct questions, saying he preferred to report to the entire court when it next met in council, which would be in October. Furious at being rebuffed, Jones called Rives. Wadsworth had been Rives's law clerk in Montgomery before becoming clerk of the Fifth Circuit. By the end of the day, Judge Tuttle and Judge Rives had each spoken with Wadsworth and told him that "he must tell the truth." Wadsworth called Judge Jones back later that afternoon to tell him that he had recalled his deputy clerk, Gilbert Ganucheau, from vacation, and they would prepare a detailed report.[24] When Jones asked, "Did Judge Brown direct or suggest that any segregation or other civil rights cases be assigned to or kept from any particular panels or judges?" Wadsworth answered "Yes."[25]

Jones continued to press both Rives and Wadsworth for more information. On August 12 he received a letter from Wadsworth. "It is bad enough but not as bad as I feared," he wrote in his diary. "Further data is to be furnished." He called Judge Rives, who told him Tuttle was in Greeley, Colorado, awaiting a part for his car. According to Jones's diary, Rives asked Jones if he thought Tuttle should return at once so that the judges could meet or whether a date in mid-September would suffice. Given the gravity of Cameron's charges, Tuttle's apparent lack of urgency is surprising but likely explained by his assumption that his own actions were being challenged and his comfort with the steps he had taken. Jones thought time was of the essence. When Rives agreed and expressed concern about whether Judge Cameron's health would allow him to attend a meeting, Jones offered to call Cameron. Cameron, Jones wrote, "seemed surprised that his dissent in the Birmingham case had touched off such a furor" and "expressed his regret that Senator Eastland had 'blasted off.'" He told Jones that "he would not, in all likelihood, expose himself to the hazards [the strain affecting his health] of attending" a council meeting, whether it was held in the next few weeks or deferred.[26]

Tuttle called a meeting of the judges to commence on August 22 in Houston; he selected Houston to make it easier for Judge Hutcheson, the most senior member of the court, to attend. On August 16 Tuttle called Judge Jones from Fort Collins, Colorado; he was leaving for Houston, and he asked Judge Jones to meet him there on August 21. Jones pointed out that his interest was no greater than that of his colleagues on the Fifth Circuit. Jones "inferred," however, that "Tuttle seemed to think . . . that since the information had been developed as a result of my inquiry, that I had a greater interest or greater knowledge." When the two men met, Tuttle told Jones that "he wanted [him] to know that he had never regarded [him] as an anti-desegregationalist." Jones recorded that Tuttle felt "the Cameron charges [were] unfounded and directed at him personally" but that he also realized there were serious questions about some of Judge Brown's actions.[27]

To describe the mood as tense at the Houston conference, as the meeting has come to be known, is a considerable understatement. The integrity of the court had been seriously challenged, and the dark shadow of an investigation by Senator Eastland lay over it. The clerk, Ed Wadsworth, was so nervous that he told one reporter, "I have no comment, and that's off the record."[28] Although the judges agreed to maintain the confidentiality of the proceedings, both Judge Jones and Judge Wisdom kept a written record. The relevant portions of Judge Jones's diary begin on August 7, 1963, the day he received a copy of the *Houston Chronicle* article of August 4 in the mail. Judge Wisdom's notes were taken during the two-day meeting, August 22 and 23.[29]

At Tuttle's request, Judge Rives opened the meeting with a prayer. Tuttle then addressed Cameron's charges regarding three-judge district courts head-on and without apology. He had declined to appoint Cameron in *Bailey v. Patterson*, a case in which black plaintiffs challenged laws that mandated racial segregation on common carriers, because, in his opinion, Judge Cameron "had disqualified himself."[30] Instead, Tuttle had appointed Judge Rives. Although Judge Jones's diary indicates that Tuttle also defended his refusal to appoint Mississippi district court judges to three-judge panels, Wisdom's notes do not mention that, and in *Bailey v. Patterson* Tuttle had in fact appointed a Mississippi district court judge, Claude Clayton.[31] Tuttle stood by his decision not to appoint Cameron, maintaining that, pursuant to the statute that created the authority of the chief judge of the circuit to appoint judges to three-judge district courts, the appointments were judicial, not administrative, acts.[32] Neither of the diaries suggests that anyone contested Tuttle's understanding of the scope of his authority when making appointments to three-judge district courts, nor did anyone challenge his conclusion that Cameron had disqualified himself by indicating he would not follow *Brown*, but there were also concerns about ordinary appellate panels.

Tuttle explained that he had directed the clerk not to assign Judges Bell and Gewin to civil rights cases while their confirmations were pending. Both Bell and Gewin received recess appointments on October 5, 1961; those temporary commissions expired at the end of the next Senate session. The expectation with recess appointments is that the president will nominate the appointee for a permanent commission when the Senate returns because the nomination is subject to confirmation by the Senate.[33] According to Tuttle, in September 1961 Griffin Bell had come by his office to discuss Walter Gewin's concern that if he accepted an interim appointment and sat on controversial civil rights cases, his vote in those cases would be used to block his confirmation. Tuttle assured Bell that if he and Gewin did receive recess appointments, he would not put either of them on race cases until after their confirmations.[34] Jones thought this decision so unremarkable that he recorded that Tuttle "reminded us that Gewin and Bell had been excused in race cases while serving under interim appointments."[35] In later years Tuttle came to believe that, because of the jurisprudential problems they present, he had been wrong to help facilitate recess appointments. In 1985 he said so in a letter to Judge William Norris of the Ninth Circuit after Norris dissented from an opinion holding that recess appointees could exercise judicial power.[36]

> [I] was quite embarrassed over the fact that I had made an agreement with Judge Bell for the benefit of Judge Gewin and himself that no civil rights cases would be assigned to them pending their final confirmation by the Senate. The mere fact that Griffin Bell spoke of the difficulties faced by such interim judges for my consideration before he and Judge Gewin would accept appointment should have made it plain to me that it is entirely inappropriate, as you say in your dissent, for a judge to be looking over his shoulder at the time he is deciding cases which may dissatisfy members of the Senate Judiciary Committee when they come around to the question of his confirmation.[37]

Tuttle's mea culpa notwithstanding, insulating Judges Bell and Gewin until they could be confirmed did not further Tuttle's interest. He was wary of Griffin Bell because Bell had been Governor Ernest Vandiver's chief of staff after Vandiver won office with his slogan "No, Not One," and Tuttle found it troubling whenever Senator Eastland assured an easy confirmation, as he did for both Bell and Gewin. But Tuttle himself had come to the court through the political process. His work building a Republican Party in Georgia and his support of Eisenhower for president led directly to his nomination. He believed in that process just as he believed in the rule of law; in large part because of that, he insulated Bell and Gewin until they could be confirmed.

Tuttle no doubt hoped his explanations would settle the matter, but several judges remained concerned. On the one hand, even on the surface there were problems with Judge Cameron's accounting. He had selected "The Four" from the split over whether Governor Ross Barnett was entitled to a jury trial on contempt of court charges. To be sure, the decision had practical implications: no one thought that Barnett would be convicted of contempt by a Mississippi jury. That said, the legal question was complex and unsettled, and its appropriate resolution did not flow from one's understanding of the import of *Brown*, or the equal protection clause, or federal civil rights legislation. The Barnett decision was not a good or fair proxy for how judges would vote in more typical civil rights cases of the era, as Judge Cameron's own list showed. Judge Hutcheson sat with Tuttle and Wisdom in *United States v. Lynd* and joined in granting the plaintiffs the extraordinary relief of an injunction issued immediately by the circuit court itself against the obstructionist Mississippi registrar.[38] Judge Jones and Bell sat together, along with Judge Rives, in *Hanes v. Shuttlesworth* and unanimously decided in one short paragraph that the continued segregation in Birmingham's parks was unconstitutional.[39] On the other hand, Jones and Bell also sat with Tuttle, and all three agreed that a black student's petition for emergency relief with respect to his application to attend Ole Miss was premature.[40]

In these early years, the black citizens' claims were often compelling, the history of deliberate denial of fundamental constitutional rights overwhelming. Only an obstructionist such as Cameron himself could be reliably predicted to vote against civil rights plaintiffs. Tuttle was the most aggressive in taking steps to provide as much immediate relief as was possible, but black litigants and their attorneys did not shudder to see Judge Jones's name or Judge Hutcheson's on a panel. Judge Griffin Bell worried the civil rights community mostly because of his political pedigree. Neither he nor Governor Vandiver of Georgia, for whom Bell served as chief of staff, would ever completely overcome Vandiver's notorious campaign slogan. On the other hand, Bell had been Jack Kennedy's campaign manager in Georgia, and while it was clear he was no Tuttle, it was also clear he was not an obstructionist on the order of Cameron. Nor was Walter Gewin, although Gewin was closer to Cameron, both personally and jurisprudentially, than anyone else on the court.[41]

Not only were the ideological differences not as sharp as Cameron suggested, but, as Tuttle had explained, other factors affected the assignments. Cameron himself refused to sit with Tuttle. Hutcheson's age and ill health limited his ability to sit, especially when travel was required. Jones did not like to sit with Cameron, nor did he like to travel to Montgomery because of "transportation difficulties." For the period Cameron surveyed, only Brown, Rives, Tuttle, and Wisdom could sit without restriction. And yet, once the matter was aired, it had become clear that several judges were skeptical about how case assignments were handled—not by Tuttle but by Judge John Brown. Suspicions were not alleviated by a lengthy letter, written on August 9, 1963, by the clerk, Ed Wadsworth, to Chief Judge Tuttle, with copies to all judges. In his letter Wadsworth spoke of Judge Tuttle's instructions that Judge Cameron should not be scheduled to sit during a bout of ill health (but, Wadsworth noted, as soon as Cameron recovered he did sit, beginning with the Governor Barnett hearings). Wadsworth also recalled Tuttle's instruction not to schedule Gewin and Bell to "any race cases" until they were confirmed. With those exceptions, Wadsworth declared, "I am certain you have since instructed me . . . to 'let them fall' when, where, and before whom they will." Moreover, he wrote, he could assure the court that among himself and his senior deputies there had "never been any conscious effort, intention or design on the part of anyone in this office to pick any of our Judges for, or to exclude any of our other Judges from, panels assigned to hear any type case."[42]

The letter went on, and Wadsworth's defense of Judge Brown was not so ringing. Judge Brown, he wrote, "directed the hearing date for the Houston school case, as Judge Wisdom by formal order entered for the Court directed the hearing date for the Louisiana voter registration cases."[43] Because the panels for those dates had already been selected, picking the date equaled picking the panel. The distinction between how Wisdom and Brown handled the scheduling is significant. Judge Wisdom had entered an order that became part of the record and was provided to the parties. Judge Brown sent Wadsworth a note, typed on his letterhead stationery. "Ed," it read, "before the Houston school case is fixed on the calendar, let me know so I can give you some suggestions."[44] While the note was in the case file, it was not part of the record, nor was it provided to the parties.

The most damning part of Wadsworth's letter came next:

> Judge Brown has recently made other suggestions to me about not calendaring these type cases while Judge Cameron or District Judges were sitting, or at Montgomery [where Judge Gewin would likely be on the panel], which have not been followed as directives, insofar as I recollect and my records reveal, since under the traditional practice the Clerk of this Court has always calendared all type cases subject to the approval of and consistent with the directives of the Chief Judge only. Never at any time has any Judge of this Court, by inference or otherwise, even intimated, much less suggested or directed, that I "pick panels" of particular Judges in assigning these cases in order to produce a desired result.[45]

In addition to the note about the Houston school case, Wadsworth attached a note from Judge Brown dated February 9, 1962, that read: "Dear Ed: For your confidential use, I suggest that none of the touchy cases be assigned for the week of June 4. They can easily be distributed through earlier weeks." The panel scheduled to sit that week consisted of Judges Cameron, Gewin, and Bell.

Bell questioned Brown aggressively; the conversation was tense, and Brown was unable to explain himself to anyone's satisfaction. He tried to explain away the note of February 9 by saying he was simply trying to continue Tuttle's policy of protecting Bell and Gewin until their confirmation—but they had both been confirmed four days earlier, on February 5. Bell wanted Brown to stop all involvement with docketing and for Tuttle to assume it. According to Judge Jones's diary, "Judge Bell [wanted] the Chief Judge to sit only half time if he takes on the task of assigning judges."[46] Judge Rives suggested that either Bell or Jones might take over. Rather than letting Tuttle be overwhelmed by the workload of handling all assignments, Rives was suggesting to those who were most outspoken that they should be part of the solution. When Judge Wisdom expressed the position that they should continue with Brown, no one commented. Judge Rives again took the floor. Because the meeting had been the subject of considerable attention by the media, the judges realized it would have to end with a press statement. Judge Rives proposed that they should make the statement that "no improper assignments had been made in race cases" and suggested that Jones, Gewin, and Bell work on a first draft together that evening.[47]

The next morning, Tuttle opened the meeting with a dramatic offer to step down from his post as chief judge in favor of Judge Jones, who stood next in seniority. Because Tuttle alone had been named as the target of Cameron's and Eastland's charges, and because Jones was not one of "The Four" in Cameron's lexicon, if Tuttle stepped down it would presumably take the pressure off the court. None of the judges spoke in favor of that option; instead, there was a consensus that Tuttle had not abused his discretion and that he would remain chief judge.[48] With that settled, Judge Gewin urged the "adoption of a tolerant attitude" toward Judge Cameron, and Judge Jones opined that because Cameron had "recently denied that he had refused to follow the Supreme Court or to enforce the Fourteenth Amendment, he should be credited with good faith and good intentions."

Both the Jones and the Wisdom diary notes reflect that Tuttle indicated he would give consideration to possibly appointing Cameron to three-judge district courts hearing civil rights cases.[49]

With some difficulty, the judges agreed on a statement to be issued to the press: "The problems alleged to exist in this court have been considered by the court. The court believes that in no given case has there been a conscious assignment for the purpose of obtaining a desired result. Action has been taken to avoid any appearances of inconsistency in the assignment of judges or the arrangement of the docket."[50]

The question remained whether Brown would retain his administration of assignments. He could not explain the memos Ed Wadsworth had produced, particularly the note of February 9, but he was "abject in his penitent apologies and profuse in his promises of good behavior," according to Judge Jones. Before leaving for lunch, Judge Jones, who had been as relentless in his questioning and as severe in his criticism of Brown as any of the judges, told Gewin and Bell he had decided to move that Brown continue to handle panel assignments. Gewin agreed, but Bell demurred. Jones pointed out that Brown had the support of Judges Hutcheson, Rives, Tuttle, and Wisdom; that he would make his motion in the interest of harmony on the court; and that he was convinced Brown had seen the error of his ways and intended to "live right." After lunch the meeting reopened, and Judge Jones was pleasantly surprised when Judge Bell seconded his motion.[51]

One other accommodation was made in order to defuse the situation. At the time of the conference, a massive voting rights case was pending before Mississippi District Court Judge Harold Cox and Judges Brown and Wisdom; Tuttle had appointed Judges Brown and Wisdom to the three-judge district court. Judge Cameron apparently felt that because this was a Mississippi case, "a semi-promise" had been made that he would replace Wisdom; he was backed up by Senator Eastland, who within days revived talk of an investigation of the court.[52] Tuttle replaced Wisdom with Cameron—a decision that carried a high cost. Judges Cameron and Cox promptly dismissed the government's complaint.[53] Brown's forceful dissent was replete with shocking statistics and analysis. The United States had set forth facts that mandated proceeding to trial, he wrote. The government simply sought to prove what everyone knew: the disenfranchisement of black voters in Mississippi was not the result of accident or happenstance; "it has happened because it was meant to happen." Two years later, Justice Hugo Black wrote for a unanimous Supreme Court.[54] By then, Judge Cameron had died; he did not have to suffer the Court's curt yet eloquent assessment. "The allegations of the complaint were too serious, the right to vote in this country is too precious, and the necessity of settling grievances peacefully in the courts is too important for this complaint to have been dismissed. The case should have been tried. It should now be tried without delay."[55]

Moving On

If Senator Eastland thought his charge of court packing would intimidate Elbert Tuttle, he quickly learned that he was wrong. The man who survived hand-to-hand combat in the Pacific theater was not about to be intimidated by the sound and fury of his detractors, even when they included a U.S. senator. Tuttle, who had already mapped the way with his pathbreaking orders, continued to show his frustration with the painfully slow pace at which desegregation litigation proceeded.

Georgetown, Texas, lies just twenty-six miles north of Austin on the historic Chisholm Trail. In 1960 its three schools accommodated approximately 1,064 white and 165 black children; of the black students, 40 or 45 were in high school. White students attended either an elementary or a high school; black students attended a single school that housed grades one through twelve. An accreditation committee of the Texas Education Agency visited Georgetown in 1960; the committee reported that all three schools were crowded and in need of updating and that the black school was markedly inferior with reference to both its physical plant and its academic program. The city fathers responded with a bond issue, authorized by a July 1962 election, in the amount of $525,000. They planned to erect a new junior high school for white students only, to expand the whites-only high school facility, and to erect a new twelve-grade school for black students only. The black citizens of Georgetown had been waiting since 1955 for some move toward compliance with *Brown*; it now appeared they would wait forever. They filed suit, seeking an injunction against the expenditure of public funds for segregated schools. The school board argued that it was simply complying with a Texas statute that mandated racially segregated schools, and the Texas trial court judge denied relief. The Texas

Court of Appeals quickly reversed, noting that the Texas Supreme Court had held all such statutes to be unconstitutional.[1]

On September 5, 1962, a group of some twenty black schoolchildren filed suit in federal district court seeking to enjoin the school board from continuing to operate racially segregated schools. When the case came on for trial on June 24, 1963, the board offered a plan for desegregation: beginning with the first grade in September 1964, it would desegregate one grade a year. By 1975 all twelve grades would be desegregated. Federal District Court Judge Ben Herbert Rice Jr. entered the board's plan as his order.[2] The children appealed. Judge Gewin wrote the opinion for the Fifth Circuit panel that heard the appeal. Joined by Judge Hutcheson, he affirmed the opinion with one modification: writing in February 1964, the judges saw no reason why both the first and second grades should not be desegregated in the fall term.

Tuttle dissented. He agreed with the modification, but he thought it offered too little too late. He noted that the small number of black students made desegregation relatively easy to achieve. Moreover, seventy-seven white students who were not residents of the Georgetown District were allowed to attend its schools; that made "overcrowding" a specious argument. What really mattered was not in dispute: the black schools were deficient in every way. The board had long been derelict in its duty to offer separate but equal educations and derelict in its duty to dismantle Jim Crow segregation. The plaintiff children, to Tuttle's mind, had offered forbearance. After giving the board eight long years, they had not asked for immediate desegregation but rather offered a three-year plan. What was most galling was the fact that the eleven-year snail's pace plan approved by the court meant that not one of the plaintiffs would ever be in a desegregated class.

Tuttle tried hard for Hutcheson's vote, and when he didn't get it, he tweaked him with a reference to one of his favorite allusions: "Over the years of my association with my esteemed colleague Judge Hutcheson, he has occasionally commented very effectively that a court should not 'keep the word of promise to (the) ear, and break it to (the) hope.'[3] I had hoped that in the circumstances here present he would, as would my brother Gewin, realize to what degree this Court would be guilty of such a charge if we were to affirm the judgment of the trial court."[4] Hutcheson responded in a special concurrence, and in his response one can see plainly the difference between Tuttle and so many of his colleagues. Where Tuttle found it easy to discern hostility to desegregation in the board's failure to act at all for seven years, followed by its determination to build new, segregated facilities, Hutcheson saw nothing to indicate that the school board or the trial judge had been "animated by a feeling of opposition as such to desegregation and a determination to continue segregation indefinitely." Indeed, he protested, had there been any such indication, he and Judge Gewin would have been "quick to sense this and to reverse the decree accordingly."[5]

In Savannah, Georgia, Federal District Court Judge Frank Scarlett left no room for doubt in anyone's mind about his animus to the mandate of *Brown*. In January 1962 a number of black schoolchildren filed a class-action lawsuit seeking to enjoin the Savannah–Chatham County Board of Education from continuing to maintain its rigidly segregated school system because it caused them irreparable harm. The board denied the harm but conceded the dual system. Then a group of white students moved to intervene, alleging that they would be badly harmed if segregation ceased. Race, they argued, was only a proxy for "traits of educational significance" that made it impossible to effectively educate white and black students together. They produced a parade of experts who testified to the inherent intellectual inferiority of black people. The well-publicized hearing was nothing less than a frontal assault on *Brown*—an attempt to prove the pernicious theory that propped up Jim Crow segregation, the theory that the "Negro race" was inherently inferior to the "white race." On May 13, 1963, Judge Scarlett entered preliminary findings of fact and conclusions of law. Yes, the Savannah–Chatham County Board of Education operated a dual, racially segregated system, he found, but a dual system would be permissible if the distinctions it made were reasonable classifications. Because of the "distinguishable educability capabilities" of white and black children, the Savannah system's classifications were reasonable. A final order would be issued in thirty days.[6] The black plaintiffs did not wait. Their attorney, Constance Baker Motley, filed a notice of appeal and asked for an injunction pending appeal. On May 24 Judge Tuttle, writing for himself and Judges Bell and Rives, granted her motion. Injunctions pending appeal, he noted, although authorized by the All Writs Act, were only appropriate "in the exceptional case where there is clear abuse of discretion or usurpation of judicial power."[7] This was such a case. Once Judge Scarlett found, Tuttle wrote, that Savannah was operating dual, racially segregated school systems, the mandate of *Brown* stepped in. Judge Scarlett had no business second-guessing the Supreme Court; he had no authority to deny the plaintiffs their hard-won constitutional rights. Not trusting Scarlett, Tuttle drafted an injunction and ordered the clerk to issue the mandate forthwith. The school board was directed to cease requiring or permitting segregation and to submit to the court, not later than July 1, 1963, a plan to desegregate the school system, one grade at a time, beginning in September 1963.

On June 28 an intransigent Judge Scarlett entered his final order. In twenty numbered paragraphs he found as fact that blacks were inherently inferior to whites as a result of different hereditary physiological and psychological characteristics; in three numbered paragraphs he entered as conclusions of law that while white and black students had equivalent rights before the court, reasonable classifications were constitutionally permissible, and because both races would be harmed by lumping together "coherent groups having distinguishable educability capabilities," racial segregation in the schools was a reasonable classification. He dismissed the complaint and denied the prayer for an injunction. All that said and done, he made the one concession to reality that Tuttle had forced upon him. "Orders heretofore entered under mandate from the Court of Appeals with respect to a preliminary injunction," he wrote, "remain of force and effect."[8] It was 1963, and the Savannah–Chatham County school system was finally under a desegregation order. The system would be held hostage, however, for another four years. The Savannah litigation was the darling of a national movement to overturn *Brown* itself, and the interveners, supported by Judge Scarlett, managed to forestall effective desegregation by a series of unprincipled stratagems. Finally, in December 1967 Tuttle wrote again for a panel (Tuttle, Gewin, and Robert Ainsworth) of the Fifth Circuit. By then the Savannah–Chatham County Board of Education had aligned itself with the black plaintiffs. "This is the fourth or fifth appearance of this case in this court," Tuttle wrote, pointedly declining to be specific. "We simply do not consider it worthwhile to take the time to canvass the exact number of times in which we have been called upon to correct the actions of the District Court for the Southern District of Georgia, which have been brought to us for review."[9] Citing the recent decision in *United States v. Jefferson County Board of Education*, the court ordered immediate desegregation of the system.[10]

Jefferson, a landmark of civil rights jurisprudence, wasn't just one case, it was nine cases from school districts in Alabama and Louisiana that had been consolidated on appeal. The *Jefferson* litigation made obvious how elusive the promise of *Brown* remained. Judge Wisdom, writing for himself and Judge Homer Thornberry over an angry dissent by District Court Judge Harold Cox of Mississippi, filed his opinion in the last days of 1966. He began by noting that the class of 1966, those students who had just graduated from high school, had not yet started first grade when *Brown I* was decided. And yet, in the fall of 1966 less than ½ of 1 percent (0.43 percent) of the black students in Alabama attended integrated schools; in Louisiana less than 1 percent did (0.69 percent). The numbers were dismal. Wisdom wrote elegantly and at great length. Not everyone was persuaded; Judge Cox asked that the matter be heard en banc, that is, by the entire Fifth Circuit. It was reheard, and it was affirmed, with Judge Coleman writing a special concurrence and Judges Bell, Gewin, and Godbold each writing dissents.

At the heart of *Jefferson* was the Fifth Circuit's succinct disavowal of "expressions in our earlier opinions distinguishing between integration and desegregation," which the court attributed to the *Briggs* dictum, the statement by a panel of the Fourth Circuit that the Constitution does not "require integration; it merely forbids segregation." In a circumstance where the state had never imposed segregation, the court now held, that might be meaningful. But in the Deep South, in the states of the Fifth Circuit, where each school district had deliberately operated a dual system in order to enforce rigid racial segregation, it was the school boards' "affirmative duty under the Fourteenth Amendment to bring about an integrated, unitary school system in which there are no Negro schools and no white schools— just schools."[11] Suddenly, from the point of view of the recalcitrant school districts involved in the *Jefferson* litigation, finally, from the point of view of the African American litigants, all grades in all schools had to be desegregated by the commencement of the 1967–68 school year. School systems could no longer rely on the absence of rules mandating segregation, nor could they hide behind "choice"—an offer to let students apply to transfer.

The en banc court emphasized the fundamental point Tuttle had made a year earlier in *Davis v. Board of School Comm'rs of Mobile County*.[12] After noting that it was the fourth appearance of the same case before the Fifth Circuit, Tuttle added, "It must also be borne in mind that this school board ignored for nine years the requirement clearly stated in *Brown* that the School authorities have the primary responsibility for solving this constitutional problem." Throughout his long career, nothing frustrated or angered Tuttle more than the failure of public officials to shoulder their constitutional responsibilities and to comply with the rule of law. Neither he nor any other judge of the Fifth Circuit (or likely of any court) wanted to oversee the administrative operations of local schools; indeed, he deplored "the utter impracticability of a continued exercise by the courts of the responsibility for supervising the manner in which segregated school systems break out of the policy of complete segregation into gradual steps of compliance and towards complete compliance with the constitutional requirements of *Brown*."[13]

Although Tuttle had finally let his frustration with Judge Scarlett show in the Savannah school desegregation litigation, he managed, as was his custom, to maintain a cordial professional relationship with him. No trace of a lack of regard, let alone enmity, can be found in Tuttle's letters to Scarlett, written from time to time in his capacity as chief judge. In the occasional letter to other judges, however, he let his feelings show. In an October 29, 1966, letter to Judges John Brown and John Godbold, Tuttle transmitted his opinion for their panel in *Rewis v. United States*, a case in which the parents of a fifteen-month-old girl had sued the United States, alleging that malpractice by an army doctor had led to her death.[14] Judge Scarlett had entered judgment for the defendants. Tuttle proposed to reverse. His opinion was dependent on a close reading of the record in the case; in order that his colleagues could evaluate it fully, he was circulating the record to them. "I am sending the original record . . . so that [you] can read Judge Scarlett's opinion, which is about in line with his usual treatment of a case," he wrote dryly. Judge Frank Scarlett was first among equals of the obstructionist politicians and judges who successfully forestalled the dismantling of Jim Crow segregation. Two years after he died in 1971, having served twenty-five years on the federal district court, Senator Herman Talmadge introduced a bill to name the federal building in Brunswick, Georgia, the Frank M. Scarlett Federal Building. Senator Sam Nunn cosponsored the bill. It passed easily.

Breaking the back of Jim Crow segregation was an extraordinarily difficult task, rendered all but impossible by the determination of so many highly placed public officials—including more than a few United States senators and representatives, federal judges, and governors of several states—to maintain it. Under Tuttle's leadership, the historic Fifth Circuit stayed the course, remained faithful to its responsibility to recognize and protect the constitutional rights of black Americans, and managed to prevail. Just as *Jefferson* is among the handful of most critical school desegregation cases ever penned, so does *United States v. Louisiana* stand as a landmark of voting rights jurisprudence. Both were written by Judge Wisdom; both built on the extraordinary work of federal district court judges like Frank Johnson in Alabama, Bryan Simpson in Florida, William A. "Gus" Bootle in Georgia, and Skelly Wright in Louisiana and of Department of Justice officials like John Doar and Burke Marshall; both depended on the body of law that had been laboriously developed in the Fifth Circuit. As Burke Marshall put it, speaking of Tuttle, Wisdom, Rives, and Brown, "If it hadn't been for judges like that on the Fifth Circuit, I think *Brown* would have failed in the end."[15] Tuttle took quiet, deep pride in the work of the court. "We became what I consider a great constitutional court," he allowed in 1969, ". . . and I think we largely have to thank the black plaintiffs for that."[16]

CHAPTER TWENTY-THREE

The City Almost
Too Busy to Hate

Although Tuttle joined the Fifth Circuit in 1954, he had carried a low pro-file until late in 1960, when, almost simultaneously, he became chief judge and he entered the order that desegregated the University of Georgia. Then he became the iconic activist judge. Tempers ran hot, and he, along with his colleagues, was the target of increasing animosity over the next several years. His daughter-in-law, Ginny, would never forget a call to her home in the aftermath of that order. "I have a daughter at the University of Georgia, and if anything happens down there you had better watch out for your kids at Westminster," a man's voice told her. Ginny had three children in grade school at Westminster. For a few weeks they were not left unattended; then that danger seemed to have passed. At their home, the judge and Sara suf-fered crank calls and crackpot letters. Moreover, the antipathy of many of their friends was quietly apparent. Still, compared to some of Tuttle's col-leagues, they were largely insulated from the worst of it.

Judges Richard Rives and Frank Johnson were less fortunate. They had the misfortune to be on the cutting edge; it was their ruling that inte-grated the Montgomery buses in late 1956. Geography and demograph-ics may have mattered more than timing. In Montgomery, a smaller and less sophisticated city than Atlanta, virtually no one stood by the federal judges—even in church. Richard Rives had been among the most highly and most affectionately regarded lawyers in Alabama until the civil rights cases; then he became a pariah. It hurt profoundly when old friends would change pews in church to avoid sitting near him and his wife. It was far worse when vandals desecrated his son's grave with paint and garbage. Yet when *Time* magazine blamed the incident on Rives's "fellow Alabamians," it was Richard Rives who wrote in defense, pointing out that no one knew who had committed the act, but whoever had "must have been mentally ill. Certainly it should not be charged to my fellow Alabamians, the overwhelming majority of whom are as fine, decent, and fair-minded people as can be found anywhere."[1]

Unlike Richard Rives, who was a native of Montgomery, Frank Johnson was born and raised in Winston County in northwestern Alabama, a county that opposed secession. When the South seceded from the Union, there was some talk of Winston County seceding from Alabama; that earned the county its enduring nickname, the "Free State of Winston." Winston did not secede from Alabama, but it did send more than twice as many men to fight for the Union than for the Confederacy. After the Civil War, Winston became a Republican pocket in an otherwise solidly Democratic region.[2] Accustomed to being an outsider, Johnson reacted differently than Rives when friends at church gave him and his wife, Ruth, too wide a berth. They simply stopped attending. Johnson minded, but being ostracized hurt him less than it did Rives in part because he had not felt as much a part of the circles they traveled in in the first place and in part because, unlike Rives, while Johnson enjoyed the company of good friends, he was not by nature sociable in a broader sense. Still, his temperament could not insulate him entirely. Even Frank Johnson, a man of great physical and moral courage, was shaken when his mother's home was bombed.

Atlanta was just up the road from Montgomery, less than two hundred miles away. In 1960 it was still in the grip of Jim Crow segregation. Not only schools but also hotels, restaurants, and cabs were segregated. There were perhaps a dozen black lawyers in Georgia in 1950, all of whom had been forced to go out of state for their legal education. One of the oldest, T. J. Henry, took the bar exam at the same sitting as Tuttle and was admitted one day before him, on July 9, 1923. Still, the Atlanta Bar Association as well as the State Bar of Georgia remained segregated until 1964 and 1963, respectively. Most black attorneys of the era were known by their initials: T. J. Henry, A. T. Walden, E. E. Moore. One of the insulting traditions of Jim Crow segregation was never to call a black man "Mister"; using initials was a stratagem to prevent white lawyers from being able to use black men's first names.

And yet, Atlanta was different. Perhaps the single most distinguishing factor was the work of one man—Ralph McGill, the editor of Atlanta's morning newspaper, the *Atlanta Constitution*. One year younger than

Tuttle, McGill was born in Tennessee in 1898. Unlike Tuttle, he had grown up with segregation, and for many years he expressed little if any quarrel with the doctrine of separate but equal. But he was a reporter, and he had a reporter's eye for the facts, and he could not abide the inequality of Jim Crow segregation. As early as 1938, he was decrying the South's failure to hold up its side of the bargain. In 1944 he was one of the founding members of the Southern Regional Council, an interracial group dedicated to attaining "through research and action the ideals and practices of equal opportunity for all peoples of the region."[3] On April 9, 1953, a year before *Brown I* was decided, he foresaw it. "Days come and go," he wrote, "and Monday is among them, and one of these Mondays the Supreme Court of the United States is going to hand down a ruling which may, although it is considered by some unlikely, outlaw the South's dual school system, wholly or in part."[4] Until the 1960s, in print McGill "repeated over and over that neither he nor anybody else in Georgia, black or white, was advocating any form of social equality, or any breaking down of the old patterns of segregation in the schools."[5] Even so, his constant commitment to equal treatment and to the rule of law and his opposition to violence in the service of ideology and to the pervasive mistreatment of black citizens changed and raised the level of discourse in Atlanta.

Even in Atlanta, few dared to raise a public voice in support of *Brown* and its implementation by the federal courts. One who did was Rabbi Jacob Rothschild, who presided at the Temple, Atlanta's main Reform Jewish congregation, from 1946 to 1973. Rabbi Rothschild was an early friend and constant supporter of Martin Luther King Jr.; when the Temple was bombed on October 12, 1958, most thought it a result in part of his open advocacy for full civil rights for black Americans. Later, the Roman Catholic archbishop of the Atlanta Diocese from 1962 to 1968, Paul Hallinan, stood out for his open support of civil rights. But it was McGill, with his voice amplified by his platform, the *Atlanta Constitution*, who mattered the most.

Tuttle and McGill knew each other socially, but they did not regularly socialize together. They admired each other deeply, as their correspondence over the years reflects, and their friendship thrived despite the fact that they chose different political camps. Tuttle was deeply involved with Eisenhower's campaign for the presidency, while McGill was completely committed to Adlai Stevenson. In 1952 Tuttle wrote McGill to complain that the *Atlanta Constitution*'s news coverage was biased toward Adlai Stevenson. Both the morning and afternoon papers endorsed Stevenson editorially; he was, after all, the Democratic candidate. Tuttle accepted that. But he had counted headlines and columns, and, he protested, the coverage was not balanced. The exchange between McGill and Tuttle was respectful but pointed.

Once Eisenhower was elected, McGill was quick to lobby him on Tuttle's behalf. McGill knew Eisenhower, having met him at Robert Woodruff's south Georgia plantation, Ichauway. Less than a week after Chief Justice Fred Vinson died on September 8, 1953, McGill wired his advice.

> I hope you will pardon the intrusion, but if the decision is yet to be made, I would like respectfully to suggest the name of Elbert Tuttle for consideration in the Supreme Court vacancy. No man in our state or region enjoys greater respect than he. Our State Supreme Court would, I am sure, unanimously endorse him, as would all Democrats, Republicans and Independents.
>
> Warm personal regards, Ralph McGill, Editor, *Atlanta Constitution*.[6]

However, the decision had already been made, and the seat went to Earl Warren.

Their respect was mutual. When McGill was named publisher of the *Atlanta Constitution* in May 1960, Tuttle sent a handwritten note from New Orleans, where he was sitting with the court.

> Dear Ralph:
>
> I got away to New Orleans before I could write and tell you how pleased I was over your being made Publisher of the Constitution. At first I thought you would be a silent publisher and I hated that. Now I am glad to see that you will continue your column.
>
> You have undoubtedly been the nearest thing to being the Conscience of the South and the Oracle of the South than any other person or group of persons. It must be very satisfying to know how *right* you have been, not because of any pride in being proved right, but because what you have done has been *right for Georgia*.
>
> Sara and I send affectionate regards.
>
> Cordially yours, Elbert

Among the most touching, and telling, pieces of correspondence is Tuttle's letter to McGill of August 17, 1967, thanking him for his generous letter on the occasion of Tuttle's retiring as chief judge and taking senior status. Tuttle replied, "Truly and frankly, I would rather feel that my official conduct has met with your approval than that of anyone on the public scene." Tuttle goes on to ponder whether his feeling of compatibility comes from the coincidence that they both started their careers as sports writers. "In any event," he closes, "we have shared many things in common and I have felt that your support both for the court I have served and for me personally has been like that of a thousand."[7] McGill's stalwart support of Tuttle's work and his clear-eyed condemnation of Jim Crow segregation and demagoguery no doubt felt like that of a thousand because he was among the few who would stand up and be counted in the 1950s and 1960s. His very public presence magnified his impact.

Another Atlantan who had a constraining influence on racial conflict in Atlanta was Robert W. Woodruff, president of Coca-Cola. In contrast to McGill, Woodruff maintained an extremely low public profile. Only thirty-three years old when he took over Coca-Cola in 1923, Woodruff led the global growth of Coke. He was a man of vision and a marketing genius. Part of that genius was recognizing that as an international company, Coke could not have its corporate headquarters in a provincial city that practiced a kind of apartheid or one that was rocked by the kind of racist violence that afflicted Birmingham. Arguably the most powerful man in the city, Woodruff was a behind-the-scenes player, but he had no difficulty letting others know what he thought, and he was more progressive than most of his colleagues. When Mayor Ivan Allen decided to testify in Congress in 1963 in favor of Kennedy's civil rights legislation, he didn't tell many of his constituents or his peers in the business community. As Allen put it, policy declarations by the Chamber of Commerce notwithstanding, he "knew where they stood." He did tell Robert Woodruff, and Woodruff supported Allen's decision. "It's going to be a very unpopular thing to do," he said, "but you've made up your mind and you're probably right about it, and I think you should go." Other than a "handful of liberals," Allen recalled, "Woodruff was about the only white person in Atlanta who told me I should go to Washington and support the bill."[8] In Washington, Ivan Allen stood alone; he was the only elected official from the entire South who testified in support of the legislation.

Allen was fourteen years younger than Tuttle, and by the time his political career was ascendant, Tuttle was on the bench; the two men never developed a relationship. Woodruff, born in 1899, was eight years older. For decades Tuttle and Woodruff both belonged to Atlanta's most exclusive private club, the Piedmont Driving Club, yet they rarely spoke. Tuttle recalled only two occasions. In 1952 Woodruff used Bobby Jones as an intermediary to place the call to Tuttle asking him to meet with Eisenhower's secretary of the treasury, George Humphrey—the meeting that led to Tuttle's appointment as general counsel to the Treasury Department. Nearly a decade later, when Atlanta's still-segregated public schools were facing desegregation orders, Woodruff again used an intermediary to approach Tuttle while he was having dinner at the Piedmont Driving Club. Mayor William B. Hartsfield asked Tuttle if he would step into an adjacent room with him. Robert Woodruff was waiting, and Hartsfield introduced the two men. Woodruff got right to the point: "I hope you won't integrate the schools in Atlanta in such a way as to cause any local rioting," he said. Tuttle replied, "Well, Mr. Woodruff, I'm sorry I can't discuss that with you" and returned to his dinner.[9]

It must have been one of the few times Woodruff was rebuffed; he was a solitary, powerful man with a reputation for arrogance, and he was used to getting his way. Tuttle meant no insult; he simply never discussed the work of the court. In fact, Tuttle counted Woodruff, along with Ralph McGill, as one of those who had done the most for Atlanta. In large part, Woodruff's contributions were financial; objects of his philanthropy still dominate the city—from Central City Park, to Emory University, to the Woodruff Arts Center. Because his economic impact was so critical, his determination to moderate Jim Crow segregation in Atlanta made a huge difference. When Atlanta was to celebrate Martin Luther King Jr.'s Nobel Peace Prize with a dinner, tickets went unsold and embarrassment loomed until Woodruff's emissary, Paul Austin, uttered a simple sentence at a gathering at the Piedmont Driving Club: "The boss wants the dinner to be a success." Then tickets became unattainable. Fortunately, Elbert and Sara Tuttle had already purchased theirs. After Dr. King's assassination, Woodruff called Mayor Ivan Allen from Washington, where he had been visiting with President Johnson. Noting that King's body was to be brought home the next day, he told Allen: "Atlanta, Georgia, is going to be the center of the universe." After a pause, he went on. "I want you to do whatever is right and necessary, and whatever the city can't pay for will be taken care of. Just do it right."[10]

By the mid-1960s Ralph McGill and Elbert Tuttle were attending the same church, All Saints' Episcopal Church in downtown Atlanta. McGill had belonged to the Episcopal Cathedral of St. Philip, in Atlanta's exclusive Buckhead neighborhood, until 1963. The dean of the cathedral also served as chairman of the board of the Lovett School, a prestigious private academy in Buckhead. When the school turned down an application for admission from one of Martin Luther King Jr.'s sons, McGill withheld judgment; some suggested the denial was not about race but religion—the King family was Baptist. Then two children of black Episcopalians applied and were denied admission. Surprised and disappointed, McGill moved his church membership to All Saints', where the progressive views of the rector, Frank Ross, were reflected in the good works of the parish.[11] At about the same time, Tuttle moved his membership from Peachtree Christian Church, which was near his home in Brookwood Hills, to All Saints'. He had joined Peachtree Christian because it practiced the religion of his childhood, he had baptized his own children there, and he had long been an elder, but he had become increasingly aware that churches were among the most persistently segregated institutions in the South. It had long been a tradition at Peachtree Christian that at the end of each service the pastor, Dr. Bricker, would ask anyone who wanted to join the church to come forward. Tuttle had sat on a case where blacks were prosecuted under Mississippi's malicious trespass and interference with divine worship statutes.[12] He began to wonder how Dr. Bricker would treat a black supplicant, so one day after services he asked, "Suppose a black person came forward?" Dr. Bricker said he would tell him to wait until after the service. "But why?" asked Tuttle. "Well, I would talk to him and try to decide if it was a political move or if he was serious." "You wouldn't do that to a white person, would you?" "Oh no, of course not." His suspicions unhappily confirmed, Tuttle resigned from the church.[13]

Elbert and Sara had been married in an Episcopal church, but that had been her choice, and it had been all but a whim. Elbert had attended church regularly as a child, as he would for most of his adult life, but in those early years after college he did not. Sara had never attended church regularly, but she had enjoyed chapel services at Florida State College for

Women (now FSU) that had been conducted by an Episcopalian priest, so when she needed a church, she picked an Episcopalian one. Now Elbert would turn to an Episcopal church, but the fact that he had been married in one had little or nothing to do with it. All Saints' offered a religious home not in conflict with his work on the court, and besides, his son-in-law, John Harmon, was an Episcopal priest.

Family and Friends

As the chief judge of the Fifth Circuit from 1960 to 1967, as the leader of a court that took the constitutional rights of black Americans seriously and insisted they be recognized, Tuttle was something of a pariah. Still, as he was quick to point out, he had it comparatively easy. It helped that Atlanta was perhaps the most progressive city in the Deep South, and it helped that everyone knew he was not a native southerner, that he had actually gone to an integrated school. "They didn't expect much of me," he would explain. Being a veteran of hand-to-hand combat and being known as a man of absolute integrity helped as well. But nothing was as important as the support of his family and friends.

Throughout his decades on the bench, Tuttle recused himself from any matters in which Sutherland, Asbill & Brennan participated. That disqualification had a salutary effect on his social life. He never had to worry that his deep friendships with his former partners would be viewed with suspicion. When he stepped down as chief judge at age seventy, he took up golf for the first time. When he wasn't playing with other judges or with his grandson David Tuttle, Tuttle's most frequent companions were two of the first associates he and Bill Sutherland had brought into the firm, Randolph Thrower and Jim Wilson. Tuttle had once been their mentor; as time went on, they became his best friends. They were first among equals in a disappointingly small group of Atlanta attorneys who steadfastly supported Tuttle's bold leadership of the Fifth Circuit. To the undying shame of the profession, during the difficult years of the civil rights revolution not one bar association or law faculty in the South stepped forward and spoke up in defense of the work of the federal courts.

In addition to a few stalwart friends, Tuttle had the constant support of his family. In the beginning, Sara would not have chosen the path they took. She was comfortable with the mores of the old South in which she had been raised, and she worried about offending her friends, whose attitudes toward blacks she understood and, for a time, had shared. But Sara Tuttle loved her husband, and she knew him very well. By the time he went on the court in 1954, they had been married thirty-five years; together they had weathered the Great Depression and World War II. She brooked no criticism of her husband because she lived by one driving principle: whenever Elbert did something, it was the right thing to do.

Tuttle was also graced by the complete understanding and support of his children and their spouses. When Tuttle joined All Saints' Episcopal Church, there were no black members, as best he could recall. Still, he felt confident that All Saints', unlike Peachtree Christian, would readily accept black members. Tuttle believed this in part because All Saints' was an in-town church with a progressive pastor, Frank Ross, and in part because of Tuttle's exposure to the Episcopalian religion through his son-in-law, the Reverend John Harmon. A pacifist, John had joined the British Field Service as an ambulance driver and left Princeton for World War II before finishing his senior thesis. His topic was the magazine the *Christian Century*, and his approach was encyclopedic—besides conducting voluminous research, he read every issue. When he came home on a three-month leave in 1944, the leave during which he and Nicky were married, he stuffed his research in a big ammunition box and took it back with him. He never opened the box. Too much had changed, and he could not get his heart back in the project. On the way home, one day out of New York harbor, in the dead of night he dumped the whole box over the side of the ship.

John went back to Princeton to finish his thesis and earn his degree, but he struggled over what career to pursue. Before the war he had considered history as a profession; now he was uncertain. By Labor Day, 1946, Nicky was seven months pregnant with their first child. In need of advice, John decided to seek out an Episcopalian priest he knew named Norman Pittenger. In 1951 Pittenger, by then becoming recognized as an important process theologian, would join the faculty of the General Theological Seminary in New York as a professor of Christian apologetics. In 1946 he was at a seminary in Red Bank, New Jersey. Pittenger welcomed the Harmons warmly and responded directly to John's question. Your calling is the priesthood, he told him. John and Nicky agreed, and John enrolled in the Episcopal Theological Seminary in Cambridge. The seminary required a college degree, so his enrollment was contingent on his earning his bachelor's degree, which meant finishing his thesis. When he returned to Princeton after the war, with Eric Goldman as his advisor John had started work on Algie Martin Simons, a prominent American socialist. His motivation renewed, John finished his thesis, graduated from Princeton cum laude, and finished seminary in 1950. By then Betsy, who was born in 1946, had been joined by Cappy, born in 1948. When Nicky was eight months pregnant with Cappy, she was confirmed at All Saints' Episcopal in Atlanta, the church her father would later join. The young family moved to Rochester, New York, where John served as curate at a parish for two years; a third daughter, Sally, was born there.

John Harmon had been committed to social justice since he was a young college student toting George Seldes's leftist political newsletter *In Fact* around. He and Nicky became involved with a group of Episcopalians (Paul Moore, later the bishop of New York, among them) committed to staying with the churches in the cities instead of following parishioners to the suburbs. In 1952 John was called to St. John's Episcopal Church in Roxbury, Massachusetts, an inner-city, mostly black parish in an economically depressed neighborhood in Boston. Later that year the Harmons' fourth and last daughter, Peggy, was born. Sara Tuttle was not happy about the move to Roxbury. In fact, as Nicky put it, "She was appalled." Sara had spent her earliest years in the plantation-like setting of turpentine camps where her father and mother were the lord and lady of the manor, her high school years in Jacksonville, and most of the rest of her life in Atlanta. She had grown up steeped in the southern version of the "War of Northern Aggression." Like virtually all white southerners of her era, she accepted the conventions of Jim Crow segregation. Race mattered, and class mattered, and she feared that John and Nicky were ruining their children's lives.

Elbert did not share Sara's sense of alarm. His parents had deplored discrimination on the basis of race and openly criticized segregation. He had spent his childhood in California; Washington, D.C.; Nogales, Arizona; and, during his most formative years, multiracial Hawaii, where he often walked by the home of the deposed last queen, a native Hawaiian, which is to say, a woman of color. He had been appalled at the harsh, unfair treatment of blacks since he first set foot in Atlanta in 1921. Moreover, he knew a number of blacks of great stature, men he respected. In the *Downer* case, Tuttle had worked with A. T. Walden, a graduate of the University of Michigan College of Law; in his long drive to create a viable Republican Party in Georgia, he had worked with John Wesley Dobbs, whose daughter was a world-class opera singer and whose grandson would become the first black mayor of Atlanta; he had worked on civic affairs with Dr. Benjamin Mays, president of Morehouse College; and as a member of the board of trustees for Morehouse, he had come to know Martin Luther King Sr. Elbert Tuttle understood, as very few of his friends and colleagues did, that black people were not inherently inferior, and he understood the extent and brutality of their oppression.

To Sara's credit, as unhappy as she was about Nicky and John's choice, she was not about to let it stand between them. Nor were Nicky and John. Mama Tut and Pop, or Poppa Tut, as they were known to the children, sent an array of presents for their first Christmas at St. John's; John wrote to thank them on December 26, 1952 (or, as he put it, Saint Stephen's Day). "Dear Mama and P. Tut," he wrote. "This isn't a thank you for all the Christmas presents for the Harmons (I haven't gotten reorganized enough for that)—but I so want to thank you for *St. Francis*!! It's a book I never hoped to have—but still wanted, terribly. God bless you for sending it— you're awfully kind." Still, Nicky was worried about her mother's first visit. She remembered coming home from Wellesley her freshman year, excited about how she had learned in sociology that white people and black people were absolutely the same and should be treated the same. Her mother, she recalled, "had a fit." Now Nicky and John were committed to his ministry to the people of Roxbury. Dinner drew the usual multiracial mix. Nicky was somewhat surprised and very relieved when her mother simply sat down and visited with their black guests.

In retrospect, Nicky pointed out that her mother "moved a long, long, long way in her lifetime. Absolutely amazing when I think about it, because she grew up in the South. . . . [S]he was thoroughly indoctrinated." Sara was also highly intelligent and a thoughtful person. In the beginning she was a product of her upbringing; as time went on she was a product of her experience. Nicky recalled one pivotal event. In 1956 or 1957 Sara went with Elbert to a dinner for the trustees of Atlanta University. Sara was seated beside Alberta King (Mrs. Martin Luther King Sr.); Martin

Luther King Jr. had just come to prominence. As a result of his leadership of the Montgomery bus boycott, his home had been bombed. His mother was "worried to death" about her grandchildren; it was all she could think about. "That," Nicky recalled, "hit my mother right where she could relate to it."[1]

A letter from John, dated March 20, 1958, captures the closeness they all cultivated. He begins by thanking them for a birthday check, which he plans to use to buy a much-needed suit as soon as he gets "brave enough to go down to Jordan Marsh and get pushed around by all those women." "I'm afraid," he adds in an aside directed to Sara, "my contact with 'your' Rich's has spoiled me for other stores." He writes of his happiness with his work, knowing it will fall on understanding ears. "Parish life is better than ever—at least as far as my spirits are concerned. It's really wonderful to be doing something & to know so certainly that you wouldn't be any other place in the world. Sort of like P Tut [Papa Tuttle] and the law." He writes of the great joy of seeing Sally take to reading and Betsy appear as Mary in the school Christmas play. Then he closes with two more expressions of gratitude.

> I'm sure Nicky has told you how grateful we are for the FM radio—but I must tell you again—especially since it's on right now—I'm listening to a Bach cantata, than which, for me, there is nothing finer. And this with the wind beating against the wall and filling the street with snow.
>
> Please pardon the paper. [He had written on lined three-hole notebook paper.] Much much love to you both and my thankfulness for being blessed with such wonderful parents by marriage.

John's letter to his in-laws usually opened with "Dear M & P Tut" and closed with "much love" or "much much love." Nicky's more frequent letters home always were addressed to "My Dearest Ones" and closed with an expression of love such as "All my love and kisses to all."

Sometimes the letters touched on the issues of the day. On January 10, 1961, just after the UGA rulings, John sent a short typed note.

> Last night I was out speaking . . . and when I came home Nicky told me about what had been happening and your part in it. I clapped! And she said that's just what the children did when she told them! But you deserve more than our claps,—you deserve our prayers,—and you shall certainly have

them. . . . I will never know why I was blessed with the privilege of marrying into the Tuttles; but I shall never cease to be thankful for it. It's so wonderful in an age so markedly lacking in personal integrity to have it so strikingly exhibited in people like the two of you.

Still, there were tensions, if only from protectiveness. On November 11, 1963, Nicky wrote to tell her parents that John was one of a group of eleven clergymen and four seminarians who had gone to Williamston, North Carolina. "They quite possibly will be jailed," she wrote, "but feel these people need all the support, moral & otherwise, that they can get. . . . I'm reasonably sure that you all will think this is a terrible idea but it is something these men feel they must do & probably will do again if they feel it's helpful to the Movement (although Johnny will never take part in anything in the Fifth Circuit), so that's the way it is." Nicky enclosed printed material about the Williamston group. She closed with "Love & kisses" and a postscript: "I'm all in favor of Johnny doing this so don't think I'm just suffering."

Nicky's news was apparently received with more equanimity than she expected. On March 23, 1964, she wrote to tell her parents that Johnny and several others were going back to Williamston. "The situation there is completely unchanged since last November, the promises made to the Negro community in December were completely empty & haven't been honored," she explained, "so it seemed necessary for them to go back." "Nobody knows what form or forms the action will take except that they're probably going to concentrate on the churches at least during Holy Week since they're going specifically as Christians themselves." This news was casually inserted in a four-page handwritten letter after a description of how the girls had begun to spend the $15 each their grandparents had sent and before a description of how very busy things were at the rectory.

One of John's fellow clergymen who went to Williamston, the Reverend Paul Chapman, had opened Packard Manse in Stoughton, Massachusetts, in the 1950s. Chapman described Packard Manse as a "free wheeling center of renewal in the church." Now John and Chapman began to question having located Packard Manse in suburban Stoughton. In 1961 they opened another Packard Manse in Roxbury. John, Jane, and the four girls moved in. They lived there ten rich years; when they left, John's place was taken by Sarah Small, an African American woman who had been the local president of the Southern Christian Leadership Council in Williamston, North Carolina, when John and his colleagues had traveled there to give them support.

The elder Tuttles visited often, first at the rectory at St. John's and later at Packard Manse. They became accustomed to an integrated setting unheard of in Atlanta. "Tons of people," Nicky recalled, most of them black, flowed in and out. One close friend, a black social worker named Charlotte Dunmore who would later teach at the University of Pittsburgh, lived with the Harmons in Roxbury from 1954 to 1960. Meals were jumbles of black and white friends. In turn, when the Harmons visited Atlanta, Nicky and John would gracefully join in dinners at the Piedmont Driving Club, where not only black members but even black guests were not allowed until the 1970s.

By the judge's own account, the Harmons' influence was great. On January 30, 1981, he wrote to thank Reverend Austin Ford, an Episcopalian priest who ran an inner-city mission for the poor and homeless in Atlanta, for the sentiments Ford had expressed in a letter of congratulations upon Tuttle's receipt of the Presidential Medal of Freedom. Tuttle shared with Ford that at this event "I had the pleasure of telling my daughter, Jane Harmon . . . that there is no way of telling how much of my judicial and other philosophy is attributed to her and John Harmon, who have been a great influence in my life." That same year he inscribed a copy of *Unlikely Heroes*, Jack Bass's history of the Fifth Circuit during the civil rights years, for Nicky and John: "For Nicky and John, our children who are more responsible than they know for much that is praised in this book. Elbert Tuttle—'Pop.'"

Elbert and Sara never had to travel to visit Elbert Jr. and his family. In 1956, as Buddy's graduation from Harvard Medical School approached, he and Ginny decided to move back to Atlanta. By then they had three children—Guy, born in November 1952; David, born in January 1954; and Jane, born in February 1955. Their family would grow. Another daughter, Beth, was born in July 1959, and their youngest son, Richard, who suffered from a severe case of Down's Syndrome, in 1962. In 1956 the combination of three small children and the financial circumstances of just finishing medical school meant that travel to Atlanta to shop for a house was out of the question, so Sara Tuttle took on the task of finding a home for them. She visited every house for sale in their

Ansley Park neighborhood and settled on a gracious, three-story frame house on the Prado, just down the street from the entrance to the Atlanta Botanical Garden. It remained home to Buddy and Ginny for over half a century.

Dr. Tuttle accepted a residency in internal medicine at Grady Memorial Hospital—the public hospital, founded in 1890, that serves Atlanta. Like everything else in Atlanta, Grady was segregated until the 1960s; it had been built with two wings, one for black and one for white patients, a history that accounts for it being known as "the Gradies" in the black community. Both wings were staffed by doctors from the Emory University School of Medicine who also staffed the Emory Hospital; once Morehouse opened its College of Medicine in the 1980s, its doctors joined in staffing Grady. When Dr. Tuttle finished his residency, he became head of the Department of Nephrology at Grady and joined the faculty at Emory. Widely regarded as a brilliant diagnostician, Dr. Tuttle spent his entire career at Emory and Grady, somewhat to his mother's frustration. Sara longed for him to open his own practice; now and again, she "encouraged" him to take that route. Ginny Tuttle remembered one evening at the Tuttles' Peachtree Circle home when Sara was particularly insistent, to no avail. Finally, to make her point clear, she told her son, "I would sell this house to raise the money to help you open an office." Judge Tuttle, who had been sitting quietly in a rocking chair, finally spoke up. "Honey," he said, "the house is in my name."

Born and raised in Wisconsin, Ginny Tuttle found Jim Crow segregation shocking and unacceptable. Her sense of civic responsibility had led her to try to enlist in the war effort; her understanding of the importance of public hospitals like Grady and the value she attached to research and teaching meant she supported her husband's career choices unreservedly, even to the extent of sacrificing her dishwasher. Grady Hospital owned one of the first-generation dialysis machines, the Kolff-Brigham, introduced in 1948. In 1956 Dr. Tuttle spent his first Christmas Eve back in Atlanta at Grady dialyzing a three-year-old patient. At first, dialysis was restricted to patients with acute renal failure. In the early 1960s, dialysis machines for patients with chronic renal failure were developed. Dr. Tuttle worked with a series of experimental machines at Emory's Department of Physiology, and he was impatient to get one for his patients. At Grady, which operated with public subsidies, there was no money in the budget for the expensive equipment, so he built a dialysis machine himself, using the stainless steel tub from Ginny's portable GE dishwasher. Not only did it work, it could be moved around. Instead of putting his African American patients on a gurney and taking them through the tunnel to the white wing of Grady for dialysis, he could bring the machine to their bedside. The dishwasher's remarkable second life lasted at least five years.

Ginny's unflagging support did not mean that she didn't sometimes feel pinched. Compared to many, they were very well off. Still, raising five children on a teaching doctor's salary wasn't easy—even with the help of Elbert Sr. and Sara, who covered most of Richard's expenses. The movement ended up leading her to a partial solution. When Martin Luther King Jr. was assassinated, several Atlanta churches pledged to help care for the throngs of mourners who were making their way to Atlanta. Central Presbyterian, located on the edge of downtown only a block from the state capitol, became the headquarters. Ginny went there to help. After organizing volunteers to sort the huge amount of donated food that had accumulated on the loading dock, she headed for the kitchen. That first night she stayed at the church cooking until 2:00 a.m. and brought home for the night three Agnes Scott College students who were helping. They all went back early the next day. Dr. Tuttle was busy manning first-aid tents; Sara Tuttle took care of the grandchildren. The next day, April 9, was the day of the funeral. Ginny was at home when her friend Betty Weltner called to tell her that a crowd of mourners at Wheat Street Baptist, just down the street from Ebenezer Baptist, where the funeral was being conducted, hadn't eaten. Ginny called friends and neighbors, asking them to bring whatever food they had to her house. In a few hours she made and delivered more than a thousand sandwiches. Things were slowing down until Dr. Tuttle got home after a long day volunteering at a medical emergency tent that had been set up by Grady staff. He reported that huge crowds at the stadium, waiting for buses to take them home, hadn't eaten. By the time Ginny got there, someone had made a plea on the radio, and food had started flowing in. Once again it was nearly 2:00 a.m. before Ginny started for home.[2]

After the funeral, Betty Weltner called again. Because of Lester Maddox's open racism, in 1966 Weltner's husband, Charles Longstreet Weltner, had resigned his congressional seat rather than take an oath of office that he would support Maddox as governor. In the aftermath of that, Betty Weltner had become friends with Coretta Scott King, and Coretta needed help. She had just lost her husband, she had her small children to care for, and every day found her meeting with celebrities and members of the press. Could Ginny possibly cook for her? She could and she did, taking dinner for fifteen or sixteen people, including Easter dinner, for almost a week. After those experiences of cooking for crowds, Ginny began a catering business. The Woodruff Arts Center, home to the Atlanta Symphony and the High Museum, was located on Peachtree Street just blocks from her home.[3] Working from her kitchen, she started by catering buffet dinners for the Atlanta Symphony Society every Thursday night. On occasion she catered receptions for the High. When the Emory University Women's Club renovated the Houston Mill House and opened it for meals and receptions, Ginny Tuttle was the first caterer on the list; wags noted that that made the Emory Women's Club the only club in town whose cook belonged to the Piedmont Driving Club.

October 22, 1969, marked Elbert and Sara Tuttle's fiftieth wedding anniversary. Their children decided to celebrate with a party at Buddy and Ginny's home; they included Dr. Benjamin Mays, the president of Morehouse College, and his wife on the guest list. Sara's reaction was negative. It was not that she herself did not think highly of the Mayses and could not socialize comfortably with them. The problem was that having interracial gatherings just was not done; her friends would be insulted. She put her foot down. Usually, when Sara Tuttle put her foot firmly down, that was the end of the matter. But this time Buddy and Ginny and Nicky and John would not give in; they were hosting the party, and they knew how highly the judge regarded Dr. Mays. They knew this was a friendship that mattered deeply to him. Finally, Sara gave in. It was hard for her; she was, as Ginny explained, "born and bred a southern belle." But she also "truly believed" in what her husband was doing.[4]

The party went off gloriously—but without Dr. Mays. He called the next week to explain his absence. His wife, Sadie, had died on the day of the event.

A Jurisprudence of Justice

Judges sit to decide cases, and for more than four decades on the bench, that is what Elbert Tuttle did. He published more than twenty-three hundred opinions during his tenure on the court; the overwhelming majority carefully applied precedent to precise facts and resolved legal disputes in matters critical to the parties but not of general public interest. He rarely found it necessary or appropriate to speak of his judicial philosophy.

In a 1971 case, however, Tuttle found himself explaining his dissent. Two prisoners had filed a class-action lawsuit against the director of the Texas Department of Correction, alleging that conditions of imprisonment, in particular of solitary confinement, violated the Eighth Amendment guarantee against cruel and unusual punishment.[1] While Judges Thornberry and Ingraham found the conditions of confinement "deeply troubling," they stopped short of concluding that they were unconstitutional, in part because similar conditions had been approved by other courts. Tuttle bluntly disagreed. "For myself," he wrote, "I do not hesitate to assert the proposition that the only way the law has progressed from the days of the rack, the screw and the wheel is the development of moral concepts, or, as stated by the Supreme Court in *Trop v. Dulles*, the application of 'evolving standards of decency.'"[2] Later, in a 1988 interview with former law clerk Fred Aman, Tuttle expanded on this.

> It may be "dangerous" to state what your judicial philosophy is in a few words, but in spite of that, I think I can say that my judicial philosophy is that I look at a record that comes before me from a trial court and if it looks to me as if an injustice has been done, then I do everything I can to correct that injustice. Now obviously, I can't always do it because of some precedent that prevents me, and obviously also, other people would disagree with me on whether it was an injustice. That all depends on your own moral precepts,

and of course therefore, I guess you could say that my judicial philosophy is based pretty much on my own moral precepts. I guess I have to say that's true, except that I am bound by precedent. But where there's no precedent that says I can't give relief and it appears that an injustice has been done, I'll try every way I can to correct that injustice.[3]

No cases exemplify Tuttle's commitment to correcting injustice more than the "removal cases." From 1954 to 1964, as Tuttle and others struggled to put an end to the gross injustice of Jim Crow segregation and to protect the constitutional rights of black Americans, they worked not only without political support but also despite the sworn opposition of almost every elected official in the Fifth Circuit. The Civil Rights Act of 1964 changed all that—suddenly the Constitution was backed up by Congress. Using its commerce clause power, Congress outlawed discrimination on the basis of race in facilities open to the public. When Heart of Atlanta, Inc., a corporation that operated the Heart of Atlanta motel in downtown Atlanta, challenged the constitutionality of the law, in a per curiam opinion Judge Tuttle and federal district court judges Frank Hooper and Lewis R. "Pete" Morgan ruled there was sufficient contact with interstate commerce to support the assertion of jurisdiction by the federal government.[4] *Heart of Atlanta Motel v. United States* was quickly affirmed by the United States Supreme Court.[5] Now when Constance Baker Motley came to argue at the Fifth Circuit, she could stop for coffee at the shop across the street. But all across the South prosecutions for the violation of Jim Crow laws were pending, and scores of protestors were in jail.

Again a case that arose in Atlanta became the standard-bearer for civil rights. Thomas Rachel was one of a number of defendants who alleged that they had been arrested for a violation of Georgia's criminal trespass statute when all they had done was seek to purchase food or accommodations at restaurants and hotels in Atlanta. Their arrests, they claimed, were motivated by racial discrimination. On February 17, 1964, they filed a petition for removal in federal court, seeking to have the prosecutions moved from state court to federal court. On February 18, Federal District Court Judge Boyd Sloan decided he did not have jurisdiction, sending the cases back to state court. The protestors appealed, and on March 12, Judges Tuttle and Wisdom entered an order staying Judge Sloan's remand, pending a decision on the merits of the appeal.[6]

By then, at least one of the defendants had been languishing in jail for more than two months. On January 11, 1964, Prathia Laura Ann Hall had dared to accompany white friends to the Heart of Atlanta Hotel; when she tried to order food, she was asked to leave, and when she did not leave, she was arrested for trespass. Fulton County Superior Court Judge Durwood Pye, an ardent segregationist who had been tapped by Governor Marvin Griffin to lead the state's efforts to resist integrating the schools, set her bond at forty-five hundred dollars, staggeringly high at that time and for that offense. Prathia Hall was unable to post it. As soon as Tuttle and Wisdom entered their order indicating that he should retain jurisdiction of the cases, Judge Sloan ordered Prathia Hall's prosecution removed to federal court and reduced her bond to one thousand dollars. A federal marshal served the Fulton County sheriff, who had custody of Hall, with notice of Judge Sloan's order. Fulton County Judge Durwood Pye immediately countermanded Judge Sloan's order with an order of his own—he directed the sheriff to ignore the federal court order.[7] *Time* magazine quoted Pye as having declared the cases "were still his, 'hide, hair and talon.'"[8]

The next day, March 20, Prathia Hall and the other defendants filed a motion for further relief with Judge Sloan. After a hearing he entered an order restraining the Fulton County solicitor, the Fulton County sheriff, and any other persons "acting by order of the Honorable Durwood T. Pye" from prosecuting or taking into custody any of the petitioners. That did not help Prathia Hall; she was already in custody. In her case, Judge Sloan issued a writ of habeas corpus ordering the sheriff to bring her to his courtroom. This time the sheriff honored the federal court order. Judge Sloan again ordered her bond reduced to one thousand dollars. Not taking any chances, he ordered her held by a commissioner of the federal court, not by the sheriff, for the time it took her to post the bond.[9] Judge Pye was undeterred. On March 23 he entered a lengthy opinion holding that the cases were not subject to removal, the order of remand entered by Judge Sloan was not appealable, and the order entered by Tuttle and Wisdom staying the remand to his court was a nullity.[10]

The state continued to prosecute civil rights demonstrators under the trespass statute. In April another group of defendants sought removal, and again the state of Georgia asked that the cases be remanded for trial. Judge Sloan held the motion to remand in abeyance pending the decision in the *Rachel* litigation and on April 17, 1964, entered an order restraining Judge

Pye from going forward with the prosecutions. The state responded by filing a motion in the United States Supreme Court asking that the court direct the Fifth Circuit to keep its hands off Georgia's prosecutions of protestors.[11] The motion was captioned *Georgia v. Tuttle*; it was denied by the Supreme Court quickly and without comment.[12] By the time the state's appeal in *Rachel* was decided by the Fifth Circuit the Civil Rights Act of 1964 had been enacted; President Johnson signed the landmark law on July 2, 1964. In December the Supreme Court ruled that state prosecutions that violated the Civil Rights Act of 1964 and had not been finalized before its enactment abated upon its enactment.[13] Civil rights leaders were ecstatic; they estimated that some three thousand people might be affected. John Lewis, chairman of the Student Nonviolent Coordinating Committee (SNCC), called the ruling "the most heartening thing since SNCC was founded."[14] On March 5, 1965, after oral argument, Tuttle filed an opinion for a divided three-judge panel. The defendants had adequately alleged that the prosecutions under the Georgia criminal trespass statute were a deprivation of rights that were protected by the Civil Rights Act of 1964, he ruled, and they were entitled to remove the prosecutions to federal court. If the federal district court judge determined that these arrests and prosecutions were motivated by racial discrimination, he should dismiss the indictment.[15]

Judge Griffin Bell, later to serve as President Carter's attorney general, dissented. Unless the defendants could "demonstrate . . . that the Georgia court would not fairly accord them their rights," the district court should not dismiss the prosecutions but instead should remand them to state court, to Judge Pye. Bell wasn't suggesting that the trial court judge, Durwood Pye, would protect the defendants' constitutional rights; everyone knew that he would not. Bell relied instead on the fact that the Georgia Supreme Court had, at least once, ordered similar prosecutions abated. In light of that, he wrote, "I doubt that appellants can point to any right that would be jeopardized by remand to the state court. . . . [A] federal court should not lightly intrude into a sphere of activity left to state and local government under the Constitution: the maintenance of local order."[16]

Tuttle thought Judge Bell was overlooking a critical point. If the defendants could prove in federal district court that "the request to leave was based upon a policy of racial discrimination," to send the cases back to Georgia courts and make the defendants continue to defend before an openly racist judge was itself a continuing deprivation of equal protection of the laws, a burden they should not have to bear.[17] Tuttle, as usual, was thinking of the people involved. Many of his friends thought the sit-in protestors were hooligans at best and had little concern for how they were treated. Tuttle saw brave young people willing to face arrest and imprisonment in the cause of fundamental fairness. He worried about their physical safety and their disrupted lives and about the economic and emotional burden of defending against criminal charges. The United States Supreme Court agreed with Tuttle, unanimously.[18] In a footnote that appears to respond to Judge Bell's concern about interference with local law enforcement, the Court noted: "The statistics on the number of criminal cases of all kinds removed from state to federal courts in recent years are revealing. For the fiscal years 1962, 1963, 1964, and 1965, there were 18, 14, 43, and 1,192 such cases, respectively. Of the total removed criminal cases for 1965, 1,079 were in the Fifth Circuit."[19] In other words, the data strongly suggested that federal courts ordered removal only sparingly, except in the Fifth Circuit in 1965, when hundreds had been arrested for racially motivated reasons in a last-ditch effort to maintain Jim Crow segregation.

When Tuttle credited the black plaintiffs for the Fifth Circuit's evolution into a great constitutional court, for the most part he had in mind the legions of African Americans like Herbert Lee and Prathia Hall who risked all to end Jim Crow segregation. In one case in the mid-1960s, the plaintiff was already a public figure in Georgia and well on his way to becoming a national figure. With the white Democratic primary a thing of the past, a special election had been held to fill seats in the General Assembly created by court-ordered reapportionment.[20] Julian Bond was elected to the Georgia House of Representatives. When sworn in on the first day of the 1966 legislative session, Monday, January 10, Bond and six colleagues would be the first blacks to sit in the Georgia House in fifty-eight years. But on Thursday, January 6, the SNCC, of which twenty-five-year-old Julian Bond was communications director, issued a statement outlining the organization's opposition to the war in Vietnam and encouraging draft avoidance— do civil rights work instead, the SNCC suggested. John Lewis, then chair of the SNCC, announced the statement. Almost immediately, Julian Bond was asked if he supported it, particularly its "expression of sympathy and support for those 'unwilling to respond to a military style draft.'"[21] When he said yes, Representative Jones Lane from Statesboro, Georgia, started a drive to bar Julian Bond from taking his seat in the House. By the time the body convened, at least two petitions had been filed challenging his qualifications. One charged him with treason and giving aid and comfort to the enemies of the United States, another with advocating violation of federal draft laws.

Martin Luther King Jr., who lived in Bond's district, rushed home from Los Angeles to support him. Governor Carl Sanders tried to derail the movement against Bond but was unsuccessful—the House voted, 184–12, to bar Julian Bond from taking his seat.[22] Three days later, on Bond's twenty-sixth birthday, a thousand supporters marched to the state capitol to protest his ouster.[23] The next day, eight Republican members of Congress issued a statement calling the refusal to seat Bond "a dangerous attack on representative government." A week later, Bond was the guest of honor at a UN luncheon given by chief delegates from fifteen African nations.[24] National and international attention notwithstanding, the real action was in court in Georgia. Bond had filed suit in the Federal District Court for the Northern District of Georgia on January 13, two days after the House refused him his seat. The suit was assigned to Judge Lewis R. Morgan, who promptly wrote Tuttle, in his capacity as chief judge of the Fifth Circuit, to inform him that the matter required appointment of a three-judge court. Tuttle wrote back the next day, January 15, notifying Judge Morgan that he had appointed himself and Judge Griffin Bell to sit with Morgan. The three-hour hearing took place on January 28. At one point, Bond's lawyers argued that race had been the determinative factor, that he would not have been punished had he been white. Tuttle countered that: "There is nothing in the record to indicate to the court that he was denied a seat on account of race," he said.[25] Both Bell and Morgan nodded in agreement.

Georgia's attorney general, Arthur Bolton, first argued that state legislatures, like Congress, had almost unlimited authority in determining their own membership and suggested that the federal court might lack jurisdiction to try the matter. Tuttle questioned that: if the court found that denying Bond's right to say what he said would violate his First Amendment rights, wouldn't it follow that the Georgia legislature could not deny him his seat on that basis? "Yes," Bolton replied. "That simplifies the issue," Tuttle responded.[26] But Bolton did not concede the larger point: Bond's statements, he argued, were not protected by the First Amendment because they presented a clear and present danger to the security of the nation and the state. In fact, as the Supreme Court held when the case finally reached it, the SNCC statement and Bond's support of it were well within the realm of political speech at the heart of the First Amendment's protection. In the court of public opinion, however, feelings ran high. Many considered opposition to the war in Vietnam unpatriotic and an expression of sympathy for Communism. J. Edgar Hoover had long tried to link Martin Luther King Jr. and the civil rights movement to Communism, as had the notorious Senator Eastland. Strong feelings about race heightened the tension and the anger. Tuttle's distinguished military service and his unquestioned patriotism served him and the country well. Many national news stories mentioned that he was a brigadier general; they stopped short of noting the irony that among the various key players, it was the war hero who was most determined to protect the war protestor's rights.

On February 10 the court released its opinion. Judges Bell and Morgan agreed that the Georgia General Assembly had acted legitimately when it denied Bond the seat to which he had been elected. They concluded that the legislature did have the power to determine qualifications of its members, subject to limitations imposed by the due process clause of the Constitution. The hearing conducted by the General Assembly, at which Bond and his attorney had spoken, provided procedural due process. As for substantive due process, it protected only against arbitrary action. If the decision not to seat Bond had a rational evidentiary basis, it did not violate substantive due process. Moreover, his First Amendment "right to speak and dissent as a private citizen is subject to the limitation that he sought to assume membership in the House." The crux of the matter, as Bell and Morgan saw it, was that Bond's support of the SNCC statement conflicted with the oath of office to "support the Constitution of this State and of the United States." Because the SNCC statement supported "those men in this country who are unwilling to respond to a military draft," it could "reasonably be said to be inconsistent with and repugnant to the oath which he was required to take."[27]

Tuttle disagreed. He dismissed out of hand the legislature's argument that it had plenary power to determine qualifications for office. Qualifications for office were established by the Georgia Constitution, and Bond met them. He met the age and residency requirements; he had not been convicted of treason or embezzlement of public funds or any other enumerated offense; he was demonstrably not an idiot or an insane person; and he did not hold any other military or public appointment that disqualified him. Bond had challenged the Georgia General Assembly's action denying him his seat on both state and federal grounds. Tuttle concluded that under the Georgia Constitution, Bond prevailed. It was not necessary to go further and determine whether the action of the General Assembly also violated the federal Constitution. The question of whether Bond had been denied rights protected by the First Amendment was grave, Tuttle noted, "since it is clear that it was for expression of his views that Bond was denied his seat."[28] It is also clear that had he needed to reach that issue, Tuttle would have held that Bond's exclusion violated the First Amendment. Instead, he rested his opinion squarely on the Constitution of Georgia.

Bond appealed to the United States Supreme Court. In the interim, Governor Sanders called a special election to fill Bond's seat. Bond won overwhelmingly. Again he declined to recant and was barred from taking the oath of office. In November 1966, with the seat from the 136th still vacant, he won the general election by overwhelming margins. Again he was barred from the General Assembly. Finally, on December 5, 1966, a unanimous Supreme Court reversed. The Court held that the Georgia General Assembly could not exclude Bond from his seat because of his exercise of his constitutionally protected right of free speech, the point Tuttle had made at the hearing.[29] The Supreme Court found it unnecessary to address the point Tuttle had made in his dissent, one that went straight to the heart of our democratic form of government. Bond was the people's choice; as long as he met the qualifications for office, Tuttle recognized, the people who had elected him were entitled to have him sworn in. Three years later, addressing Congress's exclusion of Adam Clayton Powell for alleged financial improprieties and applying the United States Constitution, the Supreme Court reached the same conclusion Tuttle had in the Bond case. Just as the Georgia General Assembly could not exclude an elected member who satisfied the Georgia Constitution's requirements to hold office, Congress could not exclude an elected member who satisfied the federal constitutional requirements to hold office.[30]

As much attention as was focused on Julian Bond due to his opposition to the war in Vietnam, far more was directed at Cassius Marcellus Clay Jr., the name by which he was known to his draft board and to the federal courts. By 1968, when his case got to the Fifth Circuit, everyone else knew him as Muhammad Ali, the heavyweight champion of the world.

Born in 1942, Ali registered for the draft in 1960, when he was eighteen, and was classified 1-A by Local Selective Service Board No. 47 in Louisville, Kentucky. Over the next two years he unsuccessfully sought reclassification as a conscientious objector or as a minister of the Nation of Islam (Black Muslims). Finally, on April 27, 1967, Muhammad Ali reported for induction at Local Board No. 61 in Houston, Texas. When his name was called and he refused to step forward, he was indicted for knowingly and willfully refusing to report for and submit to induction into the armed forces of the United States.[31] At his trial the jury deliberated only twenty minutes before finding him guilty. He received the maximum allowable sentence—a ten-thousand-dollar fine and five years in prison. He appealed, arguing that the statute establishing the Selective Service System was unconstitutional as applied to him because of the "systematic exclusion" of black men from membership on draft boards. Ali's conviction was affirmed by a panel of the Fifth Circuit (Judges Robert Ainsworth, James P. Coleman, and David Dyer) on May 6, 1968.[32] The court found no merit in the "systematic exclusion" argument, especially given that his final internal appeal had been to the three-member Presidential Appeal Board, and one of the three members was black. On June 6, 1968, his motion for rehearing en banc was denied.[33] No judge in active service voted that it be heard. Tuttle still carried a full case load, but when he reached age seventy he had taken senior status. As a result, he did not have a vote on the motion for rehearing.

In short order, Tuttle found himself writing in the case of Cleveland Sellers, a young black man from South Carolina who filed suit to enjoin his induction using the systematic exclusion argument. At the time, only one of South Carolina's 161 local draft board members was black. Sellers was supposed to report for induction on March 13, 1967; on March 12 Federal Judge Lewis Morgan, sitting in Atlanta, denied his request for an injunction. Sellers needed to file an application for a stay pending appeal immediately; if a stay were not granted in twenty-four hours, he would be subject to being inducted. His attorney, Charles Morgan, called Tuttle and explained that he did not have time to get the stay papers to New Orleans, the headquarters of the Fifth Circuit. Tuttle told him to bring them directly to his chambers. As the day wore on into evening, Morgan was still hard at work—but not finished. He called Tuttle again, apologetically, and asked if he could wait a little longer. Tuttle's response was firm. "I get paid to wait, Mr. Morgan. I get paid to decide the cases you get paid to prepare. We both get paid to work late hours. I'll be here when you are ready."[34] Later that evening, Tuttle granted the stay.

Sellers was then prosecuted, convicted, and sentenced to serve five years.[35] Judges Griffin Bell, Bryan Simpson, and Tuttle sat on the panel that heard Sellers's appeal, which was based in part on the same systematic exclusion argument Muhammad Ali had raised. Laughlin McDonald, cocounsel for Sellers, recalled that Bell's outrage at the "attack" on the Selective Service System dominated the hearing, Tuttle's efforts to interpose himself between Judge Bell and the attorneys notwithstanding.[36] On July 23, 1968, the panel ruled against Sellers in a brief per curiam opinion.[37] Tuttle filed a separate opinion, explaining why he concurred in the judgment. He was in an unusual position. The opinion in *Clay v. United States* had established the law of the circuit. Tuttle had been unable to dissent in that case because he was not a member of the three-judge panel that heard the appeal, and by the time the motion for rehearing was circulated, he had taken senior status. If he had dissented in that case, he could continue to express his dissent. Instead, he was bound by the law of the circuit it established, that is, "neither the federal constitution nor the Selective Service Act deprives a local draft board of the power to perform all of the services required of it under the Act by reason of the fact that, although as many as one third of the draft eligible persons dealt with are Negroes, the boards themselves are all white, or with a token number of Negro members."[38] Tuttle noted that there was a distinction between the two cases. Ali had been appealing from his conviction.[39] Sellers had filed suit to enjoin his draft board from inducting him prior to receiving an order to report for induction. Tuttle thought that even if the systematic exclusion argument did not give rise to a defense in a criminal prosecution, as the *Clay* panel held, it should be viable as a direct attack on the legitimacy of the draft boards. He read the *Clay* opinion as foreclosing that argument, however, so he concurred in the judgment of the panel denying relief.

Sellers's petition to the United States Supreme Court for writ of certiorari was denied, with Chief Justice Warren and Justices Douglas and Marshall dissenting. Justice Douglas noted that "in 1966, twenty-three States maintained draft boards without a single Negro member, among them being States in which Negroes constituted up to 42% of the population."[40] In a gesture showing the respect with which Tuttle was held, Douglas referred to him by name and quoted his conclusion that the statute and the

Constitution "forbid the practice which produces selective service boards of an entire state whose members are substantially all white, while classifying and ordering into service citizens of the state, approximately one-third of whom are Negroes."[41] Douglas, joined by Warren and Marshall, would have granted the writ. "This is a case we should hear and decide," he wrote.[42] The Supreme Court did not, however, then or subsequently, hear and decide the merits of the systematic exclusion argument. On June 28, 1971, Muhammad Ali's conviction was vacated because of mishandling of his request for classification as a conscientious objector.[43]

The litigation that pitted citizens against the government on matters related to the war in Vietnam led Tuttle to reconsider the way he had organized his courtroom. When he joined the court in 1954, he put both his general's flag and the American flag in the courtroom, flanking the bench. That had been customary in offices at the Treasury Department during his tenure; virtually everyone displayed an American flag, and those who had a general's flag or the like displayed it as well. After a few years, as World War II receded into history, he removed his general's flag. It was not until the Vietnam era that he removed the American flag as well. Tuttle was a patriot of the first order; he loved his country and stood ready to defend it at any cost, as he had during World War II. When he sat as a judge, however, he was pledged to neutrality, pledged to give each party a fair and equal hearing: "I realized I was handling a lot of military type cases so I decided I would take the American flag out too, so nobody would get the wrong impression."[44] Tuttle was not alone in that decision. The crusty former chief judge of the Fifth Circuit, Joseph Hutcheson of Texas, had never displayed an American flag in his courtroom either. To him it represented the executive branch, he explained to Tuttle. Like Tuttle, he wanted to avoid any impression that the court had already taken a side.

The mid-1960s in the United States were also the years of the British Invasion. They came not with tanks and guns but with guitars and drums— and long hair. When W. W. Samuell High School in Dallas, Texas, opened for the fall semester on September 7, 1966, most of the students went to pre-assigned homerooms. Paul Jarvis, Phillip Ferrell, and Stephen Webb went directly to the principal's office. They were members of a band—Sounds Unlimited. In homage to the Beatles and in compliance with a clause in their contract, all three usually sported a bowl-shaped haircut allowed to grow long—down to the eyebrows in front and down to the collar in back.

Principal Lanham informed the boys that their hairstyles violated a rule he had drafted governing appearance. It was his opinion that "the length and style of the boys' hair would cause commotion, trouble, distraction, and disturbance in the school."[45] He would not allow them to attend until they cut it.

The boys went to seven different schools seeking admission, with no luck. On September 12, 1966, they filed suit in federal court alleging that failure to let them enroll violated Texas law, constituted a denial of due process under the United States Constitution, and was discriminatory and in violation of civil rights legislation. Federal District Court Judge William Taylor ruled against them.[46] They appealed to the Fifth Circuit. The panel consisted of Judges Walter Gewin, John Godbold, and Tuttle. Judge Gewin wrote for himself and Judge Godbold. In view of the testimony that long hair, or Beatles-style haircuts, caused students to react with insults and obscenities directed at the long-haired boys and sometimes to take matters into their own hands and attempt to forcibly trim the offending hair, the judges found that the school's regulation was not arbitrary or capricious, or unreasonable. The principal had wide discretion, and he had not abused it. For the same reasons, the regulation did not offend the due process clause of the Fourteenth Amendment. Moreover, even though it could be assumed that one's hairstyle is a medium of expression protected by the First Amendment, the disruptions caused by reactions to long hair were a compelling reason to regulate that hairstyle.[47]

Tuttle dissented. He enclosed a letter with his dissent when he mailed it to Judge Gewin and Judge Godbold. "I hoped I could just let this go by," he wrote, "but I don't feel it is possible."[48] The issue, he noted in his dissent, was "something of a tempest in a teapot," and yet "three teenage school children in Dallas [are] being denied a high school education because the length of their hair did not suit the school authorities."[49] If, he pointed out, the majority were correct in their assumption that "a hairstyle is a constitutionally protected mode of expression," then the reactions of other students could not justify suppressing it. If a speaker can be silenced because others respond inappropriately to his or her message, the right to free speech is trumped by every rabble-rouser. Tuttle went on to argue that the real issue arose from the constraints of the equal protection clause of the Fourteenth Amendment. Similarly situated citizens should be treated the same. Reasonable classifications can be made; for example, those under sixteen can be denied the right to a driver's license. But this was not a reasonable classification. The three suspended long-haired students were not the problem; those who committed the disruptive acts were the problem. "It is these acts that should be prohibited," he concluded, "not the expressions of individuality by the suspended students."[50]

Three years later, another school hair case—*Glover v. Pettey*—reached the Fifth Circuit.[51] In the interim, the Supreme Court, after distinguishing *Ferrell v. Dallas Independent School District* and other "deportment cases," had ruled that high school students wearing black armbands as a protest of the war in Vietnam were engaging in protected speech.[52] The panel that decided *Glover* affirmed the trial judge's decision that the plaintiff's hair was "a disruptive influence . . . for which he could be suspended from school."[53] Judges Bell, Gewin, and Morgan affirmed without an opinion. After reviewing Glover's motion for rehearing, Judge Bryan Simpson wrote Judge Bell asking for a poll on the question of whether the case should be reheard. He found the principal's testimony disturbing. When asked whether he thought long hair had the effect of disturbing the classroom, the principal had responded, "I think any deviation from the norm causes disruption in the classroom."[54] Perhaps that was so, "but are we going back to Hitler youth standards?" Judge Simpson asked. Moreover, on similar facts another panel had affirmed a district court judge who had ruled that no disruption adequate to justify hair regulations had been shown. *Ferrell*, he wrote, "badly needs to be re-examined in the light of *Tinker*, in the light of later cases and in the light of what we see all about us." If he only had pictures of the thirty or so law clerks presently serving the court, "with the varying hair styles they affect," he would have attached them as exhibits. "I hope," he concluded, "that other judges will procure and read the record in *Glover v. Pettey* with an open mind."[55]

Judge Simpson sent his letter directly to all active judges because all active judges were entitled to vote on the motion for rehearing. He took the liberty of sending a copy to Judge Tuttle, who, as a senior judge, did not have a vote. In short order, Tuttle wrote to thank him. The passage of time had only made Tuttle's feelings about the matter stronger. Now, he explained, the question was personal to him. Two weeks earlier, his oldest grandson had graduated from Westminster, an elite private high school in Atlanta. In addition to being captain of the swim team and president of the chorale, holding a pole vault record, and winning the Bible prize for studies in the New Testament, young Guy Tuttle had shoulder-length hair. His grandfather was pretty sure that had he been required to cut his hair in order to graduate, he would have declined the diploma. "When I have personal knowledge of as well rounded young men as this feeling as strongly as this about matters of personal grooming," Tuttle wrote, "I think it borders on the fantastic to think that a boy in public school can be denied an education under the theory . . . that the state has an 'important state interest' to protect."[56] Six months later Judge Simpson had the last word. On December 14, 1971, he sent each of his colleagues on the court a photocopy of a newspaper story, complete with a picture, announcing William Rehnquist's confirmation for a seat as an associate justice of the United States Supreme Court. Simpson added a note: "Conservative or not, this boy would be barred from most high schools in the Fifth Circuit—sideburns below ear lobes are no-noes."[57]

More serious litigation came out of the Mississippi Delta from the town of Shaw, incorporated in 1886 and located in Bolivar County. From the 1930s until the late 1960s, Shaw was home to between two thousand and twenty-five hundred people, approximately 60 percent of whom were black. Many of the black people lived in a neighborhood called the Promised Land. Perhaps that gave them hope; perhaps it accounts in part for the 1969 decision of a small group to sue the city fathers. Andrew Hawkins and his friends and neighbors had grown weary of seeing municipal services provided to better-off white neighborhoods while black neighborhoods were ignored. They filed a class-action lawsuit alleging that decisions about the quantity and quality of municipal services were the product of racial discrimination.[58] After a three-day evidentiary hearing, Federal District Court Judge William C. Keady dismissed the complaint.[59] In essence, Judge Keady accepted all of the city fathers' explanations. Paving decisions had been made "on the basis of general usage, traffic needs and other objective criteria." New, improved streetlights had been provided, without regard to race, to "those streets forming either a state highway, or serving commercial, industrial or special school needs, or otherwise carrying the heaviest traffic load." As for sanitary sewers, until 1963 none existed in Shaw. All but "the more prosperous inhabitants" of Shaw relied on septic tanks; in most black areas, open-ditch sewage was the order of the day. Admittedly, the modern system installed in the 1960s had been routed to "practically all of the white residential areas," but it served "the more recent Negro subdivisions" too.[60] While it was true that older black areas remained unserved, the decision to prioritize new development had nothing to do with race. Because Judge Keady did not see evidence of discrimination based on race, he applied the rational basis test. In other words, he sought to determine whether there was a rational basis for the decisions that had been made with reference to the provision of municipal services. Finding that there was, he dismissed the complaint.

On appeal, Tuttle wrote for a three-judge panel.[61] Rather than relying on the explanations, Tuttle simply stated the facts.

> There are 451 dwelling units occupied by blacks in town, and, of these, 97% are located in neighborhoods in which no whites reside. . . . Nearly 98% of all homes that front on unpaved streets in Shaw are occupied by blacks. Ninety-seven percent of the homes not served by sanitary sewers are in black neighborhoods. Further, while the town has acquired a significant number of medium and high intensity mercury vapor street lighting fixtures, every one of them has been installed in white neighborhoods. . . . [S]imilar statistical evidence of grave disparities in both the level and kinds of services offered regarding surface water, drainage, water mains, fire hydrants, and traffic control apparatus was brought forth and not disputed.

The Fifth Circuit, Tuttle pointed out, had "long adhered to the theory that 'figures speak and when they do, Courts listen.'"[62] These figures, he ruled, made out a prima facie case of racial discrimination in violation of the equal protection and due process clauses of the Fourteenth Amendment. The only way the city fathers could justify decisions that discriminated on the basis of race would be to show a compelling state interest that justified their actions. They had not carried that burden, and the plaintiffs were entitled to relief. Rather than attempt to determine precisely how the city could make amends, Tuttle directed that on remand the "town of Shaw, itself, submit a plan for the court's approval." Judge Griffin Bell concurred in the result but disagreed with Tuttle's analysis. He would not have found that the facts established racial discrimination, only that they established racial classifications. Because he agreed that racial classifications could only be justified by a compelling state interest and that none had been established, he agreed that the plaintiffs were entitled to relief. He praised Tuttle's remedy, calling on the local governing authorities to resolve the problems, as a wise decision "in the highest tradition of Federalism."[63]

The conflict between Tuttle and Bell seems to indicate that Bell thought proof of discriminatory impact was sufficient to make out the constitutional claim, while Tuttle thought proof of discriminatory motive or intent was required—but he also thought that egregious discriminatory impact could suffice as proof on that issue, because "actual intent or motive need not be directly proved."[64] In other words, the facts could carry the day, the figures could speak, and the court would listen and draw the appropriate inference. That reading of Tuttle's opinion is clouded by the en banc opinion. Tuttle's decision was adhered to, although the sixteen-member panel produced six separate opinions. Eight judges, including Bell and Tuttle, joined the per curiam opinion of the court. Wisdom wrote a special concurrence. He completely agreed with Tuttle's opinion for the panel, he wrote, and he agreed with the result reached by the court en banc, but he thought the en banc opinion erroneously implied that "proof of motive, purpose, or intent [to discriminate] is necessary to establish a base for relief in a case such as this."[65] Notably, Tuttle did not join Wisdom's opinion, which purported to explain Tuttle's own position; rather, he joined the en banc opinion.

Thus understood, the significance of Tuttle's opinion in *Hawkins v. Town of Shaw* flowed from two holdings: first, that racial discrimination could be proven by disparate racial impact, even absent direct proof of discriminatory motive or intent; and second, that where it was proven, the federal court could assume jurisdiction and order that relief be provided by the responsible party even when that party was a unit of state government. The opinion did not go unnoticed. Within a month, Tom Wicker devoted a column in the *New York Times* to the opinion, noting that it was written by "the respected Elbert P. Tuttle" and musing about its applicability to Washington, D.C.[66] The *Houston Post* ran an editorial titled "Justice Well Done." "There are thousands of Shaws scattered across the face of the United States," the paper noted. "But now in the decision on Shaw a strong legal precedent has been laid down to correct these long-existing inequities. We salute Judge Tuttle."[67] Within a year an article in the *Tulane Law Review* called it brilliant and revolutionary, and Judge Henry Friendly, writing for a panel of the United States Court of Appeals for the Second Circuit, called it "path-breaking."[68] In time, it would spawn a book, *The Wrong Side of the Tracks: A Revolutionary Rediscovery of the Common Law Tradition of Fairness in the Struggle against Inequality*.[69]

And then, in 1976, the first issue reached the United States Supreme Court.

In *Washington v. Davis* the Court addressed a challenge to a qualifying test for applicants for the District of Columbia police force. The test disqualified a disproportionately higher number of black applicants than white applicants—four times as many. The black officers who sued alleged both a violation of Title VII of the Civil Rights Act of 1964 and a violation of their right to due process under the Fifth Amendment. The Court held that the constitutional claim, unlike the claim arising under the Civil Rights Act, could not be made out by a showing of disparate impact alone; direct proof of discriminatory motive or intent was required. *Town of Shaw* was among the cases listed in note 12 with which the Court expressed disagreement, suggesting that the majority agreed with Wisdom's understanding of Tuttle's opinion for the panel.[70]

Not all the justices agreed, however. Justice Stevens thought a finding of purposeful discrimination essential to a finding of a constitutional violation. He pointed out, however, echoing Tuttle's insistence that direct evidence of intent was not essential, that "frequently the most probative evidence of intent will be objective evidence of what actually happened rather than evidence describing the subjective state of mind of the actor." In other words, he agreed with the majority's statement of "the general rule," but he was not sure he agreed with each application. "Specifically," he wrote, "I express no opinion on the merits of the cases listed in n. 12 of the Court's opinion."[71]

Before the decade ended, the Supreme Court entrusted Tuttle with bringing a just resolution to the oldest case on the Court's docket. On January 9, 1979, the justices of the Supreme Court entered a per curiam opinion and order in *Arizona v. California*, which had been an open matter since 1952, when Arizona sued California seeking to limit California's use of water from the Colorado River.[72] Because it was a suit between states, the litigation fell under the Court's original jurisdiction, pursuant to which the Supreme Court sits as a trial court. The Court allowed the federal government to intervene in order to represent the interests of five Indian tribes that have reservations in the Colorado River Basin.

The first phase of the litigation ended in 1964, twelve years after it began. Based on the amount of potentially irrigable acreage on the reservations, the Court gave the five tribes a priority entitlement to about one-eighth of the water and divided the rest among Arizona, California, and Nevada. In 1977 several tribes petitioned the Court for more water, claiming that the "Federal Government had failed to claim water rights for all the irrigable land it knew existed."[73] The government agreed with the tribes, but the states opposed any additional allocation. The Supreme Court turned to Tuttle, appointing him as special master, charged with presiding over hearings and making a recommendation to the Court. Tuttle filed his 315-page report on February 22, 1982. In it, after "rejecting the States' strong objections to reopening the question of whether more practicable irrigable acreage actually existed" than had been delineated in the 1964 decree, Tuttle determined that it did exist and that the Indian tribes were entitled to additional allocations.[74] The states excepted, and the Supreme Court declined to accept Tuttle's recommendations, because "the principles of res judicata advise against reopening the calculation of the amount of practically irrigable acreage."[75] Three justices dissented (Justice Marshall did not participate because he had worked on the matter some twenty years earlier when serving as solicitor general). Writing for himself and Justices Blackmun and Stevens, Justice Brennan praised Tuttle for the "care with which [he] explained his conclusions" and opined that awarding additional allocations, as Tuttle recommended, "would avert a manifest injustice to the Tribes."[76]

For his part, in addition to disagreeing with the majority of the Court on the merits, Tuttle was more than a little irritated by the process. He had enjoyed the assignment; it had required that he drive west several times, a trip he and Sara always enjoyed. Always practical, however, he minded that the Court had not taken the time to rule that the allocation issue was foreclosed before they asked him to resolve it. When a former law clerk, Cam Kerry, wrote of his disappointment with the ruling, Tuttle responded: "While I am sorry the Tribes did not get the relief that they were really entitled to, . . . I am satisfied that we did our best. The one thing that really upsets me is that the Court could have decided the case on the basis of its final decision without ever referring it to a Special Master at all, so that all of the hundreds of thousands of dollars of attorneys' fees paid by the several parties . . . would have been saved."[77]

In the spring of 1979, Tuttle was thrust into the national press again when, sitting alone, he issued a stay of execution for John Spenkelink. In the years when Tuttle sat, almost all death cases that reached the Fifth

Circuit were state convictions that came by writ of habeas corpus alleging a violation of constitutional rights. When constitutional error appeared, Tuttle did not hesitate to give the defendant relief. If no error appeared, despite his personal reservations about the death penalty, Tuttle would follow the law and affirm.[78] He would be dismayed to know that in one of those cases the guilt of the petitioner, Adrian Johnson, has since come into serious question.[79]

The Spenkelink case was the subject of intense national attention because it promised to end a twelve-year-long virtual moratorium on executions.[80] John Spenkelink admitted that he had killed his traveling companion, Joseph Szymankiewicz, in their Tallahassee motel room, but he claimed to have acted in self-defense after Szymankiewicz had stolen from him and forced him, at gunpoint, to commit oral sodomy. After the jury found Spenkelink guilty of murder and recommended the death penalty, his conviction and sentence were affirmed on appeal by the Florida Supreme Court, and the U.S. Supreme Court denied certiorari. He sought executive clemency; instead, the governor signed a death warrant. Spenkelink's petition seeking collateral relief in Florida state court was denied; the Florida Supreme Court affirmed and the U.S. Supreme Court denied certiorari. Spenkelink filed a petition for writ of habeas corpus in federal district court; after a daylong hearing, the judge dismissed the petition, and in a thirty-nine-page opinion, the Fifth Circuit affirmed. Again, the U.S. Supreme Court denied certiorari. On Friday, May 18, 1979, the governor of Florida signed a death warrant that set the time of execution at 7:00 a.m. on Wednesday, May 23, 1979. On Monday Spenkelink filed another petition for writ of habeas court in a Florida federal district court; the judge denied relief and denied the petition for a stay of execution. The next day a panel of the Fifth Circuit, by a divided vote, affirmed the trial court. Spenkelink immediately sought a stay of execution from the U.S. Supreme Court. Because Justice Powell, circuit justice for the Fifth Circuit, was unavailable, Justice Rehnquist reviewed the motion and denied the stay.[81]

By the time Justice Rehnquist denied the stay, former U.S. attorney general Ramsey Clark was in Starke, Florida, near Florida State Prison, where the execution would occur, to "protest the execution and to bear witness."[82] That afternoon he received an emergency call from Atlanta attorney Margie Pitts Hames; working with Georgia lawyer Millard Farmer, head of a group called Team Defense that specialized in capital cases, she had prepared a petition for writ of habeas corpus raising a new issue: ineffective assistance of counsel. At 11:00 p.m. that night, Ramsey Clark, Margie Pitts Hames, and Millard Farmer knocked on the front door of the Tuttles' Ansley Park home. Sara Tuttle answered the door, led them to the living room, where they joined the judge, and then left them alone. Tuttle assured them he would read the petition and listen to their argument, but he also pointed out that in the twelve years since he had taken senior status he had not once granted a writ of habeas corpus. He also asked an obvious question: why had they come from Florida to bring a Florida case to him seeking emergency relief? Why had they not gone to a federal judge in Florida? The case had been in the system for six years, Clark responded, and Florida federal judges had reviewed it again and again. With the execution only eight hours away, "a new and difficult question, never raised in the case, and one that courts and lawyers alike abhor, was raised." They needed, Clark said, "a very courageous, very independent, open-minded and fair judge."[83] While Clark presented his reason for coming to Tuttle as a matter of seeking justice for his client, it can also be described as forum shopping. He was conceding that they came to Tuttle, rather than to any federal judge in Florida, because they thought it more likely he would grant the stay. Tuttle understood that. Still, two basic facts remained true: Tuttle did have jurisdiction, and time was of the essence.

Clark told Tuttle that an important piece of mitigating evidence had never been brought to the jury's attention. Spenkelink's father, a paratrooper in World War II, had served with the 82nd and the 101st Airborne Divisions. (Because of their storied heroism, it was the men of the 101st whom Eisenhower sent to escort the children who integrated Little Rock Central High in 1957.) Spenkelink's father survived the war, but he did not survive his homecoming. When Spenkelink was eleven, he found his father dead on the garage floor with a hose attached to his car's exhaust pipe in his mouth. Some prison psychiatrists attributed Spenkelink's record of minor crimes to the trauma of his father's suicide. His lawyers should have known that, Ramsey Clark argued, and they should have let the jury and the judge know too, because if they had known, they might have exercised mercy. Tuttle quietly said he would grant a stay to permit consideration of the petition for a writ of habeas corpus claiming ineffective assistance of counsel. As Millard Farmer wrote out an order for the judge to sign and the others talked, Tuttle told Clark that he did not favor abolition of the death penalty in all cases, as Clark did.[84] Then he signed the order, and the lawyers departed. The next day, Florida Attorney General Jim Smith filed a motion in the U.S. Supreme Court to vacate Tuttle's order. The state's motion to vacate was quickly denied, with Justice Rehnquist dissenting. Rehnquist had nothing but scorn for an attorney who over six years of litigation failed to file such a significant claim: "Either he does not believe the claim himself or he had held the claim in reserve, an insurance policy of sorts, to spring on the federal judge of his choice if all else fails," he charged.[85] He was caustic about Tuttle's role as well, pointing out that a federal statute, 28 U.S.C. § 2242, required that an application for writ of habeas corpus, if not presented to the district court judge in the district in which the applicant was held, should explain on its face why it was not (a defect arguably corrected by Tuttle's colloquy with Clark). The decision to take the matter to Tuttle, Rehnquist argued, looked like forum shopping.

Having been rebuffed by the Supreme Court, Florida Attorney General Smith then filed a motion to vacate with the Fifth Circuit. At seven that evening, Ramsey Clark received a phone call from the clerk, Gilbert Ganucheau; a panel had been designated to hear the motion to vacate, and Ganucheau was setting up a telephone conference call between the three judges on the panel (Judges Coleman, Fay, and Rubin), the Florida attorney general (Jim Smith), and Spenkelink's attorneys (Clark, Farmer, and Hames). In short order, the "conference" began, although Judge Fay was unavailable and did not participate. It lasted a little over an hour. At 11:30 p.m. the panel entered an order vacating Tuttle's stay. Judge Rubin reserved the right to dissent. Ramsey Clark drove from New York to Washington that night and went straight to the Supreme Court, where he met Margie Hames's husband, Bill, also an attorney. When the clerk arrived, about 7:00 a.m., they filed a discretionary writ asking the Court to reinstate Tuttle's stay. Shortly after 10:00 a.m., it was denied. John Spenkelink was dead within half an hour.

Spenkelink's execution did not end the controversy. Dean Michael Meltsner of Northeastern University School of Law read Ramsey Clark's account of these events in the *Nation* and asked Representative Robert William Kastenmeier, the chairman of the House Subcommittee on Courts, Civil Liberties, and the Administration of Justice, to investigate the panel's decision vacating the stay that Tuttle had entered. Kastenmeier, in turn, wrote Gilbert Ganucheau, the clerk of the court, requesting an inquiry.

Pursuant to the procedures adopted by the Judicial Council of the Fifth Circuit, Ganucheau referred the matter to Judge John Brown, the senior-most judge in active service.[86] Judge Brown wrote a twenty-eight-page report, with five exhibits attached as appendices. Meltsner had questioned the propriety of there being no hearing, dismissing as inadequate the telephone conference, in which, he noted, Judge Fay did not participate. He questioned whether the judges had read all of the papers submitted, and he noted their failure to allow time for briefs to be filed and their odd failure to state any reasons for vacating the stay. The order cited four cases, but none of the four had any apparent relevance; Judge Brown explained that they were cited for the simple proposition that the court could take judicial notice of earlier judicial proceedings.

The irony of an emergency ruling vacating a stay issued by Judge Tuttle was not lost on Tuttle. His own order vacating Judge Bootle's stay scant hours after it was issued and resulting in the immediate desegregation of the University of Georgia had thrust him into national prominence nearly two decades earlier. While that ruling was enormously controversial as a political and cultural matter, it was jurisprudentially sound. A notice of appeal had been filed; Tuttle presided over a hearing at which both parties appeared and argued; and he had jurisdiction under Rule 62(g), which allowed him to vacate a stay "during the pendency of an appeal." Like the All Writs Act, the rule was directed at protecting the parties and also preserving the jurisdiction of the court. In the Spenkelink matter, vacating the stay led to Spenkelink's immediate execution, which rendered any appeal moot. The order vacating the stay did not protect the court's jurisdiction; it terminated it.

Unable or unwilling to validate the actions of the panel, Judge Brown concluded that each challenged action was a judicial action and that discipline is not an appropriate response to a judicial action. He declined to "[assay] the judicial correctness or incorrectness of the action taken by the panel." But, he pointed out, there were "factors legitimately warranting the panel judicially concluding to vacate Judge Tuttle's stay." Under procedural rules prevailing at that time, however, Tuttle clearly had jurisdiction to enter the stay of execution, and the grounds on which he entered it had arguable merit. On the other hand, as Justice Rehnquist pointed out, several hundred federal judges had the power to issue last-minute stays in death cases. Rehnquist argued that judges should resist that temptation because giving in meant defeating the orderly processes of the law. He did not concern himself with the possibility that the motion raised a valid constitutional objection. He was not alone in criticizing Tuttle, in suggesting that he acted in bad faith out of opposition to the death penalty.[87]

Tuttle never regretted his ruling because he was comfortable that he was correct on the merits. He did regret that Spenkelink's right to have the issue heard was abrogated.

CHAPTER TWENTY-SIX

Hail to the Chief— and Farewell

On July 17, 1967, Elbert Tuttle turned seventy and stepped down as chief judge of the Fifth Circuit. His predecessor in office, Judge Hutcheson, had served as chief until he was eighty, but a federal statute enacted in 1958 required chief judges to relinquish the office at seventy.[1] Will Sparks, an assistant to Lyndon Johnson, sent the president a note: "We do not ordinarily recognize judicial retirements by special messages. In this case, however, Justice Department strongly recommends that you make an exception. . . . According to the Justice Department, Judge Tuttle has done more for civil rights than any other judge in the United States."[2] Johnson broke with protocol and wrote Tuttle. "Please accept my heartiest congratulations for a most distinguished career as a United States Judge. All who believe in the rule of law, and the protections it offers all citizens, owe you an enduring vote of thanks."[3]

Nearly a year later, in 1968, Tuttle decided to take senior status as well. Senior status allows for semiretirement. An age and service eligible federal judge can be designated as a senior judge by the chief judge of the circuit, and the designation can carry with it an office, an assistant, and one or more law clerks, depending on how much work the judge takes on. Tuttle had no intention of cutting back on his workload, and he did not, for the next two decades. He took senior status because by doing so he vacated his seat, gave President Lyndon Johnson an appointment, and gave the court another judge. The Fifth Circuit historically had one of the highest caseloads in the country (even before the civil rights cases expanded the dockets); more help was welcome. Judge Tuttle's first successor was Lewis "Pete" Morgan from LaGrange, Georgia; when Morgan assumed senior status in 1978, President Carter appointed Phyllis Kravitch from Savannah, Georgia. In 1997, after Judge Kravitch took senior status, President Clinton appointed Tuttle's first female law clerk, Frank Mays Hull, to the seat.

By 1967, when Tuttle stepped down as chief, the movement and its allies had won the great victories that broke Jim Crow's back. Lyndon Johnson had been one of three senators from the South who did not sign the Southern Manifesto. As president, he shepherded the landmark Civil Rights Act of 1964 and the Voting Rights Act of 1965, the legislation that signaled the end of the rigid apartheid that relegated African Americans to second- or third-class status. It did not, and could not, solve all the problems or compensate for all the inequities that flowed from a century of slavery followed by a century of Jim Crow segregation. Still, by discarding the doctrine of separate but equal and insisting on equality of treatment between races, these statutes transformed American life. As much as anyone, Judge Elbert Parr Tuttle had made that legislation possible.

Although Tuttle continued to carry a full caseload after taking senior status, having been relieved of his administrative responsibilities lightened his workload. He compensated for that by making himself available to sit and help out on other circuits. In 1969 he sat with both the Ninth and the Tenth Circuits. He particularly enjoyed sitting with the Ninth Circuit because that required him to drive all the way across the country to the West Coast. He drove, Sara read, and they talked about what she was reading, about language and word usage, about the countryside they were traveling through. Often one of his law clerks was in the back seat.

Sara never minded her husband's workload, as long as it was composed of cases. He could decide cases on a constant basis and never lose a wink of sleep. She hated, however, for him to agree to give a speech. From the time he agreed to speak until the time he actually gave the speech, he would agonize over it. As a result, by mutual agreement he committed to very few speeches. Those he did agree to give include a classic commencement address delivered at Emory University in 1957. In it, he spoke of what it meant to be a professional.

> The professional man is in essence one who provides service. . . . He has no goods to sell, no land to till. His only asset is himself. It turns out that there is no right price for service, for what is a share of a man worth? . . .

So do not try to set a price on yourselves. Do not measure out your professional services on an apothecaries' scale and say, "Only this for so much." Do not debase yourselves by equating your souls to what they will bring in the market. . . . Rather be reckless and spendthrift, pouring out your talent to all to whom it can be of service! . . . Like love, talent is only useful in its expenditure, and it is never exhausted.

Certain it is that man must eat; so set what price you must on your service. But never confuse the performance, which is great, with the compensation, be it money, power, or fame, which is trivial. . . . It is not enough that you do your duty. The richness of life lies in the performance which is above and beyond the call of duty.[4]

Those words, which express Tuttle's philosophy and describe his life, have turned out to be among his most quoted. Yet he was always a bit uncomfortable with the praise and attention they garnered. Part of that is attributable to his character; he was not unaware of his gifts or his contributions, but he resisted being lionized. In this case, he resisted being lionized in part because the credit was not all his. His son, Buddy, had pitched in and helped him draft the speech. Dr. Tuttle had been a philosophy major as an undergraduate, and he was a lifelong occasional poet. These moving words are not written in the spare style that characterized Tuttle's work. At the same time, they are very much his, down to his arcane but precise way of saying "Don't give short weight." Apothecaries' scales use a twelve-ounce instead of a sixteen-ounce pound.

Tuttle would have preferred not to take senior status, but he could hardly decline to open the way for another judge. In 1963 he had made a strong case to the Judicial Conference of the United States that the Fifth Circuit needed more judges. Around 1950 the Sunbelt states that made up the Fifth Circuit had begun their great expansion. Increased commercial activity meant more litigation. In the decade between 1950 and 1960, the Fifth Circuit's docket had increased by 41 percent, and the next three years saw a 51 percent increase.[5] Tuttle's plea did not fall on deaf ears. The judges at the conference agreed that the Fifth Circuit needed help, but they were significantly split on how to provide relief. Not everyone thought adding more judges was a good idea. Many were concerned by the vast physical territory the court covered—from Georgia to Texas. A significant few were diehard proponents of the Rule of Nine—the idea that a court larger than nine judges would be too cumbersome. The problems created by growth were not limited to the Fifth Circuit; as early as 1940 legislation had been proposed to split the Ninth Circuit (which is comprised of nine western states, including California), and Chief Justice Earl Warren had created a new committee of the Judicial Conference to address the "geographical organization of the courts." He named Judge John Biggs of the Third Circuit, a strong proponent of the Rule of Nine, as chairman. That suited Senator Eastland, Tuttle's nemesis. He wanted to see the judges he and Judge Cameron called "The Four" split up. If Eastland had his way, the circuit would be divided by a great natural boundary, the Mississippi River. Louisiana and Texas would comprise one circuit; Alabama, Florida, Georgia, and Mississippi the other. The good people of Mississippi would no longer have to endure Judges John Brown and John Minor Wisdom.

On the Fifth Circuit, for most of the judges the problems of workload superseded other concerns. If the only way to obtain more judges was to split the circuit along the lines Eastland and Biggs proposed, so be it. Two disagreed. Judge Richard Rives thought realignment "uneconomical, unnecessary, and unwise," but overriding all of that, he strongly objected to the attempt to dilute the effectiveness of the circuit in protecting the civil rights of black Americans.[6] Judge John Minor Wisdom agreed, but he described the problem differently. He saw the civil rights issue as only an example, albeit a particularly compelling one, of the policy problem the realignment proposal created. "The big question is whether judges on a national court should be drawn from a base broad enough so that they will be a more representative group," he wrote Tuttle.[7] To group Louisiana and Texas together as a circuit would be, for example, to put the oil and gas law rules of a circuit in the hands of judges exclusively from two major oil- and gas-producing states.

Tuttle was the man in the middle. He disliked the idea of realignment for the same reasons his friends Judges Rives and Wisdom did. On the other hand, he understood too well the administrative difficulty created by the size of the circuit (especially by the ever-expanding docket). He polled the nine-member court. All the judges agreed that additional judges were essential to help manage the caseload. A strong majority of six (Bell, Brown, Cameron, Gewin, Hutcheson, and Jones) would accept splitting the circuit if that were the only way to expand the judgeships. Tuttle sided with the majority, in part because as chief judge he acted in a representational capacity. No one took more pride in, indeed loved, the Fifth Circuit more than Tuttle; agreeing to break it up, and being on the other side of the issue from the two men on the court to whom he was closest, took a high toll. Judges Rives and Wisdom did not concede. Instead they mounted a campaign to persuade key players that it would be a grave mistake to address caseload problems by splitting the circuit. By the end of 1964, they had gathered support from the highest levels of the federal judiciary, from members of Congress, and from two of their colleagues on the Fifth Circuit. In July 1964 Judges Brown and Hutcheson informed Judge Biggs that they had been persuaded by the opposition, and they no longer accepted the idea of splitting the circuit. Judge Cameron had died in April, so the court was now split four to four: Rives, Wisdom, Brown, and Hutcheson opposed the split; Tuttle, Bell, Gewin, and Jones accepted it. When the national press started covering the issue, with the civil rights implications on center stage, the Biggs proposal was derailed.[8]

The controversy subsided, but the enormous caseload that had given rise to the call for a split of the circuit continued to expand. Finally, in 1980, all twenty-four judges in active service signed a petition to the Congress asking that the Fifth Circuit be divided into two circuits, one to be composed of the states of Louisiana, Mississippi, and Texas, the other to be composed of the states of Alabama, Florida, and Georgia. The first grouping would remain the Fifth Circuit, with headquarters in New Orleans. Alabama, Florida, and Georgia would become the Eleventh Circuit, with headquarters in Atlanta.[9] The Four—Tuttle, Wisdom, Brown, and Rives— all still sat as members of the court, but each had taken senior status, and none were asked to join in the petition. The Rule of Nine, for all its arguable merit, has been overtaken by history. By 2007 the Ninth Circuit had twenty-eight active and twenty-two sitting senior judges; the Fifth Circuit had seventeen active and four sitting senior judges; and the Eleventh Circuit had twelve active and four sitting senior judges. The Fifth Circuit Courthouse in New Orleans is named for Judge John Minor Wisdom, and in Atlanta the Eleventh Circuit is headquartered at the Elbert Parr Tuttle United States Court of Appeals Building.

In the spring of 1969, Tuttle was personally caught up in the tumult that characterized college campuses across the country. He had long prized his membership on the boards of Atlanta University and Morehouse College, two historically black institutions of higher education located in Atlanta.[10]

Elected to membership in 1950, he found that this service, like his work with the Republican Party in Georgia, put him in contact with the leaders of the black community at a time when racial lines were rarely crossed. Among Tuttle's cotrustees was Martin Luther King Sr. In November 1964, at a meeting at which Tuttle was not present, the Morehouse board elected Martin Luther King Jr. to fill a vacant seat—contingent on Tuttle's reaction. If King's election would trigger Tuttle's resignation, it would be held in abeyance until it could be discussed again at the next meeting. Charles Merrill, chairman of the board, and Dr. Benjamin Mays, president of Morehouse, met with Tuttle in his chambers on December 11, 1964. They reported to the board that Tuttle "stated that in any non-judicial service he must always be alert to any even apparent conflict of interest, but stated that insofar as he can look into the immediate future, he does not contemplate any termination of his service on the Board."[11] They took that to mean that Martin Luther King Jr.'s election would not cause Tuttle to resign, and they closed their report by saying, "In good faith we can now declare Martin Luther King, Jr. a member of the Board of Trustees of Morehouse College." For whatever reason—perhaps because he was overextended, perhaps because others in the movement did not want to risk disqualifying Tuttle from presiding over civil rights litigation—Martin Luther King Jr. never served.

His father, Dr. Martin Luther King Sr., remained on the board, and he and Judge Tuttle were both among the trustees at a joint meeting of the Atlanta University and Morehouse College boards on Friday, April 18, 1969. Between 9:00 and 10:00 a.m., about a dozen student demonstrators and one professor in his first year on the Spelman College faculty entered the boardroom. As many as a hundred demonstrators crowded the third-floor area outside the boardroom. They had two demands. At the time, a loose consortium of six predominantly black colleges—Atlanta University, the Atlanta Interdenominational Theological Center, Clark, Morehouse, Morris Brown, and Spelman—was known as the Atlanta University Center. The protestors wanted to change the name to the Martin Luther King Jr. University Center, and they wanted the resignations of all white board members. They intended to hold the trustees hostage until their demands were met. Most of the trustees, including Tuttle, spent a tense twenty-eight hours as prisoners of the protestors. Outside, a crowd, mostly students, ringed the building, some expressing solidarity with the demonstrators, others concerned about the trustees. Both black and white trustees were subjected to invective. Even Reverend King was repeatedly insulted, including the charge that "he had not heard what his son had said." After six or seven hours, King had had enough. He got up and simply walked out, saying he was "going to leave even if they killed him."[12] Three other trustees, including Florence Read, a former president of Spelman and the only woman in the group, were permitted to leave. The rest remained hostages until early Saturday afternoon.

That weekend saw similar demonstrations on campuses across the country, including Tuttle's beloved alma mater, Cornell, where many of the protesting black students carried rifles.[13] The situation at Morehouse had not been nearly as perilous, and Tuttle weathered it with equanimity. Still, it accentuated the possibility that his service on the board would create the appearance of partiality that would require him to recuse himself in matters that would likely come before the court. He attended one more meeting of the trustees in New York City in November 1969 and then resigned.[14]

Long an icon of the federal courts because of his integrity and courage, Tuttle became legendary for his stamina and acuity as he aged. In 1986, when he was eighty-nine, Judge Tuttle's doctors consulted with Dr. Tuttle when they realized his father needed a triple coronary bypass. Dr. Tuttle dismissed their concerns with a laugh—"Oh, he's not really eighty-nine, he's only seventy. Go ahead and do it." They did, and he came back to work full-time exactly six weeks after the surgery. Tuttle's friend and colleague Judge Thomas Clark took to coming by his office daily so the two of them could take an exercise walk through the halls of the courthouse, the judge went back to playing golf regularly at Bobby Jones with his grandson David, and in short order he bounced back. The next summer he, Sara, Nicky, and John took a road trip of some ten thousand miles. "We thought it a good time to take our daughter and son-in-law to show them something of the sights in the western part of the United States," he wrote a friend. "Incidentally, I did practically all of the driving."[15]

For nearly twenty more years after taking senior status, Tuttle carried a full load—enough so that the chief judge continued to assign him two law clerks and a secretary until 1987. Lillian Klaiss, who had come with him in 1954, stayed twenty years before retiring in 1974. Shortly thereafter, Betty (Mrs. Edward) Keener joined his staff; she would stay with him twenty years as well. Both Elbert and Sara enjoyed extraordinary good health as they aged, as did their siblings. That small group—Malcolm and Rilla, Elbert and Sara, Bill and Sarah, Mac and Jennie—all reached their sixtieth wedding anniversary. But time and age claim everyone. Elbert and Sara slowed down but remained engaged. Sara's interest in the judge's law clerks never waned—on July 30 and 31, 1991, she noted in her daybook that Rob Neis, Tuttle's last law clerk, was taking the Georgia bar exam. A week later, on August 6, Rob picked the judge up and drove him downtown for his last sitting with the court. "He came home a little sad," Sara wrote, "but we agreed it could not have been a better life."

Almost all their travels had been by car because Sara did not like to fly. Now Elbert wanted to visit Hawaii once more. Sara found the idea daunting, and they put it off, but on September 7, 1993, they left from Atlanta's Hartsfield Airport for their "wonderful trip to the Hawaiian Islands," as Sara described it after their return. "At age 95 and after a year of medical problems I knew I wasn't in shape for the long trip. However I have never seen anyone more anxious than Elbert Sr. to go once more to the islands where he grew up. After 74 years of married life with him I had always done everything he wanted me to do (except watch the Braves play Baseball) and I felt that it was no time to change now." Buddy and Ginny traveled with them, and in Honolulu Buddy drove them to his father's favorite childhood places. They paid a bittersweet visit to Leckie Mattox's grave at Punchbowl National Cemetery and enjoyed a dinner Margaret Thrower arranged for them at the Outrigger Club, hosted by the club's president. Their granddaughter Peggy Harmon and her husband, who had just moved to Maui, joined them for a luncheon at Punahou, where Judge Tuttle received the first Samuel Chapman Armstrong Award for Humanitarian Service. Afterward, he was interviewed by "two very young boys" from the *Honolulu Advertiser*, where he himself had worked as a teenager.

The Hawaii trip marked the end of their travels. Sara was now ninety-five, and Elbert was ninety-six. She suffered increasingly from back and shoulder pain and from pain in her extremities, especially her hands. Elbert remained intellectually acute and physically hale for his age. With the help of Mrs. Keener, who read the briefs to him, he continued to handle screeners. He went to the office regularly until December 1993 (by which time he was ninety-six), and even then continued with a few screeners at home. Ever frugal, in October 1992 he had informed the library that all subscriptions for his office should be canceled. Because he was entitled to his full salary as retirement pay whether he worked or not, and because Mrs. Keener helped out in other offices at the court, he felt comfortable continuing to work despite his limited contributions.

Sara's health continued to fail. She spent long hours not moving from her chair. When Bessie would come to her or walk close by, she would reach out and touch her on the back of her legs. At first it was a smack, then barely a pat. "Bessie," she had told her, "that means I love you. Remember that when I don't have the strength to say it." For the last year of Sara's life, home health care assistants were with her around the clock. Sara rarely complained, except occasionally to say, "My hands hurt." She missed reading and enjoyed being read to, especially the newspaper. Annita Rosser, a nurse's assistant who often had the night shift, remembered that "to see them was like seeing young people in love." Their bedtime ritual replicated Elbert's experience as a small boy. Every evening he would go to her bedside and say, "I love you, darling," and she would respond, "I love you too." Sara would tell Elbert, "I'm glad you are my husband," and he would respond, "I'm glad I had so many years with you."[16] Sara lingered through the summer and then the fall. On October 22, 1994, Elbert and Sara celebrated their seventy-fifth wedding anniversary with a quiet dinner at home with Buddy and Ginny. Nicky and John came down from Rochester for Thanksgiving, which fell on November 24, and to celebrate Nicky's seventieth birthday on November 26. Over the holiday weekend, Nicky read to her mother. Sara Tuttle always embraced an opportunity to laugh, so they chose Bailey White's *Mama Makes Up Her Mind: And Other Dangers of Southern Living*. It was Sara's last book. On the morning of November 26, 1994, Nicky's seventieth birthday, Elbert awoke and reached for Sara's hand. She felt cold, so he called for someone to bring a blanket. And then he caught himself and realized that Sara had died. Just leave us for a little while, he said, and stayed by her, holding her hand.

Sara's funeral was held on Wednesday, November 30, at Patterson Spring Hill Funeral Home in midtown Atlanta, not far from their Ansley Park home. In his eulogy for his mother, Dr. Tuttle explained that, more than grief, he felt a sense of completeness. Thinking of her long, grand life, he was reminded of walking past the cathedral of Notre Dame in Paris. It was beautiful, majestic, inspiring, and also complete. When one reached the end, one did not wish it to go on. Sara was cremated but not interred at once. In the mid-1970s, Elbert had confirmed that, as a retired brigadier general, he was eligible for interment at Arlington National Cemetery. Sara was eligible too, as long as she did not survive him and remarry.[17] Even so, they decided they wanted to be buried in Atlanta in the cemetery at All Saints' Episcopal Church. On March 25, 1981, they paid fifty dollars each to All Saints'; in return, the church agreed to "inter the Ash Remains when they are presented, and to furnish a proper cast bronze individual name plate." Now Sara would wait for Elbert. He survived her by a year and a half.

Time hung heavy without Sara at home, but Elbert was not alone. Bessie was there five days a week, Buddy and Ginny were just around the corner, old friends and law clerks paid occasional visits, and Dr. Tuttle installed a young premed student in one of the upstairs bedrooms. P. J. Patterson brought the vitality of youth to the household. Everyone was taken aback when he brought the judge home beaming one spring afternoon. Tuttle was by then mostly confined to a wheelchair, but he could manage the transfer to a car, and P.J. had gone one step better. The two of them had taken a spin in a golf cart around the Bobby Jones golf course Tuttle had played so often.

On May 30, 1996, Dr. Tuttle had his father admitted to Piedmont Hospital; the Atlanta papers carried news of his hospitalization. Former president Jimmy Carter sent a short, personal note. "Rosalynn and I want you to know that you are in our hearts and prayers," he wrote. "You are a hero to me, and I feel fortunate to be among those whose lives you have touched."[18] An unsigned card arrived, postmarked Valdosta, Georgia. The writer had added his or her own sentiments to a conventional verse expressing sympathy. "Tuttle—a traitor to the South," the handwritten note read. "Things have a way of evening out, you old goat." Tuttle had developed uremia, caused by a kidney blockage; the blockage itself was caused by prostate cancer. He could have surgery for the blockage, but the cancer had metastasized and might move to his bones. He declined the operation. Elbert Tuttle died peacefully on June 23, less than a month before his ninety-ninth birthday.

On June 29, 1996, more than five hundred family and friends, colleagues and clerks filled All Saints' Episcopal Church in Atlanta for Tuttle's funeral. Bessie's son, Gregory Mayfield, played a trumpet solo. Eulogies

were offered by his son, Dr. Elbert "Buddy" Parr Tuttle Jr.; by his partner at the firm Randolph Thrower; by his colleague on the Fifth Circuit
Judge Phyllis Kravitch; and by Congressman John Lewis. "As Chief
Judge of the old Fifth Circuit, of the old South, Judge Elbert P. Tuttle
did more than any lawyer, any member of the bench or bar to liberate
the South—to usher in the new South, a new America," John Lewis recalled. "This extraordinary man, so good and so decent, prevailed. He had
an inner strength—a moral strength born of righteousness—that would
not fail. It guided him. Under the rule of law, Judge Tuttle created a new
generation in the South."

LAW CLERKS TO JUDGE TUTTLE

Vaughn Stelzenmuller (1954–55)

John Ludington (1955–56)

Paul G. Szasz (1956–57)

Harold E. Abrams (1957–58)

Philip L. Evans (1957–58)

James C. Conner (1958–59)

L. Hugh Kemp (1959–60)

Lawrence B. Custer (1960–61)

Alan Shalov (1961–62)

Charles M. Kidd (1961–63)

Christopher Bond (1963–64)

Jerome I. Chapman (1964–65)

S. Philip Heiner (1965–66)

Bennett Kight (1966–67)

Arthur Howell III (1967–68)

David Jarvis (1968–69)

Bernard Parks (1969–70)

Alfred C. Aman (1970–72)

John R. Barmeyer (1971–73)

Charles Shanor (1972–73)

Frank Mays Hull (1973–74)

Rodney Johnson (1973–74)

Dennis J. Hutchinson (1974–75)

John Michael Clear (1974–75)

Melissa Clark (1975–76)

Anne Emanuel (1975–76)

Stephen J. Ellmann (1976–77)

C. Christopher Trower (1976–77)

William N. Reed (1977–78)

Judith A. O'Brien (1977–78)

James H. Wilson III (1978–79)

Cameron F. Kerry (1978–79)

Deborah Bell (1979–80)

Steven Stark (1979–80)

Sara Ellen McIntire (1980–81)

Donald A. Winslow (1980–81)

Robert McGlasson (1981–82)

Lana Sensenig (1981–82)

Michael J. Egan III (1982–83)

Gary Guzy (1982–83)

Kenneth N. Bass (1983–84)

Susan Adams (1983–84)

Jeffrey P. Sweetland (1984–85)

Beth Hornbuckle (1984–85)

Michael D. Jones (1985–86)

Charles M. Elson (1985–86)

Fred B. Codner (1986–87)

Derek M. Alphran (1986–87)

Dean W. Russell (1987–88)

Ellen K. Snyder (1988–90)

Robert J. Neis (1990–91)

MILITARY HONORS

BRONZE SERVICE ARROWHEAD, DECEMBER 8, 1945

"For participation in an amphibious landing on enemy-held territory in the Ryukyu Islands."

LEGION OF MERIT, SEPTEMBER 5, 1945

"For exceptionally meritorious conduct in the performance of outstanding service from 1 December 1943 to 22 July 1944 and from 11 August 1944 to 20 May 1945. As s-3 of the 77th Infantry Division Artillery, Colonel TUT-TLE directed the rapid and intensive training of the artillery battalions of the division before embarkation. The efficacy of his techniques was subsequently demonstrated in combat when the artillery units performed with a maximum of efficiency with minimum casualties. As a field artillery battalion commander during the Leyte Operation and later in assaults against the Ryukyus, Colonel TUTTLE led his organization in beach landings and expeditiously established it in action in support of the infantry. The superior military attainments, personal courage, and inspirational leadership demonstrated at all times by Colonel TUTTLE were important factors in the victory of our forces in the war against Japan."

PURPLE HEART, MAY 20, 1945

"For wounds received in action against the enemy at . . . Ie Shima, R I 19 Apr 45."

BRONZE STAR, OCTOBER 14, 1944

"For meritorious service in connection with military operations against the enemy from 23 July to 10 August 1944 on Guam, M.I. As Battalion Commander of an Artillery Battalion Lieutenant Colonel TUTTLE skillfully employed his organization in support of the ground action. He functioned efficiently as a Staff officer and maintained the closest liaison with the supported regiment. Forward observers were maintained with lower echelons so as to provide rapid observed fires at all time. His willing cooperation and untiring efforts to do his job well contributed materially to the success of the operation."

AWARDS AND HONORS

HONORARY DOCTOR OF LAWS, EMORY UNIVERSITY, JUNE 1958

HONORARY DOCTOR OF LAWS, HARVARD UNIVERSITY, JUNE 17, 1965

"The mind and heart of this dauntless judge enhance the great tradition of the federal judiciary."

HONORARY DOCTOR OF LAWS, GEORGETOWN UNIVERSITY, MAY 21, 1978

"A sharply divided court was faced with ingenious and tireless resistance to the Civil Rights law and decisions issued by Congress and the Supreme Court. While the Warren Court won the headlines, Judge Tuttle's court manned the battle lines in the Constitutional war for racial equality. 'Massive Resistance' required both personal courage and subtlety . . . and Judge Tuttle responded with more than full measure."

PRESIDENTIAL MEDAL OF FREEDOM, JANUARY 16, 1981

"Elbert Tuttle is a true judicial hero. At a time when it was unpopular to do so, he carried out the mandate of Supreme Court decisions and Congressional legislation to end racial discrimination in the Deep South. With steadfast courage and a deep love and understanding of the region, he has helped to make the Constitutional principle of equal protection a reality of American life."

MARTIN LUTHER KING JR. GOVERNMENT RESPONSIBILITY AWARD, JANUARY 15, 1988, MARTIN LUTHER KING JR. CENTER FOR NONVIOLENT SOCIAL CHANGE

EDWARD J. DEVITT DISTINGUISHED SERVICE TO JUSTICE AWARD, MAY 8, 1989, AMERICAN JUDICATURE SOCIETY

NOTES

CHAPTER ONE. The Legal Lynching of John Downer

1. Transcript of Habeas Hearing at 85, Downer v. Dunaway, 1 F. Supp. 1001 (M.D. Ga. 1932); "Statewide Interest in John Downer Hearing," *Elberton Star*, July 8, 1932.

2. Colonel O'Keefe and Captain Williamson testified to firing down the stairs, not out the windows. One newspaper reported that they had returned fire, which had come from the courthouse grounds, infuriating the mob and wounding two men, one so critically that his leg would likely be amputated. "Tear Gas Bombs, Rifle Fire Used to Save Negroes," *Atlanta Constitution*, May 19, 1931.

3. "Negro Suspects Are Brought to Atlanta for Safekeeping after Rifle Fire, Tear Gas Bombs Suppress Elberton Mob," *Atlanta Constitution*, May 20, 1931.

4. Transcript of Habeas Hearing at 92–93, *Downer*, 1 F. Supp. 1001.

5. "Negro Suspects Are Brought to Atlanta."

6. Ibid. At the time, Elberton had a total population of approximately 4,650. Petition for Writ of Habeas Corpus in *Downer*, 1 F. Supp. 1001.

7. Elbert Tuttle, interview by author, June 7, 1993.

8. *Downer*, 1 F. Supp. 1001.

9. See, generally, Dan T. Carter, *Scottsboro: A Tragedy of the American South*, rev. ed. (Baton Rouge: Louisiana State University Press, 2007).

10. See, for example, Carter v. Jury Commission of Greene County, 396 U.S. 320 (1970).

11. Transcript, Downer v. State, May 20, 1933, 58.

12. McCleskey v. Kemp, 481 U.S. 279, 329–30 (1987) (Brennan, J., dissenting).

13. Downer v. State, 178 Ga. 185 (1933).

14. "Asks Only Justice for Downer, Says Sutherland, Outlining Case," *Atlanta Constitution*, June 16, 1931.

CHAPTER TWO. The Great Migration

1. George Frederick Tuttle, *The Descendants of William and Elizabeth Tuttle, Biographical Notes and Sketches* (Rutland, Vt.: Tuttle & Company, 1883), 1, xxv–xxvi, xxxiv. Isabel is described as the "supposed mother of Richard."

2. Virginia DeJohn Anderson, *New England's Generation: The Great Migration and the Formation of Society and Culture in the Seventeenth Century* (Cambridge: Cambridge University Press, 1991), 15, 16–18.

3. David Cressy, *Coming Over: Migration and Communication between England and New England in the Seventeenth Century* (Cambridge: Cambridge University Press, 1987), 120. Yeomen were better off than husbandmen; "the husbandman conventionally lived closer to the subsistence line" (Roger Thompson, *Mobility and Migration: East Anglian Founders of New England, 1629–1640* [Amherst: University of Massachusetts Press, 1994], 110).

4. Thompson, *Mobility and Migration*, 118–21.

5. Tuttle, *Descendants*, l, li, lii.

6. Ibid., liv, l.

7. Ibid., 374–84. See also Ola Elizabeth Winslow, *Jonathan Edwards, 1703–1758* (New York: Collier Books, 1961), 308n35; Perry Miller, *Jonathan Edwards* (New York: William Sloane Associates, 1949), 35. William Tuttle's daughter Elizabeth Tuttle married Richard Edwards; their son Timothy, born in 1669, was Jonathan Edwards's father. According to Miller, "Elizabeth [Tuttle] proved, by the most charitable account, to be of unsound mind; at any rate, she bore a seventh child by another man, and her husband invoked a council of ministers to justify his petition for divorce. There were other scandals in the Tuttle family: Elizabeth's brother killed a sister with an ax and was hanged for it; another sister murdered her own child. However, her son Timothy was eminently sane" (*Jonathan Edwards*, 35). Winslow records that Elizabeth Tuttle suffered from mental illness even at the date of her marriage and suggests that her siblings' difficulties may have reflected mental illness as well (*Jonathan Edwards, 1703–1758*, 26–28).

8. Tuttle, *Descendants*, 464, 498.

9. Ibid., 499.

10. Ibid. Guy Harmon Tuttle's family was under the impression that his given name was Guy Bascom Tuttle but that when Uncle Bascom failed as a role model (in ways now lost to history), Guy Tuttle, a very religious Congregationalist, changed his middle name to Harmon. According to the family genealogy, however, the uncle's name was Harmon Bascom Tuttle, and he too was a religious Congregationalist. The Reverend Harmon Bascom Tuttle graduated from Union Park Seminary in Chicago and served as the pastor of the Congregational Church in Lake Mills, Wisconsin. Guy Tuttle may have simply preferred his uncle's first name to his second. Elbert "Bertie" was born April 17, 1874; Frank was born January 12, 1880.

11. One article discussing the early years of this movement, 1780–1820, describes the founders as a "collection of radicals" who acted in reaction to the "tyranni-

cal clergy, abstract theology, and restrictive church discipline" that character-ized the traditional Protestant churches. T. P. Linkfield, 1980, abstract, Nathan O. Hatch, "The Christian Movement and the Demand for a Theology of the People," *Journal of American History* 67, no. 3 (1980): 545–67. See also *World Book* (1988), s.v. "Disciples of Christ."

12. Edwin Scott Gaustad, *Historical Atlas of Religion in America*, rev. ed. (New York: Harper & Row, 1976), 64–68, 164.

13. Samuel married Lucie Caroline McEldowney on July 12, 1865; her oldest sister, Katherine, had been born in Dublin, Ireland. Lucie, Hester, Harriet, and Margaret were all born in Bakerstown, Pennsylvania. The other two children were Claude Pearl, who never married, and Nellie Amanda, who married Charles A. Miles of California. They had two children, a daughter, Lucille, and a son, Louris. Elbert Tuttle to Robert McEldowney Jr., February 20, 1964.

14. Elbert Tuttle to Bruce Kappel, April 29, 1993.

15. Earl Warren, *The Memoirs of Chief Justice Earl Warren* (New York: Doubleday, 1977), 12–16.

16. Elbert Tuttle dated the incident to 1903 or 1904. Elbert Tuttle to Bruce Kappel, April 29, 1993.

17. Committee on the Judiciary, *Report, History of the Immigration and Naturalization Service*, prepared by the Congressional Research Service, Library of Congress, 96th Cong., 2nd sess. (December 1980), 12.

18. George F. Nellist, "Men of Hawaii: A Biographical Record of Men of Substantial Achievement in the Hawaiian Islands," *Honolulu Star-Bulletin* 4 (1930): 493–95. An engineer by training, Ramsay held various positions before organizing his own company in 1923. W. A. Ramsay, Ltd., was the manufacturer's representa-tive in the islands for General Electric and many other well-known corporations.

19. Kin Hylton and Mary Hylton, "The Tuttle Brothers: Hawai'i's Aviation Pioneers and First Glider Pilots," *Hawaiian Journal of History* 24 (1990): 117–28.

CHAPTER THREE. Life Was a Breeze

1. See William Adam Russ, *The Hawaiian Revolution (1893–94)* (Selinsgrove, Pa.: Susquehanna University Press, 1959); Michael Dougherty, *To Steal a Kingdom* (Honolulu: Island Style Press, 1992); Liliuokalani, *Hawaii's Story by Hawaii's Queen* (Rutland, Vt.: Tuttle & Company, 1964); Gavan Davis, *Shoal of Time: A History of the Hawaiian Islands* (Honolulu: University of Hawaii Press, 1968); Tom Coffman, *Nation Within: The Story of America's Annexation of the Nation of Hawaii* (Kaneohe, Hawaii: Tom Coffman and Epicenter, 1998).

2. The 1913–14 *President's Report to the Trustees* listed the academy registration

by nationality. Of the 211 students, white students constituted 73.3 percent; part Hawaiians, 15.4 percent; Portuguese, 0.5 percent; and Oriental, 10.8 percent.

3. By 1950 the University Census Bureau gave up on analysis by race in the islands, finding it "impossible to list individuals even according to the race of the father." John Porter Bloom, "The Territory of Hawaii: Themes in Territorial History," *Journal of the West* 29 (1981): 22–31, quote on p. 29.

4. Judge Elbert Tuttle to Judge Bryan Simpson, December 17, 1974. They arrived in Hawaii at the end of the summer of 1907; Elbert would have turned ten that July, and Malcolm was eleven.

5. Mary Alexander and Charlotte Dodge, *Punahou: 1841–1941* (Berkeley: University of California Press, 1941), 19 (quoting an 1837 report), 9.

6. David W. Forbes, "Look to the Rock whence Ye Are Hewn: A Reappraisal of Punahou's Early History," in *Punahou: The History and Promise of a School of the Islands*, ed. Nelson Foster (Honolulu: Punahou School, 1991), 19.

7. Ibid.

8. Booker T. Washington, *Up from Slavery* (New York: Bantam Classic, 1959), 51.

9. Woody Fern, "Who Was Samuel Chapman Armstrong?," *Punahou Bulletin* 40, no. 2 (1993): 27.

10. As a student at Punahou, Tuttle had been aware of Armstrong's legacy. The school kept his memory in the forefront. In 1908 the school literary magazine, the *Oahuan*, carried a brief "Biography of General Samuel Armstrong." He had made a vow on his father's deathbed, the article reported, "to wear his father's mantle in the pulpit, but his ministry included the Negro and Indian races." Armstrong's mother, the article reported, had often remarked that "he was born with a steam engine in him." *Oahuan* 8, no. 4 (1908): 8–9.

11. *Report of the Experiment Station Committee of the Hawaiian Sugar Planters' Association for the Year Ending September 30, 1908* (Honolulu: Bulletin Publishing Company, 1908), 54.

12. *Report of the Experiment Station Committee of the Hawaiian Sugar Planters' Association for the Year Ending September 30, 1909* (Honolulu: Bulletin Publishing Company, 1909), 19.

13. *Report of the Experiment Station Committee of the Hawaiian Sugar Planters' Association for the Year Ending September 30, 1910* (Honolulu: Bulletin Publishing Company, 1910), 33.

14. *Report of the Experiment Station Committee of the Hawaiian Sugar Planters' Association for the Year Ending September 30, 1914* (Honolulu: Bulletin Publishing Company, 1914), 17.

15. Kin Hylton and Mary Hylton, "The Tuttle Brothers: Hawai'i's Aviation Pioneers and First Glider Pilots," *Hawaiian Journal of History* 24 (1990): 121.

16. Thomas Cook, a stranger to the boys although he lived nearby, put up $20 for repairs to the glider. His mother was a member of Central Union, a connection that may have led to the church asking for the use of the glider at the Christmas party. Ibid., 120.

17. Joe Brennan, *Duke of Hawaii* (New York: Ballantine Books, 1968), 129.

18. Hylton and Hylton, "The Tuttle Brothers," 121.

19. *Sunday Advertiser*, August 13, 1911.

20. Brennan, *Duke of Hawaii*, 32.

21. Ibid., 33.

22. Harold H. Yost, *The Outrigger Canoe Club of Honolulu, Hawaii* (Honolulu: Outrigger Canoe Club, 1971), 58.

23. Central Union is the largest of the more than one hundred United Church of Christ churches in the state of Hawaii and one of the largest in the national congregation.

24. Elbert Tuttle, interview by author, May 5–7, 1993.

25. Elbert Tuttle to Bruce Kappel, July 19, 1993.

26. Margie Tuttle, personal communication, March 1901 (on file with author).

27. Ibid.

28. *Odds & Ends* 14, no. 2 (1913): 37.

29. *Odds & Ends* 14, no. 6 (1914): 26.

30. *Odds & Ends* 13, no. 9 (1913): 71.

31. Elbert Tuttle to Bruce Kappel, April 29, 1993.

CHAPTER FOUR. College Years

1. Wright Bryan, "Elbert Tuttle Is the Type of Leader Who Knows What Leadership Means," *Atlanta Journal*, December 9, 1948.

2. Editorial, *Cornell Daily Sun*, April 12, 1917.

3. William A. Hammond to Elbert Tuttle, November 12, 1917, Tuttle Papers.

CHAPTER SIX. Founding a Law Firm and Raising a Family

1. Harvey H. Jackson, *Hansell & Post: From King & Anderson to Jones Day Reavis & Pogue* (Atlanta: Hansell & Post, 1989), 78.

2. Ibid., 79, 55.

3. Ibid., 78, 80.

4. Hartley v. Nash, 157 Ga. 402 (1924).

5. Old Colony Trust Co. v. Comm'r, 279 U.S. 716 (1929).

6. Graham v. Goodcell, 282 U.S. 409 (1931).

7. Fox Film Corp. v. Doyal, 286 U.S. 123 (1932).

8. Long v. Rockwood, 277 U.S. 142 (1928).

9. Woolford Realty Co. v. Rose, 286 U.S. 319 (1932); Ralston Purina v. United States, 58 F.2d 1065 (Ct. Claims 1932), *cert. denied*, 289 U.S. 732 (1933).

10. Fulton Bag & Cotton Mills v. United States, 288 U.S. 612 (1933).

11. Clifton Mfg. Co. v. United States, 293 U.S. 186 (1934).

12. Anniston Mfg. Co. v. Davis, 301 U.S. 337 (1937).

13. McEachern v. Rose, 302 U.S. 56 (1937).

14. Rufus Dorsey, voice-mail message to author, April 10, 2007.

15. See Ajay K. Mehrotra, "Envisioning the Modern American Fiscal State: Progressive-Era Economists and the Intellectual Foundations of the U.S. Income Tax," *UCLA Law Review* 52 (2005): 1793.

16. Elbert Tuttle, interview by author, March 19, 1993.

17. Elbert Tuttle, dinner address at the Omni International Ballroom, Atlanta, Georgia, September 22, 1982.

18. Judge Elbert Tuttle, interview by Fred Aman, tape 3 of 5, May 16–18, 1988, Atlanta, Georgia, on file at the Cornell University School of Law.

CHAPTER SEVEN. Gearing Up for War

1. Lillian Ledbetter Gregory, interview by author, February 6, 1995.

2. Judge Elbert Tuttle, interview by author, April 20, 1994.

3. Gregory interview.

4. Herbert Elsas, interview by author, March 25, 1993.

CHAPTER EIGHT. The War Years

1. Ronald H. Spector, *Eagle against the Sun: The American War with Japan* (New York: Free Press, 1985), 106.

2. Ibid., 321n84 (citing Phillip A. Crowl, *Campaign in the Marianas* [Washington, D.C.: Center of Military History United States Army, 1960], 365).

3. Elbert P. Tuttle, "Heroism in War and Peace," *XIII: The Emory University Quarterly*, October 1957, 129–30.

4. "The 77th was an untested division, but it had been exceptionally well trained and had an aggressive, intelligent commander in the person of Major General Andrew D. Bruce. In the fighting on Guam, the 77th did more than hold their end up" (Spector, *Eagle against the Sun*, 320).

5. Lt. Col. Max Myers, "Lookit Those Old Buzzards Go!" *Saturday Evening Post*, January 11, 1945.

6. Max Myers, ed., *Ours to Hold It High* (Washington, D.C.: Infantry Journal Press, 1947), 126.

7. "For every American soldier killed 36 Japanese died. For every American battle casualty the Japanese lost 10 men killed. It is believed that these ratios are the most favorable attained by an American Division in any major campaign in the Pacific War" (ibid., 211).

8. Ibid., 265.

9. Spector, *Eagle against the Sun*, 501.

10. Margaret Peavy, "Atlanta Marine Is First Pilot Ashore on Iwo," *Atlanta Journal*, April 9, 1945.

CHAPTER NINE. Building a Republican Party in Georgia

1. Elbert Tuttle, interview no. 1 by John Luter, Eisenhower Administration Project, June 28, 1972, 8, transcript, Oral History Research Office, Columbia University.

2. See, generally, King v. Chapman, 62 F. Supp. 639 (M.D. Ga. 1945), *aff'd*, 154 F.2d 460 (5th Cir. 1946), *cert. denied*, 327 U.S. 800 (1946).

3. Frank Read and Lucy McGough, *Let Them Be Judged* (Metuchen, N.J.: Scarecrow Press, 1978), 41.

4. Tuttle, interview no. 1 by Luter, 8–9.

5. C. E. Gregory, "National GOP Committee Seats Williams Faction: Dominant Racial Issue Flares Openly in Preconvention Contests by Georgians," *Atlanta Constitution*, June 23, 1944.

6. Ibid.

7. Tuttle, interview no. 1 by Luter, 10–11.

8. Ibid., 13.

9. Wright Bryan, "Elbert Tuttle Is the Type of Leader Who Knows What Leadership Means," *Atlanta Journal*, December 9, 1948.

10. "Fulton GOP Names Tuttle New Chairman: H. H. Turner, Long Time Holder of Office, Is Replaced," *Atlanta Journal-Constitution*, undated clipping.

11. Lewis Paul Rowan, "The Rise and Development of the Republican Party in Georgia" (master's thesis, Emory University, 1948), 95–96; "GOPs Eye Governor Candidate," *Atlanta Constitution*, September 10, 1948; Albert Riley, "State GOP Passes Up '48 Slate," *Atlanta Constitution*, September 12, 1948; Franklin Nix, "Two-Party System Move Delayed by Georgia GOP," *Atlanta Journal*, September 12, 1948.

12. Republican George E. "Sonny" Perdue III was inaugurated as governor of Georgia in January 2003.

13. Rowan, "Rise and Development," 75 (quoting *Atlanta Constitution*, May 17, 1944).

14. Ibid., 73–74.

15. Ibid., 77.

16. Gregory, "National GOP Committee."

17. "Tucker Georgia Republican Delegates Win First Round," *Atlanta Daily World*, June 19, 1948.

18. "Lily-White Ga. Unit Seeks GOP Convention Seats," *Washington Afro-American*, June 12, 1948.

19. William Wyant, "Georgia GOP Dispute before Committee," *Atlanta Journal*, June 17, 1948.

20. William K. Wyant Jr., "Pro-Dewey Cause Wins with Williams," *Atlanta Journal*, June 18, 1948.

21. Wyant, "Georgia GOP Dispute"; Louis Lautier, "Republicans Contest Seats in Philadelphia," *Atlanta Daily World*, June 18, 1948.

22. "Tucker Georgia Republican Delegates."

23. Killian Townsend, interview by author, May 20, 1994.

CHAPTER TEN. The 1952 Republican National Convention

1. Elbert Tuttle, interview no. 1 by John Luter, Eisenhower Administration Project, June 28, 1972, 18, transcript, Oral History Research Office, Columbia University.

2. Killian Townsend, interview by author, May 20, 1994.

3. "Fulton GOP Club, Office for Ike Formed by Republicans Here," *Atlanta Journal*, January 11, 1952.

4. "Shaw, Calhoun, Dobbs, Holloman Off to GOP Meet," *Atlanta Daily World*, July 25, 1952; "State's Two Opposing GOP Delegates Listed," *Atlanta Journal*, July 2, 1952.

5. "NOW, the FULL STORY of the Contested Delegates," *Washington Post*, July 8, 1952.

6. Ralph McGill, "Ike Plans Dixie Drive if He Is Nominated," *Atlanta Constitution*, June 11, 1952.

7. "Republicans: Change of Positions," *Time*, July 7, 1952.

8. Editorial, "Taft Steamroller Cannot Hide Truth," *Atlanta Constitution*, July 2, 1952.

9. Arthur Krock, "GOP Choice May Hinge on Delegate Contests: Southern Bloc Could Be Sufficient to Swing Nomination if the Present Lineups Remain Intact at Chicago: Decision up to Convention," *New York Times*, June 22, 1952.

10. "National Affairs: Marching through Georgia," *Time*, July 14, 1952.

11. Townsend interview.

12. "Tucker Slate to Fight 'Double Cross' Seat Ban," *Atlanta Constitution*, July 3, 1952.

13. Randolph Thrower, interview by author, April 12, 1994; Townsend interview.

14. George Erwin, "Sommers Likes GOP but He's No Politician," *Atlanta Constitution*, undated.

15. Ken Turner, "Committee Seats Florida Taftites: Georgia Dispute Next for Credentials Ruling," *Atlanta Journal*, July 8, 1952; W. H. Lawrence, "Delegate Test On," *New York Times*, July 9, 1952.

16. "GOP Credentials Committee Votes to Seat Foster Group," *Atlanta Daily World*, July 9, 1952.

17. Ken Turner, "Georgia GOP Fight before Credentials Committee: Arguments Center on Griffin Ruling," *Atlanta Journal*, July 8, 1952.

18. M. L. St. John, "Credentials United Backs Seating of Georgia Taftmen but Battles Rage over Texas and Louisiana," *Atlanta Constitution*, July 9, 1952.

19. Joel William Friedman, "Judge Wisdom and the 1952 Republican National Convention: Ensuring Victory for Eisenhower and a Two-Party System for Louisiana," *Washington and Lee Law Review* 53 (1996): 33, 38.

20. "National Affairs," *Time*, July 21, 1952, 15.

21. Ralph McGill, "Eastvold Called David Who Slew Taft Goliath," *Atlanta Constitution*, July 11, 1952; "Here's Inside Story of Taft's Defeat," *Chicago Daily News*, July 12, 1952.

22. "National Affairs: Marching through Georgia."

23. Jack Bass, *Unlikely Heroes* (New York: Simon & Schuster, 1981), 26–27.

24. Some sources say this advice came from Brownell, but I rely on Friedman, "Judge Wisdom," 33, and Elbert Tuttle, interview by author, March 19, 1993.

25. Herbert Brownell was a key figure in the Eisenhower campaign. He later became Eisenhower's attorney general.

26. Joel William Friedman, "John Minor Wisdom's Fight against the Political Bosses to Create a Two-Party System in Louisiana," *Tulane Law Review* 69 (1995): 1439, 1481–82; Bonnie Wisdom, interview by author, April 3, 1998.

27. Friedman, "Judge Wisdom," 71.

28. Bass, *Unlikely Heroes*, 28.

29. Friedman, "Judge Wisdom," 76.

30. Ralph McGill, "How Georgia Helped Nominate Eisenhower," *Atlanta Journal-Constitution Magazine*, August 17, 1952.

31. Earl Warren, *The Memoirs of Chief Justice Earl Warren* (New York: Doubleday, 1977), 260; Ed Cray, *Chief Justice: A Biography of Earl Warren* (New York: Simon & Schuster, 1997), 245–53; Stephen E. Ambrose, *Eisenhower: The Presidency* (New York: Simon & Schuster, 1984), 2:128–29. For his part, Tuttle recalled that Warren Burger had told him he had approached Earl Warren on Eisenhower's behalf prior to the balloting and had told Warren that if he held his votes (as he did), he could have the

first open position he wanted in the new administration. Tuttle, interview no. 1 by Luter, 71–72.

32. Wylly Folk St. John, "How Atlanta Welcomed Eisenhower," *Atlanta Journal-Constitution Magazine*, October 5, 1952; quote in Pat Watters, *Down to Now* (Athens: University of Georgia Press, 1993), 42.

CHAPTER ELEVEN. The Washington Years

1. Stephen E. Ambrose, *Eisenhower: The Presidency*, vol. 2 (New York: Simon & Schuster, 1984).

2. "The Treasury: A Time for Talent," *Time*, January 26, 1953.

3. Nathaniel R. Howard, ed., *The Basic Papers of George M. Humphrey as Secretary of the Treasury, 1953–57* (Cleveland, Ohio: Western Reserve Historical Society, 1965), 26–27.

4. "Tuttles' New Home in Colorful Spot," *Atlanta Journal*, February 9, 1949; George Erwin, "Royal Barry Wills Picture Started Home for Elbert Tuttle," *Atlanta Journal*, February 13, 1949.

5. Gladstone Williams, "Georgians Okayed for Fiscal Jobs," *Atlanta Constitution*, January 27, 1953; Ken Turner, "Senate Group Okays Tuttle, Folsom Jobs," *Atlanta Journal*, January 27, 1953.

6. The others were Bill Sutherland and Joe Brennan, Mac's father, Mac Asbill, Randolph Thrower, Herbert Elsas, C. Baxter Jones Jr., and Jim Wilson. "Tuttle Takes New Job; Firm Changes Name," *Atlanta Journal-Constitution*, February 1, 1953.

7. James H. Wilson Jr., interview with author, August 23, 2000.

8. John A. Sibley to Elbert Tuttle, January 14, 1953.

9. Elbert Tuttle to Ralph McGill, January 15, 1953.

10. Elbert Tuttle to John Sibley, January 16, 1953.

11. John A. Sibley to Elbert Tuttle, January 19, 1953.

12. "Georgia GOP Meeting; Tuttle Ouster Talked," *Atlanta Journal*, February 21, 1953.

13. Pat Watters, "Tuttle Supporting Bootle for Judge, Adding to GOP Mixup," *Atlanta Journal*, March 13, 1954.

14. Charles Pou, "W. B. Shartzer Named Georgia GOP Chief," *Atlanta Journal*, March 14, 1954.

15. "Tuttle Sworn in as General Counsel U.S. Treasury Dept.," *Georgia Republican*, February 2, 1953.

16. Elbert Tuttle, interview no. 1 by John Luter, Eisenhower Administration Project, June 28, 1972, 91, transcript, Oral History Research Office, Columbia University.

17. *Savannah Morning News*, September 4, 1953.

18. *Savannah Morning News*, October 24, 1953.

19. Tuttle, interview no. 1 by Luter, 37–39.

20. "Summerfield to Pay Tax," *New York Times*, October 11, 1953; "Summerfields Sue," *New York Times*, May 5, 1955; "Summerfields Upheld," *New York Times*, October 29, 1957.

21. Exec. Order No. 10,450, 3 C.F.R. 936 (1949–53).

22. W. H. Lawrence, "4 of 131 Treasury Ousters in Year Based on Loyalty," *New York Times*, February 16, 1954, 14.

23. Tuttle, interview no. 1 by Luter, 84–86.

24. Judge Elbert P. Tuttle, interview by author, March 24, 1993.

25. Western Union telegram from A. Walton Hall to Senator Richard Russell, February 5, 1954, series VII, Richard Russell Collection, Richard B. Russell Library for Political Research and Studies, University of Georgia Libraries, Athens.

26. Western Union telegram from Senator Richard Russell to A. Walton Hall, February 6, 1954, series VII, Russell Collection.

27. Judge John Minor Wisdom, interview by author, June 3, 1994, New Orleans.

28. Bass, *Unlikely Heroes*, 30.

29. Ibid., 1.

30. Transcript, Hearings of the Subcommittee of the Committee on the Judiciary, United States Senate, July 16, 1954, 2, 3.

31. Transcript, Hearings of the Subcommittee of the Committee on the Judiciary, United States Senate, July 30, 1954, 15.

32. Ibid., 17.

33. Ibid., 21, 23.

34. Ibid., 23–24.

35. Western Union telegram from Ralph McGill to President Dwight D. Eisenhower, October 14, 1953, Ralph McGill Papers, Manuscript, Archives, and Rare Book Library, Emory University.

36. John Sibley to Robert Snodgrass, September 11, 1956, John A. Sibley Papers, Manuscript, Archives, and Rare Book Library, Emory University.

37. John Sibley to Robert Cutler, February 5, 1957, Emory Sibley Archives, Atlanta, Georgia.

CHAPTER TWELVE. The Great Writ

1. By 1953 Tuttle was vice president of the board of trustees of Spelman. See Florence M. Read, *The Story of Spelman College* (Princeton, N.J.: Princeton University Press, 1961), app. 1, p. 377.

2. Elbert Tuttle, "A Salute to Bennie" (remarks, January 9, 1982).

3. Charles H. Martin, *The Angelo Herndon Case and Southern Justice* (Baton Rouge: Louisiana State University Press, 1976), 1–5. Much of the material about the Herndon case is from Martin's book, a thoroughly researched analysis of the Herndon litigation. Herndon told his own story in Angelo Herndon, *Let Me Live* (New York: Arno Press and the New York Times, 1969). See also Kendall Thomas, "Rouge et Noir Reread: A Popular Constitutional History of the Angelo Herndon Case," *Southern California Law Review* 65 (1992): 2599.

4. Herndon v. State, 124 S.E. 597 (1934).

5. "The State cannot reasonably be required to measure the danger from every such utterance in the nice balance of a jeweler's scale. A single revolutionary spark may kindle a fire that, smouldering for a time, may burst into a sweeping and destructive conflagration" (*id.* at 616).

6. Dan T. Carter, *Scottsboro: A Tragedy of the American South* (Baton Rouge: Louisiana State University Press, 1969), 54.

7. Martin, *Angelo Herndon Case*, 117.

8. Ibid., 140.

9. Prior to the first trial, the ILD retained Oliver Hancock, an Atlanta attorney, on Herndon's behalf. The ACLU decided to support the defense also and provided funds to retain W. A. McClellan, a Macon attorney. On June 29, 1932, Roger Baldwin, founder and director of the ACLU, wired Will Alexander of the Commission on Interracial Cooperation that Hancock was unsatisfactory. They had asked McClellan to take over and to select an attorney to assist. Baldwin asked Alexander to recommend an Atlanta attorney. On July 1 Alexander wired back recommending Bill Sutherland: "Has standing in community courage of his convictions integrity and intelligence" (wire from Will Alexander, Herndon Collection at Clark University, Atlanta, Georgia). Baldwin did not contact Sutherland at that time, and Herndon was represented at trial by two young black attorneys, Ben Davis and John Geer. Martin, *Angelo Herndon Case*, 34.

10. Martin, *Angelo Herndon Case*, 142.

11. Norris v. Alabama, 294 U.S. 587 (1935).

12. Martin, *Angelo Herndon Case*, 145.

13. Herndon v. Georgia, 295 U.S. 441 (1935).

14. Martin, *Angelo Herndon Case*, 160–61.

15. Leonard Dinnerstein, *The Leo Frank Case* (Athens: University of Georgia Press, 1987), 33 (quoting L. O. Bricker, "A Great American Tragedy," *Shane Quarterly* 4 [April 1943]: 90).

16. Frank v. Mangum, 237 U.S. 309 (1915).

17. Dinnerstein, *Leo Frank Case*, 121.

18. Melissa Fay Greene, *The Temple Bombing* (Reading, Mass.: Addison-Wesley Publishing Company, 1992), 74–76, 244–45.

19. Dinnerstein, *Leo Frank Case*, 159 (quoting Lucien Lamar Knight, *A Standard History of Georgia and Georgians* [Chicago: Lewis Publishing Company, 1917], 2:1208).

20. In 1920 Hugh Dorsey was defeated in a race for the Senate by Tom Watson. Watson served only until September 26, 1922, when he died of respiratory failure. The Ku Klux Klan sent a cross of roses some eight feet high to his funeral. Dinnerstein, *Leo Frank Case*, 161.

21. R. B. Eleazer of the Commission on Interracial Cooperation described Dorsey as "quite fair-minded in his interracial attitudes" (Martin, *Angelo Herndon Case*, 162).

22. Ibid., 163.

23. Lowry v. Herndon, 182 Ga. 582, 583–84 n.2 (1932); "Conviction Called Void by Court, Herndon Is Freed on $8,000 Bond," *Atlanta Journal*, December 8, 1935.

24. Herbert Elsas, then an associate at Sutherland and Tuttle, recalled that Kane was selected partly because he had worked on the matter and partly because he "was a hard nosed s.o.b." Whitney North Seymour had implored the firm to get Herndon to Washington safely and explained that he had planned a celebration. When the train pulled into Union Station, enthusiastic supporters, including a number of white women, embraced Herndon. "Ed Kane came back thoroughly disgusted," Elsas recalled. Elsas also recalled that everyone in the firm supported the work on the Herndon case: "We recognized that serious injustice was being done" (Herbert Elsas, interview by author, March 25, 1993).

25. Herndon v. Lowry, 301 U.S. 242 (1937).

26. At this time, U.S. attorneys were called district attorneys.

27. Bridwell v. Aderhold, 13 F. Supp. 253 (N.D. Ga. 1935).

28. Ibid., 255, 256, 254.

29. Judge Elbert Tuttle, interview by Fred Aman, tape 3 of 5, May 16–18, 1988, Atlanta, Georgia, on file at the Cornell University School of Law.

30. Although in recounting how he came to handle the case in a 1962 letter Tuttle does not mention Bridwell, he did represent both defendants on appeal. Bridwell, however, did not join in the petition for writ of certiorari. Judge Elbert Tuttle to Professor Elliott Cheatham of Vanderbilt University, August 7, 1962, Elbert P. Tuttle Judicial Papers, Manuscript, Archives, and Rare Book Library, Emory University, Atlanta, Georgia.

31. See, for example, William M. Beaney, *The Right to Counsel in American Courts* (1955; repr., Westport, Conn.: Greenwood Press, 1972), 29.

32. "An Historical Argument for the Right to Counsel during Police Interrogation," *Yale Law Journal* 73 (1964): 1000, 1003–4.

33. Beaney, *Right to Counsel*, 29–30, 32.

34. Powell v. Alabama, 287 U.S. 45 (1932).

35. Of the remaining four justices, Justice Reed concurred in the reversal but did not join the opinion; Justice McReynolds stated, without explanation, that the court of appeals should be affirmed; Justice Butler stated that in his opinion the record showed a waiver and the court of appeals should be affirmed; and Justice Cardozo did not participate. Johnson v. Zerbst, 304 U.S. 458, 469 (1938).

36. Bram v. United States, 168 U.S. 532 (1897) (arising under the due process clause of the Fifth Amendment); see also Brown v. Mississippi, 297 U.S. 278 (1936) (arising under the due process clause of the Fourteenth Amendment).

37. "A waiver is ordinarily an intentional relinquishment or abandonment of a known right or privilege" (*Johnson*, 304 U.S. at 464). Later writers describing or relying on the opinion distilled the holding into the phrase "knowing, intelligent, and voluntary."

38. The waiver of a Fourth Amendment right, at least as long as the right waived does not implicate the right to a fair trial, need only be voluntary. Schneckloth v. Bustamonte, 412 U.S. 218 (1973).

39. Tuttle interview by Aman.

CHAPTER THIRTEEN. Forming the Historic Fifth Circuit: Nine Men

1. Jack Bass, *Unlikely Heroes* (New York: Simon & Schuster, 1981), 38.

2. Joseph Hutcheson, "The Local Jail," *ABA Journal* 21 (1935): 67, 83; Joseph C. Hutcheson Jr., *Judgment Intuitive* (Chicago: Foundation Press, 1938); Joseph C. Hutcheson Jr., "Law and the Lawyer—'Then' and 'Now,'" *Baylor Law Review* 8 (1956): 26; Joseph C. Hutcheson Jr., "In Praise of Lawyers and Lawyering," *Tennessee Law Review* 21 (1949): 1; Joseph C. Hutcheson Jr., "This Thing Man Called Law," *University of Chicago Law Review* 2 (1934): 1; Joseph C. Hutcheson Jr., *Law as Liberator: The Principle of Democracy in America: The Spirit of Its Laws* (Chicago: Foundation Press, 1937); Joseph C. Hutcheson Jr., "Judging as Administration, Administration as Judging," *Texas Law Review* 21 (1942): 1.

3. Judge John Minor Wisdom, interview by author, June 3, 1994.

4. Bass, *Unlikely Heroes*, 38. This was an oft-told tale, as the book remarks.

5. Sara Tuttle, interview by Fred Aman, Tape 1, May 16–18, 1988, Atlanta, Georgia, on file at the Cornell University School of Law.

6. Charles L. Zelden, "The Judge Intuitive: The Life and Judicial Philosophy of Joseph C. Hutcheson, Jr.," *South Texas Law Review* 39 (1988): 905, 916.

7. Judge Elbert Tuttle, interview by Fred Aman, Tape 1, May 16–18, 1988, Atlanta, Georgia, on file at the Cornell University School of Law.

8. Sara Tuttle, interview by author, June 1, 1993.

9. "R. Rives, 1895–1982," editorial obituary, *Montgomery Advertiser*, October 9, 1982.

10. Bass, *Unlikely Heroes*, 70.

11. Ibid., 70–71.

12. Frank Read and Lucy McGough, *Let Them Be Judged* (Metuchen, N.J.: Scarecrow Press, 1978), 32.

13. Smith v. Allwright, 321 U.S. 649 (1944).

14. Davis v. Schnell, 81 F. Supp. 872, 879 (1949).

15. "R. Rives, 1895–1982."

16. Ibid.

17. *Davis*, 81 F. Supp. at 879 (quoting *Alabama Lawyer*, July 1946).

18. *Id*. at 880 (quoting *Alabama Lawyer*, October 1946).

19. Bass, *Unlikely Heroes*, 72.

20. Judge John Minor Wisdom, interview by author, June 4, 1994.

21. Fred Powledge, *Free at Last?* (New York: Harper Perennial, 1991), 68, 182–83.

22. Bass, *Unlikely Heroes*, 85, 86.

23. Read and McGough, *Let Them Be Judged*, 223–24; *see* Meredith v. Fair, 306 F.2d 374 (5th Cir. 1962), *cert. denied*, 371 U.S. 828 (1962) (order vacating the first stay).

24. Read and McGough, *Let Them Be Judged*, 45.

25. J. Robert Brown Jr., Allison Herren Lee, and William W. Shakely, "Judge Warren L. Jones and the Supreme Court of Dixie," *Louisiana Law Review* 59 (1998): 209.

26. Ibid., 213.

27. Ibid., 214–15.

28. Eric Page, "Herbert Brownell Jr., Eisenhower Attorney General, Dies at 92," *New York Times*, May 3, 1996; see Stephen E. Ambrose, *Eisenhower: The Presidency* (New York: Simon & Schuster, 1984), 2:142–43, 189–90, 326–28; Robert Fredrick Burk, *The Eisenhower Administration and Black Civil Rights* (Knoxville: University of Tennessee Press, 1984), 208–14; see also Michael R. Belknap, *Federal Law and Southern Order* (Athens: University of Georgia Press, 1987), 34–35.

29. Page, "Herbert Brownell Jr." See also Herbert Brownell, *Advising Ike: The Memoirs of Attorney General Herbert Brownell* (Lawrence: University Press of Kansas, 1993), 182–84; but see Burk, *Eisenhower Administration*, 199.

30. Elbert Tuttle to Herbert Brownell, November 4, 1954.

31. Ibid.

32. Attorney General Herbert Brownell to Judge Elbert Tuttle, November 6, 1955.

33. Bass, *Unlikely Heroes*, 102.

34. *In re* Texas City Disaster Litigation, 197 F.2d 771 (5th Cir. 1952) (*en banc*).

35. Nomination of John R. Brown of Texas to U.S. Circuit Judge, Fifth Circuit,

unpublished transcript of hearings before the Senate Judiciary Committee, 84th Cong. 3 (1955), microformed on CIS no. 84-SJ-T.66 (Congressional Info. Serv.).

36. John R. Brown to Judge Elbert Tuttle, June 4, 1955, Elbert P. Tuttle Judicial Papers, Manuscript, Archives, and Rare Book Library, Emory University, Atlanta, Georgia.

37. Judge Elbert Tuttle, interview by Lucy McGough, May 30, 1972.

38. Judge Elbert Tuttle to John R. Brown, June 4, 1955, Tuttle Papers.

39. Nomination of Brown, transcript, 67.

40. Ibid., 60.

41. Ibid., 61.

42. Ibid., 63.

43. Ibid., 136. In his testimony, John harked back to an earlier point. Acting on a referral from Assistant Attorney General Graham Morrison, the U.S. attorney in Houston, Brian Odem, had investigated the matter and concluded that "there had been no violation." John concurred: "In the light of subsequent events, in the light of my participation in the case, my lengthy friendship with Mr. Brown, my knowledge of his legal ability and his standing at the bar, I am inclined to agree with Mr. Odem that there was no violation. That is my opinion now" (punctuation in original transcript corrected).

44. Exhibit to the transcript.

45. Bass, *Unlikely Heroes*, 102–3.

46. Joel William Friedman, "John Minor Wisdom: The Noblest Tulanian of Them All," *Tulane Law Review* 74 (1999): 1, 19–20.

47. Wisdom interview, June 4, 1994.

48. Bass, *Unlikely Heroes*, 44.

49. Herbert Brownell, "Civil Rights in the 1950s," *Tulane Law Review* 69 (1995): 781, 788.

50. 102 Cong. Rec. 4515–16 (1956).

51. Report of Proceedings, Special Subcommittee on Nominations of the Committee on the Judiciary: Nomination of John Minor Wisdom of Louisiana to Be United States Circuit Judge of the Fifth Circuit, 85th Cong., April 29, 1957, 6, microformed on CIS no. 85-SJ-T.43 (Congressional Info. Serv.).

52. Ibid., 72–73.

53. Ibid., May 11, 1957, 25.

54. Ibid., April 29, 1957, 60, 62.

55. Jack W. Pelatson, *58 Lonely Men: Southern Federal Judges and School Desegregation* (New York: Harcourt Brace, 1961), 28.

56. Wisdom interview, June 4, 1994.

57. Read and McGough, *Let Them Be Judged*, 55–56n6.

58. Wisdom interview, June 4, 1994.

59. Joel William Friedman, *Champion of Civil Rights: Judge John Minor Wisdom* (Baton Rouge: Louisiana State University Press, 2009), 107.

60. Labat v. Bennett, 365, F.2d 698, 702 (5th Cir. 1966) (*en banc*), *cert denied*, 386 U.S. 991 (1967).

61. Judge Borah had taken senior status in 1956; he remained a member of the court until his death in 1966, but he did not sit after 1958.

62. Jimmy Carter, *Turning Point* (New York: Random House, 1992), 21–23.

63. Read and McGough, *Let Them Be Judged*, 158.

64. Bass, *Unlikely Heroes*, 155–56.

65. Read and McGough, *Let Them Be Judged*, 140; Liva Baker, *The Second Battle of New Orleans* (New York: Harper Collins, 1996), 420.

66. Read and McGough, *Let Them Be Judged*, 156.

67. Senate Executive Journal, February 5, 1962; e-mail from Dr. Betty K. Koed, U.S. Senate Historical Office, October 18, 2007.

68. Bass, *Unlikely Heroes*, 158–59; Read and McGough, *Let Them Be Judged*, 174–75.

69. Bass, *Unlikely Heroes*, 159.

70. S. Ernest Vandiver, "Vandiver Takes the Middle Road," in *Georgia Governors in an Age of Change*, ed. Harold P. Henderson and Gary L. Roberts (Athens: University of Georgia Press, 1988), 159.

71. Ibid., 159–60.

72. "Papa's Kindness and Ability Hold Community and Kin Together," *Christian Science Monitor*, May 3, 1985.

73. John Sibley, speech to Alabama and Georgia Civic Clubs, November 9, 1960, reprinted in the *Atlanta Journal*, November 10, 1960.

74. John A. Sibley Papers, "Opening Statement," Georgia General Assembly Committee on Schools Collection, Robert W. Woodruff Library, Emory University, Atlanta, Georgia.

75. *The New Georgia Encyclopedia*, s.v. "Sibley Commission," www.georgiaency clopedia.org (accessed March 9, 2010).

76. By the time Tuttle stepped down as chief judge on June 1, 1968, eight more judges had joined the court: Homer Thornberry (1965), James Coleman (1965), Robert Ainsworth (1966), John Godbold (1966), Irving Goldberg (1966), David Dyer (1966), Bryan Simpson (1966), and Claude Clayton (1967).

CHAPTER FOURTEEN. Justice Is Never Simple: *Brown I* and *II*

1. Jack Bass, *Unlikely Heroes* (New York: Simon & Schuster, 1981), 1.

2. Richard Kluger, *Simple Justice* (New York: Knopf, 1975), 57.

3. John Popham, "Reaction of South: 'Breathing Spell' for Adjustment Tempers Region's Feelings," *New York Times*, May 18, 1954.

4. William S. White, "Ruling to Figure in '54 Campaign," *New York Times*, May 18, 1954. See also Michael Klarman, *From Jim Crow to Civil Rights: The Supreme Court and the Struggle for Racial Equality* (New York: Oxford University Press, 2004), 320.

5. 1953 Ga. Laws 241; Nunan Bartley, *The Rise of Massive Resistance: Race and Politics in the South during the 1950's* (Baton Rouge: Louisiana State University Press, 1969), 54–55.

6. Bartley, *Rise of Massive Resistance*, 54.

7. Sweatt v. Painter, 339 U.S. 634 (1950).

8. McLaurin v. Oklahoma State Regents, 339 U.S. 637 (1950).

9. *Id*. at 640.

10. McLaurin v. Oklahoma State Regents for Higher Ed., 87 F. Supp. 528.

11. Mark Tushnet, *Making Civil Rights Law: Thurgood Marshall and the Supreme Court, 1936–1961* (New York: Oxford University Press, 1994), 166–67.

12. Ibid., 6.

13. Ibid., 7.

14. Ibid., 35–36, 116.

15. The Court issued a separate opinion in the fifth case, the companion case known as Bolling v. Sharpe, 347 U.S. 497 (1954), because it involved the District of Columbia and was decided under the due process clause of the Fifth Amendment rather than the equal protection clause of the Fourteenth Amendment.

16. See, for example, Mark Tushnet with Katya Levin, "What Really Happened in *Brown v. Board of Education*," *Columbia Law Review* 92 (1991): 1867.

17. *Sweatt*, 339 U.S. at 619; Henderson v. United States, 339 U.S. 816 (1950); Dennis J. Hutchinson, "Unanimity and Desegregation: Decision Making in the Supreme Court, 1948–1958, " *Georgetown Law Journal* 68 (1979): 1, 86.

18. Klarman, *From Jim Crow to Civil Rights*, 320.

19. C&H Air Conditioning Fan Company v. Haffner, 216 F.2d 256 (5th Cir. 1954); Hornbrook v. United States 216 F.2d 112 (5th Cir. 1954) (*per curiam*); Folsom v. Young & Young, Inc., 216 F.2d 352 (5th Cir. 1954).

20. Frank Read and Lucy McGough, *Let Them Be Judged* (Metuchen, N.J.: Scarecrow Press, 1978), 74.

21. Jackson v. Rawdon, 135 F. Supp. 936, 937 (N.D. Tx. 1955), *reversed*, 235 F.2d 93 (5th Cir. 1956).

22. Read and McGough, *Let Them Be Judged*, 70.

23. Avery v. Wichita Falls Independent School District, 241 F.2d 230 (5th Cir.), *cert. denied*, 353 U.S. 938 (1957).

24. *Id.* at 234.

25. Briggs v. Elliott, 132 F. Supp. 776 (S.C. 1955).

26. Read and McGough, *Let Them Be Judged*, 70.

27. Ibid., 78.

28. Borders v. Rippy, 247 F.2d 268 (1955).

29. Rippy v. Borders, 250 F.2d 690, 691 (5th Cir. 1957).

30. *Id.* at 692.

31. *Id.* at 694.

32. The district sought a declaratory judgment as to whether two Texas statutes, enacted in 1957 after the first appeal and in place at the time of the second appeal, prevented the school district from complying with the federal court order. Judge Atwell dismissed the complaint. Writing for himself, Judge Brown, and Judge Wisdom, Tuttle affirmed in a terse opinion, Dallas Ind. School Dist. v. Edgar, 255 F.2d 455 (1958).

33. Read and McGough, *Let Them Be Judged*, 112–13.

34. Bush v. Orleans Parish School Board 364 U.S. 500 (1960).

35. Bush v. Orleans Parish School Board 138 F. Supp. 336 (E. D. La. 1956).

36. Orleans Parish School Board v. Bush, 242 F.2d 156, 163 (5th Cir. 1957), *cert. denied*, 354 U.S. 921 (1957) (emphasis added).

37. James M. Washington, ed., *A Testament of Hope: The Essential Writings and Speeches of Martin Luther King, Jr.* (New York: HarperOne, 1990), 219.

38. *Orleans Parish School Board* at 164.

39. *Id.* at 166.

40. Read and McGough, *Let Them Be Judged*, 111.

41. Ibid., 154.

42. Jack W. Pelatson, *58 Lonely Men: Southern Federal Judges and School Desegregation* (New York: Harcourt Brace, 1961).

CHAPTER FIFTEEN. From *Plessy* to *Brown* to Buses

1. Brown v. Board of Education of Topeka, 347 U.S. 483, 495 (1954).

2. Browder v. Gayle, 142 F. Supp. 707 (M.D. Ala. 1956), *aff'd*, 352 U.S. 903 (1956).

3. Fred Gray, *Bus Ride to Justice* (Montgomery, Ala.: Black Belt Press, 1995), 56.

4. Brooks Barnes, "From Footnote to Fame in Civil Rights History," *New York Times*, November 26, 2009; Phillip Hoose, *Claudette Colvin: Twice toward Justice* (New York: Farrar, Straus & Giroux, 2009).

5. Gray, *Bus Ride to Justice*, 49.

6. Ibid., 78.

7. Jack Bass, *Taming the Storm: The Life and Times of Judge Frank M. Johnson, Jr., and the South's Fight over Civil Rights* (New York: Doubleday, 1993), 108; Jack Bass, *Unlikely Heroes* (New York: Simon & Schuster, 1981), 64.

8. Frank Sikora, *The Judge: The Life & Opinions of Alabama's Frank M. Johnson, Jr.* (Montgomery, Ala.: Black Belt Press, 1992), 34.

9. Ibid., 35, 36.

10. Plessy v. Ferguson, 163 U.S. 537 (1896).

11. Sikora, *Judge*, 36.

12. Dawson v. Mayor and City Council of Baltimore, 220 F.2d 386, 386–87 (4th Cir. 1955).

13. Taylor Branch, *Parting the Waters: America in the King Years* (New York: Simon & Schuster, 1988), 196.

14. Clayborne Carson, David J. Garrow, Bill Kovach, and Carol Cosgrove, comps., *Reporting Civil Rights: Part One, American Journalism, 1941–1963* (New York: Library of America, 2003), 356.

CHAPTER SIXTEEN. The Desegregation of the University of Georgia

1. Frank Read and Lucy McGough, *Let Them Be Judged* (Metuchen, N.J.: Scarecrow Press, 1978), 183.

2. J. Clay Smith Jr., "Celebrating Fifty Years of Desegregation Jurisprudence: The Road to *Brown v. Board of Education* and Its Aftermath," *Howard Law Journal* 47 (2004): 1075, 1076.

3. North Carolina and Louisiana were exceptions. See Ludley v. Board of Supervisors of LSU, 150 F. Supp. 900 (D. La. 1957), *aff'd*, 252 F.2d 372 (1958), *cert. denied*, 358 U.S. 819, 820 (1958). See also Read and McGough, *Let Them Be Judged*, 200.

4. Lucy, a library science student, had been convinced to apply by her friend Pollie Anne Myers. Myers was an ambitious young journalist, working for a black newspaper and the NAACP; she wanted to study journalism at the University of Alabama. When Lucy was finally admitted, Myers was rejected because she had, in 1952, become pregnant before marrying. Gene Roberts and Hank Klibanoff, *The Race Beat* (New York: Knopf, 2006), 52, 128–29.

5. Lucy v. Adams, 134 F. Supp. 235 (N.D. Ala. 1955), *aff'd*, 228 F.2d 619 (5th Cir. 1955). Judge Grooms had entered an injunction restraining the university from refusing admittance to Lucy and Myers on August 26, 1955; on motion of the university, he stayed his order pending appeal. Lucy and Myers asked a judge of the Fifth Circuit to vacate the suspension, but their motion was denied. They then filed the same motion in the United States Supreme Court, where it was granted

on October 10, 1955. Lucy v. Adams, 350 U.S. 1 (1955). The Fifth Circuit per curiam opinion affirming Judge Grooms was rendered on December 30, 1955; rehearing was denied on February 1, 1956. *Lucy,* 228 F.2d 619.

6. Roberts and Klibanoff, *Race Beat,* 128–32.

7. Calvin Trillin, *An Education in Georgia* (New York: Viking, 1964), 13.

8. 1959 Ga. Laws 20.

9. Trillin, *Education in Georgia,* 11.

10. Dr. Hamilton Holmes, interview by author, August 15, 1994.

11. Ibid. According to Trillin (*Education in Georgia,* 28), Albert Holmes was the United Golfers Association champion in 1947 and 1958. According to Calvin H. Sinette, author of *Forbidden Fairways: African Americans and the Game of Golf* (Farmington Hills, Mich.: Gale Gengage, 1998), he was the amateur champion. Howard Wheeler, who had caddied for Bobby Jones, was the champion of the pro division in 1947 and 1958. Dr. Sinette, interview by Harold Franklin, April 8, 1999.

12. E. E. Moore, a graduate of Howard University Law School, where he had studied under Charles Hamilton Houston, was lead counsel in the litigation. Moore, who had moved to Atlanta in 1946 at a time when there were only three black attorneys in Atlanta, handled much of the NAACP litigation, including the attempt to desegregate Georgia State University, until 1960–61, when Donald Hollowell began to play a more prominent role.

13. Holmes v. City of Atlanta, 350 U.S. 879 (1955).

14. *Report of Proceedings of the 73rd Annual Session of the Georgia Bar Association,* May 24–26, 1956, Savannah, Georgia. Interposition was a form of outright defiance of the Supreme Court that purported to be within the law. First promulgated in the context of *Brown* in 1955 by James Jackson Kilpatrick, editor of the *Richmond (Va.) News Leader,* interposition was a completely discredited theory that each state could interpose its own sovereignty between the national government and the people of the state. In other words, the southern states could simply refuse to comply with the mandate of *Brown v. Board of Education* or, for that matter, any other decision of the United States Supreme Court. See, for example, Mark Tushnet, *Making Civil Rights Law: Thurgood Marshall and the Supreme Court, 1936–1961* (New York: Oxford University Press, 1994), 240–41.

15. General Appropriations Act of 1956, 1956 Ga. Laws 753.

16. Board of Regents of the University System of Georgia, minutes, February 11, 1959, 30, Atlanta.

17. In 1979 Horace Ward was appointed to the federal bench by President Carter. He is presently a senior judge of the Federal District Court for the Northern District of Atlanta, headquartered in Atlanta.

18. Dr. Hamilton Holmes, interview by author, August 15, 1994.

19. When Franklin Roosevelt became president, Bootle resigned, as is customary for U.S. attorneys. Explaining this, Bootle later said, "He and I had some philosophical differences. They were resolved when it was agreed that I would resign as U.S. attorney and he would remain president. He construed that agreement that he would remain president for life. And he did" (Eric Velasco, "Judge Bootle, Who Was in 'Vortex of the Civil-Rights Movement,' Honored," *Macon Telegraph Online,* June 30, 1998).

20. The August 29, 1960, issue of *U.S. News and World Report* headlined an update, "South Still Holds Out—It's the Seventh Year and Few Schools Are Mixed."

21. "As Schools Opened—Most Everywhere in South: Calm—and Still Segregated," *U.S. News and World Report,* September 19, 1960, 60–62. In the spring of 1951, the trustees of the UNC adopted the policy that administrators would admit "any qualified student to graduate or professional schools of the University 'without regard to race or color' in cases where the State did not provide separate facilities for minority races, and admitted a negro to the Medical school—the first time a negro student had been admitted to a white southern university absent a court order" (Neal Cheek, "An Historical Study of the Administrative Actions in the Racial Desegregation of the University of North Carolina at Chapel Hill, 1930–1955" [PhD diss., University of North Carolina at Chapel Hill, 1973], 145). Subsequently, in June 1951 three students who had sued and won were enrolled in the law school (ibid., 147). See also James Herbert Vaughan Jr., "The Integration of Negroes into the Law School of the University of North Carolina" (master's thesis, University of North Carolina at Chapel Hill, 1952).

22. Aaron v. Cooper, 163 F. Supp. 13 (E.D. Ark. 1958). An immediate petition for writ of certiorari to the United States Supreme Court was denied in an order remanding the case to the Eighth Circuit. Aaron v. Cooper, 357 U.S. 566 (June 30, 1958).

23. "Educators in a Squeeze," *Newsweek,* July 14, 1958.

24. Aaron v. Cooper, 257 F.2d 33 (8th Cir. 1958).

25. Aaron v. Cooper, 358 U.S. 1 (1958).

26. See *Ludley,* 150 F. Supp. 900, *aff'd,* 252 F.2d 372 (1958), *cert. denied,* 358 U.S. 819, 820 (1958); see also Read and McGough, *Let Them Be Judged,* 200.

27. William H. Robinson, "Desegregation in Higher Education in the South," *School and Society,* May 7, 1960.

28. Louise Hollowell and Martin C. Lehfeldt, *The Sacred Call: A Tribute to Donald Hollowell—Civil Rights Champion* (Winter Park, Fla.: Four-G Publishers, 1997), 213.

29. Trial transcript, Holmes v. Danner, 191 F. Supp. 39 (M.D. Ga. 1961).

30. *Id.* at 394.

31. For descriptions of the search of university records, see Hollowell and Lehfeldt, *Sacred Call*, 6; Trillin, *Education in Georgia*, 38.

32. *Holmes*, 191 F. Supp. at 406, 407.

33. "Holmes interview record discloses that he was marked 'average' on physical appearance, poise, maturity, seriousness of purpose, and social adaptability, and 'poor' on verbal expression and cooperativeness" (*id*. at 408).

34. *Id*. at 408.

35. "Here Is Chronology of Events Leading Up to Integration Crisis at Georgia," *Macon Telegraph*, January 15, 1961; Bruce Galphin, "U.S. Court Demands Desegregation Now," *Atlanta Journal-Constitution*, January 7, 1961.

36. Hollowell and Lehfeldt, *Sacred Call*, 8–9; Trillin, *Education in Georgia*, 52–53; see also "Dean Tate Battles to Prevent Riots," *Macon Telegraph*, January 12, 1961.

37. "Bootle Hanged in Effigy near Mercer Campus," *Macon Telegraph*, January 10, 1961. The effigy was hanged from an arch at the entrance to the park, directly in front of Mercer University. Nearly four decades later, Bootle would enjoy a rare honor when the federal courthouse in Macon was named for him. Eric Velasco, "Courthouse Will Bear Name of Noted Civil-Rights Era Judge," *Macon Telegraph Online*, June 30, 1998.

38. Hollowell and Lehfeldt, *Sacred Call*, 10–11.

39. Judge William A. Bootle, interview by author, August 30, 1994.

40. Donald Hollowell, interview by author, July 21, 1998; Hollowell and Lehfeldt, *Sacred Call*, 12.

41. Jack Bass, *Unlikely Heroes* (New York: Simon & Schuster, 1981), 217.

42. Larry Custer, interview by author, January 29, 1997.

43. *Holmes*, 191 F. Supp. at 411.

44. *Lucy*, 134 F. Supp. 235.

45. Read and McGough, *Let Them Be Judged*, 202. One might assume it was Judge Rives, as he was the circuit court judge sitting in Alabama.

46. *Lucy*, 350 U.S. 1.

47. Fred Powledge, "Profiles: Charles Morgan, Jr.," *New Yorker*, October 25, 1969.

48. Fed. R. Civ. P. 62 (emphasis added).

49. Hollowell interview.

50. Ibid.

51. Larry Custer, interview by author, January 29, 1997. More than three decades later, Donald Hollowell did not recall Cook's turning his chair. But, he remarked, "Gene was not above antics." Hollowell interview.

52. Constance Baker Motley, *Equal Justice under Law* (New York: Farrar, Straus & Giroux, 1998), 121.

53. Ibid.

54. Holmes v. Danner, 5 Race Rel. L. Rptr. 1091 (5th Cir. 1961); see also "Judge Tuttle's Edict Setting Aside Stay," *Atlanta Constitution*, January 10, 1961.

55. *Lucy*, 350 U.S. 1. Justice Black had the advantage of having his colleagues in the same building so that he could expeditiously obtain their vote. In all likelihood, he presented it to the entire Court in order to increase the effect of the order.

56. Hollowell and Lehfeldt, *Sacred Call*, 13; Marion Gaines, "Judge Tuttle Kills Delay at University," *Atlanta Constitution*, January 10, 1961, 1, 9. They returned to pay their fees the next day. Bruce Galphin, "U.S. Judge Bars Fund Cutoff; Supreme Court Denies Delay," *Atlanta Constitution*, January 11, 1961, 1.

57. S. Ernest Vandiver, "Vandiver Takes the Middle Road," in *Georgia Governors in an Age of Change*, ed. Harold P. Henderson and Gary L. Roberts (Athens: University of Georgia Press, 1988), 161. This puts the total at fifty. S. Ernest Vandiver, interview by Kathleen Dowdy, 10, McGill Collection, Robert W. Woodruff Library, Emory University, Atlanta, Georgia. This puts the total at fifty-six.

58. See Calhoun v. Latimer, 217 F. Supp. 614 (N.D. Ga. 1962), *aff'd*, 321 F.2d 302 (5th Cir. 1963), *vac'd & rem'd*, 377 U.S. 263 (1964).

59. Vandiver interview, 10. See also Vandiver, "Vandiver Takes the Middle Road," 161; James F. Cook, *The Governors of Georgia, 1754–1995* (Macon, Ga.: Mercer University Press, 1996), 268–69.

60. "Legislative Delay Has Proved Costly," *Atlanta Constitution*, January 9, 1961; "Sanders, Twitty Oppose Closing of University," *Macon Telegraph*, January 9, 1961. "'I don't like to see any mixing of the races,' Sanders said, 'but we are not going to adopt a head-in-the-sand attitude'" (ibid.).

61. 1961 Ga. Laws 103. See also "Vandiver's Declaration Is Praised," *Atlanta Constitution*, January 10, 1961.

62. 1961 Ga. Laws 102–3.

63. Governor Ernest Vandiver to Lieutenant Governor/President of the Senate and the Speaker of the House, January 9, 1961, 1961 Ga. House Journal at 113; Charles Pyles, "S. Ernest Vandiver and the Politics of Change," in Henderson and Roberts, *Georgia Governors*, 149.

64. Cook, *Governors of Georgia*, 266. Charles Weltner, who would in 1966 decline to run for reelection to his seat in Congress rather than pledge loyalty to a Democratic ticket headed by Lester Maddox, recalled that Vandiver had, in his inaugural "No, not one" speech, pledged "to resist the 'tyranny' of the Supreme Court at every crossroad and every hamlet in Georgia, and to preserve segregated education by going to jail, if necessary. . . . Nevertheless, he was attacked by his opponent, a Baptist minister from Ty Ty, Georgia, as being weak on segregation" (Charles Weltner, *Southerner* [New York: Lippincott, 1966], 25).

65. A gospel singer named Lee Roy Abernathy also ran for the nomination. Vandiver, "Vandiver Takes the Middle Road," 146.

66. Ibid., 157.

67. Governor Vandiver to Lieutenant Governor/President and Speaker, 114.

68. Ibid., 149; *Holmes*, 191 F. Supp. at 416.

69. Two days later, after a full hearing, he entered a preliminary injunction, again ordering the governor and the auditor not to restrict the flow of state funds to the university.

70. Gene Britton, "Bootle Order Is Denounced by Vandiver," *Macon Telegraph*, January 11, 1961.

71. Vandiver interview, 10–11.

72. Celestine Sibley, "Students Rally in Chapel to Keep University Open," *Atlanta Constitution*, January 9, 1961.

73. "Vandiver Denies Delay in Rushing Aid to Athens Police during Riot," *Macon Telegraph*, January 13, 1961.

74. "2 Negro Students Suspended by University for Own Safety as Violence Develops," *Macon Telegraph*, January 12, 1961.

75. Tommy Johnson, "Students at Georgia Await Negroes," *Macon Telegraph*, January 14, 1961.

76. Dave Anderson, "Yanks Chase the Ghosts of 1906 Cubs," *New York Times*, August 7, 1998.

77. Judge William A. Bootle, interview by author, August 30, 1994, Macon, Georgia.

78. Bass, *Unlikely Heroes*, 17.

79. Charlayne Hunter-Gault, *In My Place* (New York: Farrar, Straus & Giroux, 1992), 176.

CHAPTER SEVENTEEN. The Costs of Conscience

1. United States v. St. Joe Paper Co., 284 F.2d 430 (1960); McCarty v. Runkle, 285 F.2d 144 (1960); Laskey v. United States, 285 F.2d 98 (1960).

2. St. Helena Parish School Board v. Hall, 287 F.2d 376 (5th Cir.), *cert. denied*, 368 U.S. 830 (1961); East Baton Rouge Parish School Board v. Davis, 287 F.2d 380 (5th Cir.), *cert. denied*, 368 U.S. 831 (1961).

3. Paul H. Roney, "Chief Judge Charles Clark and Court Collegiality," *Mississippi College Law Review* 12 (1992): 359, 361.

4. Clifford M. Kuhn, Harlon E. Joyce, and E. Bernard West, *Living Atlanta: An Oral History of the City, 1914–1948* (Athens: University of Georgia Press, 1990), 201.

5. Stephen G. N. Tuck, *Beyond Atlanta: The Struggle for Racial Equality in Georgia, 1940–1980* (Athens: University of Georgia Press, 2001), 122–23.

6. Kuhn, Joyce, and West, *Living Atlanta*, 98.

7. Harry G. Lefever, *Undaunted by the Fight* (Macon, Ga.: Mercer University Press, 2005), 33–36; David Garrow, *Bearing the Cross* (New York: William Morrow, 1986), 131, 144.

8. Garrow, *Bearing the Cross*, 143.

9. Ibid., 144.

10. Ibid., 151.

11. Claude Sitton, "Atlanta Integrates Restaurants Calmly," *New York Times*, September 29, 1961.

12. Herbert Elsas, interview by author, March 25, 1993.

13. John K. Train III to Miles J. Alexander, April 27, 1971, in author's possession.

14. Miles J. Alexander to the Directors of the Piedmont Driving Club, March 23, 1973, in author's possession.

15. Hearings on the Prospective Nomination of Griffin B. Bell, of Georgia, to be Attorney General before the S. Comm. on the Judiciary, 95th Cong., 1st sess., at 472 (1977).

16. Herbert Elsas, memo to Elbert Tuttle, January 28, 1953.

17. Fritz W. Glitsch & Sons v. Wyatt Metal & Boiler Works, 224 F.2d 331 (5th Cir. 1955).

18. North Carolina Utils. Comm'n v. Fed. Communications Comm'n, 537 F.2d 787 (1976), *cert. denied*, 429 U.S. 1027 (1976).

19. Elbert Tuttle to Honorable Roy W. Harper, March 17, 1975, Elbert P. Tuttle Judicial Papers, Manuscript, Archives, and Rare Book Library, Emory University, Atlanta, Georgia.

20. San Marco Shop, Inc. v. Comm'r, 223 F.2d 702 (5th Cir. 1955).

21. Judicial Conference of the United States, *Report of the Proceedings* (September 1963), 62.

22. See Robert A. Ainsworth Jr., "Judicial Ethics—a Crisis Abates," *Tulane Law Review* 45 (1971): 245, 250–51.

23. Joseph F. Spaniol Jr., *The Code of Judicial Conduct for the United States: A Review of the Activities of Judicial Conference Committees Concerned with Ethical Standards in the Federal Judiciary, 1969–1976* (Washington, D.C.: AOC, 1976).

24. Judge Cornelia Kennedy to Anne S. Emanuel, July 20, 2009, Tuttle Papers.

25. Judge Elbert Tuttle to Chief Justice Warren Burger, November 18, 1976, Tuttle Papers.

26. Chief Judge Irving Kaufman to Judge Elbert Tuttle, May 13, 1976, Tuttle Papers.

CHAPTER EIGHTEEN. Oxford, Mississippi: The Battleground

1. James Meredith, *Three Years in Mississippi* (Des Moines, Iowa: Meredith Publishing, 1996), 54.

2. Meredith v. Fair, 298 F.2d 696, 698 (5th Cir. 1962).

3. Constance Baker Motley, *Equal Justice under Law* (New York: Farrar, Straus & Giroux, 1997), 162–63; Meredith, *Three Years in Mississippi*, 55.

4. Meredith v. Fair, 199 F. Supp. 754, 757 (S.D. Miss. 1961).

5. *Meredith*, 298 F.2d at 701.

6. Jack Bass, *Unlikely Heroes* (New York: Simon & Schuster, 1981), 177.

7. Meredith v. Fair, 202 F. Supp. 224, 226 (S.D. Miss. 1962).

8. Meredith v. Fair, 305 F.2d 343 (5th Cir. 1962).

9. Jack W. Pelatson, *58 Lonely Men: Southern Federal Judges and School Desegregation* (New York: Harcourt Brace, 1961), 147.

10. *Meredith*, 305 F.2d 343. Quintus Fabius Maximus, nicknamed *cunctator*, or "delayer," became legendary for his successful use of delaying tactics in the Second Punic War. See http://www.brittanica.com/EBchecked/topic/199706/Quintus-Fabius-Maximus-Verrucosus.

11. *Id.* at 351–52.

12. *Id.* at 361.

13. Pursuant to Rule 32 of the Rules of the Fifth Circuit, the mandate (the injunction requiring the registrar to enroll Meredith) would issue at any time after twenty-one days after the date of the opinion, unless an application for rehearing had been made and was either pending or had been granted. Moreover, under Rule 32, "a mandate once issued will not be recalled except by the court and to prevent injustice." The university did not apply for rehearing or for a stay of the mandate.

14. Boman v. Birmingham Transit Co., 292 F.2d 4 (5th Cir. 1961) (Cameron, J., dissenting).

15. Browder v. Gayle, 142 F. Supp. 707 (M.D. Ala. 1956), *aff'd*, 352 U.S. 903 (1956).

16. Boman v. Birmingham Transit Co., 280 F.2d 531, 533 (1960).

17. Boman v. Morgan, 4 Race Rel. L. Rptr. 1027 (N.D. Ala. 1959).

18. *Boman*, 280 F.2d 531.

19. *Id.* at 536.

20. *Boman*, 292 F.2d 4.

21. United States v. Wood, 295 F.2d 772, 788–89 (1961).

22. The statute has since been amended, and a three-judge court is now only required in cases involving the apportionment of legislative districts. 28 U.S.C. § 2284 (2006).

23. Edward W. Wordsworth to All Counsel in Meredith vs. Fair, July 20, 1962,

Elbert P. Tuttle Judicial Papers, Manuscript, Archives, and Rare Book Library, Emory University, Atlanta, Georgia.

24. Meredith v. Fair, 306 F.2d 374 (5th Cir. 1962).

25. Frank Read and Lucy McGough, *Let Them Be Judged* (Metuchen, N.J.: Scarecrow Press, 1978), 223.

26. Meredith v. Fair, 83 S.Ct. 10 (1962).

27. "This Righteous Cause," *Time*, September 21, 1962.

28. Yasuhiro Katagiri, "With the Aura of Sophistication and Respectability," paper delivered at the 2004 Annual Meeting of the Organization of American Historians, Boston, March 27, 2004. For an excellent history of the commission, see Sara Rowe-Sims, "The Mississippi State Sovereignty Commission," *Journal of Mississippi History*, Spring 1999, 29–58.

29. Read and McGough, *Let Them Be Judged*, 226, 183.

30. "Step by Step: How Crisis Developed in Mississippi," *U.S. News and World Report*, October 15, 1962; Read and McGough, *Let Them Be Judged*, 227.

31. Meredith v. Fair, 313 F.2d 532 (5th Cir. 1962) (*en banc*).

32. Meredith v. Fair, 7 Race Rel. L. Rptr. 759 (1962).

33. Transcript of record at 7, 10, *Meredith*, 313 F.2d 532 (No. 19,475); Hearing on Order to Show Cause Why Governor Ross R. Barnett Should Not Be Cited for Civil Contempt, September 28, 1962, New Orleans. For an eyewitness account of this hearing, see Jack Greenberg, *Crusaders in the Courts* (New York: Basic Books, 1994).

34. Transcript of record, 10–14.

35. Ibid., 14–43.

36. *Meredith*, 313 F.2d 532.

37. Transcript, supra note 502, at 76.

38. Ibid., 90.

39. Arthur Schlesinger Jr., *Robert Kennedy and His Times* (New York: Ballantine, 1978).

40. Read and McGough, *Let Them Be Judged*, 239.

41. "The Mississippi Tragedy—What It All Means," *U.S. News and World Report*, October 15, 1962.

42. Victor Navasky, *Kennedy Justice* (New York: Atheneum, 1977), 237.

43. Meredith v. Fair, 330 F.2d 369, 381 (1963) (*per curiam*).

44. *Id.* at 390.

45. United States v. Barnett, 376 U.S. 681 (1964).

46. United States v. Barnett, 346 F.2d 99, 101–2 (5th Cir. 1965) (Tuttle, J., dissenting).

47. *Id.* at 101, 104, 107, 108, 109.

CHAPTER NINETEEN. The Fight for the Right to Vote

1. Frank Read and Lucy McGough, *Let Them Be Judged* (Metuchen, N.J.: Scarecrow Press, 1978), 283.

2. Guinn v. United States, 238 U.S. 347 (1915); Read and McGough, *Let Them Be Judged*, 283–84. *See also* United States v. Louisiana, 225 F. Supp. 353 (E.D. La. 1963).

3. Claude Sitton, interview by author, February 1, 1994, Atlanta, Georgia. Sitton covered civil rights in the South for the *New York Times* from May 1958 through October 1964. See also Claude Sitton, "Negro Vote Drive in Mississippi Is Set Back as Violence Erupts," *New York Times*, October 24, 1961.

4. Philip Dray, *At the Hands of Persons Unknown: The Lynching of Black America* (New York: Random House, 2002), 426.

5. Taylor Branch, *Pillar of Fire: America in the King Years 1963–65* (New York: Simon & Schuster, 1998), 222–23.

6. Civil Rights Act of 1960, Pub. L. No. 86-449, § 601, 74 Stat. 86 (1960); 5 Race Rel. L. Rptr. 240–41 (1960).

7. In addition to understanding tests, strategies used to block registration by black citizens included literacy tests, demonstrations of good moral character, and vouchers from registered voters. Read and McGough, *Let Them Be Judged*, 308.

8. Reddix v. Lucky, 252 F.2d 930, 936 (5th Cir. 1958).

9. *Id.* at 937, 933, 936.

10. *Id.* at 938.

11. *Id.* at 943.

12. Pursuant to federal legislation enacted in 1910, a three-judge federal court (usually composed of one circuit judge and two district court judges) was convened whenever a state statute was challenged as unconstitutional under the federal Constitution. They are now only required in cases involving reapportionment. 28 U.S.C. § 2284 (2006). For a history of this law, see S. Rep. No. 94-204 (1976).

13. Jack Bass, *Unlikely Heroes* (New York: Simon & Schuster, 1981), 231–37; Read and McGough, *Let Them Be Judged*, 268–76.

14. Sharp v. Lucky, 252 F.2d 910 (5th Cir. 1958).

15. *Id.* at 913.

16. In March 1956 101 members of Congress (every senator and congressman from a southern state except Senators Gore and Kefauver and Representative Lyndon Johnson) signed the Southern Manifesto, in which they excoriated the Supreme Court for the *Brown* decision and commended "the motive of those States which have declared the intention to resist forced integration by any lawful means" (102 Cong. Rec. 4515–16 [1956]). Mark Tushnet, *Making Civil Rights Law: Thurgood*

Marshall and the Supreme Court, 1936–1961 (New York: Oxford University Press, 1994), 240–41.

17. Sharp v. Lucky, 165 F. Supp. 405 (W.D. La. 1958).

18. Sharp v. Lucky, 266 F.2d 342 (5th Cir. 1959).

19. *Id.* See Matthew 23:23: "You give a tenth of your spices—mint, dill and cummin. But you have neglected the more important matters of the law—justice, mercy and faithfulness. You should have practiced the latter, without neglecting the former" (New International Version).

20. Anne S. Emanuel, "Forming the Historic Fifth Circuit: The Eisenhower Years," *Texas Forum on Civil Liberties and Civil Rights* 6 (2002): 233, 254.

21. Bass, *Unlikely Heroes*, 45.

22. United States v. Louisiana, 225 F. Supp. 353, *aff'd*, 380 U.S. 145 (1965).

23. *Id.* at 378–79.

24. Ausberry v. Monroe, 456 F. Supp. 460 (W.D. La. 1978).

25. Sanders v. Gray, 203 F. Supp. 158 (N.D. Ga. 1962) (three-judge district court: Tuttle and Bell of the Fifth Circuit, Hooper of the Northern District; Bell writing), *vac'd and rem'd*, 372 U.S. 368 (1963).

26. Toombs v. Fortson, 205 F. Supp. 248 (1962) (three-judge district court: Tuttle and Bell of the Fifth Circuit, Morgan of the Northern District; Tuttle writing), *vac'd in part and rem'd*, 379 U.S. 621 (1965).

27. See chapter 14.

28. Sara Tuttle, interview by author, June 1, 1993.

29. *Sanders*, 203 F. Supp. 158 (primaries); *Toombs*, 205 F. Supp. 248 (general elections).

30. Baker v. Carr, 369 U.S. 186 (1962).

31. Williams v. Wallace, 240 F. Supp. 100, 104, 106 (M.D. Ala. 1965).

32. United States v. Alabama, 171 F. Supp. 720, 729 (M.D. Ala. 1959).

33. United States v. Alabama, 192 F. Supp. 677 (M.D. Ala. 1961), *aff'd*, 304 F.2d 583 (5th Cir. 1962), *aff'd*, 371 U.S. 37 (1962).

34. *Id.* at 683.

35. United States v. Penton, 212 F. Supp. 193 (M.D. Ala. 1962).

36. 5 Race Rel. L. Rptr. 241 (1960).

37. See *United States v. Penton*, 212 F. Supp. 193.

38. Jack Bass, *Taming the Storm: The Life and Times of Judge Frank M. Johnson, Jr., and the South's Fight over Civil Rights* (New York: Doubleday, 1993), 152.

39. Frank M. Johnson Jr., "In Defense of Judicial Activism," *Emory Law Journal* 28 (1979): 901, 907, 912.

40. Bass, *Taming the Storm*, 134.

41. Ibid., 107.

42. Bass, *Unlikely Heroes*, 164–68; Victor Navasky, *Kennedy Justice* (New York: Atheneum, 1977), 245–51.

43. Juan Williams, "Marshall's Law," *Washington Post Magazine*, January 7, 1990.

44. Bass, *Unlikely Heroes*, 166.

45. United States v. Lynd, 301 F.2d 818, 821 (5th Cir.), *cert. denied*, 371 U.S. 893 (1962). See also regarding *Lynd* et al., 7 Race Rel. L. Rptr. 1171 (1962).

46. *United States*, 301 F.2d at 822.

47. *Id.* at 823.

48. *Id.* at 818.

CHAPTER TWENTY. But for Birmingham

1. Other cases he might mention included the series of opinions involved in the litigation surrounding James Meredith's attempt to register at Ole Miss as well as Becker v. Thompson, 429 F.2d 919 (5th Cir. 1972) and Bond v. Floyd, 251 F. Supp. 333 (N.D. Ga. 1966), cases in which his dissenting position was adopted by the U.S. Supreme Court.

2. John Lewis, *Walking with the Wind* (New York: Simon & Schuster, 1998), 186.

3. Henry Hampton and Steve Fayer, *Voices of Freedom* (New York: Bantam Books, 1990), 106.

4. Lewis, *Walking with the Wind*, 186.

5. Ibid.

6. Victor Navasky, *Kennedy Justice* (New York: Atheneum, 1977), 256–57.

7. Ibid., 257.

8. Ibid.

9. All Writs Act, 28 U.S.C. § 1651(b). *See* Kelly v. Page, 335 F.2d 114 (5th Cir. 1965); Thomas E. Baker, *Rationing Justice on Appeal* (St. Paul, Minn.: West Publishing Company, 1994), 138–40.

10. Constance Baker Motley, *Equal Justice under Law* (New York: Farrar, Straus & Giroux, 1998), 140.

11. Diane McWhorter, *Carry Me Home* (New York: Simon & Schuster, 2001), 108; NAACP v. Alabama, 357 U.S. 449 (1958).

12. NAACP v. Alabama, 377 U.S. 288, 307 (1964) (quoting *NAACP*, 357 U.S. at 460).

13. McWhorter, *Carry Me Home*, 109.

14. Ibid., 73–75, quote on 114.

15. At the mass meeting that closed the conference, King gave the main address. Baker also spoke, reminding the students of the importance of the lunch counter

sit-ins; they were, as she often said, about larger issues, issues "bigger than a hamburger." Joanne Grant, *Ella Baker* (New York: John Wiley & Sons, 1998), 126–31.

16. Taylor Branch, *Parting the Waters: America in the King Years 1954–63* (New York: Simon & Schuster, 1988), 689–90.

17. McWhorter, *Carry Me Home*, 323–24.

18. Gene Roberts and Hank Klibanoff, *The Race Beat* (New York: Knopf, 2006), 50–51. The Scott family also owned the *Atlanta Daily World*, the nation's only black daily paper, and the *Memphis World*.

19. McWhorter, *Carry Me Home*, 341–42.

20. Ibid., 355.

21. Four years later the United States Supreme Court upheld the convictions and the five-day sentences imposed. Walker v. Birmingham, 388 U.S. 307 (1967).

22. McWhorter, *Carry Me Home*, 359–61.

23. Branch, *Parting the Waters*, 755.

24. Ibid., 757.

25. Everyone criticized MLK Jr. for using children, from Attorney General Robert Kennedy, to Mayor Boutwell, to Malcolm X: "Real men don't put their children on the firing line" (David B. Oppenheimer, "Martin's March," *ABA Journal* 80 [June 1994]: 54).

26. Branch, *Parting the Waters*, 759.

27. Ibid.

28. McWhorter, *Carry Me Home*, 433.

29. Ibid.

30. Michael Dorman, *We Shall Overcome*, quoted in Clayborne Carson, David J. Garrow, Bill Kovach, and Carol Cosgrove, comps., *Reporting Civil Rights: Part One, American Journalism, 1941–1963* (New York: Library of America, 2003), 814.

31. Glenn T. Eskew, *But for Birmingham* (Chapel Hill: University of North Carolina Press, 1997), 118–19, 308–9; McWhorter, *Carry Me Home*, 449.

32. The school board used both the term *expelled* and the term *suspended*. Students over sixteen were expelled; those under sixteen were suspended. The effect was the same. None could finish the two weeks left in the term; no one would graduate or be promoted. All could "make application" for summer school and attempt "to make up the time lost and receive credit for this year's work" (Woods v. Wright, 8 Race Rel. L. Rptr. 444 [May 22, 1963]). Otherwise, they could come back in the fall and complete the full grade or semester from which they had been expelled or suspended.

33. The Reverend Calvin Woods, interview by Dr. Horace Huntley, May 12, 1995, Oral History Project, Birmingham Civil Rights Institute.

34. Judy's memory, more than four decades later, was that she and her sisters

hid in the back of the car and popped up when they arrived at the church that morning. Her father, she recalled, "was livid," but at that point there was nothing he could do but let them join the protestors. Judy Woods, interview by Dr. Horace Huntley, March 19, 1997, Oral History Project.

35. The Reverend Abraham Woods, interview by Betty Hanson, April 30, 1998, Oral History Project.

36. Marion Woods, interview by Dr. Horace Huntley, June 28, 1996, Oral History Project.

37. Woods v. Wright, 334 F.2d 369 (5th Cir. 1964).

38. Motley, *Equal Justice under Law*, 136.

39. Woods v. Wright, 8 Race Rel. L. Rptr. 444 (N.D. Ala. 1963).

40. Motley, *Equal Justice under Law*, 136.

41. Ibid.; Claude Sitton, "U.S. Appeals Judge Orders Birmingham to Reinstate Pupils," *New York Times*, May 23, 1963.

42. Motley, *Equal Justice under Law*, 136. In her autobiography, Motley indicates that she was accompanied by Leroy Clark of the LDF and Donald Hollowell, the Atlanta attorney who assisted in the UGA desegregation litigation.

43. Sitton, "U.S. Appeals Judge."

44. *Woods*, 334 F.2d at 374.

45. Sitton, "U.S. Appeals Judge"; *Woods*, 8 Race Rel. L. Rptr. at 445.

46. Sitton, "U.S. Appeals Judge."

47. His law clerk at the time, Charles Kidd, recalled that calling the radio stations had been Tuttle's idea; it was not an aspect of relief requested by Constance Baker Motley. Charles Kidd, interview by author, April 5, 1994.

48. In three of the cases, although the arrests were for trespass, there was a municipal ordinance requiring racial segregation at lunch counters. Peterson v. City of Greenville, 378 U.S. 153 (1963); Lombard v. Louisiana, 373 U.S. 267 (1963); Gober v. City of Birmingham, 378 U.S. 374 (1963). In the fourth, there was no ordinance, but both the mayor and the chief of police had made highly publicized statements indicating they would not tolerate sit-ins at lunch counters by blacks, and there were no desegregated lunch counters in the city of New Orleans. Avent v. North Carolina, 378 U.S. 375 (1963).

49. *Woods*, 8 Race Rel. L. Rptr. at 447–48.

50. President John F. Kennedy, news conference, May 22, 1963, 56, State Department Auditorium, Washington, D.C., John F. Kennedy Presidential Library and Museum, www.jfklibrary.org.

51. President John F. Kennedy, radio and television report to the American people on civil rights, June 11, 1963, the White House, Washington, D.C., John F. Kennedy Presidential Library and Museum, www.jfklibrary.org.

CHAPTER TWENTY-ONE. The Houston Conference

1. Judge Griffin Bell to Judge Elbert Tuttle et al., May 23, 1963, 7, Elbert P. Tuttle Judicial Papers, Manuscript, Archives, and Rare Book Library, Emory University, Atlanta, Georgia.

2. Judge Walter Gewin to All Fifth Circuit Judges, May 24, 1963, Tuttle Papers.

3. Armstrong v. Board of Education of Birmingham, 323 F.2d 333, 356 (5th Cir. 1963) (Cameron, J., dissenting).

4. Jack Bass, *Unlikely Heroes* (New York: Simon & Schuster, 1981), 226.

5. Woods v. Wright, 334 F.2d 369 (5th Cir. 1964).

6. In Rios v. Wigen, 863 F.2d 196 (2nd Cir. 1988), after expressing concern about judge shopping, the court noted: "Nevertheless, authority to issue an extraordinary writ appears to be conferred upon an individual judge by the 'all writs' statute."

7. 28 U.S.C. § 46.

8. See Federal Rules Appellate Procedure, Rule 8.

9. See Boman v. Birmingham Transit Co., 292 F.2d 4 (5th Cir. 1961) (Cameron, J., dissenting).

10. Elbert and Sara Tuttle, interview by Fred Aman, tape 1 of 5, May 16–18, 1988, Atlanta, Georgia, on file at the Cornell University School of Law.

11. 323 F.2d 333 (5th Cir. 1963).

12. 220 F. Supp. 217 (S.D. Ala. 1963).

13. Armstrong v. Board of Education, 323 F.2d 333, 336–37 (5th Cir. 1964).

14. *Armstrong*, 323 F.2d at 353. For an analysis of the series of events triggered by Judge Cameron's dissent, see J. Robert Brown Jr. and Allison Herren Lee, "Neutral Assignment of Judges in the Court of Appeals," *Texas Law Review* 78 (2000): 1037.

15. *Woods*, 334 F.2d 369.

16. *Armstrong*, 323 F.2d at 353 n.1.

17. Cameron's list of twenty-five opinions represented only twenty matters, because five arose from James Meredith's attempts to matriculate at the University of Mississippi and two arose from a single voting rights matter.

18. *Armstrong*, 323 F.2d at 357.

19. "Feud over Racial Cases Flares in U.S. Appeals Court in South," *New York Times*, July 31, 1963, 12.

20. Saul Friedman, "Appeals Court Facing Revolt," *Houston Chronicle*, August 4, 1963, 1.

21. See Allison Herren Lee, William W. Shakely, and J. Robert Brown Jr., "Judge Warren L. Jones and the Supreme Court of Dixie," *Louisiana Law Review* 59 (1998): 209.

22. Frank Read and Lucy McGough, *Let Them Be Judged* (Metuchen, N.J.: Scarecrow Press, 1978), 272.

23. Jones diary, August 7, 1963. The author is grateful to Professor J. Robert Brown of the University of Denver College of Law and William Shakely, Judge Jones's grandson, for access to Judge Jones's diary. It is on file with Mr. Shakely.

24. Report of Edward W. Wadsworth, clerk of the court, United States Court of Appeals for the Fifth Circuit, 1959–63. According to Judge Jones's diary, the judges agreed to turn in all copies of the report with the understanding that they would be delivered to Judge Tuttle and that he would destroy them (Jones diary, August 23, 1963). A diary entry made three days later, on August 26, indicates that Tuttle had told Jones he would keep all the materials, as he did (Tuttle Papers). Judge Jones and Judge Wisdom each retained a copy also. See Brown and Lee, "Neutral Assignment," 1045; Friedman, Champion of Civil Rights, 258n35.

25. Jones diary, August 7, 1963.

26. Ibid., August 12, 1963.

27. Ibid., August 16 and 21, 1963.

28. Read and McGough, Let Them Be Judged, 270.

29. Judge Wisdom's diary is on file with his biographer, Professor Joel Friedman of Tulane University Law School, and is available at http://www.law.du.edu/index.php/neutral-assignment-of-judges/1963-houston-conference-notes.

30. Bailey v. Patterson, 199 F. Supp. 595 (S.D. Miss. 1961); Wisdom diary, August 22, 1963.

31. Clayton, along with his colleague Judge Harold Cox, has been described by one historian as a "die hard white supremacist." Steven F. Lawson, Black Ballots: Voting Rights in the South, 1944–1969 (Lanham, Md.: Lexington Books, 1999), 272; Jones diary, August 22, 1963.

32. See 28 U.S.C. § 2284.

33. William Ty Mayton, "Recess Appointments and an Independent Judiciary," Constitutional Commentary 20 (Winter 2003–4): 515, 530.

34. Wisdom diary, August 22, 1963.

35. Jones diary, August 22, 1963.

36. United States v. Woodley, 751 F.2d 1008 (9th Cir. 1985) (en banc).

37. Judge Elbert Tuttle to Judge William Norris, May 29, 1985.

38. United States v. Lynd, 301 F.2d 818 (1962).

39. Hanes v. Shuttlesworth, 310 F.2d 303 (1962).

40. Greene v. Fair, 314 F.2d 200 (1963).

41. Joel William Friedman, Champion of Civil Rights: Judge John Minor Wisdom (Baton Rouge: Louisiana State University Press, 2009), 255, 269; Bass, Unlikely Heroes, 242; Read and McGough, Let Them Be Judged, 275.

42. Edward Wadsworth to Judge Elbert Tuttle et al., August 9, 1963, Tuttle Papers.

43. Ibid.

44. Brown to Wadsworth.

45. Wadsworth to Tuttle et al.

46. Jones diary, August 22, 1963.

47. Ibid.

48. Wisdom diary, August 23, 1963.

49. Jones diary, August 23, 1963; Wisdom diary, August 23, 1963.

50. Bob Tutt, "Appeals Court Denies Stacking," *Houston Chronicle*, August 24, 1963.

51. Jones diary, August 23, 1963.

52. Ibid., August 26, 1963.

53. United States v. Mississippi, 229 F. Supp. 925 (S.D. Miss. 1964), *rev'd*, 380 U.S. 128 (1965).

54. *Id.* at 144.

55. 380 U.S. 128 (1965). Justice John Harlan concurred specially, noting that he would have relied solely on the Fifteenth Amendment.

CHAPTER TWENTY-TWO. Moving On

1. C. J. Kreger v. Board of Trustees of Georgetown Ind. Sch. Dist., 8 Race Rel. L. Rptr. 561 (Tex. Civ. App. 1963).

2. Miller v. Barnes, 8 Race Rel. L. Rptr. 1035 (W.D. Tx. 1963).

3. *Macbeth* 5.8 is cited in note 1 in the opinion.

4. Miller v. Barnes, 328 F.2d 810, 815 (5th Cir. 1964) (Tuttle, J., dissenting).

5. *Id.* at 816, 817 (Hutcheson, J., concurring).

6. Stell v. Savannah–Chatham County Board of Education, 5 Race Rel. L. Rptr. 514, 515 (S.D. Ga. 1963).

7. *Id.* at 528.

8. *Id.* at 528.

9. Stell v. Board of Education, 387 F.2d 486 (5th Cir. 1967).

10. United States v. Jefferson County Bd. of Education, 372 F.2d 836 (1966), *corr'd and aff'd en banc*, 380 F.2d 385 (1967); *cert. denied, sub nom.* Caddo Parish School Bd. v. United States, 399 U.S. 840 (1967).

11. *Id.*

12. Davis v. Bd. of School Comm'rs of Mobile County, 364 F.2d 896 (5th Cir. 1966).

13. *Id.* at 898, n.1.

14. Rewis v. United States, 369 F.2d 595 (5th Cir. 1966).

15. Jack Bass, *Unlikely Heroes* (New York: Simon & Schuster, 1981), 17.

16. Frank Read and Lucy McGough, *Let Them Be Judged* (Metuchen, N.J.: Scarecrow Press, 1978), 296.

CHAPTER TWENTY-THREE. The City Almost Too Busy to Hate

1. "The Fascinating and Frenetic Fifth," *Time*, December 4, 1964; Jack Bass, *Unlikely Heroes* (New York: Simon & Schuster, 1981), 79.

2. Jack Bass, *Taming the Storm: The Life and Times of Judge Frank M. Johnson, Jr., and the South's Fight over Civil Rights* (New York: Doubleday, 1993), 4, 15, 16–17; Frank Sikora, *The Judge: The Life & Opinions of Alabama's Frank M. Johnson, Jr.* (Montgomery, Ala.: Black Belt Press, 1992), 51–53.

3. See http://www.southernregionalcouncil.org/history.html#1919.

4. Ralph McGill, "One Day It Will Be Monday," *Atlanta Constitution*, April 9, 1953, reprinted in *The Best of Ralph McGill: Selected Columns*, ed. Michael Strickland, Harry Davis, and Jeff Strickland (Atlanta, Ga.: Cherokee Publishing, 1980), 108–9.

5. Harold Martin, *Ralph McGill, Reporter* (Atlanta, Ga.: Little, Brown, 1973), 132. See also Leonard Ray Teel, *Ralph Emerson McGill: Voice of the Southern Conscience* (Knoxville: University of Tennessee Press, 2001), 238–39.

6. Ralph McGill, telegram to President Dwight D. Eisenhower, September 14, 1953, Ralph McGill Papers, Manuscript, Archives and Rare Book Library, Emory University.

7. Ralph McGill and Elbert Tuttle correspondence, May 13, 1960, and August 17, 1967, Elbert P. Tuttle Judicial Papers, Manuscript, Archives, and Rare Book Library, Emory University, Atlanta, Georgia.

8. Ivan Allen Jr., *Mayor: Notes on the Sixties* (New York: Simon & Schuster, 1971), 108.

9. Judge Elbert Tuttle, interview by author, March 24, 1993.

10. Allen, *Mayor*, 205.

11. Ibid., 147.

12. Poole v. Barnett, 336 F.2d 267 (5th Cir. 1964).

13. Judge Elbert Tuttle, interview by author, May 5, 1993.

CHAPTER TWENTY-FOUR. Family and Friends

1. "Jump Jim Crow: Out of the Segregated South: Oral Histories from the Great Migration," *Rochester City Newspaper*, May 29 and June 6, 2002.

2. Eugene Patterson, "Mrs. Tuttle Sliced the Ham," *Atlanta Constitution*, April 25, 1968.

3. At the time, the Woodruff Arts Center included the Alliance Theater and the Atlanta College of Art.

4. Ginny Tuttle, interview by author, May 9, 1997; Dr. Tuttle and Mrs. Ginny Tuttle, interview by author, March 7, 2008.

CHAPTER TWENTY-FIVE. A Jurisprudence of Justice

1. Novak v. Beto, 453 F.2d 661 (5th Cir. 1971) (Tuttle, J., dissenting).

2. *Id.* at 672.

3. Elbert and Sara Tuttle, interview by Fred Aman, May 16–18, 1988, Atlanta, Georgia, on file at the Cornell University School of Law.

4. Heart of Atlanta Motel v. United States, 231 F. Supp. 393 (N.D. Ga. 1964), *aff'd*, 379 U.S. 241 (1964).

5. *Heart of Atlanta Motel*, 379 U.S. 241.

6. Judge Harold Carswell dissented because in his view the order of remand was not appealable. Rachel v. State of Georgia, 9 Race Rel. L. Rptr. 838 (1964).

7. See Georgia v. Hall, 9 Race Rel. L. Rptr. 860 (1964).

8. "Shoofly Pye," *Time*, April 17, 1964.

9. Georgia v. Hall, 9 Race Rel. L. Rptr. 864 (1964).

10. Georgia v. Rachel, 9 Race Rel. L. Rptr. 839 (1964).

11. The motion sought "leave to petition for mandamus and/or prohibition to the Fifth Circuit Court of Appeals to prevent that court's further exercise of jurisdiction in the removed cases." Georgia v. Tuttle, 9 Race Rel. L. Rptr. 868 (1964).

12. Georgia v. Tuttle, 377 U.S. 987 (1964).

13. Hamm v. Rock Hill, 379 U.S. 306 (1964).

14. Fred Powledge, "Ruling on Sit-ins May Free 3,000, Mostly in the South," *New York Times*, December 15, 1964.

15. Rachel v. Georgia, 342 F.2d 336 (5th Cir. 1965).

16. *Id.* at 346.

17. *Id.* at 341.

18. Georgia v. Rachel, 384 U.S. 780 (1966).

19. *Id.* at 788 n.8.

20. The case that ended the white Democratic primary is Toombs v. Fortson, 205 F. Supp. 248 (N.D. Ga. 1962).

21. "ACLU Aiding Negro in Fight to Take Seat in Georgia House," *New York Times*, January 9, 1966.

22. "Special Election Asked in Georgia," *New York Times*, January 12, 1966.

23. "1000 Stage March on Georgia Capitol; Back Ousted Negro," *New York Times*, January 15, 1966. Among the twelve who voted to seat Bond were Kil Townsend, who had been Tuttle's aide de camp at the 1952 Republican Convention, and Mike Egan, a partner at the law firm Tuttle founded, Sutherland, Asbill & Brennan. They too were newly elected; it was the first vote they cast. Kay Powell, "Kil Townsend, 89, 'Voice of Moderation' in Georgia House," *Atlanta Journal-Constitution*, March 27, 2008.

24. "Bond Hailed at UN Luncheon Given by Africans of 15 Nations," *New York Times*, January 22, 1966.

25. Gene Roberts, "Racial Issue out in Bond Case; Court Weighs Free-Speech Plea," *New York Times*, January 29, 1966.

26. Ibid.

27. Ibid.; Bond v. Floyd, 251 F. Supp. 333, 344 (N.D. Ga. 1966).

28. *Bond v. Floyd*, 251 F. Supp. at 357.

29. Bond v. Floyd, 385 U.S. 116, 137 (1966).

30. Powell v. McCormack, 395 U.S. 486, 533 (1969).

31. 50 U.S.C. § 462.

32. Clay v. United States, 397 F.2d 901 (5th Cir. 1968).

33. *Id.* at 913, 901.

34. Charles Morgan, *One Man, One Voice* (Austin, Tex.: Holt, Rinehart & Winston, 1979), 165.

35. See Sellers v. Laird, 395 U.S. 950, 951 (1969).

36. Laughlin McDonald, interview by author, October 3, 2003.

37. Sellers v. McNamara, 398 F.2d 893 (5th Cir. 1968).

38. *Id.*

39. As Tuttle noted, in the case decided in the Fifth Circuit, Ali was appealing his conviction. Like Sellers, however, he had filed suit to enjoin his deduction in both Kentucky and Texas. *Id.* at 907–9.

40. *Sellers*, 395 U.S. at 950.

41. *Id.* at 951 n.3.

42. *Id.* at 952.

43. Clay v. United States, 403 U.S. 698 (1971).

44. Judge Elbert Tuttle, interview by author, July 8, 1993.

45. Ferrell v. Dallas Indep. Sch. Dist., 392 F.2d 697, 699 (5th Cir. 1968) (Tuttle, J., dissenting), *cert. denied*, 393 U.S. 856 (1968).

46. Ferrell v. Dallas Indep. Sch. Dist., 262 F. Supp. 545 (N.D. Tx. 1966).

47. *Ferrell*, 392 F.2d at 697, *cert. denied*, 393 U.S. 856.

48. Judge Tuttle to Judges Walter Gewin and John Godbold, March 18, 1968, Elbert P. Tuttle Judicial Papers, Manuscript, Archives, and Rare Book Library, Emory University, Atlanta, Georgia.

49. *Ferrell*, 392 F.2d at 705, *cert. denied*, 393 U.S. 856.

50. *Id.* at 706.

51. Glover v. Pettey, 447 F.2d 495 (5th Cir. 1971), *aff'd*, without opinion.

52. Tinker v. Des Moines Indep. Cmty. Sch. Dist., 393 U.S. 503 (1969).

53. Judge Bryan Simpson to Judge Griffin Bell, June 21, 1971, Tuttle Papers.

54. Quoted in ibid., 2.

55. Ibid., 2, 3.

56. Judge Elbert P. Tuttle to Judge Bryan Simpson, June 23, 1971, Tuttle Papers.

57. "Senate Kills Delays, Approves Rehnquist," *Dateline* (AP), Washington, D.C., Tuttle Papers.

58. The complaint alleged economic discrimination as well, but that claim was dropped on appeal. Hawkins v. Town of Shaw, 437 F.2d 1286 (5th Cir. 1971).

59. Hawkins v. Town of Shaw, 303 F. Supp. 1162 (N.D. Miss. 1969).

60. *Id.* at 1169, 1165–66.

61. Judge Goldberg joined Tuttle's opinion, and Judge Bell wrote a special concurrence.

62. Hawkins v. Town of Shaw, 437 F.2d 1286, 1288 (5th Cir. 1971) (Bell, J., concurring specially).

63. *Id.* at 1295.

64. *Id.* at 1292.

65. Hawkins v. Shaw, 461 F.2d 1171, 1174 (5th Cir. 1972) (Wisdom, J., concurring specially).

66. Tom Wicker, "A Tale of Two Cities," *New York Times*, February 7, 1971.

67. "Justice Well Done," *Houston Post*, February 10, 1971.

68. Beal v. Lindsay, 468 F.2d 287, 288 (2d Cir. 1972); Lawrence P. Simon Jr., "Equal Protection in the Urban Environment: The Right to Equal Municipal Services," *Tulane Law Review* 46 (1972): 496.

69. Charles M. Haar and Daniel William Fessler, *The Wrong Side of the Tracks: A Revolutionary Rediscovery of the Common Law Tradition of Fairness in the Struggle against Inequality* (New York: Simon & Schuster, 1986).

70. Washington v. Davis, 426 U.S. 229, 245 n.12 (1976) (Stevens, J., concurring).

71. *Id.* at 253, 254.

72. Arizona v. California, 439 U.S. 419 (1979).

73. Linda Greenhouse, "Court Refuses to Increase Water Rights of 5 Tribes," *New York Times*, March 31, 1983.

74. See Arizona v. California, 460 U.S. 605, 615 (1983) (Brennan, J., dissenting).

75. *Id.* at 626.

76. *Id.* at 655.

77. Judge Elbert Tuttle to Cameron Kerry, June 16, 1983.

78. See Shriner v. Wainwright, 715 F.2d 1452 (5th Cir. 1983); Johnson v. Ellis, 296 F.2d 325 (5th Cir. 1961).

79. Adrian Johnson was one of seven black teenagers charged with the sodomy and murder of a twelve-year-old white boy. Keven McAlester, "The Icebox Revisited," *Houston Press*, March 11, 2004.

80. "Florida Ends the Nation's Moratorium on Executions," *Time*, June 4, 1979.

In 1972 the Supreme Court held Georgia's death penalty statute unconstitutional in an opinion that cast serious doubt on the viability of the statutes in other states. Furman v. Georgia, 408 U.S. 238 (1972). Not until 1976 did the court hold that new statutes adopted in Florida, Georgia, and Texas were constitutional, opening the door to the resumption of executions. Gregg v. Georgia, 428 U.S. 153 (1976); Proffitt v. Florida, 428 U.S. 242 (1976); Jurek v. Texas, 428 U.S. 262 (1976). The twelve years date from the execution of Luis José Monge in the gas chamber at Colorado State Penitentiary on June 2, 1967; Gary Gilmore was executed on January 17, 1977, but his was a "voluntary execution"; he had directed his attorneys to cease all efforts to block it.

81. For citations to all decisions, see Spenkelink v. Wainwright, 442 U.S. 1301 (1979).

82. Ramsey Clark, "Spenkelink's Last Appeal," *Nation*, October 27, 1979, 399.

83. Ibid.

84. Ibid.

85. Wainwright v. Spenkelink, 442 U.S. 901 (1979).

86. See "Report of John R. Brown on Alleged Complaints as to Action of James P. Coleman, Now Chief Judge and Peter T. Fay, Alvin B. Rubin, Circuit Judges," July 16, 1980, Tuttle Papers.

87. Robert A. Burt, "Disorder in the Court: The Death Penalty and the Constitution," *Michigan Law Review* 85 (1987): 1741, 1811.

CHAPTER TWENTY-SIX. Hail to the Chief—and Farewell

1. Act of August 6, 1958, Pub. L. No. 85-983, 72 Stat. 597 (1958).

2. Wills Sparks to Lyndon B. Johnson, June 27, 1967, Ex ME 1, WHCF, LBJ Library, Austin, Texas.

3. Lyndon B. Johnson to Elbert P. Tuttle, June 29, 1967, Ex ME 1, WHCF, LBJ Library.

4. Elbert Parr Tuttle, "Heroism in War and Peace," *Emory University Quarterly* 13 (1957): 129–30.

5. Deborah J. Barrow and Thomas G. Walker, *A Court Divided: The Fifth Circuit Court of Appeals and the Politics of Judicial Reform* (New Haven, Conn.: Yale University Press, 1988), 4. This book provides an excellent, comprehensive overview of the split of the circuit.

6. Ibid., 76.

7. Ibid., 77.

8. Ibid., 88–120.

9. Ibid., 153.

10. Elbert Tuttle to Dr. Rufus E. Clement, president, Atlanta University, January 5, 1950.

11. Charles Merrill and Dr. Benjamin E. Mays to trustees of Morehouse College, February 5, 1965.

12. Judge Sidney A. Jones Jr. to Judge Tuttle, undated, 9, 5.

13. John Kifner, "Armed Negroes End Seizure; Cornell Yields," *New York Times*, April 21, 1969.

14. Elbert Tuttle to Lawrence McGregor, March 3, 1970, AU Center Archives.

15. Judge Elbert Tuttle to Judge Osgood Williams, August 24, 1987.

16. Annita Rosser, interview by author, March 8, 1996.

17. R. J. Costanzo, superintendent, Arlington National Cemetery to Brannon B. Lessene, H. M. Patterson and Son, Atlanta Funeral Home, December 2, 1977.

18. Former resident Jimmy Carter to Judge Elbert Tuttle, June 6, 1996.

INDEX

on, 159–60; Fifth Circuit's approach
to, 161–62; Georgetown school
board's plan for, 268–69; Hunter
and Holmes litigation on University
of Georgia, 174–92; *Jefferson*
ordering, 270–71, 273; *Lucy* case
on University of Alabama, 170–71,
174–75, 184, 185, 187, 353n5; *Meredith*
case on University of Mississippi,
136, 190, 203–15; NAACP focus on,
168; New Orleans school cases on,
164–67; obstructionist tactics to delay, 179–92; "public placement plan"
to appease, 179; Savannah-Chatham
County Board of Education's dual-
system rejected for, 269–70; and
"token integration," 179. See also
*Brown v. Board of Education (Brown
I)*; desegregation
school hair cases, 302–5
Schwartz, Mrs., 96
Scott, Hugh, 87
Scott Newspaper Syndicate of Atlanta,
241
Scottsboro boys cases, 4, 120, 126
Second National Bank of Saginaw, 45
segregation: Boswell amendment to
continue Democratic Party, 134–35;
Briggs dictum on voluntary, 161–62,
163; of Georgia's Democratic Party,
133–34; *McLaurin v. Oklahoma State
Regents* rejection of, 154, 155–56;
NAACP litigation against, 156–57;
Plessy v. Ferguson rejection of, 154–
55, 156, 157, 172; Rives and Tuttle's
understanding of evils of, 161–62;
Savannah-Chatham County Board
of Education's dual-system as,
269–70; Sibley Commission's hear-

ings on, 150–52; *Smith v. Allwright*
decision on Democratic Party,
133–34; *Sweatt v. Painter* rejection
of, 154, 155, 156. See also *Brown v.
Board of Education (Brown I)*; Jim
Crow laws; racial discrimination
Seldes, George, 53, 284
Selective Service System: Ali's litigation
over, 299–300, 301; Sellers's litiga-
tion over, 300–302
Sellers, Cleveland, 300–302
Sellers, Clyde, 171
Seventy-Seventh Division, 62–77
Seymour, Whitney North, 120, 123
Sharp, James, Jr., 222–23
Shartzer, W. B., 105
Shaw, Stan, 35, 37
Shaw, W. J. "Bill," 88
Sheppard Air Force Base, 160
Shivers, Allan, 160
Shuttlesworth, Fred: civil rights leader-
ship of, 238, 239, 244; encourages
King to challenge injunction against
marching, 241–42; files petition to
stage mass protest march, 242–43;
King welcomed to Birmingham by,
240
Shuttlesworth, Hanes v., 262
Sibley, John, 103–4, 114, 115, 116, 151
Sibley Commission, 150–52
Sierra (steamship), 13
Simms, Otis M. "Jack," 48, 200
Simons, Algie Martin, 284
Simpson, Bryan, 14, 200, 273, 304–5
sit-ins, 196–98
Sitton, Claude, 219, 246
Sixteenth Amendment, 50
Sixteenth Street Baptist Church bomb-
ing (1963), 252